"The publication of the letters of Dorothy Day, founder of the Catholic Worker, is a significant event in the history of Christian spirituality. Like her journals, these letters—by turns personal, frank, earthy, joyful, frustrated, contrite, hopeful, funny, and, above all, unmistakably human—will change the widely held belief that Dorothy was interested only in her 'movement.' Instead she is revealed as a woman deeply involved with her family, her friends, her church, her country, and her world. Her love letters to her common-law husband, Forster, will also challenge the popular notion of sanctity, which sometimes equates 'real' holiness with a disinterested and disembodied love. Love is, in fact, the hidden theme of the letters of this astonishing woman: love for the poor, love for her fellow human beings, and love for God. Read these remarkable letters and come to know a saint. Study them and come to know what Christian action is about. Take them to heart and come to know God more fully."

—JAMES MARTIN, SJ, AUTHOR OF *MY LIFE WITH THE SAINTS*

"These wonderful letters (wonderful even in a merely human sense) can almost startle us with their revelation—natural, unpretentious, non-preachy—of what it means to be holy. Dorothy Day loved our Lord in the darkness of a real world, one where she met with distrust, betrayal, grinding poverty, and anxiety. These sorrows did not keep her from God. They drew her into His own redemptive suffering. There are no letters like these."

—SISTER WENDY BECKETT

"Editor Robert Ellsberg has supplied masterful context and commentary to give a good summary of her life at the Catholic Worker, but it is for the intimate Dorothy and her friends that one should read *All the Way to Heaven*. In these letters, we see a Dorothy Day who falls in love with God, and with God in the thousands of people who came into her life. Savor and delight in these letters, the last of her once-unpublished words we're going to get."

"Readers continue to encounter Day in her own books and a growing number of thoughtful assessments of her life and work. In those we find an impressive, even saintly, journalist observer, a remarkable Christian witness and spiritual guide. But in her letters we meet her as a person very much like ourselves. . . . If saints are people who, over a lifetime, try very hard to live out the gospel message of love and forgiveness, in the first instance with those whom they meet every day, then these letters provide a lot of evidence of Dorothy Day's saintliness. But be warned: holiness in action, at least in the case of Day, is not an easy path."

"These letters, along with her diary entries, give clear evidence of an extraordinary woman, one who herself spent a long life living the Christian Gospel, and one who undoubtedly deserves to be called 'saint.' "

"This book reveals a portrait of a remarkable Christian, one who throughout her life worked fiercely and relentlessly to 'put on Christ,' to conform her life to his. From the beginning in 1933 until her death she chose to live with the poor and serve them, tirelessly performing the works of mercy. She spoke up faithfully and courageously against violence and oppression. All of this was rooted in and sustained by the prayer life of the church. The American Catholic church is floundering and deeply in need of heroes and models. This great and holy woman should be one of them."

"Taken together, the diaries and letters afford us a fuller appreciation of Dorothy Day's spiritual genius, her courageous and loving heart, the depth of her suffering, and the gratitude that undergird her rigorous but ultimately triumphant life."

"Thirty-five years after her death, Dorothy Day remains one of the most compelling and transformative personalities in the history

American Catholicism. . . . Robert Ellsberg has performed a monumental service by editing selections of her diaries and now her letters. . . All future studies of Dorothy Day will necessarily take the letters and diaries into account, and even libraries that serve casual readers rather than researchers will find this inspiring and revealing collection to be a worthwhile acquisition."

—DAN McKANAN, *CATHOLIC LIBRARY WORLD*

"These letters offer an incomparable window into the heart and mind of one of the most inspiring spiritual leaders of the twentieth century. They are a treasure trove, the fruit of truly counter-cultural consciousness. Read them if you can. Most of us will not be Dorothy Days, but all of us can benefit immensely from her 'upside down' understanding of the tasks to which God calls us in the world."

—*FRIENDS JOURNAL*

"This splendid collection of Dorothy Day's letters offers a doorway into the ups and downs of her daily endeavors. Inside this wealth of correspondence both Day's ordinary human struggles and her deep spirituality are revealed. I rejoiced at being able to peer inside this enriching view of Dorothy Day's life. There I found a woman who both inspires and challenges me toward further peace and justice."

—JOYCE RUPP, AUTHOR OF *FRAGMENTS OF YOUR ANCIENT NAME*

"Diaries are one thing, letters often quite another. After reading Dorothy Day's diaries (published in 2008 as *The Duty of Delight*), I couldn't have imagined a more unobstructed gaze into the heart and mind of this extraordinary woman. But this selection of her letters, stretching across almost sixty years, augments them wonderfully. Every letter is written to a particular individual—her daughter Tamar, an old friend, a wayward Catholic Worker, a bishop, a poet—so the tone and level of discourse alter almost kaleidoscopically from one page to the next. She is warm, funny, passionate, high-minded, withering, desolate, fierce, and self-effacing by swift turns, and before long you realize, as her reader, that you are in the presence of an absolutely human being who is evolving in plain sight—and that it is an enormous privilege to be there watching. I cherish this book."

—CAROL LEE FLINDERS, PH.D., AUTHOR OF *ENDURING LIVES:
PORTRAITS OF WOMEN AND FAITH IN ACTION*

ALL THE WAY TO

Heaven

Dorothy Day with her grandchildren, 1950s.

ALL THE WAY TO
Heaven

❦The Selected Letters of Dorothy Day

EDITED BY ROBERT ELLSBERG

IMAGE BOOKS   NEW YORK

Published in the United States by Image Books,
an imprint of the Crown Publishing Group, a division
of Random House, Inc., New York.
www.crownpublishing.com

IMAGE and the Image colophon are registered trademarks of
Random House, Inc.

Originally published in hardcover in the United States by
Marquette University Press, Milwaukee, Wisconsin, in 2010.

Library of Congress Cataloging in Publication Data
Day, Dorothy, 1897–1980.
  All the way to heaven: the selected letters of Dorothy Day /
edited by Robert Ellsberg.
  Includes bibliographical references and index.
  1. Day, Dorothy, 1897–1980—Correspondence.   2. Catholics—
United States—Correspondence.   3. Catholic Worker Movement.
I. Ellsberg, Robert, 1955–   II. Title.
  BX4705.D283A4 2010
  267'.182092—dc22
  [B]
                                                    2010031892

ISBN 978-0-7679-3281-3
eISBN 978-0-7679-3282-0

Cover photograph © Bob Fitch

146983092

TO JIM FOREST

Our lives are open to all.

We belong to a Kingdom not of this world, tho we are in it.

May you be a constant reminder, a witness, of this other

Kingdom, this glorious and beautiful Kingdom

where we are willing and obedient and joyful subjects.

Remember St. Catherine of Siena said, "All the way to Heaven

is heaven, because He said, 'I am the Way.'"

So may heaven be in your heart this day.

—DOROTHY DAY TO CHARLES BUTTERWORTH, JUNE 10, 1959

CONTENTS

PREFACE

This volume and its companion, *The Duty of Delight: The Diaries of Dorothy Day*, complete the publication of Dorothy Day's personal papers, part of the Dorothy Day–Catholic Worker Collection housed at Marquette University's Raynor Memorial Libraries in Milwaukee, Wisconsin. According to her wishes, these materials were sealed for twenty-five years after her death in 1980.

After receiving an invitation from the University in 2005 to edit these writings, I chose to begin first with the diaries. That project was a greater editorial challenge, both in terms of the sheer quantity of material to be transcribed and the difficulty of deciphering Day's handwriting. In contrast, it was a positive relief to turn to the letters. As these were intended to be read, at least by their recipients, they were mercifully legible—many of them typed. The relatively limited number of letters, however, was a disappointment.

While she spent little time each day writing in her diary—sometimes only a few minutes—Day evidently spent many hours writing letters. Many of these were short notes, postcards, polite acknowledgments, and the like. But in many other letters she poured out her thoughts and feelings in a personal way, quite different from her public writings. With the exception of letters of an official character, she did not keep carbons or drafts. Thus, the extent of the letters available for this collection reflects the choice of her correspondents to preserve them and their willingness, or that of their heirs, to make them available. I have no illusions that these letters represent any more than a small fraction of the many thousands of letters she wrote in her lifetime. Many letters to close friends, colleagues, and even family members were lost or discarded. Fortunately, a wealth of material remained, including her precious early letters to Forster Batterham, to her daughter Tamar, to Ammon Hennacy, Thomas Merton, Catherine de Hueck Doherty, and many other lifelong friends and fellow travelers. In making the selection for this book, I included only those that seemed to hold particular interest. All were edited to omit repetition and inconsequential detail.

Many people helped with this project. I am particularly grateful to those who stepped forward, in response to my appeals, to share their letters from Dorothy Day. These include the Woodcrest Bruderhof, Sidney Callahan, Jeff Dietrich and Catherine Morris, Jim Douglass, Francisco Fernandez, Eric Gauchat (the son of Bill and Dorothy Gauchat), Judith Gregory, Father Paul Lachance, Karl Meyer, and the family of Karl Stern. I am immensely grateful to Kate and Martha Hennessy for their consistent encouragement of this project and for sharing Dorothy's many cards and letters to her grandchildren. Johannah Turner, who grew up in the Catholic Worker, was exceptionally generous with her talents as a proofreader. Other careful readers were Tom Cornell and Jim Forest, whose long personal memories of the Catholic Worker story and many of its fabulous characters were an invaluable resource. Rachelle Linner and Julie Pycior helped track down sources. Pat Jordan and Frank Donovan offered critical assistance on numerous points. Thanks also to Rosalie Riegle, Claudia Larson, Jim Martin, Jim Allaire, George Horton, Michael Harank, and Gabrielle Earnshaw.

This project would not have been possible without the expert assistance of Phil Runkel, the dedicated archivist of the Dorothy Day–Catholic Worker Collection at Marquette University's Raynor Memorial Libraries. It was he who obtained and catalogued the majority of the letters selected here. For this work, as well as his tireless willingness to pursue all leads, no matter how unlikely, and for his patient attention to any and all questions, he has been a true partner in this project. I am grateful to Matt Blessing, Head of Special Collections and Archives at Marquette, for initially entrusting this project to me and for his many years of support. It has been an honor to work again with Andrew Tallon, director of Marquette University Press, who, together with Maureen Kondrick, oversaw every aspect of this publication. In addition, once again I wish to thank the Archdiocese of New York and Marquette University's Edward Simmons Religious Commitment Fund for their generous financial support.

I am glad for an opportunity to thank Dorothy's daughter, Tamar Hennessy, who preserved so many of these letters, and who was generous, in the final months of her life, in sharing memories of her parents. Readers of *The Duty of Delight* as well as this book will appreciate that some of these memories were not particularly happy. Tamar deeply loved her mother and treasured her association with the Catholic Worker. But she was initially apprehensive about publishing private materials that stirred up complicated emotions. In the end, I am glad that she made her peace with the past and with this project, and I am grateful for the trust she placed in me.

Finally, it is only right to acknowledge my debt to Dorothy Day, whom I met in 1975 when I was nineteen and who asked me, just a few months later, to take on the job of editing the *Catholic Worker*. I could not know at that time just how significant this assignment would be, nor how much her example and her spirit would dominate the rest of my life. I possess only one letter from Dorothy, a picture postcard—like countless others she wrote, too insignificant to include in this collection. I received it while fasting in a jail cell in Colorado where I was confined as a result of an anti-nuclear protest. It was an aerial picture of Cape Cod. On the reverse she had written:

> *Dear Bob—Hope this card refreshes you and does not tantalize you. We all love you and hold you in our prayers. Dan Mauk will feature you on the first page in CW. Love in Christ, Dorothy*

I knew that Dorothy's bedroom wall was covered with postcards like this: pictures of mountains, deserts, tropical birds, and polar bears. . . . I hung her card on the wall of my cell and I have remembered it many times since. It has never ceased to refresh me.

—ROBERT ELLSBERG

ACKNOWLEDGMENTS

The publisher gratefully acknowledges the cooperation of the following sources, who provided copies of letters in their collections:

The Bancroft Library, University of California: William Everson Papers, Banc Mss 7/5, The Bancroft Library, University of California, Berkeley.

Bellarmine University: Thomas Merton Center, Bellarmine University, Louisville, Kentucky.

Catholic University of America: John Brophy Papers, John Cort Papers, Paul Hanly Furfey Papers, and CIO Records, The American Catholic History Research Center and University Archives, The Catholic University of America, Washington, DC.

College of St. Catherine: Ade Bethune Collection, College of St. Catherine Library.

Columbia University: Allen Ginsberg Papers, Rare Book & Manuscript Library, Columbia University.

Connecticut College: Sheaffer-O'Neill Collection. Reproduced from the original held by the Linda Lear Center for Special Collections and Archives, Connecticut College.

Cornell University: Daniel and Phillip Berrigan Papers, #4602. Courtesy of the Division of Rare and Manuscript Collections, Cornell University Library.

Georgetown University: Donald Powell Papers, Special Collections, Georgetown University Library.

Harvard University: American Birth Control League Records, MS Am 2063 (110). By permission of the Houghton Library, Harvard University. Judith Palache Gregory Papers, Schlesinger Library, Radcliffe Institute, Harvard University.

Library of Congress: Clare Boothe Luce Papers, Manuscript Division, Library of Congress.

McMaster University: William Ready Papers, William Ready Division of Archives and Research Collections, McMaster University Library, Hamilton, Canada.

Princeton University: "Caroline Gordon Papers," Department of Rare Books and Special Collections, Princeton University Library.

Sinsinawa Dominican Archives: Letters to Sr. Thomas Aquinas O'Neil.

Tamiment Library: Virginia Gardner Papers, Tamiment Library, New York University.

University of Arizona: Ada Peirce McCormick Papers, University of Arizona Library Special Collections.

University of Delaware: "Emily Holmes Coleman papers," University of Delaware Library, Newark, Delaware.

University of Maryland: Katherine Anne Porter Papers, Special Collections, University of Maryland Libraries.

University of Michigan: Ammon Hennacy Papers, Labadie Collection, University of Michigan.

University of Mississippi: Marjorie Baroni Papers, Archives and Special Collections, J.D. Williams Library, University of Mississippi.

University of Notre Dame Archives: Letters to Nina Polcyn Moore; Gordon Zahn. Archives of the University of Notre Dame, South Bend, Indiana.

Yale University: Claude McKay Collection, Yale Collection of American Literature, Beinecke Rare Book and Manuscript Library.

Thanks also to these individual donors: Bernice Butterworth, Thomas Cornell, Dorothy Day, Frank Donovan, Harvey Egan, Sr. Peter Claver Fahy, Dorothy Gauchat, Mary Hope Griffin (letters to Gerry Griffin), Patrick Jordan, Robert MacNeil (letters to Dixie MacMaster), William Miller, Fr. Leo Neudecker, Nina Polcyn Moore, Deane Mowrer, William Oleksak, Katherine Skorzewska (letters to Karl Stern), Chuck Smith, Robert Steed, Elinor Stetson, Jacques Travers, Johannah Hughes Turner, Joseph Zarrella, Jim Forest, Toni Eichenberg, Tamar Hennessy.

INTRODUCTION

The arrival of mail at the Catholic Worker house in New York City was always an event. Given what Dorothy Day called the "precarity" of life at the CW, the donations that came with each day's mail—whether five dollars, a check for a hundred, or a pile of "25¢ per year" subscriptions to the *Catholic Worker*—might make the difference in buying beans for the morning soupline, mailing out thousands of bundles of newspapers, or forestalling the shut-off of utilities. But for Dorothy the mail also brought *news*: about what was happening at Catholic Worker communities across the country, the story of a labor strike or some experiment in nonviolence, a report from old friends, or a family's account of their struggle to practice their faith and to live out the works of mercy.

As Dorothy opened the mail, she would share the contents with anyone at hand. Jim Forest, a former editor of the paper and one of her biographers, describes his first meeting with Dorothy at the Catholic Worker farm on Staten Island. "In the large, faded dining room of an old farmhouse, I found half a dozen people gathered around a pot of tea and a pile of mail at one end of a large table. Dorothy Day was reading letters aloud."

Although the only letter Forest remembered from that day

was one from Thomas Merton, the famous Trappist monk, he could vividly recall after many years the impression she made as she read aloud from assorted letters and related stories about the people who had sent them. "At the core of each story there were always just a few people, maybe just one person, for whom following Christ was the most important thing in the world."

In her monthly column in the *Catholic Worker* she often employed a similar device, sharing with her readers a sampling of the letters on her desk. She did the same in an article from 1941 entitled "The Apostolate of Letter Writing," in which she noted, "Whenever I sit down to write an article I do so with the oppressive sense of having many letters that have come in the Catholic Worker mail bag waiting to be answered. I wake up with letters to answer and I go to bed with letters to answer. When I go out on a speaking trip, I take a bundle of letters with me, and even on a social call bring a few of the longer letters we have received to read on the subway and meditate on the answers to be given."

Her article goes on simply to note and comment on the letters of the day. "Here is a letter from a rabbi in Cleveland. . . . A few cheering letters from the Houses of Hospitality . . . A letter from a priest enclosing quotations from Leo the Great . . . A beautiful letter from [CW artist] Ade Bethune . . . A letter condemning us for defending three seamen in San Quentin . . . A letter from a former soldier in the Abraham Lincoln Brigade . . . Letters from a priest in the Philippines . . . A letter from an American born Slovak, a poet and a waitress, who has known hunger and hardship and loneliness and wants friendly correspondence. . . ."

Many of these letters, she noted, "demand thought and prayer, so that an hour in the presence of the Blessed Sacrament is necessary before presuming to answer some of them. But with all the toil and shared suffering of letter receiving and letter answering, there is joy and happiness too, the happiness of seeing the lay community—which is the Catholic Worker movement—growing and reaching out and touching many lives."

Dorothy Day is primarily known for her role as co-founder, with Peter Maurin, of the Catholic Worker. First a newspaper, launched on May 1, 1933, and eventually a movement centered in houses of hospitality and farming communes around the country, the Catholic Worker represented an effort to put into practice the radical social message of the Gospel. Day's inspiration drew in particular on the Gospel text where Jesus ties our salvation to our treatment of our neighbors. "I was hungry and you fed me. . . . I was homeless and you sheltered me. . . . I was imprisoned, and you visited me. . . . Insofar as you did these things to the least of my brothers and sisters, you did them to me." For Day, that meant not just practicing the works of mercy—feeding the hungry, sheltering the homeless in her house of hospitality—but also protesting and resisting the social structures and values that were responsible for so much suffering and need. The Catholic Worker movement was not intended to resolve the problems of poverty and violence in the world, but to provide a model of what it might look like if Christians truly lived out their faith in response to the challenges of history and the needs of their neighbors.

For almost fifty years, from 1933 until her death in 1980, Dorothy Day lived out her life in this movement. That involved the day-in, day-out challenge of living among the poor, sick, and sometimes crazed individuals who made up the Catholic Worker family. It involved resolving conflicts and rivalries, assigning tasks, and overseeing the management of a newspaper along with multiple urban and rural households. It involved representing the movement through travel and speaking across the country, both to spread the message and to generate funds. It involved protests against war, racism, and injustice that occasionally landed her in jail. All this was sustained by resilient faith and a discipline of prayer. As documented in her diaries, her days usually began at dawn with an hour of prayer, followed by Mass. When possible she tried to read the daily prayers from her breviary, and she usually found time to recite the rosary. As she often liked to say, when describing the disparate elements of her life, whether commonplace or sacred: "It all goes together."

Her life also involved constant letter writing: acknowledging and thanking contributors, responding to queries from priests and church officials, answering critics, exhorting and encouraging fellow Catholic Workers around the country, writing letters to editors and city agencies, letters of support to prisoners of conscience, advice on practical aspects of hospitality, or pastoral responses to young people coping with existential crises and spiritual struggles. When she traveled there were also letters home, or letters to her daughter Tamar and her grandchildren. There were letters to old friends and to innumerable strangers. In every case she connected intensely with the needs of her correspondents, just as she did with the people close at hand. In reading and replying to letters, Dorothy responded not just to the particularities of the moment; she saw her correspondents' struggles, their yearnings, their sufferings in relation to the universal human condition, and as part of a drama that linked this life and the life to come. As she liked to quote St. Catherine of Siena, the fourteenth-century mystic, "All the way to Heaven is heaven."

A reading of her diaries, *The Duty of Delight,* suggests that writing letters was in fact a major part of her day: "Letters all morning . . . Night of letters . . . Letters for me all day." In one year—surely not an exception—she estimates having written over a thousand letters. Sometimes this was a truly Sisyphean labor. She notes in one entry the burden of "an immense correspondence that I cannot keep up with, always leaving me with a feeling of great uneasiness at neglecting so much of my duty."

In her column one month she writes, "I know I will never catch up on my mail. Forever there will be letters left unanswered, except for the prayers I say as I open my mail in the morning or read all the mail which has piled up while I am away on my pilgrimages. 'To breathe prayers over them as I read them' sounds trite and pietistic, but I mean it. I do pray out loud but [*here referring to some of her companions at the Catholic Worker*] there are enough people around here talking to themselves. Some of it irritates, some of it is heart-rending, a lot of it is cheery and bright."

As overwhelmed as she could be by the enormous volume of mail, ultimately she was sustained and energized by contact and connection with other people. Life at the Catholic Worker often left one gasping for peace and quiet, but Dorothy had no natural taste for solitude. She thrived on conversations over a cup of coffee or around the kitchen table. She enjoyed exchanging stories, discussing novels, or hearing the news of the day. She enjoyed the back and forth debate at Friday night meetings "for the clarification of thought," as much as she savored the communal ritual of evening prayer. And through the cartons of mail that awaited her on her return from a trip, she wrote, "I feel as though I were talking to our readers and they to me, and I think of all the things I would like to say to them personally which are hard to get down on paper, but which come so readily when one is face to face with others."

In that spirit, there was often little distinction between the quality of her correspondence and the personal style she employed in her newspaper columns. In her column for October 1950 she noted, "The reason we write is to communicate ideas, and the reason for getting out the *Catholic Worker* each month is to communicate with our brothers. We must overflow in writing about all the things we have been talking about and living during the month. Writing is an act of community. It is a letter, it is comforting, consoling, helping, advising on our part, as well as asking it on yours. It is a part of our human association with each other. It is an expression of our love and concern for each other."

. . .

Most of the letters included in this volume span the years of her life in the Catholic Worker. As with her diaries, the letters reflect her reaction to the events of history and the shifting cultural tides of the day. So the letters from the 1930s chronicle the early years of the Catholic Worker. Set against the backdrop of the Depression, her letters chronicle the back and forth exchange with readers, critics, allies, and diocesan officials, all trying to comprehend just what this movement was about. With the 1940s and the Second World War, Dorothy's unpopular commitment to pacifism ensured a certain marginalization within the church and American society. At the same time, her exposure to Fr. John Hugo's retreats, which emphasized the universal call to holiness, intensified her already demanding spirituality.

With the 1950s the Catholic Worker's emphasis on voluntary poverty, peace, and social justice ran against the mood of postwar prosperity and Cold War patriotism. The arrival of Ammon Hennacy on the Catholic Worker scene initiated a new era of nonviolent witness. With the 1960s, especially with the civil rights movement, the Second Vatican Council, and the rising protests against the Vietnam War, the Catholic Worker embodied the mood of idealism and protest. At the same time, Dorothy reacted with concern against elements of the counterculture and the general revolt against traditional moral values.

With the 1970s she sustained a prophetic balance between her traditional piety and her radical social critique. She was arrested for the final time while picketing with the United Farm Workers. She stood up to the IRS in her refusal to pay federal taxes for war. She was invited to address the Eucharistic Congress in Philadelphia, and she reported happily on her experiences with the Catholic charismatic renewal. Finally, in these years, she began to receive the respectful attention from the church and the media accorded to "venerable survivors."

Of course, one of the striking features of this volume is the inclusion of letters from the decade preceding the founding of the Catholic Worker. The letters from 1923 to 1932 offer a refreshingly new picture of a period that is otherwise known chiefly through Dorothy's accounts in her much later autobiographical writings. Here is a glimpse of Dorothy as a young woman, giddy with excitement over the publication of her first book and filled with future writing schemes. Readers of *The Long Loneliness* (1952) already know the story of her love affair with Forster Batterham and how her experience of pregnancy and the birth of her daughter Tamar in 1926 prompted her conversion to Catholicism. When he refused, on principle, to get married, they parted ways. Now, however, the publication of her many letters to Forster, unavailable to previous biographers, provides a much more vivid picture of this story. They offer a moving and often heart-rending reflection of the depth of her love, and thus the cost of her vocation. They invite the question of how different her life would have been, not to mention history, had Forster acceded to Dorothy's desires, had he given up his "pig-headedness" and agreed to marry her.

Instead, her lonely years in the "desert," raising Tamar on her own, while struggling to discern her vocation, led with a decisive suddenness to her meeting with Peter Maurin at the end of 1932 and her plans, only a few months later, to launch the *Catholic Worker*. At that point her life assumes a course of astonishing direction and consistency. Having found, through Peter Maurin, her essential program and spiritual compass, she steered a path that carried her for the next forty-seven years, one of the most tumultuous and dramatic periods in both American history and the life of the church.

The range of her correspondence is wide—from famous Catholics like Thomas Merton, Clare Booth Luce, and Eunice Shriver, to the Beat poet Allen Ginsberg. The letters chronicle her long friendship with spiritual comrades like Catherine de Hueck Doherty, founder of the kindred Friendship House in Harlem, as well as activists like Daniel Berrigan and Cesar Chavez. In one letter she is interceding on behalf of convicted atomic spies Ethel and Julius Rosenberg, while in the next she is describing her desire to write a biography of St. Therese of Lisieux. She is forthright in challenging Cardinal Francis Spellman's role in opposing a strike by Catholic gravediggers, and in another letter explaining to a chancery official the great scandal it would cause were she obliged to drop the word *Catholic* from the name of her newspaper. There are letters that reflect her attraction to the desert spirituality of Charles de Foucauld, while others discuss her adventures in jail, or explain to an assortment of college presidents her refusal to accept any honorary degrees.

The letters display a range of attitudes and dimensions of her personality. Her letters to Jack English, a former Catholic Worker who entered the Trappists and who struggled for years with alcoholism, display her deep compassion and sensitivity for human frailty. (A series of letters document her efforts to establish a retreat house for alcoholic priests.) In writing to Ammon Hennacy, a swashbuckling radical who was inspired by Dorothy's example to become a Catholic, we see her admiring his courage and principles, while deflecting his romantic intentions and admonishing his tendency to hero worship.

She held friends to her own high standards. To a former *CW* editor, after learning that he planned to remarry without seeking an annulment, she advised him to resign as secretary of a Catholic peace organization. "You are certainly going through the sorrowful mysteries. But if you don't go through them to the glorious, you will be a hollow man, and considered an opportunist and a fraud. I am putting it as strong as I am able, and hate doing it, but to me the Faith is the strongest thing in my life and I can never be grateful enough for the joy I have had for the gift of Faith, my Catholicism." (In a subsequent letter, years later, she writes him to apologize for her "critical attitudes.")

Writing to a distinguished figure in the Catholic peace movement, whose faith was threatened by the failings of the hierarchy, she writes, "As a convert, I never expected much of the bishops. In all history popes and bishops and father abbots seem to have been blind and power loving and greedy. I never expected leadership from them. It is the saints that keep appearing all thru history who keep things going. What I do expect is the bread of life and down thru the ages there is that continuity."

Not all the qualities on display are entirely admirable. In her diaries she reproaches herself for impatience, anger, judgment, and self-righteousness, qualities she often brought to confession, and which enter into some of her letters. The letters to her daughter Tamar, in particular, reflect all the complexity of any parent–child relationship. On the one hand she was devoted to Tamar and her family, offering considerable assistance and support over the years, including much of the income from her writing. She was a particularly doting grandmother for Tamar's nine children. And yet, in earlier years, certain letters show just how much Dorothy struggled—like any mother—to find the appropriate balance between support and *control*. The final word for Dorothy was always *love*. But here, as in other relationships, there were often other words and questionable judgments along the way.

In her diaries, Dorothy wrote directly of her sufferings, both physical and spiritual. In the letters, she is mostly reticent about personal troubles, not wanting to add to others' burden or to invite their pity. Nevertheless, certain frank glimpses of CW life peek through: "Yesterday I had to drive the station wagon down for bread and it smelled of vomit and human excrement from the people sleeping in it at night. We spent the day scrubbing out the thing at the farm. Drunkenness and madness and filth and ugliness. A picture of hell." In another letter she writes, "You must know the deep unhappiness I felt and do feel. I have felt so many periods of dryness and heaviness and confusion myself, but also felt that I could only keep saying, 'Lord, I believe, help thou my unbelief.' And to try to keep my own deep sadness and discouragement from others."

But sadness and discouragement are certainly not the dominant notes. After reflecting on the many failures that abound she notes: "And yet—and yet—there are so many strong and amazingly good and hard-working young people continually coming to the Catholic Worker, both at the farm and the city. And when I look at the vices of some, I can say their virtues outweigh their vices, and my own sloth and self-indulgence should provide my mind and heart with occupation. . . ."

Her own struggles and sorrows increased her compassion: "I was thinking how often and how many of us feel unloved, unwanted, on many and many occasions during our lives—all the misunderstandings there are in families, even between husband and wife. We all want heaven here and now, no patience, no waiting. Don't think I don't understand how you feel, because I have felt the same many a time. How many times I have felt even a wall of hatred and resentment around me—sometimes over little things, and also over the big ones."

She reacted strongly against the loose sexual mores of the 1960s' counter-culture, and resisted their intrusion at the Worker. In one letter she writes of her efforts to purge the Worker of a group of "beats" who "reversed all standards, turning night into day," and proudly proclaimed their freedom from bourgeois morality. "This is not reverence for life. . . . It is a great denial and is more resembling nihilism than the revolution which they think they are furthering."

At the same time, the memory of her own youthful struggles made her particularly sensitive to the searching and sufferings of youth. To a young woman in distress she wrote, "Please forgive me for presuming to write you so personally—to intrude on you and your suffering, as I am doing, but I felt I had to—because I have gone thru so much the same suffering as you in the confusion of my youth and my search for love. I cannot help but feel deeply for you and for your mother, your family, because now I go through these sufferings over my grandchildren—one or another of them. In a way, to use old-fashioned language, I feel you are victim souls, bearing some of the agony the world is in, Vietnam, the Third World, 'the misery of the needy and the groaning of the poor.' But just the same it is a very real agony of our own, wanting human love, fulfillment, and one so easily sees all the imperfections of this love we seek, the inability of others ever to satisfy this need of ours, the constant failure of those nearest and dearest to understand, to respond."

Even as she aged, she retained her idealism, her spirit of adventure, and an instinct for the heroic. It gave her an uncanny youthfulness, and it is no wonder that young people were attracted to her, or that they have continued in large numbers to take up her mission. As Jim Forest notes, recalling that first meeting around the kitchen table, she had the ability "to focus on the person she was talking to, not to see just a young face but *your* face, not discerning just a vague, general promise but *your* particular gifts. Through Dorothy, you saw exciting possibilities in yourself you hadn't seen before. Also you saw what it meant to lead a life that was relentlessly God-centered."

In titling her memoir *The Long Loneliness,* Dorothy alluded to the essential loneliness that is part of the human condition and a feature of any vocation. But the major theme of her life was the search for community—whether in love and family, among friends and neighbors, in solidarity with all who struggle for a better world, or, on the supernatural plane, in the Mystical Body of Christ. Both in her youthful participation in the radical movement and later, as a Catholic, she resonated with the words of St. Paul: that we are all "members one of another."

For Dorothy, the experience of community—with its griefs as well as its joys—was a foretaste of heaven. And that experience was reenacted in every occasion of genuine human connection—whether face to face, or through a letter. In the conclusion to her memoir, she wrote, "Heaven is a banquet and life is a banquet, too, even with a crust, where there is companionship. We have all known the long loneliness, and we have learned that the only solution is love, and that love comes with community."

Her letters are more than the reflection of a life. They are an invitation to community and to an ongoing conversation. As she noted: "It all happened while we sat there talking, and it is still going on."

—ROBERT ELLSBERG

PART I

A Love Story

1923–1932

The letters in this first section, written in a period of ten years before the launch of the Catholic Worker, reflect a time of searching and transition. Since quitting college in 1916, Dorothy had lived in New York, working on a succession of left-wing journals, including The Call and The Masses. Her friends had included radicals and rebels of all stripes, as well as artists and writers like the playwright Eugene O'Neill. In 1917, with a group of suffragists, she was arrested for picketing the White House and spent eighteen days in a penal workhouse in Washington.

Later, while working as a nurse trainee at Kings County Hospital, she fell under the sway of a charismatic writer named Lionel Moise. It was, as she later wrote, a "fatal attraction," which left her constantly tormented by fears of losing him. When she became pregnant she acceded to Moise's insistence that she have an abortion. He left her anyway.

On the rebound from this affair, she married a wealthy man named Berkeley Tobey, traveled with him to Europe, and there began work on an autobiographical novel. The marriage did not last a year.

Returning home, Dorothy settled in Chicago, apparently hoping—without success—to rekindle the relationship with Moise. Among other jobs, she found work on The Liberator, *a Communist journal. The humiliating capstone of this time was her arrest one night during a "Red Squad" raid on a hangout for radicals where she was spending the night. She was charged with being an occupant of a "disorderly house"—that is, a prostitute.*

The decision to leave Chicago in the fall of 1923 brought an end to a period of her life marked by "almost desperate unhappiness." At the time of these earliest letters she was eagerly awaiting publication of The Eleventh Virgin. *The novel ends with a fictionalized version of her affair with Moise and its tragic aftermath. Now having written that story and, to some extent, gotten it out of her system, Dorothy was eager for a fresh start. All that she knew for certain was that she intended "to go on writing."*

TO MARGARET SANGER

Dorothy Day's first extant letter is to Margaret Sanger, founder of the American Birth Control League—the precursor of Planned Parenthood. Sanger and her sister Ethel Byrne were repeatedly arrested for trying to open a birth control clinic in the slums of New York, a story Dorothy had covered as a reporter for The Call. *Dorothy's younger sister Della at one point worked for the League and remained for the rest of her life a strong supporter of the cause.*

CHICAGO, SEPTEMBER 2, 1923

I am sorry the League does not feel that it can afford a regular publicity director, as I am so interested in the work. I should have liked the job. But it is probably better for me that I'm not going to get it, for it would take all of my time and I need some hours a day for my writing and proofreading on my books.

Delafield [*Dorothy's sister, Della*] arrived yesterday and we are going to have a very frivolous two weeks. We shall pay you an

unofficial call at the Drake [Hotel] when you arrive and I hope
that you'll have time to see us.

It was certainly sweet of you to contribute to her vacation
with the berth and breakfast money, for the silly child was going
to sit up all night and eat sandwiches on the train, and part of
the fun of traveling (when you don't do it often) is to have a
sleeper and breakfast in the dining car.

TO LLEWELLYN JONES
Llewellyn Jones was literary editor of the Chicago Evening Post
from 1914 to 1932.

NEW YORK, [FALL] 1923
As Mary has probably told you, *The Eleventh Virgin* will be out
October 10, and I am very much thrilled. [Maxim] Lieber [*her
publisher*] wants to know if you will contribute a line or two of
praise to be used in catalogues and on the jacket. I have Eugene
O'Neill, Mary Heaton Vorse, and Floyd Dell, and I wonder if you
wouldn't add your little comment too.* If you could telegram it,
or night letter it, I should say, I'd appreciate it very much, because their catalogue goes to press the first of the week.

What is even more exciting to me is the fact that I've finished the second book (it isn't named yet) and it will probably be
out in January. I've worked like a fiend since I came back to New
York, and I have cramps in both arms from typing so much. But
I must sublimate my emotions, don't you know, and that's the
only way I get any writing done.

Lionel [Moise], in a fit of pique, left town with another woman
a few weeks after I left [Chicago], but he wrote me a letter in

---

* Dorothy knew all these writers personally. The playwright Eugene O'Neill
was her close companion for a brief period in the winter of 1918. Mary Heaton
Vorse was a suffragist and feminist writer. Floyd Dell was a progressive writer
and Dorothy's former editor at *The Masses.*

which he said he had gotten rid of his incubus and was going to be sober and alone all summer. That's what I came to New York for,—to get him sober and to get some writing done.

I'll be seeing you soon at afternoon tea, one of these days,— probably in the fall.

P.S. You're a darling, if you do this for me.

In December Dorothy traveled to New Orleans "to have a change and to work there for a time" while awaiting publication of her novel. She easily found work writing "sensational articles" for the New Orleans Item. *Aside from Della, her companion in this adventure was a woman named Mary, a friend from her "disorderly life" in Chicago, whom she later described as a "big gold-haired, pink-cheeked girl with an irresistible sense of humor and a huge appetite for a 'good time.'" She would also remember Mary, gratefully, as the source of her first rosary.*

NEW ORLEANS, DECEMBER 4, 1923

Well, we got here—arrived last night at ten and stopped at the Y.W. for the night. We spent all today looking for rooms and found one for eight a week—2 rooms and bath. So you see how cheap rents are. Paying only five dollars deposit leaves us only two to last thru the week on. Do you think you could let me borrow five? If you sent it special I'd get it Saturday, and I'll be tired of bananas by then.

P.S. Will write more later but this is an s.o.b. of a pen.

UNDATED 1923

You certainly are a darling. We weren't quite driven to bananas for the milkman delivers two quarts of milk a day and we had bought lots of rice and oranges—the latter ten cents a dozen. We had a gorgeous time this afternoon shopping in the French market along the wharves. It took the three of us to carry our purchases home—cabbage, potatoes, ground artichokes (did you ever taste them?), pounds of flour, and lard with which to make biscuits in the morning, and, most delectable of all—shrimps, which are fifteen cents a pound and huge and luscious. Food is cheap here as room rent is. And the weather is perfect. We walked all afternoon exploring the docks dressed only in serge dresses, for no coats were necessary. The cold I had has disappeared entirely and I feel glorious.

Mary has a job beginning Monday, selling lingerie in a big shop on the main street—fifteen a week with a bonus on sales. The salaries are smaller down here but you can live so much cheaper and better than you can in Chicago. We are going to live on fish and vegetables alone. I'm so glad I'm here, because I was getting sick of cold northern winters and they left me a wreck by spring, and the cold gave me another excuse to keep drinking, and you know I never needed much excuse when the liquor flowed free as it generally did in Chicago. Fortunately we know of no place to get it here and there is no one to drink with, so we never think of it.

Besides us, there is only the French landlady and her daughter in the house, and every evening I go downstairs to read French to her. I'll learn lots from her.

Write to me sometimes when you have a chance and tell me the latest gossip from Chicago.

Among her other colorful assignments as a journalist, Dorothy went undercover to investigate the work of "taxi dancers"—women employed by bars and dance halls to dance with the male patrons.

C. 1/9/24

I received news from Albert and Charles Boni [publishers of *The Eleventh Virgin*] last week that they had taken over the business of Lieber and Lewis and that my book would come out on or before the fifteenth of January. Great news! What's more, their letter was most encouraging and complimentary, telling me how much they liked *The Eleventh Virgin*, and that they wanted some weeks longer to consider "Moon" because they think that they'd like to go on with my books, etc. The cover is going to be dark green, with orange lettering and orange the top of the pages, and a bright orange jacket. I told them that you'd like an advance copy as soon as possible, and they said they'd send one.

My work down here is going splendidly, thanks to the fact that I've been taken off the column. The man who had it before has been on the job for the last fifteen years and threatens to resign, etc., and I told them I'd rather do daily feature stories than this column, because it takes up all my energy and initiative, going out and getting material for it, especially as they wanted all New Orleans stuff. So now I'm doing Sunday stuff, a double page in the magazine section each week, and daily features. They don't mind working you like hell for very little money. However, the work is fun, and keeps me occupied so that I don't miss liquor and the bright lights.

My latest assignment, however, will bring me in contact with these, I fear. I'm requested to go to one of three dance halls, which are under the same management. These dens of vice cater only to men, and many girls are hired to dance with them. They pay ten cents a dance, and the girl gets four of it. Working hours, from eight to twelve. I'm to investigate, under assumed name, and disguised as a flapper, to see if this wild night life doesn't lead to vice and crime amongst our young womanhood of the South. I shall enjoy myself immensely. Tonight I try for this job, and if I don't get in at one place I will at one of the other two.

Della, not being able to get work down here, and finding time to hang heavy on her hands, succumbed to the repeated requests of the family to leave my evil influence and return to New York. 'Tis only for the time being, however, because I think Mary and I'll be wandering up there, via the Southern Pacific steamers, steerage, around in April. Pop sent Della first class passage of course and all the money she needs to travel with, and also informed Della that if I wanted to return to New York and honest womanhood, he'd send me the fare, and supply me with money to live in some respectable rooming house "provided any would have me," and would do this with the same spirit that he would help out any Godforsaken bum that he met along the race track. Thank God, I've never had to take advantage of father's kindly offers. I prefer appealing to friends, whose spirit is somewhat different.

Dorothy's series, "Dance Hall Life of a City Revealed," stirred up a good deal of attention. But by the spring she was ready to return to New York. The Eleventh Virgin was published in April by Albert and Charles Boni. Though the reviews were disappointing, there was good news—the publisher had managed to sell the movie rights for $5,000. With her share she bought a fisherman's cottage in Huguenot on Staten Island where she could "settle down to study and to write."

UNDATED 1924

Please excuse my delay in writing you and thanking you for your lovely review which some friends sent on from Chicago. I nearly died over the picture. I looked like a rugged forest. God knows what he would make of me now since I cut off my hair like a boy's and have bleached it beside,—did both, by the way, under the influence of liquor. Della and I always get this maudlin impulse to beautify ourselves. However, everybody likes it, so no harm done, and it is very convenient since I am swimming every day.

I have thought of you often and affectionately, even though I didn't write, and expected any time to see you in New York. I do hope you will be here this fall, and don't fail to call up Boni and get my telephone number, and no matter what I am doing, swimming, digging clams, or fishing, I shall cast all to the winds and come rushing in to see you.

My book, now that it is in cold print, doesn't please me, but

I console myself by remembering that I wrote it when I was twenty-two. Neither has it pleased my friends. I have heard much adverse criticism, and people who liked the book in manuscript, changed their minds when they saw it in print.

Boni turned down my [novel] "Joan Barleycorn," asking me to rewrite it. I had disapproved of some comments they made, and very foolishly wrote them the enclosed letter, which to my amazement they took with all seriousness and asked me to rewrite the book according to my plan. I am not doing it, but I am doing a rather wild popular novel which they think they are going to get. But I don't know whether I'll turn it over to them or not. In spite of the fact that I'm using the same name, "Joan Barleycorn," it is so entirely another thing, that I can consider it a third novel.

However, I'm having a lovely time,—lots of pretty boys around and wish you were here and so forth. I weigh 135 (last year at this time it was 108), am very tan, am drinking a little but not too much, and in general am being godly and righteous according to my lights.

TO CHARLES BONI (publisher of *The Eleventh Virgin*)
Dorothy's imagination was bubbling with writing projects. Apparently this proposal for "Joan Barleycorn" was written in jest. But when her publisher took it seriously she actually wrote the novel (never published).

The time my brain is most active is in the small hours of the night when I awaken to listen to the waves on the shore and contemplate all the things I intend to write in the future,—my detective story, my interviews with obscure people, and a child's history of Marco Polo. But last night when I woke up, I thought of none of these things, but of "Joan," and gradually my mind devolved the story as I should have written it. I remembered as I lay there that I had not given any credit to Robert W. Chambers in my preface, and I am sure he would be very much hurt and immediately begin writing letters to the newspapers about it. Do you remember the story,—I can't remember the name of it,—of the beautiful young society woman who had inherited a thirst from her mother or father, and was addicted to soaking lumps of sugar in cologne and eating them one after another until she fell into a stupor after the fifth, perhaps? And how her fiancé, with grief in his eyes, would carry her prostrate form to her boudoir, there to deposit her on her bed until the effects of her debauch had worn off? She cured herself in the end, I don't know how, of this vicious habit, and they married and lived happily ever after, and Chambers doesn't say whether or not her children inherited her propensities.

I thought of this story, as I say, and I thought too of the serial story which is running in my morning paper and which I await with great anxiety every morning. Indeed my breakfast doesn't taste the same without it. And as I realized the appeal which both these stories has for the public mind, the inspiration came over me in a gust—just what I could have made of Joan Barleycorn.

Joan of course had to be a woman with a propensity for drink, but Mallory, her husband, should have been a teetotaler. Regardless of feminine psychology, Joan would continue drinking after her marriage with her sober husband, and regardless of masculine psychology, Mallory would have stuck by her through thick and thin, undressing her and putting her to bed at night,— getting up to make tea for her when she had a hangover in the morning and endeavoring to wean her away from the bottle gradually, rather than abruptly, with a clout over the head, for instance. The plot of the story as it should have been written is this.

Overcome with despair, Mallory, who is one of these strong, silent men, takes his wife on an ocean voyage, and arranges with the captain, who is in his confidence, that they be put off on a desert island, where there is no alcohol,—nothing but the barest necessities, such as mussels and clams, and bananas and cocoanuts. There is the possibility of many appealing situations here,—how Joan walks the shore night after night, craving the stimulants she was used to, gritting her teeth, wringing her hands, and recalling, only to torture herself, her bibulous friends, and the parties when everybody had been jovial and happily intoxicated. You can imagine the strong and silent Mallory diverting her mind, in his strong and silent way, seeking to provide other interests for her, the primitive and wholesome interests which go with God's great outdoors.

To make Mallory's job more complicated, Joan finds out how to make cocoanut brandy, by piercing the cocoanuts and allowing them to remain in the sun, and a moment of terrific intensity would come when Mallory discovers his addict-wife's fiendish ingenuity and punishes her by cutting down all the cocoanut trees and scattering the fruit thereof in the ocean.

And then gradually the craving leaves her; she finds a great interest in making baskets and pottery, and adorning their rude home. She realizes that Mallory, worn out by his attempts to cure her, has begun to look on her with an indifferent eye, and an agony comes over her, a yearning for the love of the strong and silent man which she has so foolishly sacrificed. She frantically spends hours and hours, devising means to increase her scanty wardrobe, searching over the island for beauty clays and pollen which can be used for face powder and rouge. Then when he is unable longer to withstand her lures,—lures far more potent than those she wielded in the days of their courtship,—he is enabled to continue his pose (for it is only that to win her back to him and away from the demon rum) by the return of the ship to rescue them. They are brought back to civilization.

After a few more months to try her out, our strong and silent hero is able to keep silent no longer, and falls into his wife's arms just as she is about to commit suicide. There is a general reunion in which he confides in her that the reason he practiced his cruel deceit was because he discovered that he was about to become a father, and that he wished to make her worthy to be a mother at any cost. Whereupon they live happily ever after.

Doubtlessly this is just the sort of book both you and Mr. [Franklin] Spier [*publicist for Boni and Dorothy's future brother-in-law*] would like to have, so if you will return my manuscript I shall set to work immediately.

TO FORSTER BATTERHAM

The conclusion to The Eleventh Virgin *has Dorothy, in the voice of her fictional alter-ego, talking with her sister and imagining her future happiness with a home, a husband, and children. In the spring of 1925 that happy image began to take shape in her relationship with Forster Batterham, the brother of her friend Lily Burke. In* The Long Loneliness *she describes Forster, "the man I loved," in somewhat elegant terms, as "an anarchist, an Englishman by descent, and a biologist." Actually, he was from North Carolina. His "anarchism" was chiefly expressed in opposition to the institution of marriage. And though he was fascinated by natural history and anything to do with fishing, it was a stretch to call him a biologist; he worked in a factory making gauges and later owned a store in Manhattan. Nevertheless, within a short time of their first encounter, he was spending weekends with Dorothy on Staten Island, and she was passionately in love.*

FRIDAY, APRIL 3, 1925

You simply must come on down for a couple of days Monday if you can't get down Saturday to stay until Monday. There is plenty of room and plenty to eat, and plenty of room in the woods so you must get out. And if you don't I'll be coming back Monday. I miss you so much. I was very cold last night. Not because there wasn't enough covers but because I didn't have you. Please write me, sweetheart, and I won't tear the letter up as I did the last one (but I saved the pieces) because I was mad at you.

I love you muchly.

TO LLEWELLYN JONES

APRIL 14 [1925]

In spite of a cold which has made me sniff and blow and sneeze for the last two weeks, I've been spending most of my time in the garden and woods. This morning I gathered field horse tails which like the skunk cabbage are most exotic, even phallic, in spite of their names, violets, adder's tongue, spring beauty, butter cups, arbutus, etc., so you can see what lovely months we're having. It's a shame it wasn't a decent day when you were down, but it's good we had a visit anyway.

I finished "Joan B" a few days after I saw you, and was so disappointed at the inadequacy of my ending, and its clumsiness that I sat and wept for three hours, not able to stop. However, I felt that I had worked long enough on it and brought the book to Liveright where it has been 3 weeks next Monday. Here's hoping.

I am now engaged in a book for children and the first 5,000 words are done. It will be long and leisurely and full of moral lessons, as all children's books should be. That's the way I enjoyed them when young and more or less vicious. This little exercise will rest me until I'm prepared to start on a novel which will be as fraught with emotion as Dostoevsky's. I've been jotting down scenes and conversations for it during the winter. Living down here and knowing that you're not going to be forced to pick up and move every few weeks makes one terrifically prolific.

MONDAY, MAY 25 [1925]

The book ["Joan Barleycorn"] has already come back from Liveright's with a little note saying that three or four had read it, that all agreed it was disjointed and that they didn't like realistic novels anyway. Which is rather discouraging since as far as I can make out I'll never write anything but what they call realistic novels.

Do write and let me know what you think of it. Shall I send you the last forty pages, or can you judge from what you have? And what would you advise me to do next? I can't tell you how I appreciate your encouragement. After the rejection of Liveright I was all ready to throw it in the attic, but thinking of you I decided to wait and see what you have to say. For God's sake don't tell me to put it aside and wait a few years and then see what I think of it. After rewriting it three times, I do want to send it around.

I am working half-time for a real estate man up in our little village, for twenty a week. It doesn't interfere with my work and pleasures in any way, and I am having a lot of fun showing people around bungalows and cottages and preaching the pleasures of the simple life.

Do let me hear from you soon. I'm sending you a picture of me and my country view. It was taken from the attic window and doesn't it give a lovely idea of the view I have from my windows?

I have made two gallons of dandelion wine and three of raison, and now some rhubarb and parsnip wine are making. I found the recipes in an old English cookbook. I'm going to try your apricot wine today.

Aside from working on various unpublishable novels, Dorothy wrote articles on gardens for the Staten Island Advance *and occasional pieces for* The New Masses. *Otherwise she was quite occupied by domestic life with Forster—what she liked to call her "common-law marriage." The passionate love expressed in her letters to Forster certainly corresponds to her account in* The Long Loneliness: *"I loved him in every way, as a wife, as a mother even. I loved him for all he knew and pitied him for all he didn't know. I loved him for the odds and ends I had to fish out of his sweater pockets and for the sand and shells he brought in with his fishing. I loved his lean and cold body as he got into bed smelling of the sea, and loved his integrity and stubborn pride."*

It was not long before Dorothy detected the first signs of pregnancy—a development that presaged a major turning point in her life. As she would later write in From Union Square to Rome, *"For a long time I had thought I could not have a child."* Reading Silas Marner *she had felt "a great longing in my heart for a baby. . . . No matter how much one is loved or one loves,"* she wrote, *"that love is lonely without a child. It is incomplete."* And now: *"I know that I am going to have a baby."* With this happy secret, she traveled that fall to visit her mother in Florida.

TO FORSTER BATTERHAM

MIAMI, SEPTEMBER 21, 1925

Dearest,

I am having a nice restful time, but oh, how I am looking forward to seeing you and Huguenot again. Mother is much dismayed at the idea of my starting back the first week in October, wanting me to stay until November but Lordy, I'd die, away so long. I rather think that I shall never travel again in all my life. I used to love it, gallivanting from one place to another, seeing new sights and new cities, but now I contrast every place with Huguenot and like it better than them all. And I keep thinking that frost will be coming on in another month, and there is so much to do, and I do want to see the garden in its fall glory.

Well, I didn't draw pictures of the specimens, leaving that for John [*Dorothy's younger brother*] to do, but he was so enamored of his own handiwork that he pasted them all in his scrapbook instead of sending them on to you. I put the specimens in a huge jar of alcohol and shall bring them back with me. Unfortunately, I put some lovely seaweeds in with them and the alcohol turned green from them, and the color of the butterfly fish is all gone, but it is interesting all the same.

Yesterday morning we all went over to the beach and swam and had a great time, but the water was warmish although delightfully clear, and the sands, in spite of bits of coral and interesting shells, nowhere's near so interesting as our own. I keep making these contrasts and drive Mother and Della crazy. Della loves Florida and says she would just as soon live down here all the year round, but Mother and I gasp with the heat and think of the delightfully contrasted seasons of the North.

I've driven around so much down here that I am much at home in an automobile and thinking of maybe perhaps driving back to New York by car. Every day there are advertisements of people going to Niagara Falls, Chicago, St. Louis, Los Angeles, and New York by car and will take a couple or one passenger for twenty bucks or expenses. It will cost me a hundred to get back by train, seventy-five by boat and I figure approximately fifty by auto. However all this is just speculation. I only know I wouldn't stay down here if I had to walk back.

This visit really had to be paid, for the family would have died if I hadn't come [for] Christmas and that of course would be impossible. I got a book on the expectant mother from the library and figured that I had figured wrong in the matter of dates. One should figure ten menstrual months or nine calendar months and I had figured nine menstrual months. That makes the date around March 5 instead of February 15 as I had estimated. Have you heard whether Caroline Tate had hers yet? All of Mother's friends are having babies, and also one of my aunts. Mother and Della sure will be surprised when I produce one for their inspection next summer, though of course Della will know before since she is coming up in March.

I think of you much and dream of you every night and if my dreams could affect you over long distance, I am sure they would keep you awake.

I love you lots and lots, sweetheart. Write soon.

MIAMI, MONDAY [SEPTEMBER 1925]

Dear Darling,

Another tropical storm and the rain is coming down in torrents. We have one or two a day now, and after they are over you feel as tho you were sitting in the steam room of a Turkish bath.

I haven't heard from you for days and days. I've written three times since I've heard from you. Your last letter was the long newsy one which you were so proud of.

I can hardly wait till next week, sweetheart. Next Monday at this time I'll be on the train speeding toward you.

Yesterday we all went swimming and the surf was tremendous, also the undertow. Della almost got drowned due to the undertow and waves breaking over her head.

I had a marvelous haircut today. They call it a pineapple bob. Next time I'll call for a cocoanut or an avocado bob. My ears are fully exposed but there are locks of hair before my ears so I can still look good in a hat. I am sure all this is of great interest to you—or do you love me because my legs meet together above the knees? Or because they don't?

Since I have refused to write (fiction) during the last two weeks in all this heat I've been sewing industriously. I have made two beautiful padded handles to grasp hot things with from off the stove. Especially the spoon you leave sticking up out of sauce pans to get hot and burn my fingers on purpose. Also I have made sachet bags with iris root to perfume the baby's clothes, also my own. Also I have made four egg cozies after the fashion of our tea cozy—to keep our soft-boiled eggs hot in the morning. Not that we need four. Two are to impress company with. I couldn't do all these silly things up there. I'd keep thinking I had to clean the kitchen shelves or wash windows, or something useful like that.

What a letter! You'd think I was writing to a female like Peggy [Cowley, *wife of the writer Malcolm Cowley*] instead of to my best beloved. I've written Peggy once—enough for her. You are the only, only one I want to write to. Do you still want me or are you used to being without me? However, notwithstanding, cold weather is coming, so fight as you may against it you'll have to sleep with me to keep warm, and who knows in my luring nightgown, you might be seduced into doing something besides sleep. Huh?

THURSDAY [SEPTEMBER 1925]
Dearest,

Yes, I guess the delay is at this end. When the postman brings the mail twice a day, he takes our outgoing mail, and the Miami post office here is awfully tied up. The postmen here look like street cleaners and so do the policemen, they go around so dishabille. In fact we all go around that way. I haven't worn shoes and stockings once down here except to go out, and my usual costume is a pair of pants—did I mention that I made two pair, trimmed in lace?—and a dress—and at least three times a day I go sit in the bathtub to cool off. Because of course the beach is fifteen miles away. Your various allusions to your intentions toward me are very disturbing. In fact, as I read your letter this morning I turned pale and faint and dizzy. My desire for you is a painful rather than pleasurable emotion. It is a ravishing hunger which makes me want you more than anything in the world and makes me feel as though I could barely exist until I saw you again.

However, be that as it may, I shall go on in this numb trance until a week from Sunday. My train leaves in the evening, and I'll arrive Tuesday afternoon at one thirty. More details of that later. Anyway, it's only a little over a week that I'll see you. If you meet me at the station we can go straight to the ferry from there. And Tuesday afternoon makes it pretty sure that there will be no visitors—I hope not at Freda's place either. And you can tell Peggy and Malcolm [Cowley] I'll be home Wednesday, so that we can have ourselves to ourselves.

I wouldn't be able to abide the slow boat trip getting to you. And the train costs little more than the boat I find.

Do have a plate of pickled eels, squash, and tomatoes for my supper when I come home. I have had plenty of summer squash down here, thank goodness, but there isn't a bit of fruit worth a damn. I don't care for guavas, nor [blank], nor [blank], the only three fruits there were on the market aside from grapes and watermelon. Grapefruit and alligator pears aren't in yet. Mother is giving me some jars of guava jelly to take back with me, and it's the most marvelous stuff you ever tasted. Nothing like the glue they sell and call jelly. Hers is just like honey and very delicate. I refused it for several weeks, then sampled a jar which was on the table, and after supper, retired to the couch with it and a spoon and my book and ate the whole thing. And when I like jelly it must be good.

I am rather more obvious than when I left, and although Mother has remarked on my size several times, she doesn't waste time in conjecture. I think she could guess if she wanted to, but it's just one of those facts she is going to ignore until the brat appears on the scene.

Strangely enough, Della guessed immediately, on account of the size and color of my breasts, but I laughed her off until a week ago when I told her. It was silly to keep on denying obvious symptoms such as my girth—none of her dresses will fit me—my occasional illnesses, and the most obvious fact of all that I can't wear a dress at all without a pad in front to keep my breasts or rather one of them from wetting everything. That's a strange symptom and I'll be glad to see a doctor when I get back to New York. Doesn't all this sound clinical?

Anyway, Della is delighted, and isn't making any difference in her plans except to come back in February instead of March. It would be too mean to do her out of half the fun which one has in expectations of this sort. And she is so healthy and normal in every way now—you wouldn't know her. She says she was an awful fool all last year, and it's a healthy fact that she realizes it and laughs at herself. Anyhow all young gals go through stages like that—I had my turbulent months when I was an utter ass and a nuisance to everybody, only younger—and we should not blame her.

The name of the little one, I've decided, will be Carol, which I've remembered is one of my favorite names. Don't you think it's an awfully happy name? The alternative is Michael. I've wasted no thought on that.

I do long for you, but it's only a little over a week, I keep assuring myself. That will just give you time to do the ceiling and floor, won't it darling love, she said hintingly. But the ceiling is most important and the floor could really be put off since I can help with that. There are so many things to do and I am so anxious to be there. Manure for the garden, and I've been thinking of strawberry plants. Do you put them in in the fall or spring? One of Mother's friends comes from Connecticut and had a farm there, and last week on a visit, we got together and bored everybody to death talking gardens. Anyway, she said that a spot as big as our front porch would produce an awful amount of strawberries and I'm wild about the idea.

You end your letter saying that your page and a half is all you will "inflict" me with, and here I am gossiping on and on when I should punish you for it. Especially for insinuating things in your letter which torture and torment me. I have never wanted you as much as I have ever since I left, from the first week on, although I've thought before that my desires were almost too strong to be borne. From the first, I've kept thinking how wonderful it will be to be back with you alone, but to have you completely to myself. Also no morning sicknesses which came on at all times of the day. I really feel marvelously healthy and plagued only by the heat. But that doesn't bother my appetite which is for three or four, not two.

Enough for you now, you undeserving wretch who probably doesn't miss me half as much as I do you. Always, all my love and kisses.

P.S. What does your brother want Mike's place for? Is he going to present it to you to farm? That's the only thing I could think of. If he did, and you did, I'd give up Huguenot and come down there with you and raise ten children. I'd not be so efficient as Lily but the children could help. Isn't Mike's place nearer to that other lake?

It may be a sentimental notion but I think it would be wonderful to live entirely off the land and not depend on wages for a livelihood. Don't snort. At least there wouldn't be any $30 grocery bills with a garden like Lily's.

MIAMI, OCT 2 [1925]
Dearest Forster,

Two more days and I shall be starting North, laden with avocado pears, guava jelly, cocoanuts, angel fish, and fish and porcupine fish, egg cozies, new clothes, love, etcetera, especially the love.

Pop is meeting me in Washington Tuesday morning at 7:30, where the train stops for half an hour and shall unload some of the pears and jelly on him. Most sweet and affectionate of him to get up so early for half an hour's visit. He sent me a hundred this morning for my ticket and I'll have enough over to pay $15 on the grocery bill which was thirty when I left.

Oh dearest darling, I can hardly wait to be with you to hug the life out of you. I do love you so much I shall never be away from you for more than a week again.

I had a terrible dream of your not meeting me and of me going weeping and heavy laden to Huguenot by myself only to find you lackadaisically out fishing, saying it was too much trouble to come into town. I awoke in a fine rage, but was so scared that I sent you the telegram or night letter right after getting my ticket. I thought of writing Sasha [a neighbor in Huguenot] and Peggy, one in town and the other out in the country, to make sure you heard when I'd be in, since I was afraid you might not be in your office again before Tuesday.

P.S. Call up and find whether train is late or not.

Dorothy's return to New York in October interrupts the record of her correspondence with Forster. By the time of the next surviving letter to her friend Llewellyn Jones her daughter, Tamar Teresa, was already seven months old and much had occurred. In fact, these missing months correspond to the most significant chapters in The Long Lone-liness, *the description of how her pregnancy and Tamar's birth decisively turned her heart to God. And yet, as her letters make clear, this overpowering conversion did not dim her longing for commercial success as a writer.*

TO LLEWELLYN JONES

LABOR DAY, FIVE P.M. [1926]

It will amuse you much to hear that "Joan Barleycorn" is also coming out as a serial. . . . I've also got sixty thousand words of another novel done, but it's going to be two hundred thousand probably so I expect to be another year or so on it, especially since I've thyroid trouble just now and may have to be operated on. I haven't a bulbous throat or anything but they say I have too much thyroid, etc., and since I've been losing weight steadily for six months now I suppose I must do something about it.

The baby is wonderful, the cutest little thing I've ever seen. I never cease to marvel at having such an adorable *Ladies Home Journal* baby. I always rather expected an ugly grotesque thing which only I could love; expecting perhaps to see my sins in the child. You see I'm still religious, reading my missal faithfully, pinning medals on the baby and going to Mass. And when I go walking, I mutter over my beads and feel my soul growing strong through exercise. But I have not yet attained contrition for my sins, so I guess I am still lacking.

A nice sober Labor Day, having celebrated last week with a lovely party on the beach where I, inspired by the example of some laboring men digging sand on the beach who threw off their clothes in the heat of the day and rushed in nude, was impelled to do likewise. But I did it at night, since my bosoms, as I have nicknamed them, have hung like sacks since nursing the baby, though the rest of my figure is still sweet, so I must retain some vestiges of modesty. Also I was inspired to think I should have been a dancer instead of a writer, and draped myself in lace shawls and danced in the moonlight for the assembled multitude who played on guitars and sang Russian gypsy songs. Forster had been out fishing and reappeared on the scene in time to see me disappearing in the water again, and his concern for my safety—I was swimming out too far—infected several of our Russian friends who rushed into the water after me with their clothes on. A gay time, indeed.

While Dorothy's letters offer no chronicle of her conversion to Catholicism, they do shed considerable light on her painful separation from Forster. The intimations of a gulf between them were present from the beginning. Forster, she wrote, "had always rebelled against the institution of the family and the tyranny of love. It was hard for me to see at such times why we were together, since he lived with me as though he were living alone and he never allowed me to forget that this was a comradeship rather than a marriage."

And yet the greater tension between them arose from Dorothy's increasing attraction to Catholicism. It had begun with an impulse to pray—an instinct inspired by her happiness and a desire to offer thanks. With that gratitude "came the need to worship, to adore." The very delight in nature, which Forster had helped awaken, drew her heart to God and the life of the spirit. Forster, meanwhile, "did not believe in bringing children into such a world as we lived in." He certainly recoiled from her decision that "I was going to have my child baptized, cost what it may."

For herself she put off the day of decision. "A woman does not want to be alone at such a time. . . . Becoming a Catholic would mean facing life alone and I clung to family life. It was hard to contemplate giving up a mate in order that my child and I could become members of the Church. Forster would have nothing to do with religion or with me if I embraced it. So I waited."

The real impediment was Forster's refusal to get married before officials of either Church or state. To become a Catholic, Dorothy recognized, would mean separating from the man she loved. "It got to the point where it was the simple question of whether I chose God or man." This was no easy choice. Radical friends insinuated that her turn to God was because she was "tired of sex, satiated, disillusioned." But this was quite far from her feelings. "It was because through a whole love, both physical and spiritual, I came to know God."

By the winter of 1927 Dorothy and Forster separated, and when he tried to return she would not let him. "My heart was breaking with my own determination to make an end, once and for all, to the torture we were undergoing." The next day, on December 27, she was received into the Church.

That is the familiar story recounted in her memoir. But, as the following letters make clear, this did not, by any means, mark an end, "once and for all," to her relationship with Forster, to her passionate love for him, or to her desire that he would in the end come around and agree to marry her and that they might be a happy family at last. Meanwhile, the ongoing attachment between them, broken as it was, provoked pain and resentment on both sides. Though they did not live together, Forster continued to drop in, both to visit the baby and to check on Dorothy, evidently in hopes that her attitude might show signs of softening. It did not.

TO FORSTER BATTERHAM

STATEN ISLAND [MARCH? 1928]
Dearest Forster—

The baby is as happy as the day is long and remembers every detail of her life down here. Yesterday it was sunny enough for her to spend the entire morning on the porch and in the afternoon we sat on the beach after her nap until five o'clock, the sun was so warm. As soon as she got down the other day she went out on the porch and I fixed up the swing for her and she lay down on it, covered herself up and took a nap. And on the beach she started right away to cover herself with sand. She remembers Smiddy all right, and Betty, but she's scared to death of her. Of course there being no other children down here, Betty leaps all over her and she was frightened blue in the face. But as long as I hold her hand, she laughs and screams with joy and calls "Beh-beh" to her.

The dock weed is one inch high. . . . Tamar has found her way off the porch and wandering around the yard.

The wind is blowing a gale out, but it isn't cold,—forty on the porch. Tamar's cough gets worse instead of better. She had about five spasms both last night and the night before. From the descriptions in the baby books down here, it looks as though she has whooping cough all right. If it's bronchitis she'll be well within a week, so time will tell.

I forgot your bedroom slippers and left them under the bed in Elizabeth's front room. You need them yourself so next time you're by why don't you get them.

I miss you a lot, but I'm not going to talk about it. I'll wash windows instead. Besides, spring isn't here yet.

Love,

P.S. Most of this letter was written with the baby under hoof, so it's probably incoherent.

FRIDAY [MARCH? 1928]

Dear Forster,—

I wish you wouldn't come down Saturday night but would come Sunday morning instead. —That is, if you were coming down at all. I have been trying all week to write this letter and it is almost impossible for me to write it now. You make it much harder when you are kind to me. But we can't go on in any but a friendly relation and I suppose you will say we can't even have that. Quite aside from my religious instincts, which you refuse to recognize, we weren't getting on at all last year as you know. We had any number of mean, ugly quarrels which are enough to corrode anyone's existence and the quarrels were not only about religion but there were resentments about the baby and about finances and Lily and then finally about my moving into town.

It is terribly hard to even mention my religious feelings to you because I am sure you do not think I am sincere. But it is not a sudden thing, but a thing which has been growing in me for years. I had impulses toward religion again and again and now when I try to order my life according to it in order to attain some sort of peace and happiness it is very hard but I must do it. Because even though it is hard, it gives me far more happiness to do it, even though it means my combating my physical feelings toward you. The strength of our physical attachment never led you to make any sacrifices or capitulations of your principles. You were always very hard about maintaining your independence and freedom. You would never marry even when I begged you to some years ago. And you always held yourself somewhat aloof from me. It is only now when I wish to give you up that you hold on to me.

Before, after every quarrel you fought against coming back to me and never did unless I went after you. You say that I went after you this time, but I only did that once when I went over to your room after your sister's party. And that was because Della shouted at me when I came home and said that she didn't want you coming in and sitting around when she was taking care of the baby, and I was afraid she had said something to hurt you and came over to see if you were angry at me. I told you afterward that I was sorry I came, but you have been coming after me ever since. I do not think you would pursue me, if you did not think I was sincere in my desire to break away,—you are so contrary. If you thought I was bound to have you you would run away from me and shun me.

I do not see why we can't be friends, but if you insist on not being friends with me, I'll just have to put up with it, no matter how unhappy it makes me. After all, the present unhappiness is not unbearable because I at least have the peace of knowing that I am doing what I think is best. And it's a bearable unhappiness because it has in it none of those horrible resentments I had toward you last year so often.

Please do not be angry at me. You know I love you and as a matter of fact always did love you more than you loved me.

THURSDAY [APRIL 1928]

Dear Forster,—

The wind is almost blowing the house away today but it is much warmer, thank goodness.

Please, Forster, do not come down this weekend. We just make each other miserable, and I really can't help the unutterable gloom I fall into which is only the result of mental conflict. When I am alone here by myself I am perfectly happy. Things will work out alright some way or another, but just now please leave me by myself, won't you?

You certainly ought not to mind staying away from me, you have such a rotten opinion of me anyway. Our last two weekends have been anything but pleasant, as you said yourself, so please, please, stay away from me.

WEDNESDAY, MAY 16 [1928]

Dear Forster,—

The baby must be getting some more back teeth for her cold persists and she is as cranky and hellish as she can be. Yesterday she went through the garden and broke off half the iris buds and I could have wept. I shut her up on the porch for the first time and made her stay there, trying to impress on her the fact that she was in disgrace. This morning she went around touching the sweet william and iris buds very gently and saying, "Bad girl," very definitely. But the trouble is, even though she understands, she just wants to be hellish every now and then and do something to rile you.

I dreamt the other night that you were marrying a rich widow who lived down the beach somewhere, and I thought desperately that I must have one last night with you before the wedding. You were very cold to me and kept saying, "Well this is what you get."

Love,
Dorothy

Thank you for the contribution, darling, but why don't you send a word with it? Do you insist on hating me so much?

Aside from her writing, Dorothy—with help from her neighbor Freda—brought in a little income by taking care of young children in the neighborhood. Forster also made regular contributions, though Dorothy felt his support was grudging.

TUESDAY [MAY 1928]
Dear Forster—

I am paying no attention to your taunting letter, in the first place because I rather expected it, and in the second place because I have no pride where the baby is concerned. I shall continue to beg, as you call it, in order to keep me going until Charlie is out of school. I heard from him the other day about coming down and he says he wants to but his mother isn't sure yet. Freda and I are going to take three or four kids between us and we'll probably make out very well all summer.

Thank goodness the rain is almost over. It is dull and cloudy today but warm. We almost froze last week, because even over on Schram's beach there was very little wood and that so damp of course that it was almost impossible to start a fire and when you did, it smoked so it drove you out.

The baby has a cold and was fretful last night what with her nose being stopped up, but she is fine this morning.

Love from both of us, Dorothy

In spite of the manner in which it was sent, I thank you very much for the money you sent last week. Sasha tells us that your business is very slow, but I hope you do not get discouraged. If you are terribly broke, don't bother about us. Freda will feed Tamar and I can get along on salt fish and oatmeal. The salt fish, by the way, is delicious, or would be if one was not eating it every day. I am sending some jam in to you by Freda.

WEDNESDAY MORNING [MAY 1928]
Dearest Forster—

I've been agonized with poison ivy since last Thursday now and it seems to get worse instead of getting better, new patches appearing every day. I'm covered from head to foot with one side of my face all swollen. That's what I get for going out in the woods after violets and that barberry bush we saw. No more woods for me this year. I've been too nerve racked to write and thank you for the money last week. Both Freda and Sasha say your business is most slow and discouraging, and I appreciate the fact that it's a sacrifice on your part to send it.

It's a rainy cold day again and the fire is going merrily. There hasn't been a day that we could go without one. And there is plenty of wood now on the beach.

The baby's cold is over, thank goodness—for her whoop came back with it and she was coughing badly again, says a lot of words now, like Rock-a-bye, and "sweet kitties wetting bed," and she calls Smitty "Mish," which delights him.

I shall send you in some more of the jam next time Freda goes in, for you know I do not eat it and I'd rather you had it than company.

The New Masses accepted my Bellevue article on the birth of a child and it is coming out on the fifteenth.*

---

* Dorothy's article, "Having a Baby," appeared in the June 1928 issue of *The New Masses*. A joyous account of motherhood, it was reprinted in workers' pa-

Don't be discouraged about your business, dearest. After all it is very young. Sasha brings most discouraging reports as to your discouragement, and I don't know whether it is his pessimism or whether it is true.

THURSDAY [MAY 1928]

Dearest Forster—

It is hard to write you when you just preserve this gloomy silence. Why don't you take unto yourself a concubine and then perhaps you won't have this feeling of rancor toward me.

The baby is feeling fine. She is not picking any more irises and the garden is full of them. Did I tell you I got that poison ivy while going out and digging up that barberry bush which you said you liked? I didn't get it because I liked it but because you said you liked it. The bush, not the poison ivy.

I finished my book and it is now in the hands of Coward McCann.

SUNDAY NIGHT [1928]

Dearest—

Every morning when the baby climbs in the window to me she gives me a good morning kiss, imitating you, and pressing her face to mine for a long time. It is too sweet. And now she insists on kissing the cat goodnight, chasing her around the room until she can grab her by the ears and plant a kiss on her nose.

She is sitting in the bathtub now and I just had to jump over and rinse the soap with which she was washing her hair and which she gets in her eyes.

I suppose you will sneer at me for writing to you but I can't help wanting to keep in touch with you some way. I suppose the best thing for both of us would be if you contracted an alliance with some nice fat Jewish girl (your ideal of beauty)

---

pers around the world, including in the Soviet Union, and eventually also in the *Catholic Worker* (December 1977).

even though I would be racked with jealousy if you did. I dream of you every night—that I am lying in your arms and I can feel your kisses and it is torture to me, but so sweet, too. I do love you more than anything in the world, but I cannot help my religious sense, which tortures me unless I do as I believe right.

I wish you would write to me now and then.

Let me know if you find out anything about those beads, and if you can sell them for ten dollars, do, for it would keep me for two weeks. You mustn't think I am mean and bitter when I reproach you about money matters. I really do think you ought to send me five dollars a week, which I could live on so easily down here with the baby, but if you don't want to contribute to my delinquency, as Della would consider it (I don't exactly understand what way you have of looking at it)—I shan't mention it again but get along some way or other until school closes and I have some kids to take care of.

You said I didn't appreciate anything you had ever done for me, but you are absolutely wrong. Just because I don't gush with sweetness like Libby you condemn me. In fact you are always condemning me because I am not like your sisters.

But I remember all the things you have done for me, the dearness and the kindness of all the little everyday things you did. I should like to hold you and kiss you and kiss you, but I can't and my arms ache for you. I do love you.

Dorothy spent her winters in the city, returning with spring to Staten Island. In these years she was gradually adjusting to the discipline of Catholic life, including daily Mass and weekly confession, reciting the Little Office of the Blessed Virgin, and reading books by a range of Catholic authors. She began to sell the occasional story to a Catholic magazine. Still, she reassured Forster, if he would only marry her she would not impose her piety. "I would have nothing around the house to jar upon you,—no pictures and books," she wrote. "I am really not obsessed as you think I am."

MARCH 15, 1929

Dear Forster,

I got your note and the check last night and thank you very much indeed. If it would not be just as mean and bitter as your note, I would send it back to you. Instead I will use it to catch up on, since I'm always about fifty dollars behind my salary.

I'm sorry about what happened Saturday night. I knew nothing about it until the next morning, strange though it may seem. Charlie had been in a most depressed mood the week before, and I was sitting there expressing my general feeling of melancholy and depression, most of which was due to the fact that I had finished my play. Anyway, he being a sentimentalist was very sympathetic and went out and got me a bottle of liquor. I took a few drinks and after a few more gloomy remarks went to bed and fell right to sleep. I had no idea that he was so idiotic and foolish as to go down to get you. He had said, earlier in the evening, that doubtless my feeling of depression was due to not being with you, and should he go down to get you. I vetoed the idea of course. But as I say, he is a most sentimental German.

What he did just deepened my feeling of depression, of course, so that it hung on all the next day.

One of the reasons I was so tired that I didn't hear you and Peggy [Cowley] in the next room was that I had gone to the *Masses* ball the night before, not getting home until almost three, and then got up early and went with Lily and the kids over to Rose's for the day. It was being with them and seeing their happy home life which made me feel that life was very black indeed. I wonder how you would feel if one of your sisters had to go through the struggle that I do. I'm sure you would feel that marriage was a very slight concession to make and that the man was indeed a most pig-headed idiot to ruin their two lives.

I have told you again and again that you would be involving yourself in nothing if you married me. I assure you of that because you mention in one of your letters "who knows what entanglements you would drag me into? Etc." You would of course have to agree to allow the children to be raised Catholics, but the ceremony is as simple as that of going before a justice of the peace. Religion would be obtruded on you in no way except that you would have to see me go to church once a week, and five times a year on various saints' days. I would have nothing around the house to jar upon you,—no pictures and books.

I am really not obsessed as you think I am. You might say that far more about my writing. And I would try my best to understand your irritation with me just as you had to put up with my irritation of you when you were mildly obsessed with fishing and stamp collecting.

But I suppose it is no use. No use at all of going over these old arguments.

The baby speaks of you often, and only the other day she gave me a sweet fervent kiss and said "Forster kisses you like that."

TO KATHERINE ANNE PORTER

The writer Katherine Anne Porter would earn fame for her novel Ship of Fools. *She was part of the Greenwich Village literary set that included Dorothy's friends the Burkes (Lily and Kenneth), the Tates (Allen and Caroline), and the Cowleys (Malcolm and Peggy). In later life she too would embrace Catholicism.*

SEPTEMBER 1929

Just got your Tuesday letter and urge you to come immediately, Friday evening when you get this. I'm leaving here Sunday afternoon for good, going in to town to spend three days with Della, before going on Wednesday. So you see the time is short, the night is far spent, etc.

If you can't possibly get down here this weekend, I'll see you at Della's, since she says she's going to have a little supper and liquor for me before I go, Tuesday night.

And if you can't see Father McKenna, you'll enjoy dropping in at the church of Our Lady of Guadalupe on Fourteenth Street, and on either Thursdays or Saturdays, ringing Father Zachary's bell to call him to talk to you. You don't have to go to confession just because you ring the confessional bell. Father Zachary is the sweet dear who, after giving absolution in the confessional, whispers impiously to me each time, "Did you sell your play yet?" He told me it was passionate but very good. I do wish I had a chance to talk to you about some stranger supernatural incidents. So try to come on down.

In August 1929, Dorothy received a surprising call from Pathé Films, the movie studio in Los Angeles. They had liked a play she had sent some months before and now they were offering her a job writing dialogue and reading novels for possible film adaptation. Apart from the promise of a paying job, the move offered an escape from the constant attraction to Forster and the tension this caused her. In September Dorothy and Tamar departed for the Coast.

TO FORSTER BATTERHAM

[SEPTEMBER 1929]

PENNSYLVANIA RAILROAD

Dearest [Forster]—

I realized afterward that it was cruelty to us both to ask you to see me off. You might better have said goodbye over the telephone and gone right down to the Island. I felt so terribly to leave you—I can't tell you. I do love you so much sweetheart. Tamar wants to know when you're coming to take us off the train.

Much, much love from both of us, darling one,
Dorothy

CULVER CITY, CALIF.

TUESDAY NIGHT [10 SEPTEMBER 1929]

Dearest Forster,

Lord, what a deplorable place this is. Ugly, —barren and sub-urban. And not a single playschool or nursery for Tamar. After hunting all day since 9:30 this morning, the best I could do was to find an Englishwoman around the corner from the studio who will board her. The house is nice but with a tiny yard. In fact it is all desert except for tiny patches of garden around the houses. And as for the beach which is twenty minutes away, for miles and miles it is just like Coney Island or Rockaway, unspeakably dreary.

Culver City, to do it justice, is the prettiest spot around here—18 miles away from the station in Los Angeles. The city itself spread for miles and miles and *flat*. Scarcely a hill in sight. They say there are hills over on the Hollywood end of the city but that is ten miles from here. Culver City is much like the nice suburbs around Miami. In fact the whole place reminds me of Florida, except it's just warm, not hot.

The studios themselves are magnificent. The administration buildings look like the White House and most luxurious inside, and the studios themselves stretch for blocks and blocks.

I just got Tamar to bed. She has the most angelic disposition. With all the dragging around she remains cheerful, and only shows her fatigue by becoming obstreperously lively. As for me, I'm as blue as indigo. I told you it was much harder for those who went away than for those who stayed. I have felt nothing but a blank loneliness since I left you. Life is indeed a most miserable affair. Why don't you become reasonable or indulgent or what-ever you want to call it and tell me to come back and marry you? We could be so happy together. And even if we fought it would be better than this blank dead feeling. You know I love you and it isn't just loneliness which makes me long for you so.

Do write me, c/o the hotel here, where I'll probably stay a

week or so. It's a small family affair, right across from the studio and more cheerful than any of those lousy bungalows which can't compare with mine.

I'll run up now and see if the little imp is asleep. If I'd known how desolately ugly this place was and the total absence of nurseries I almost think I'd have left her with Freda or Gert for three months. But perhaps she doesn't mind it as much as I do.

All my love, Dorothy

The job in California did not have much glamour. In fact it was not much of a job at all. "I was cooped up in my own office, with chaise longue, having nothing to do all day and every day, except to wait for mail from home and read." She was "dead lonely" and the distance from Forster only intensified her longing. As she noted in The Long Loneliness, *"I would have gone back to New York . . . but to me at that time New York was an occasion of sin. I hungered too much to return to Forster."*

PATHÉ STUDIOS, INC.

CULVER CITY, CALIFORNIA

MONDAY MORNING [16 SEPTEMBER 1929]

Dear Forster,

I got your letter mailed Friday night, this morning. That was certainly quick enough, wasn't it? I've been longing to hear from you, so it was sweet of you to write at once.

I am feeling much better now that I've been assigned an office to myself, looking out over a swimming pool and lawn and bush geraniums. Although I've only been given three scripts to read and criticize—much like that awful work I had at Metro Goldwyn,—I've worked out the first pages of a synopsis of a story of my own, which I hope they let me go to work on. Usually they assign you to something idiotic like a society drama with no plot, or a detective story which they have bought up from somewhere and feel they have to use, for you to write the dialogue. If they let me do my own stuff I'll get along better.

I do love you so much, sweetheart, and miss you more than I thought possible. Even if we weren't together before, I at least had hopes of seeing you, and knowing you were there. Now, God knows when I'll see you again. Can't you realize how much happier we'd be together, in spite of differences of opinion, than we are apart? And you know this job, no matter how much money it pays, means nothing to me. I'd rather live with you, no matter how poor we were or how little we had; just as long as the bills got paid, I'd be perfectly happy. The only misery I had before about financial matters was having to borrow from friends to pay such things as grocery and milk bills. I don't mind going without things as long as I have a roof over my head and enough to just live on.

Well, perhaps someday I can bulldoze you into marrying me. I certainly don't want to ever marry anybody else. Do I have to be condemned to celibacy all my days, just because of your pig-headedness? Damn it, do I have to remind you that Tamar needs a father? And you needn't think I'm sentimental, because I'm not. She keeps asking after you,—and you know how she loves you. She used to say that things such as automobiles and dogs, etc. were going home to their mothers, but now she says fathers. And whenever she sees a child with its father she points it out. She was telling Mrs. Lavelle, the woman who is taking care of her, that her father was coming out here next Sunday (you know how she says everything is next Sunday). So you see, she wants you as much as I do.

I won't talk about this any more. It's foolish to, and I've talked enough about it. But you know that no matter how miserable or lonely it makes me, I can't ever be with you again,—to live with you.

Got to read a most awful script now. Do write to me dearest sweetest, because I think of you and want you night and day.

All my love,
Dorothy

[SEPTEMBER 23, 1929]

Dearest Forster,—

Depending on your regularity, I knew I would get a letter from you this morning, another piece of paper, but a sweet one, only I'd like a marriage license more. As for your being a father, a hell of a lot of good you are as one, or ever have been except for the first year and a half. A father separated some thousands of miles isn't much, you must admit.

I delight in hearing of the frost here in this balmy weather where it is not too hot and yet not cool enough for a coat. If I only had something to do I'd be quite content and sink into an idyllic existence and prepare to stay here for the next five years, you being what you are, a stubborn mule. But as one of the girls here says, life in this place broadens the fanny and narrows the mind. I must expect to sit here doing nothing for a month. There are twelve writers, I the only woman, and half of them are doing nothing. Why they have them on the payroll I don't see . . .

For the last two days, I've been taking the car out alone and have enjoyed it immensely. We can have long trips and explorations this fall, and maybe drive down to Mexico for a weekend.

The woman who is taking care of Tamar is a dear. She drops every "h" and sticks them in front of all vowels, as I've never heard done before, "me h'eye," for instance, and "Gawd bless me 'ome," in the most approved cockney style, which I thought existed only in books. Helen Crowe would die at the influence over our little one. From Eighth Avenue she'll be changing to another dialect. I like her because she is such a gay and lively creature full of bustling and laughter, and Tamar took to her immediately, within a week kissing her as though she'd known her as long as she had Freda. There is a houseful of people, a young son and daughter, a sister, and since the neighborhood is full of friends of theirs, all English, they are always sitting around drinking tea.

Darling, I don't know how to be otherwise than restrained when I want to put my longing for you on paper. It seems so damned inadequate. How can I tell you how I long for our long evenings down there in Huguenot, interspersed with buttered toast and tea and books and the New York *Times* not to speak of our passionate hours together.

I am not restrained when I am lying in your arms, am I? You know I am not a promiscuous creature in my love. I've never loved anyone but you and Lionel [Moise] and that early affair seems but the dimmest adolescent crush compared to the love I have for you. But it is all so damned hopeless that I do hope I fall in love again and marry since there seems to be no possibility for a happy outcome to our love for each other. It will either be that or a single life for me from now on so it is no use your nursing any hopes as to anything else. So what is the use of your expecting any impassioned phrases from me on paper? My letters to you can only be friendly ones, so stop writing if you want to, and go find yourself some other affair.

Dorothy and Tamar were joined in California by Lallah Rogers, an older woman friend from New York whose son had recently committed suicide. Dorothy welcomed the companionship. But in almost every letter to Forster she entreated him to give up his pig-headedness and agree to marry her.

SEPTEMBER 30 [1929]

Dearest Forster,—

After I am away a few years long, you'll wish you did have the old fashioned kind of love for me which made you want me by your side. When I'm residing down in Mexico City, you'll be sorry. Tamar will have forgotten all about you by then. Now she talks about you all the time. When I told her Lallah was coming, she insisted you were coming too, since she saw you both on weekends. "My friend Lallah and Forster are coming," she keeps saying. We saw a movie the other day in which the father scolds his son loudly, and Tamar said "My father doesn't scold me." And she has the most fascinated interest in watching other children with their fathers.

You don't seem to have the slightest idea what I'm complaining about—and that is, for one that I haven't you,—and the other is that I have no work to do. You tell me to be satisfied that I am at last engaged in writing, which I've always wanted to do, etc. Everything is marvelous except that I am not working. I'm doing nothing around here and I'm afraid, every now and then, that the entire three months will pass this way and then I'll be let out. It has happened to many others. They just don't seem to find a story for you to work on. And though you rack your brain for synopses and ideas, they are all greeted with indifference, and you hear nothing from nobody from one week to the next.Don't talk so much about my complaining. If you don't want to hear how I feel about things, my worries about instability, etc., I'll write you blah letters telling you nothing about myself. That seems to be what you'd prefer.

I'll read Tamar your letter but it will only make her wonder more than ever why you don't come around. As for a present, why don't you pay Gert to make her a little winter coat. She will need one quite light and warm because it is chilly and sunny here in winter and she can play out every day. You know Tamar loves clothes almost as much as she does toys.

Lots of love, sweetheart,—*your friend* (How do you like that?),
Dorothy

SEPTEMBER 1929

Dear Forster,—

Sure,—to everybody else but you and Freda, I tell the nicest of things, and to you, I tell my deep fears of landing on my ear in three months after not having a chance to do a single lick of work. But even that fear is evaporating, since just this morning one of the "ideas," "suggestions," or "plots" which I turned in was sent back with approval and they may set me to work on that.

I complain of not being married to you, not of not being with you. If you should drop in and want a bed, you would indeed, as you surmise, find a very chaste one on an army cot. But I shall complain no more. I'll be very glad to stay five years out here, and by that time you will have found yourself a new weekend affair, since that is all you want, and when I want to come back and live in my little house by the water, I shall not be plagued by you.

Give my love to everybody on the beach and a friendly, and perhaps slightly impassioned kiss to yourself.

PATHÉ STUDIOS, CULVER CITY, CALIF.

NOVEMBER 4, 1929

Dearest Forster:

Tamar and I sat on the beach all yesterday afternoon in our bathing suits and basked in the sun and waded, though we didn't go in. Mussels are about eight inches long out here and the seaweed comes in long tough ropes just like the tubing for a bath shower and people jump rope with it and lasso each other, it is so tough. The beach is all sand, but what shells there are are huge. We drive down in about ten minutes from the house and today or tomorrow I'll go down about four and take some pictures of Tamar and the sea birds for you. My camera costs 85 cents and these are the first pictures I've taken.

I certainly hope the stock market won't affect your business the way it has affected the movie business. It is completely dead around here. No work at all. Only three writers left out of twenty-four there were a few months ago. I'm hoping they keep me on and my hopes are based on the fact that my salary is a comparatively small one.

I wish you would give in. I can assure you I would not bother you and your own opinions in the least as long as you granted me religious liberty,—that is, me and the numerous other children we'd have. I haven't been writing because of the seeming hopelessness of it all, but perhaps it shows a lack of faith in miracles to be so hopeless. Anyway, I do miss you terribly, and I want nothing more in life than to be with you again. Tamar frequently mentions you in her monologues, as her Forster father, so that it sounds as though she had adopted you rather than that you produced her. When I went to get her the other day she was telling the little boy she plays with about her Forster father and the motor boat and fishing, etc. She is getting browner and browner and gaining weight steadily.

"As ever,"

Dorothy

MONDAY [NOVEMBER 1929]

> *Forster is my foster-father*
> *He has no hair.*
> *He threw it in the garbage.*
> *He has just a little bit of hair.*
> *He has black eyes,*
> *a blue nose,*
> *a white mouth.*
> *He says fish.*
> *I had a little fish, a rotten fish, it was dead.*
> *My Forster Forster Forster.*
> *He is away, away, away, away, away.*
> *Pretty soon he will come in this door, in this window.*
> *He's gone over to Hoogayack.*

This is a little poem which I took down at Tamar's dictation last night. She was singing it to her dolls as she put them to bed.

In three weeks my contract will be up and I doubt whether it will be renewed. They are producing nothing and every idea I have is sent back to me, though some they have said are "pretty good." I have three more plots in my head—all in all I've evolved more plots in these three months than I have in all the rest of my life—which I'm going to put in short story form to hand in to them, so that if they don't want them, I'll have them almost in shape to send out. It makes you feel rather hopeless when you realize that they have a whole staff of readers here and in the East, who are going over everything that's being published in books and magazines, as well as everything that is being produced. They choose none of these, so what hope is there that they'll select one of my ideas? None at all. I'm looking forward to a nice leisurely drive down to Mexico City.

Two sweet letters from you last week. I wish I were there to scold you and clean the house up after you and find your cap for bed. We would take a bath together so as not to waste the hot water—the bathroom could be heated easily with the oil stove which heats the water, and if the nights are cold I would keep you very warm indeed. As it is, I'm cold every night and I need very much my electric pad which I left up in the attic. Could you send it on to me, together with the shawl Della brought me from Riga? Also that brown wool suit with wooly trimming which looks like fur but which is worsted? Would it be too much trouble for you to do this: Or do you need the electric pad yourself?

Where are you living or where are you going to live this winter?

Do you notice Tamar's sweet boyish bob in the picture? She is going to dancing school twice a week and consistently has refused to work with the other children. But she likes to go, and when she gets home she does the exercises all over the floor and insists on my playing the phonograph so she can dance.

Love from both of us, dearest.

Dorothy

Approaching the end of her contract with Pathé, Dorothy began making plans to travel to Mexico.

NOVEMBER 25, 1929

Dear Forster,—

Of course I'm not coming back to New York. What's the use? As you say there is only one thing that stands between us, but that one thing is insurmountable. I shall probably be away for two or three years, maybe longer. We have found that when we get down into the middle of Mexico there is no road into Mexico City, so we have to change our destination, choosing Tampico as our terminal. It has the advantage, too, of being on the Gulf, which I'll like. I've contracted with an automobile club which publishes a monthly magazine for a monthly article on touring in Mexico, and that will help out expenses some. I will have two hundred to start out with and a portable typewriter and phonograph besides a new winter coat and shoes and hat.

If you should write to me between now and the next two weeks, and said we'd get married, I'd drive back across country. Or no! that would be way too slow for me. They would pay my fare of course and I'd dash madly back as quick as I could get there, and we'd get married and live happily ever after, etc. That line will make you laugh at me. But oh, what happiness it would be to be with you again. But I must not think about it.

As always, I miss you terribly, dearest one, but there is certainly no use in my coming back and continuing the struggle to make a living in New York. Out here in this climate and in Mexico, it will be easy though the wage may be small, after the princely moving picture pay. Of course nothing is settled yet. They may keep me on, but I doubt it much.

FRIDAY [DEC 1929]

Dearest Forster,—

Next Friday, a week from today, we are on our way to Mexico City. There has been a terrific upset around the studio, Ralph Block and all the other studio heads being let off, all the writers and readers, secretaries, and everything. I had a feeling that this was coming by the gossip ever since I've been here, as I told you.

I feel as though I had accomplished much out here, but I cannot say that I've enjoyed being with Pathé. It really is unbelievable, the way these studios operate. Every day I've sat around with a slightly sick feeling at the pit of my stomach, just as you feel when you're looking for a job or going to borrow money from someone—waiting for something to happen, and nothing has happened. There has never been one moment when I haven't felt uncertain and absolutely lacking in confidence. Only last week I finally knew where I stood. And that I learned through the newspapers which came out with the story that Pathé was changing management and that thirty of the executives at the head were out and new ones coming in. Which means that all the writers and readers and secretaries are out too.

I miss you so much darling, and it will be such a long time till I see you again. I'll probably stay down there until Tamar is seven when she can go to school winters. Only then I'll come back to New York. And by that time you'll have a sweetheart, but just the same we must stay friends so do write to me and to Tamar. She is always writing a letter to you, but it is so formless yet I don't send her scribbles.

MEXICO CITY
JANUARY 4, SATURDAY [1930]
Dearest Forster,—

We are nicely settled now, Lallah in one big room at the other end of the apartment of some Mexican people, and me with two lovely little rooms, one for sleeping and the other for a sitting room. The roofs are the scene of general activity here. You see turkeys and chickens and cats wandering around most amiably together, and I suppose if we were in a less respectable neighborhood there would be also pigs. It is a poor neighborhood, but a grade above poverty.

Tamar and I are both happy here. The weather is ideal, and

the place is incredibly beautiful. It is a big valley, 7,000 feet high, and all sides are still higher ranges of mountains, white capped, and tremendous. We take a bus out to the outskirts every day or so and walk over the hilly roads and through the little villages, where the people kindly answer questions and are very polite about your poor Spanish, and do not stare at you as tourists. Tamar says, "Now, we have no more thank yous, only Gracias. And we have no more goodbyes, only Adios." She is picking up words very quickly, and if I can find a kindergarten which will take her, young as she is, she'll learn the language fast.

All the newspapers have English sheets, so I'm hoping to land a job on one of them. I have fifty dollars left. I met an artist I knew in New Orleans, and Diego Rivera, the other day, but no other Americans.

Do write me when you have time.

Love, Dorothy

Dorothy remained in Mexico for several months, writing a number of articles for America and The Commonweal. *She might have remained there indefinitely, had Tamar not come down with malaria. This prompted a return to New Jersey, where they stayed with friends and family.*

TO KATHERINE ANNE PORTER

ANDOVER, NEW JERSEY, JULY 5, 1930

I'm staying down with Kenneth Burke and his wife Lily, as you see, and from here I shall go down to Della's (my sister) next week.

Tamar was in the hospital eleven days with her malaria, taking twenty grains of quinine a day. Now she is down to four, has gained four pounds, and looks as though she were never sick in her life. She's having a great time with Kenneth's kids. Forster (the father of Tamar—his illegitimate child) paid her hospital bills which were thirty-three dollars, and is only too pleased to take care of her board all summer. He is going to take up the matter with his sister himself. I'm pulling the completely helpless female stunt, leaving everything to him. If he is going to foot the bills, it is only just for him to make all the decisions as to what should be done. So I find myself playing a new role in life and a hard one, as it is difficult to keep from making plans and tending to things myself.

TO FORSTER BATTERHAM

GLEN GARDEN, NEW JERSEY, AUGUST 7, 1930

Dearest Forster,

Della and Franklin are in town and all is peace and quiet. The kids are fed and Tamar is playing in the hammock and John Simon on the porch. They enjoy each other very much. When Johnny takes his bath, Tamar insists on sitting naked by the side of him so that he can splash her.

I picked enough elderberries in ten minutes last night to start a couple of gallons of wine, so Tamar and I will go out and get a few more gallons. The blackberries still are going strong, and I shall make a few gallons of that just to see what it is like. (I am getting so used to being homeless that I am making myself at home wherever I am, though I thought at the beginning of the summer I'd never be able to stand it. I am increasing in philosophical wisdom, evidently.)

I hope you haven't had too nerve-racking a week and that you are catching weakfish. We all send our love, even John Simon who loves everybody promiscuously already.

TUESDAY, MARCH 3, 1931

Dearest Forster,—

Got your note yesterday and the money and thank you so much. I paid the milkman for two weeks in the morning which left me with a quarter in the morning. . . . Well darling, you will think I'm an indefatigable letter writer, but I do miss you down here. I miss you always and continually. Everything I do is connected with you in my mind. And I cannot help thinking how wonderful it would be if you would come back to me, and how cheap and convenient. We three could live on the same amount you send me, there would be no rent, and you wouldn't be getting along on the bare margin you do now. It's so hellish to work as hard as you do for a bare existence. Oh well, maybe a few years from now you will be more used to my Catholicism. I do not give up hope you see.

Much much love, sweetheart.

The country was now in the thick of the Depression. In the fall of 1931 Dorothy and Tamar moved to Coral Gables, Florida, to live with her mother. Her letters chronicle her constant anxiety over money at a time when $2 was a windfall.

CORAL GABLES, FLORIDA, NOV 1931

Dearest Forster,—

Got your letter and the money last night and thank you ever so much.

I learned to drive the car last week. Father's cousin lives down here a mile away and he came over with his two kids and leaving the children sliding on the polished floor we went out and had a lesson. He instructed me for about fifteen minutes, and the next day with a feeling of great daring, I got in the car myself and ventured out. After driving around the block a dozen times, I became very venturesome and went down through the mangrove swamps to the beach. The next day I drove twenty-five miles down the coast and back. But I still need practice in traffic. That beach is the most beautiful I have ever seen and I must take some pictures and send them to you.

Pop is here now, arriving yesterday and staying only until tomorrow when he will go on to Havana.* The house is so big

---

* John Day, Dorothy's father, was a sportswriter who covered horse racing in Cuba.

and has such a nice large garden around it that Tamar has no chance to get in his way. He is very sweet. He told Mother not to let me do any housework and that he sent me down here so that I'd have a chance to write all winter. And how I revel in the prospect of three months of leisure with no idea of work and paying bills. I'm concentrating on magazine stuff and given a winter of that, I'll be perfectly content to go back to work on the [Staten Island] Advance in the spring if I can get it.

Do write me when you can, dear. Tamar sends her love and wishes you were with us. Give my best to Lily and the kids when you see them.

CORAL GABLES, FLORIDA
FRIDAY, NOVEMBER 26, 1931
Dearest Forster,—

It is two weeks today since I have heard from you and I'm wondering if your Christmas business is starting already. I know that this is your busy season and that you seldom get a chance to write.

We are about a mile from the water and Aunt Jenny and Tamar and I drive down every day and sit in a little pine tree park and fish off a breakwater, but so far with no success. But Tamar just likes to hold a line in her hand anyway.

I am sending, or rather have sent a feature story up to the Advance and am going to see if they won't take one a week, for five dollars, but so far I have not heard from them. We are all very broke down here, so if you could only send the five regularly every week it would be a great help. Pop just gets his expenses and seems to be very broke just now. Mother hasn't had a cent in the house for a week, so I had to stall off the school fees and the milk man. And Tamar does need shoes, she wears them out so quickly, and outgrows them too. She has grown an awful lot this summer. She says she wants to send you her copy book when it is filled and every day she proudly brings it home with "one hundred" in blue pencil over her letters and numbers.

I have written two new stories since coming down, and sent out three old ones, besides my long one, and am hoping something comes of them. I'm having a glorious time working and the water is just right.

Love, Dorothy

C. NOV 1931

Dearest Forster,—

Though I hate to trouble you, I'm sending you the enclosed bill which came to me when I inquired from the electric people as to whether Pat had paid that bill or not for his last week's board. He didn't, of course, and now it has increased to eight dollars and they'll be shutting off the electricity in their usual manner if it isn't paid. So can you attend to it for me? I hate to mention it, but you have only sent the five dollars twice in the five weeks I've been here, and I really don't see how I'm going to get along sending Tamar to school and I do want her to now that she is beginning to learn to read and enjoys it so much. Mother is unbelievably broke. Pop sends her $25 every two weeks and she has a hard time getting along on that. And sending Tamar to school means six a month and the school is three miles away so I have to drive the car every day and sometimes we haven't had money for gas and had to charge it and that's something Mother never does. And Mother lives on canned milk and gets milk only for Tamar and so that bill runs up.

I got two dollars (unbelievable sum) for a tiny review (book note) for the *New Republic* yesterday which took care of the milk. It seems that Pop is getting his living at the Havana track, with room in the clubhouse and that's all but he expects to be making more after the season opens on the 19th. But just now, I can't expect any help from him in these extra things. So please don't get angry at my asking you to help, dear, and let me hear from you soon.

Love, Dorothy

News arrived of the marriage of Dorothy's younger brother John to Tessa de Aragon, a young Spanish woman. Dorothy contemplated remaining in Florida, it being "easier to be poor in a warm climate."

[3 DECEMBER 1931, CORAL GABLES]
Dearest Forster,—

Got your letter this morning, and thanks dear, for the money.

Mother is reconciling herself to John's marriage though she was most awfully shocked and surprised of course. We are expecting Pop in from Havana tonight or tomorrow and I suppose he will raise hell at the news.

I dreamed of you and Nannette last night. We were all living together most amicably down in the bungalow. I'm not worried about your occupancy of it, my dear, I was just repeating reports about Freda and Dickie and Tina. As I understood it, Pat drove you and Nannette to the station and he said he left it as Freda and Dick had left the house, so I had visions of a most ungodly mess. I had the place all cleaned up and in good shape, and Pat when he stayed with us this summer was always a tidy soul. He was paying me six a week before I left, and he said he paid the electric bill for his last week's tenure, though he is such a liar I don't know whether it is paid or not.

Aunt Jenny and Tamar are clamoring to go to the beach, so this will be all. Much love, darling, from both Tamar and me.

DECEMBER 25, CHRISTMAS DAY [1931]
Dearest Forster,

It was so sweet of you to send the money in time for me to buy Tamar some little gifts. I owed Mother five of it, and I spent two dollars on Tamar, getting a little doll with real eyelashes and eyes which close and real hair and a crib. She has named the doll Eileen Batterham and is so tickled. Mother got her a doll's house with three rooms and electric light in it, a breakfast nook and curtained windows, and Aunt Jenny bought the furniture for it, and she is so delighted she doesn't know what to do. She plays with it all the time and goes around saying "I got everything I wanted and I didn't know I was going to get them!"

Tamar is not at all hard up for children to play with. There is a little boy across the street who plays with her and she has two second cousins down here, one six and the other three. She loves it here and doesn't ever want to move away she says. She tells me to tell "her fadder" to come down here and fish with her. And she says "My fadder sent you money to give to Santa Claus, didn't he?"

I get very lonely occasionally and wonder whether I shall live alone for the rest of my life with no real home of my own, but after all, this is the best place for Tamar so am content. Mother wants me to sell the house up there and buy a little place down here and settle here and I am seriously thinking of it. There is no reason why I should live in New York with the long cold winters and the poverty which necessitates nurseries for Tamar. Property is as cheap as dirt down here. Of course it would be lonely, away from all my friends, but I would be doing the best thing for Tamar and there is always my writing which I can do anywhere.

Do write when you can, dearest.

Much love, Dorothy

MONDAY, DECEMBER 28 [1931]

Dearest Forster,—

Of course I do not let Tamar forget you. I told her you sent me the money for her doll and crib and she said, "Yes, he sent you the money to give to Santa Claus." She is very particular that everything should come through Santa Claus and all the presents she gets have been given to him first to pass on to her. She had a lovely Christmas and went around saying, "I got much more than I thought I was going to get," in the most appreciative way.

I'm getting a lot of writing done, three short stories and one article since I've been down. The short stories are longish ones. Did I tell you that Tamar has started to read? I find it very thrilling to hear her. I cannot say she is very quick or unusually brilliant, however. But as I said before, she has all her life to read and I wouldn't care if she didn't start until she was ten. She continues to draw and I think she has a real talent in that line.

Got to go and make supper for the rest of the family now. Cabbage with cheese sauce, cucumber salad, toast, and tea. Wish you were here to eat it with me. I miss you, always.

Much love, dearest, from us both,

Dorothy

TO JOHN DAY

Dorothy's younger brother John was living in New York, hoping to break into the newspaper business.

NEW YEAR'S DAY, 1932

Mother got your letters yesterday and was so happy to hear from you. She was so touched at Tessa's gift. I had told her how wicked it was to worry and she said, yes, John might have married at twenty-five and gotten a trollop, and now at least he has a lovely girl for his wife. She is looking forward to meeting the de Aragons when she comes up in the summer. I do hope you get work of some kind soon so that she will have nothing at all to worry about.

I feel the aloneness very much down here. We have lovely times, Aunt Jenny, Mother, and I, but of course there is a sameness and a monotony about life and I do enjoy people and cities so much. However, I am enjoying the complete quiet and relaxation down here, and I am actually getting fat. One of my dresses is becoming tight around the hips and I think I am actually getting a figure. The luxury of warmth, continual baths, clean clothes without having to pay laundry bills, delightful food and fruits, a marvelous car to drive around in and all this beauty of scene round about. I am having the nicest time I have had in years. I do not think I'll come back until May first when it is time to get the bungalow ready for sale or rent. I wish I could sell it.

Do write often as we enjoy your letters so much, darling boy. I'm so glad you and Tessa are so happy. I feel sure you will get work soon. Tamar and I both pray for you every night that you will get something soon. Give Tessa my love and tell her to drop me a line when she has time. Also my love to the rest of the family.

SATURDAY MORNING, JAN 9 [1932]
After two weeks of grey chilly weather the sun is out again hot as blazes and everybody is cheerful. Mother hasn't been at all well, droopy, melancholy, and nervous, totally unlike herself. Though she seems totally reconciled to your marriage now. I hear her telling people over the telephone what a lovely young wife you have, how different she is from other young girls of her age and how she thinks it is probably just as well you settled your fate so young. I really think she is beginning to be happy about it.

When I read her your lovely letter and Tessa's, and they both gave her such a charming family picture of happiness, she was absolutely delighted and said what a splendid surrounding for you and what sane and wholesome pleasures you were now having and had to look forward to, instead of racing around at tracks, drinking and betting and associating with trash.

Anyway,—she has now got to the state where she listens delighted and happily to accounts of you and your new relatives, instead of cutting me short and getting sore at me. I have had rather a difficult time of it, darling, and so perhaps my own letters to you have not been so happy as they should have been.

And here now, is a great piece of news, though I haven't sold a story so don't get excited in that way. But Mother IS GOING TO MOVE NORTH TO SETTLE! This is in view of the fact that you are never going to come home no more, never no mo', and Sam is settled there, and Della and me,—four of us, to be exact. When she moved to Florida you were a little boy and due to stay home for some years and Della came home for a year, and Sam [*Dorothy's elder brother*] was down for months. Now she realizes that we are all put up in N.Y. she sees no necessity of being here. Pop is in Havana three months, and the rest of the time he is in and out of New York so she thinks of getting a three-room apartment on Staten Island in St. George, and I am delegated to find the place so that she can ship the stuff up that she wants in June and be all ready to move in. She has quite definitely decided, though she hasn't told Pop yet. She says he will say that she wants to take you in, and he will throw such fits that he will not support her if she does, so she will only take a little apartment, big enough for her and him.

I do think, John, now that you are definitely out of the family life, that Mother and Pop will get along better. You were a bone of contention for those last years and Pop has always been jealous of his sons and Mother's attentions to them. Mother has told me a great many things, and I didn't realize before how bad things were between them, but I think that now that you are gone, and won't be living with Mother any more Pop will be nicer to her. She was saying that when Donald [*Dorothy's eldest brother*] was with them over on Plaza Street, Pop tried to put him out of the house because she, Mother, ran his bath for him. He is a strange man, Pop is.

I sent ten stories out on New Year's Day and six of them have come back, hells bells. "The Fleet Companion" has been at Scribner's since December 14, a new story, "Storm and Tressa Serenade" is at the *Chicago Tribune* Short Story syndicate. Let us hope and pray. I am now working on a Mexican article for one of the women's magazines and in view of the parlous times in Mexico, the closing of the churches again, it may be taken. It is not a Catholic article, but the story of a lady adventuress in Xochimilco.

TO FORSTER BATTERHAM

JANUARY 12 [1932]

Dearest Forster—

Got your letter this morning just when I had begun to dream about you. Whenever I don't hear from you in two weeks, I start having dreams. Tamar says she misses you and Dickie and John Simon but no one else, and sends her love to you.

Our life is very quiet. I eat, sleep, bathe, sew, play solitaire, and write. We can't take trips in the car because it eats up too much gas and we are cutting down all around. But I'm getting a great deal of writing done and am very happy and satisfied about it. I sent out ten stories and got all but two back and one of those has been gone since December 11 so I'm hoping. It's that long three-part serial, which of course takes much longer to get a decision on.

This morning I finished an article on Easter in Xochimilco which will be sent out just in time for Easter this year, I hope. But just in case it's late for Easter numbers, I'm calling it "Spring Days in Mexico." Also I'm finishing up a novelette, ONE MORE ADVENTURE, about an American woman having an affair with a Mexican ranchero and when he finds out she regards him as one more adventure he smothers her. It is very wild and I hope it will go. It's not bad either, as a piece of literature. I feel that sooner or later all these things I'm doing now are bound to sell and it costs me nothing but time and energy to put out my commodity and I have plenty of both. You are helping me a great deal this winter and I do appreciate it.

Do write again soon, dearest. I'm sending you the kiss I dreamed I gave you last night.

Love from both Tamar and me,

Dorothy

Evidently Forster came down to Florida for a visit, reawakening old feelings and the dream, once more, of spending a happy life together.

SATURDAY [JANUARY 1932]

Dearest Forster,—

My feeling about our night together was one of sadness because we couldn't be always together. I feel that Tamar and I belong to you and when I am with you in that way it leaves me with a feeling of our close presence in my heart for weeks afterward.

Aren't we ever going to be together again, sweetheart? There are the nicest little bungalows on the experimental station, and I think often how nice it would be for you and me to settle down here, and live in this delightful climate, working out of doors, not so far from the water. What do you say you marry me when I come up in the spring, and then I'll sell or rent the house and we'll come down here to live? Huh?

Do go over to see Lily oftener, dear, for she isn't having such a smooth time now I believe from what she has said to me. Della thinks that there actually may be a separation, and I know she is very very unhappy. Certainly everybody is having their troubles in personal as well as financial arrangements. But speaking of us, I do not see why you can't let me and Tamar be Catholics and be happy with us just the same. You know I love you, and I always think of us belonging together in spite of us being four years apart.

I know how hard you are working, but write when you can, dearest.

Much love from us both,

Dorothy

FEBRUARY 2 [1932]

Dearest Forster,—

It made me happy to think that you missed not hearing from me, for it seems that I wrote two weeks ago and every two weeks just as I always have. But maybe you missed that letter, tho letters seldom go astray. I've been as busy as a cat having kittens, getting a twenty-five thousand word story off to Scribner's by February first when a contest for novelettes closed. The story was seventy-five pages, about Mexico, and had to be written twice. The very work of copying it was arduous. But now it is off and I am sitting back for a week doing nothing. I've had another story in that contest since December 11th and I haven't heard from it yet. They had a contest like this a few years ago. They buy about twenty-four of these short novels for publication, and then one is selected for a five thousand dollar prize.

All this talk of war worries me to death. It looks as though another large mess were brewing. The world certainly is in a befuddled state. The people down here are all ready to believe in a yellow peril and jump to arms in defense of their country, etc.; and even in defense of the Americans in charge of big interests over there.

Much love to you from both of us.

TO TESSA [DE ARAGON] DAY, *Dorothy's new sister-in-law*

TUESDAY, FEB 5, 1932

I was so delighted to hear from Donald [Day, *a successful newspaperman*] that he was sending John letters of introduction to various editors. It was such a nice sympathetic letter, so appreciative of John's talent and desires to be a newspaper man. I do hope John is doing something with his leisure while he is waiting for the letters and looking for work. There are so many little feature stories to write that he could be sending off to newspapers and to the Sunday editors.

He ought to tramp the streets, absorbing the atmosphere of the city, sit in Union Square and Madison Square for hours and listen and observe what goes on as O. Henry and other feature writers did. You don't need money to gather material. And if he doesn't use it now, it will all come in handy later. He ought to be turning out a certain number of words every day, and sit at the typewriter for an hour or so at least. He just can't sit around waiting for inspiration to come to him. Look up books of journalism at the library—down at the Second Avenue branch—and see their suggestions for features, and write them out as though he were doing exercises for a theme class in college.

Keep after him, Tessa, and do these things with him. Remember, an awful lot depends on you and what you do for him. And you know how much I love both him and you and want him to get along.

I have accomplished wonders this winter. I have learned to make tatting to put on Tamar's pants, I have learned to play bridge, and won a cake for a prize at a bridge luncheon given at the church, and I have learned to tell fortunes from tea leaves. There was a check in my cup this noon and several letters, not to speak of a tall blond man in spectacles striding with great rapidity toward me.

P.S. Is John studying the papers every day and catching the features? Sometimes you see something that can be followed up. You see this is just as much a letter to John as you, Tessa, but you are to be thought of together nowadays. It wouldn't be a bad idea for John to have some stories to submit when he goes in to look for a job. If he had a story, he could generally get in to see the Sunday editor—they are easier to see than city editors—and take a good deal of freelance material, not paying much it is true.

TO FORSTER BATTERHAM

SUNDAY, FEBRUARY 14, 1932

Dearest Forster,—

Times continue hard down here, but it's easy to be poor in a warm climate with fruit lying around on the ground. Pop will finish his job at Havana in a month now and won't go back next year and he's through on the Miami tracks, done out of them by dirty business, and will be looking for work up north. So it looks like a sure thing that Mother is coming north. I don't know when I'm coming. If she moves, she will want me to stay and help her so that may mean that I'll be here until April or the end of it.

With the "spring," which means that we now have summer heat, the snakes are coming out and you can't drive along the roads without passing several at every block. This morning I saw three, a long black snake, a chicken snake, and a grass snake, and the poor grass snake had been run over and was trying to pull his besmattered body from the road. It just made me sick—with pity, I mean. We have found five scorpions in the house, one in Tamar's bed, and yesterday I found her grabbing a foot-long black lizard by the tail out in the garage. Cousin Clem says he was bitten by one and it made him sick for a day.

Do write me, dearest. In your last letter you addressed me as "Dear Dorothy" not "Dearest"? Don't do it again. I notice such things.

Lots of love from both me and Tamar.

Dorothy

Dorothy returned to New York in April. She continued to focus on writing novels, stories, and plays. That summer she was working on "a social novel with the pursuit of a job as the motive and social revolution as its crisis." It would feature "the struggle between religion and otherworldliness," and it would be "replete with a heroine and hero and scores of fascinating characters." But at the same time, she also tried to widen her contacts in the Catholic literary world.

TO R. W. ZIMMERMAN, *editor of*
The Catholic Encyclopedia

SEPTEMBER 22, 1932

In reply to your letter of September 20, I am especially interested in biography and hagiography. There is but brief mention in the old edition of the encyclopedia of Margaret Bosco, the mother of the Blessed John Bosco. I should like also to write about Rose Hawthorne, and about the Catholic authors, [Sigrid] Undset, Sheila Kaye Smith, Agnes Repplier, and others. Willa Cather, whose last three books are Catholic in spirit, though she herself is not a Catholic, is deserving of mention also. I notice also that although there are very comprehensive articles on Catholic schools, there is little space devoted to day nurseries, which I think in this modern age a very important branch of parochial educational work. So much attention is being paid by educators to the pre-school child that it would be good to call attention to all the Church does for infants and small children in day nurseries whose mothers and fathers go out to work.

I should be very glad to hear from you soon in regard to this work.

By the fall of 1932 Dorothy was sharing her apartment with her brother John and his wife Tessa. In December she accepted an assignment from Commonweal *to travel to Washington, D.C., to cover a "Hunger March of the Unemployed." In* The Long Loneliness *she describes this demonstration, organized by many of her old Communist comrades, as the occasion for the critical turning point in her life. On December 8, Feast of the Immaculate Conception, she visited the Basilica of the Immaculate Conception and there offered a prayer that God would*

show her some way to combine her Catholic faith and her commitment
to the cause of the poor and oppressed. She was thirty-five years old.
Soon after her return to New York—by some accounts, the very day of
her return—she met Peter Maurin, the French peasant philosopher
who inspired her to launch the Catholic Worker *and whose ideas would*
dominate the rest of her life. Whether there was any relation between
this new door opening and her decision finally to close the door on
hopes of marrying Forster, her letter to him of December 10 would be
her last for many years.

TO FORSTER BATTERHAM

10 DEC, 1932

Dear Forster—

I got your letter Friday afternoon and I've been pondering
since whether or not to answer it. It doesn't seem much use, but
still I can't let some of your statements go without telling you
what I feel.

As to my feeling about sex, I do indeed now feel that sex is
taboo outside of marriage. The institution of marriage has been
built up by society as well as the Church to safeguard the home
and children as well as people who don't know how to take care
of themselves. Of course anyone who is sane and sound mentally will agree that promiscuity and looseness in sex is an ugly
and inharmonious thing. You have always in the past treated me
most casually, and I see no special difference between our affair
and any other casual affair I have had in the past. You avoided,
as you admitted yourself, all responsibility. You would not
marry me then because you preferred the slight casual contact
with me to any other. And last spring when my love and physical
desire for you overcame me, you were quite willing for the affair
to go on, on a weekend basis.

Sex is not at all taboo with me except outside of marriage. I
am as free and unsuppressed as I ever was about it. I think the

human body a beautiful thing, and the joys that a healthy body have are perfectly legitimate joys. I see no immediate difference between enjoying sex and enjoying a symphony concert, but sex having such a part in life, as producing children, has been restricted as society and the Church have felt best for the children.

I believe that in breaking these laws one is letting the flesh get an upper hand over the spirit, so I do not want to break these laws.

St. Augustine says, "If bodies please thee, praise God on occasion of them." And I feel no sorrow for all the joys we have had in the past together.

When I laughingly spoke about many a young girl holding out—you should have understood what I meant. You seem to think that one should always succumb immediately to any promptings of the flesh, and you think of it as unnatural and unhealthy to restrain oneself on account of the promptings of the spirit. What I meant was that many people in the past have observed the conventions and rules, for the sake not only of convention but of principle. It is hard for me to talk to you seriously,—you despise so utterly the things which mean so much to me. I wish you'd read more of Aldous Huxley, and imbibe a little of his rational tolerance.

You think all this is only hard on you. But I am suffering too. The ache in my heart is intolerable at times, and sometimes for days I can feel your lips upon me, waking and sleeping. It is because I love you so much that I want you to marry me. I want to be in your arms every night, as I used to be, and be with you always. I always loved you more than you did me. That is why I made up with you so many times, and went after you after we had had some quarrel. We always differed on principle, and now that I am getting older I cannot any longer always give way to you just because flesh has such power over me.

Of course I understand your allusion to smoking and drinking and such indulgences, and as I said before, I do agree with you and would give them all up for you. I really don't think I over-indulge very often. I consider drink only sinful inasmuch as it affects one's health, and I'm most ashamed for every time I do over-indulge. Sex and eating and drinking may easily be put in the same class since they are both physical gratifications. Still, even the slightest sexual lapse may have terrible and far-reaching consequences and so these laws have been built up. Of course all intelligent people can say—Oh, I'm so smart this doesn't apply to me, but I think that such laws, whether one considers them human or divine, have to be obeyed by all. It all is hopeless of course, tho it has often seemed to me a simple thing. Imaginatively I can understand your hatred and rebellion against my beliefs and I can't blame you. I have really given up hope now, so I won't try to persuade you any more.

Dorothy

PART II
House of Hospitality

There are, unfortunately, few letters to document the early days of the Catholic Worker. This gap merely accentuates the contrast between the previous letters to Forster, friends, and family members and her new voice a year later—now as the editor of her own newspaper, the leader of a lay movement, a recognized name in both church circles and the social movements of the day. Instead of short stories and novels, she was writing editorials and articles about labor issues, poverty, and social justice.

What accounted for this dramatic shift? Certainly the catalyst was her meeting with Peter Maurin, the French peasant philosopher, twenty years her senior, who appeared at her door in December 1932. He had been sent by the editor of Commonweal, who sensed that the two of them had something in common (despite all the obvious differences)—namely, a passion to connect their faith with the pressing social issues of the day.

Maurin had refined his vision over the course of many years, while otherwise tramping around the country performing hard manual labor. Upon introducing himself to Dorothy, he began at once to indoctrinate her, quoting from an assortment of thinkers such as Eric Gill, Peter Kropotkin, and Jacques Maritain. Maurin had a whole program laid out, beginning with the need for a newspaper to promote the social teachings of the Church, houses of hospitality to practice the works of mercy, farming communes where "workers could become scholars and scholars could become workers." He had even formulated his ideas in sing-songy verses, ideal for street-corner declamation: "The world would become better off/ if people tried to become better. / And people would become better/ if they stopped trying to become better off."

Maurin had preached this message for many years before finding anyone who would take him seriously. In fact, it would be some time before Day herself fully appreciated his ambitious vision. (And even then, she had to ask herself whether she really liked him.) But she was quickly won by his notion of starting a newspaper that would offer solidarity with the workers and a critique of the social system from the radical perspective of the Gospel. Maurin, as she later put it, had given her "a program," a "Catholic view of history," broader than the "class struggle" framework in which she had been formed. Drawing on the lives of the saints he showed her that it was not necessary to await official permission to live by the teachings of Christ. One could begin today, with the means at hand, "building a new world in the shell of the old." In effect, he gave her permission to invent her own vocation.

Five months later, on May 1, 1933, the Catholic Worker newspaper was launched at a Communist rally in Union Square. If Maurin provided the "program," it was Dorothy who set it in motion. Before long the paper was the organ of a growing movement based in houses of hospitality—first in New York, and then in other parts of the country—where lay Catholics lived in community among the poor, feeding the hungry, offering shelter to the homeless. Through these works of mercy, the Catholic Workers responded to the needs of their neighbors. But through the paper and other forms of direct action they also challenged the values, the structures, and the institutions that gave rise to so much poverty and need.

By the time of the first letter below the Catholic Worker *was already six months old. A small community of volunteers had been drawn to the work, operating a house of hospitality on East 15th Street, and putting out a paper, which by this time had reached a circulation of 75,000, selling (as it always would) for "a penny a copy." Much of Dorothy's time was spent answering letters from priests, contributors, and readers of the paper eager to learn more about this new movement.*

TO CATHERINE DE HUECK

Catherine de Hueck (1896–1985) was a colorful and charismatic figure whose career in some ways paralleled and at times overlapped with Dorothy's. A Russian baroness by marriage, she had fled the Soviet Union soon after the Revolution and settled first in New York, and then Canada. After a powerful experience of conversion, she embraced the Gospel and dedicated herself to living out and promoting its radical social message. In Toronto she established Friendship House, a community that shared much in spirit with the Catholic Worker, though Catherine always set a higher value on order, discipline, and cleanliness. After learning of the Catholic Worker she contacted Dorothy Day, and they became lifelong friends.

DECEMBER 19, 1933

Dear Mrs. de Hueck:

Your letter made us very happy and we are sending the paper as you suggested to the place you mentioned.

The Archbishop [McNeil of Toronto] has already sent us his subscription and a very kind letter. If you can use more copies to distribute among your friends, we will be very glad to send you a dozen.

Trusting that you will remember us in your prayers, and we need them especially for the House of Hospitality.

I am, sincerely, Dorothy Day

TO A MOTHER SUPERIOR

JANUARY 1 [1934]

Dear Mother Imogen Ryan,

We want to thank you very much for your generosity and cooperation and we wish also to apologize for not answering you promptly. The holiday work included so many more things than attending to the work of the paper and the correspondence that we were pretty rushed. We were around visiting poor families in the neighborhood and all our charitable friends used us as distributing agents so that we were on the go all the time bringing clothes, food, and coal to those who needed them.

Your suggestion about paying the rent for an apartment for one month is an overwhelming one and I pray God to bless you for your generosity. I would be very glad to come up to the convent and talk to you further about this if you will drop me a line and make an appointment for me. Mrs. Kelly came down and very kindly offered to cooperate with us and made suggestions regarding advertising. She fell into the hands of Peter Maurin who delivered a broadside against drives and advertising and modern technique in business which might well have discouraged her but I hope it didn't and that she will come again. Since she left Miss [Eileen] Corridan, who is taking Dorothy Weston's place for the present, drew up a plan about advertising and we would be very glad to talk it over with Mrs. Kelly.

Thanking you again for your kindness.

TO THE EDITOR OF INTERRACIAL REVIEW

Interracial Review *was the organ of the Catholic Interracial Council of New York, founded by Fr. John LaFarge, SJ, to foster racial justice and advance understanding between African Americans and the*

Catholic Church. Having only recently launched the Catholic Worker, *Dorothy hastened to express her support for this kindred venture. Her letter was published in the February 1934 issue of the* Review.

JANUARY 26, 1934

Dear Father [William M.] Markoe:

We have only recently become acquainted with the very excellent *Interracial Review*. Needless to say, it is highly encouraging for our new publication to find that a Catholic monthly like the *Review* has long been blazing the trail for better interracial understanding and improved conditions through programs of Catholic Social Justice.

Our paper, the *Catholic Worker*, was started in May and is a monthly selling for one cent a copy, twenty-five cents a year subscription price, in order to cover the cost of mailing. We have twenty thousand circulation now after starting with 2,500, and we are certainly pleased with the welcome the paper has received. The purpose of the paper is to combat communism and atheism by showing the social program of the Church, thus taking away from them one of the weapons communists have been using against the Church, namely, the charge that it is allied with capitalism and an enemy of the worker.

The paper is for Negro and white alike. On the masthead there is a white worker on one side and a Negro worker on the other, and in addition to handling the problems of the Negro race, we want to have Negro writers for our paper, writing not only on race problems but on social justice in general. . . .

Our idea is to have Negro artists and writers helping us to get out the paper, so that by the time we have reached two hundred thousand circulation and are well established, the fact will be well established in the minds of Catholic America (and Communist America too) that the paper is not a paper for black or white but for the Catholic Worker—all Catholic Workers. . . .

Hoping that you will bring our paper to the attention of your readers and that you will pray for us in our work.

Sincerely,

Dorothy Day, Editor, the *Catholic Worker*

TO A JESUIT PRIEST

Father Gerald Ellard, SJ, who taught seminarians in Kansas, was one of the leading figures in the liturgical movement, which linked liturgical and social reform. His book Christian Life and Worship *(1933) was a major contribution in the field.*

JANUARY 29, 1934

You are the kindest and most patient person! Here I am informed that we called attention to your book under the wrong title, and you never complained about it.

The work piles up and we are most busy what with keeping the House of Hospitality running—it is always full, and the paper, and now the workers' school. And I'm running around making speeches a couple of times a week. I am very grateful that people are so interested and responsive.

Money is hard to come by and we are always just one jump ahead of the wolf, but I don't mind that. In fact, the only phase of the work which I do mind is not being able to pay our volunteer helpers, several of whom give up all their time to the paper just in return for their meals. I am praying that a kind angel will come along to donate some salary money sooner or later. Won't you pray too? That's the thing about holy poverty. Even though you are on the best of terms with the lady yourself, others are not so conscious of her attractions.

Do write us when you can, and do not mind the belated replies.

TO MADELEINE SHERIDAN

Madeleine Sheridan, an advocate of Christian socialism who lived in Canada, was an early and frequent correspondent. She and Dorothy exchanged numerous letters on the relation between the Gospel and political action.

C. MARCH 1934

I am enjoying so much contemplating the work which you are doing up in Montreal. I should like very much to be able to throw myself into the work of a political movement, but I can't. The whole policy of our paper is against political activity. You will see by our next issue, my main editorial, our real purpose is holding up a Utopian ideal, an actual, Gospel view of life. Father Quadrapani says, "Those who seek to influence a hardened multitude ask for much in order to obtain a little and insist with vehemence on the subject with which they desire to impress their auditors, and appear to forget for the moment all else."

We have to oppose political activity, state regulations,—in that it tends to fascism and fascism is the great danger of the present day. We hold up the idea instead of individual responsibility. But that doesn't keep us from pointing out that they are wrong who oppose the C.C.F. [*Cooperative Commonwealth Federation*] on the grounds of its "Moscow" flavor.

I have received several long letters from Mr. [Franz] Wiese which I enjoyed tremendously. But I confess with shame that I have answered neither of them yet. If you could see the continual demands on our time down here,—all day long people are coming in for help and advice,—correspondence is heavy, there is the workers' school now and the House of Hospitality,—all these little activities which are so important, combining as they do theory and practice.

But perhaps you will pass this letter on to him as he said

you did another of mine and then I shall feel that I have killed two birds with one stone.

I shall write more later—just had a telephone call to go out.

TO CATHERINE DE HUECK

Catherine had sent a description of her apostolic activities.

MARCH 19, 1934

I can't tell you how interesting I found your report, and I am mailing back to you the one you marked to be returned. As to the other—the report of the social service worker (which I presume to be the result of your activities)—I am wondering if I cannot use parts of it, disguised, so that it would be applicable to any city.

Indeed, the report as it stands could apply to New York, Chicago, or any big industrial center. It would be of tremendous help in stirring things up, it seems to me. Do write at once, if only a post card, and let me know if I cannot use it for the paper. We reach so many parishes throughout the country that it might inspire some of the pastors to start the social centers which are so urgently needed.

Do excuse us if we do not write often, on account of all our activities. I know that, busy woman as you are, you understand and do not expect it.

Any reports of your work are always interesting to us, so send them on.

We have placed the names you sent on our mailing list and we are very grateful for your cooperation.

Do let us hear from you soon, and if you are ever in New York, look us up.

APRIL 11, 1934

If there is any chance of your coming to New York for a few days before the end of the month, you would have a chance to see just what little we are able to do here at our headquarters.

Our belief is, you know, to start in little ways, and our small store[front] is so humble that no one passing by on the street is afraid to come in. A larger place perhaps might intimidate. Our little school reaches from thirty to sixty people a night. What we always emphasize is beginning from the very bottom and working up—starting with nothing and living from day to day. It is the way so much has been done in the Catholic Church.

It would be wonderful if you could start a social center in Toronto such as you describe in your article. But one must always be prepared to accept the slow response cheerfully. Beginnings must be made, and women, being practical and never too optimistic, are the best ones to make these beginnings.

TO THE EDITOR OF THE *CORPUS CHRISTI REPORTER*

APRIL 16, 1934

Dear Father Cook:

You ask me for a small article, but it being near the deadline, I can only think in terms of a letter, especially since I do not know what phase of our work you wish me to write about. It is a rainy evening and our school is going on with just a few customers, with Peter Maurin making points about Social Control, Social Legislation, Political Control, State Dictatorship, and finally Proletarian Dictatorship. He is evidently in a pessimistic mood in his forecasting this evening. His discussion is carried on with the interpolations of Mr. Herman Hergenhan, an anarchist friend from Union Square and the municipal Lodging House, who is now sharing our kidney stews and sleeping on the Catholic Worker floor (on a mattress). Haig, as he has been nicknamed, is good for clarification of thought—Peter's thought, and the thought of the Catholic Workers who attend the school, according to Peter. . . .

Times must be getting better, for two of the women from the Hospice got jobs last week. The Hospice goes along smoothly, the girls cooperating in the work, and although there has been a bit of bickering now and then, nothing has occurred which upsets our theories that our shelter can get along as a cooperative, without a matron or supervisor. This is one aspect of the house which surprises everyone.

The House goes along well, the school has demonstrated by the attendance that there is a need, and a continuing need, for a center of Catholic thought, and we are still thinking and wishing and planning for a real House, a real center, some day, and we hope it will be soon. . . . We were offered a house last week, but it was a dark backyard house down on Mott Street, unheated and in bad repair. But the very fact that we are being offered houses is a hopeful sign and we shall continue to pray to Don Bosco, our new saint, who had so much trouble getting a house for himself and his homeless boys in Turin. We have no doubt but that God will send us what we need, when we need it, for His work.

This may be a bit vague—this letter—but Father Monoghan and Father Dooley in Corpus Christi parish have been so generous in their cooperation with our work that we take it for granted that your parishioners know about our paper, the *Catholic Worker*, which was started a year ago in opposition to *The Daily Worker*, the Communist sheet. It was because we felt the necessity to put into practice some of our ideals as the Catholic Worker's schools, Houses of Hospitality, etc., that we started these other activities which bear so close a relationship to our work.

TO A CANADIAN SUPPORTER

A Canadian correspondent asked about the official stand of the Church toward the Catholic Worker.

APRIL 27, 1934

Dear Mr. [Franz] Wiese,

Thank you very much for your encouraging letter. It came just as we were gong to press—a low moment full of misgivings, and it brightened me up considerably.

As for official approbation, Cardinal Hayes [of New York] told Monsignor Chidwick to write and tell us that he approved of our good work. And the Chancellor of the diocese is inviting Miss [Dorothy] Weston to speak at a communion breakfast next Sunday. And that is approval enough. Lay papers do not get the imprimatur—*The Commonweal* has not got it now and they have been in existence much much longer than we. Monsignor Chidwick says that it was to be expected that we would make mistakes, but the thing was not to persist in them.

Dr. Reilly of Hunter spoke last night on Carlyle and Ruskin and has a great admiration for each. He stressed the fact that Ruskin's thesis was that the hearts and minds of men must be changed—that they would never get anywhere by the vote, and I see nothing fundamentally wrong with that. It sounds like our Holy Father. Perhaps Father Carr was thinking of Ruskin's desire to scrap machinery. Did you read Eric Gill's article in *Blackfriar*, from which we quote this issue in regard to machinery?

What you say about spiritual hospitality is true. I often think that it is indeed very hard to extend such hospitality to everyone that comes in. It is so much easier to throw people the clothes, food or what not that they need, and so hard to sit down with them and listen patiently. There are so many people dropping in that some days I do not sit down to the typewriter once,—the work gets far behind and I have to remind myself that all those little frittering things which take up one's time are quite as important, many times more so in the sight of God, than answering letters or keeping one's files up to date.

Answering your letters is something that I have postponed because it was a pleasure. So do write when you can (since starting this letter, I have answered six telephone calls, talked to one of the girls from the House of Hospitality about a job, taken two little girls to the toilet, found some lost toys, discussed the Jewish situation with Peter Maurin, etc.). So if a long blank follows one of your letters, please excuse, and keep in touch with us.

TO MADELEINE SHERIDAN

MAY 2, 1934

Thank you for your kind note and do excuse me for not replying before. Many troubles piled up and I could not. . . . I do not
worry about the work, though often we get so low in funds. After
all, if it is the work God wants done, he will take care of us and
we must just humble ourselves, write appeals and leave it at that.
We were so low last month that we all lived on Home Relief pork
for three weeks straight, and pork day after day gets most tiring.
We have a common table in the office you know and feed all and
sundry who pass by, so food is something to think about. But the
appeal brought in enough money immediately to pay our bills for
last month and half pay for this so we are very grateful indeed.

We have a splendid article on the CCF for the next issue. Let
me know what you are doing in that line. Our paper, as I pointed
out, is not "for" any line of political action and we get a great
deal of criticism for it. After all we're just a paper, disseminating
Catholic thought, and as such we can write about all these things
without sponsoring them.

TO A JESUIT PRIEST

Father Ervin A. Stauffen taught at Marquette University.

MAY 7, 1934

Thank you for your suggestion as to the joys of Lady Poverty.
That is a thing we try to convey in the editorial columns but
we feel that it is a thing delicate and precious and hard to convey.
For instance—we are aiming to reach the embittered, fallen
away Catholic,—the man in the street,—the poor mother of
many children, the father out of work. And to hold up the joys of
Lady Poverty too blatantly is to embitter them too much. It
must be done by suggestion, rather than by outright words.

One hears too often nowadays the bitter criticism of the priest and brother—"What do they know about poverty, they who are secure,—who have food for themselves and a roof over their heads?" It is the horrible sense of insecurity for oneself and for loved ones that hardens the heart. Living in fear and doubt, a fear and doubt engendered by already having experienced days of involuntary fasting, homelessness, eviction.

Just yesterday I brought a doctor to a family around the corner, the mother a widow with nine children, and the five-year-old was ill. The doctor found he had tuberculosis and he had to go to the hospital at once. It was not inherited, but brought on from a winter of cold and too little to eat. Even the most saintly person, with the utmost faith in God, could find it hard under these circumstances to find anything but a sense of grim endurance under suffering in one's heart.

To teach faith—that is the first thing, and the joy will come afterward.

It is very good of you to write such kind things about us and being very unlearned people around here we need help and criticism. So any suggestions you have to make us will be appreciated.

TO A PRIEST

MAY 22, 1934

Dear Father [Russell] Wilbur,—

We enjoyed your letter so much and thank you for it. I was especially glad to pass on to [Peter Maurin] that stuff about him being tamed down. The fact was that he was not too well last month and we sent him up to the country, and the only stuff he had in the paper of his own was quotations and comments. I do indeed keep out some of his stuff which attacks the bishops. I just don't think it's politic. We differ on technique. I think that if we ask courteously cooperation from priests we are more apt to get it than if we point out that they are not in contact with the workers and that they are not doing anything, etc., etc., etc. There are quite a number of priests who think Peter just quaint when he verbally attacks the clergy who would, if we printed the stuff, hold up their hands in horror.

TO CATHERINE DE HUECK

MAY 22, 1934

Someone wrote and asked us to send you as many copies [of the paper] as you could use, and enclosed a check to pay for them. Did anyone else on the paper ask you how many you wanted? Anyway, ask for as many as you can use, and don't worry about paying for them. We are so glad to have them distributed. We are anxious to reach the people, and God will take care of the printing bill. This theory that people don't value what they don't pay for, and better to sell the copies than to distribute them, I just don't hold with. I believe in distributing ever more and more literature.

God bless you for your enthusiasm and for your work. We do indeed pray for your House of Friendship, and pray for us too. The main thing is never to get discouraged at the slowness of people or results. People may not be articulate or active, but even so, we do not ever know the results, or the effect on souls. That is not for us to know. We can only go ahead and work with happiness at what God sends us to do.

TO JAMES "MAC" McGOVERN

James McGovern, the first mate of a tanker, was an early friend of the Catholic Worker who spent much of his leave time at the CW in New York or on the farms. (He would later die during World War II after his ship was torpedoed.)

AUGUST 3, 1934

Wednesday ten of us distributed anti-war leaflets in Union Square and all but got mobbed by the Communists. However a few of them came to our Wednesday night meeting afterward and continued the discussion until one o'clock. It was a very good meeting. The Baroness [Catherine] de Hueck, a very charming Russian, came from Toronto that night and spoke for us too. A most interesting person, like Peter [Maurin], impatient and idealistic and driving the clergy crazy up there. Peter is not so well, by the looks of him, and I'm going to ship him away upstate for a rest.

Do send me up that [Joseph] Conrad book you mention as carrying around with you. I love Conrad and by the time I get it I'll be needing the relaxation of a good novel. We make our plans from day to day and I try not to think of the fall, and all of Peter's plans for a school every night for ten months. The prospect of such a grind, I confess, appalls me.

TO CATHERINE DE HUECK

AUGUST 14, 1934

Just a hasty note to thank you for your kindness and to remind you that I am offering up the Mass tomorrow for you. The fast day before is all part of the happiness to me. We are busy getting ready leaflets to distribute tomorrow at the doors of some of the biggest churches for the noonday Masses. In the evening there is a big meeting of anti-Communists who are also anything but Catholic, and trying to work the Catholics in on their nationalist propaganda. We have to mimeograph some stuff for them too.

We are sending you up a hundred copies of the paper for the remaining two weeks of your stay, and although that may be too much, you can always use the others, or just leave them at the vestibule of the church for distribution.

TO FATHER DANIEL LORD, SJ

Father Lord, a Jesuit priest, was a popular Catholic writer, director of the Sodality of Our Lady, and editor of its journal, The Queen's Work.

SEPTEMBER 5, 1934

Enclosed is the third article you asked for, about what college students can do for the cause of social justice. Perhaps my article is not specific enough about social justice, but the more active we are, the more we realize that it is as Mr. [Frank] Sheed said in speaking of his experiences with the Catholic Evidence Guild in England, that the man in the street is as much interested in his immortal soul as he is in the minimum wage, thank God!

And I want to do another article for you on the Negro,—may I? I couldn't handle it in one paragraph in this article. Unless you go into the subject in detail you don't get the sympathy of the readers and only antagonize them. I'll wait to hear from you before I write it, because you may have other ideas in view as to how to put over the idea of justice for the Negro and how to go about it.

TO MADELEINE SHERIDAN

SEPTEMBER 12, 1934

I do wish we could have a long talk together. Also I wish I knew more about the situation in Canada. You must remember that I judge things as a convert of only eight years standing, and a convert from Socialism and Communism at that. I *know* Socialists and I don't trust them, though I do trust you and find your reactions tremendously stimulating, and judge they would be so too to our readers.

Of the reasons why I have not written you more at length and have to continue to neglect much correspondence—one of the girls at the shelter had a baby, was sick, the baby was sick and had to have a transfusion, the mother was sick, my kid needed much attention,—we had to start her in school,—we've had some ferocious attacks directed at us by nationalists, even physical ones. There was a Catholic Action School two weeks ago and we had visitors from breakfast until late at night, etc., etc. As to the attacks, some of our friends and sympathizers were slapped and ejected from meetings, we've had detectives on our tail, we've been investigated by the Detective Bureau at Center Street on complaints that we were Communists masquerading as Catholics, and so on. All these things keep happening in addition to all our routine work. But do forgive me and write soon.

TO CATHERINE DE HUECK

SEPTEMBER 12, 1934

I was so happy to get your letter telling of the growth and progress. Will it make you mad if I ask you to write us a detailed letter for publication about the House of Friendship? And in that letter you could list the books you most want. As for the *Daily Worker* [the Communist newspaper]—what do you want that for? Sure we take it every day but not *Pravda* [from the USSR]. I'll send it on if you want it, but you can probably get it in Toronto too. About the Canadian Catholic Worker, it sounds grand and you are of course at liberty to use anything we have in the paper if you don't find our stuff too long.

You saw by our last issue that people in Australia and England would also like to start Catholic Workers and while we are glad to see the idea spreading we do think it better to keep all these projects absolutely separate. For one thing you know conditions in your own territories and know what you want to do. Another thing we don't want [is] to make ourselves responsible for policies adopted by others. We are all so far apart with no likelihood of getting together to confer, so I think this the best attitude to take. When you use our material and [illustrations], you could just give us credit, with a byline "Catholic Worker Service," for instance.

Also to avoid confusion, it would be better to call yours the Canadian Catholic Worker.

I do wish you would get in touch with Father [Joseph] Mc-Sorley for advice and help. I consider him our general spiritual advisor and he has been of tremendous help to us down here, defending us from attacks and advising as to policies.

I have your name written in my prayer book and remember you daily, as I hope you do us. Do keep us informed as to all that is happening to you.

TO FATHER JOHN MONAGHAN
Corpus Christi Rectory, New York City

SEPTEMBER 24, 1934

Thank you very much for your generosity. I have your name written down in my prayer book and I will pray for you that brother body does not fail you.

Some interesting things have been happening to us. As a result of a great many attacks Monsignor Scanlan dropped in to pay us a call and said that he was asking the Cardinal to appoint a priest as our official spiritual advisor, more to check us up on doctrinal points than on economic. He thought that would be a good way to help us in our work. He further said that they would give us the imprimatur if we did not think it would hinder us. He asked us to list the priests who were sympathetic so that a choice could be made among them. He thought that you would be good for this work. The only thing that worries me is the burden this would put upon you. However nothing is settled yet and we have not heard from Monsignor Scanlan since Saturday; I will call you when we do.

TO MONSIGNOR ARTHUR SCANLAN

Msgr. Scanlan was rector of the Archdiocesan Seminary and censor for the diocese. He was often the bearer of official tidings from the chancery. In these early years of the Worker, Dorothy was in regular contact with diocesan officials. Over time, the interaction became increasingly infrequent.

TUESDAY, SEPT 25 [1934]

I was so sorry I was not here the other afternoon when you came to see us. I should have been so happy and honored to have welcomed you. We appreciate very much the cooperation and help you are giving us.

I am enclosing a copy of the appeal we wish to send out—indeed we have to send it out before we go to press again, to raise money for the printing bill. We have caught up on almost everything else and we are sure of a response, judging by the results of our other semi-annual letters. What we want your approval for is the opening paragraphs which are most important. We are sure that many of the more timid readers who now take only a single copy will be encouraged by this news to try to spread the paper and that is why we wish to publish it. We have been queried so many times in the past as to whether we had any approbation from the Chancery Office.

Also, do I understand you to have said that the [spiritual] director appointed is to advise us on matters of doctrine, and that we are permitted to use our own judgment on matters dealing with sociology and economics, the reporting and editorializing on labor?

Even if the appointment of a director is delayed, may we go ahead and announce this projected appointment as news, in the next issue? Or are we to delay publication of the October issue until this point is settled and the priest appointed?

I am writing to you, rather than trying to telephone or waiting for you to telephone us, because some of the time I am called out of the office, and Miss Weston cannot always be here either.

If you would just "yes" or "no" the paragraphs of query and send this letter back to me, it would perhaps save you trouble.

Trusting that you do not think us importunate, and begging that you will remember us in your prayers,

TO A FRIENDLY CRITIC [C. J. KELLY]

OCTOBER 13, 1934

Thank you very much indeed for your generous contribution and also for your friendly criticism. We try to be sensible and sound according to our lights and we do indeed ask the advice of all our friends among the professors and priests. We regard very seriously the necessity for being fools for Christ's sake and since our main objective is to present the case of the worker many think that we are not well balanced. I do think that agitators have to be extreme in their presentation of the case. The situation today is extreme. If Mr. Rockefeller offered us $100,000, indeed we would not take it. We would tell him to go and give it back to the miners in Colorado from whom he stole it. We don't believe either that labor is 100% right. We feel that they have copied the technique of Big Business and the Bosses and have in many cases become as corrupt and greedy as they, and of course we agree with you that violence is not the answer.

Do write to us again and be assured we appreciate your criticism and suggestions.*

---

* In her column of September 1934, Dorothy used rather stronger language to answer criticism of her attitude toward the Rockefellers. After reviewing the facts of the Ludlow massacre (1914), she noted: "It is too bad our antagonists do not inform themselves on the subject before they take the lying statements of enemies of God and His poor as truth."

TO DONALD POWELL

Donald Powell, a lawyer, wrote to Dorothy from Washington, D.C. Despite his criticism of the Worker's social activism, he contributed a number of articles, reviews, and letters to the paper. Dorothy's letters to him are marked by much affectionate teasing. Evidently she regarded him as a close friend.

C. 11/34

Dear Fellow Worker,

By this time I suppose you will have seen Peter [Maurin], or if you haven't, you will. And when he tells you to picket with him in front of the Mexican Consulate on Wednesday, the feast day of Our Lady of Guadalupe, don't think it's just a notion of his.* We're really serious. It would be swell if you and Peter and John Doyle would do that. We've picketed every day by twos and threes in front of the consulate here, following our mass picket line on November 15, and preparing for the one on Wednesday, and even when two or three do it, it works. I know that it's a great bother to the Mexican government. So do be a sport and join in and try to get a few others to do it. I told Peter to have some signs made to carry. You do not impress me as the respectable sort of person who would object to carrying a sandwich sign.

TO A PRIEST CRITIC

NOVEMBER 13, 1934

Dear Father [Anthony] Wolf,

Thank you for your friendly letter, with which however we find ourselves only partly in agreement. Or perhaps it is the

---

* At the time the CW was protesting the persecution of the Catholic Church in Mexico.

ideology. I wish you would help us by pointing out just which articles you object to,—it would be much more helpful. Won't you do that next time? Just mark the paper and send it back in to us.

I will agree with you that the poor man also is greedy. I believe I pointed out that greed in the editorial columns last month. I do not think, however, that we are guilty of envy or begrudging a rich man his wealth if we point out the abuses of the capitalist system which allows one man to accumulate the most of the world's goods while other families suffer year after year, the aching pinch of poverty if not of actual destitution. St. Jerome and many many Fathers of the Church, and our Leader Himself condemned the rich and no one would dare breathe the word of envy in connection with them.

TO FATHER J. STANLEY MURPHY

Father Murphy was founder of the Christian Culture Series at Assumption College, Ontario. In reply to an invitation to Peter Maurin, Dorothy offered very particular instructions.

DECEMBER 6, 1934

I am answering your letter for Peter [Maurin], who is at present sitting in the front office haranguing some visitors—getting them charged up for action; as a matter of fact he is doing exactly the kind of work that you want him to come up there and do.

He will be very glad to come up and spend a week with you either in January or February—just as you say. He is very glad to go because he enjoys making these jaunts, so don't thank him but thank us for letting you have him. I don't know what we will do without him down here!

Another thing when you send his fare be sure and send him a return ticket to New York. If you give him money he is liable to spend it and go someplace else. As you mention making him an offering, I also ask you not to give him that but to send it on to the Catholic Worker—if you give it to him he might decide to visit Bishop O'Hara in Montana or some equally distant place, as he is very impulsive. We really couldn't get along without Peter down here.

TO MONSIGNOR ARTHUR SCANLAN

DECEMBER 8, 1934

On the advice of Father Cox of Fordham, I write to tell you of an incident which is very disquieting to our friends but which is the kind of thing we run up against all the time in this work. There is a man by the name of Patrick Clare who is working with Russell Dunne, an ex-Catholic and anti-Semite to an extreme degree. Mr. Clare goes about talking about the Catholic Workers and what they represent and lately he has formed an organization which he calls The Catholic Militant Workers (the group consists of two or three, I believe). Patrick Clare, being obviously unbalanced, is not taken any too seriously by those he meets or seeks out. He seeks out everyone, by the way, to tell them his views. But last week he put an advertisement in the Irish papers about his organization, giving as his headquarters, 2070 Seventh Avenue, which is the address of Peter Maurin, with whom he disagrees violently on every subject. He has given this address because Peter, who is a gentle saintly soul, never puts anyone out. He has borne him patiently when he comes in to talk of his views, which are all for militant action and a United Front with anyone who is working for social justice, whether they be Communist, Socialist, Nationalist or Anti-Semitic.

It is unavoidable in doing a work like ours, that all sorts and conditions of people should associate themselves with us if only by attending our meetings and that they should, perhaps unconsciously, and very often consciously, do us harm by misrepresenting what we stand for.

Our own attitude should be perfectly clear to any who read

the *Catholic Worker*. But Father Cox is afraid of injury to our cause, and advises me to acquaint you with the circumstances in regard to Mr. Clare. I would not have troubled you with the matter otherwise. Just in case of complaints coming to you and to the Chancery office, I am informing you of the facts.

As far as I can see there is nothing that can be done which we are not doing about Mr. Clare. We have tried every friendly means to persuade him from his tactics, but aside from bopping him on the head and so disposing of him, I can think of nothing further to do.

It would indeed be unfortunate if our work should temporarily be stopped for some reason or other. However, we can only trust to prayer, and we can only leave our work in the hands of God. Whatever happens to us, whatever comes to us, can only come through Him, and if we make mistakes, I trust that He will not let them harm us.

I ask you too, dear Father, to pray for us, most especially on December twelfth [feast of Our Lady of Guadalupe].

TO FATHER JOSEPH McSORLEY, CSP

Dorothy had known Father McSorley, a Paulist priest, for some time. He had helped her arrange for the printing of the first issue of The Catholic Worker. *When the chancery advised Dorothy to select an official spiritual advisor, she was pleased that Fr. McSorley accepted the office. She made it clear, however, that she didn't expect any interference on social topics. His role was purely to advise her on Church teaching, doctrine, and theological matters beyond her competence.*

THURSDAY, DECEMBER 23, 1934

If you are appointed as our advisor, as I hope and pray you will be, it will mean just so much more work for you, which I regret exceedingly, knowing how many demands there are made on you. In my anxiety to find out whether you would be willing, this morning, I forgot to express this regret but I am sure you know how much we appreciate your help.

I shall see you next Monday night and let you know the result of my appointment.

TO DONALD POWELL

JANUARY 24, 1935

I wasn't sore about your attitude toward the Mexican business since I realize you don't see exactly how it all fits in with our program. Getting 3,000 Catholics to picket is bound to make them take a different attitude towards labor and street tactics quite aside from the question of Mexico. For another thing, it breaks down the spirit of nationalism, which American Catholics have so strongly, and actively demonstrates the Doctrine of the Mystical Body of Christ. However, as penance for your attitude you ought to come up and picket with us some day. I would enjoy seeing you carrying a nice flamboyant sign.

As to perfume, I am only opposed to it because it is expensive. I don't believe that the senses need much cultivation. The growth of sensual tastes is rank enough as it is. I think you are very much of a pessimist when you say that life is 95% pain. As a matter of fact I welcome the fleas as a necessary offset to the enjoyment we are at the present time getting out of life.

Your fellow worker in Christ,

TO THE EDITOR, *INTERRACIAL REVIEW*

FEBRUARY 1935

In regard to your editorial, "How Liberal is a Liberal?" in the December issue of your paper, I have a suggestion.

In the last paragraph there is a rather broad criticism of the efforts of others to promote interracial justice which I do not think we Catholics are justified in making. There is a questioning of their motives which I do not think it is necessary to make. It is the part of a Catholic Review of this kind, it seems to me, to present the Catholic viewpoint, to show a positive program of action, to tell what has been done in the past—even to acknowledge mistakes in the past and confess our remissness in the work which we should have done. We have enough to do in this positive way without giving space to criticism of the kind above mentioned. If they, the liberals and Communists, are trying to win adherents to their cause of materialist philosophy—we too are trying to win them in our Catholic philosophy, by spiritual and corporal works of mercy, and by a general program of propaganda. They can always point out our mistakes, and they have been and are many, and they can also say very truly that our efforts are to win souls, just as theirs is to win them away from us. Let us take what truth there is in what they say in regard to racial justice and give them credit for what good they do.

TO MONSIGNOR ARTHUR SCANLAN

While Dorothy declared herself receptive to any correction on matters of faith or dogma, she stood her ground when it came to social themes.

MARCH 16, 1935

Yesterday I went to see Father McSorley at his request in reference to the letter you forwarded to him, objecting to some of the articles which we had in the last issue of the paper.

If you will please excuse this long letter, I should like to explain to you the reasons we had for our stand. I should prefer, of course, talking to you personally but I know how busy you are with your great responsibilities, and do not wish to bother you, so perhaps this is the better way.

As to the article on the Child Labor Amendment, the stand we take is also the stand taken by Monsignor John A. Ryan,

Father Francis J. Haas, and Father Kerby and others. It is, after all, a matter of opinion, and it has nothing to do with faith or dogma, so we did not think we were treading on dangerous ground in upholding this piece of legislation. Those of our readers who opposed us,—and they were many—were not at all acrimonious in their opposition, and their letters, while differing from us, were sympathetic and kind. We handled the matter at such length because we felt that we owed it to our readers to give them in entirety our stand on the question. Dealing with it [briefly], we felt, would smack of arrogance, and we have a respect for our readers which makes us feel it necessary to give them each and every reason we could think of for taking the stand we do.

And after all, isn't there room for a difference of opinion on this matter? It makes for clarification of thought and also brings out before the opposition all the reasons for and against, far more clearly than as if there were a unanimous objection to it.*

Then, as to the Mexican paragraph, which after all did not amount to much. We are working in close cooperation with those Mexican priests in Baltimore who are working under the supervision of Archbishop Curley, and our supposedly humorous recommendation that if the Rotarians had to go to Mexico, then Catholic Rotarians should bring all the leaflets about the persecution possible (and we offered to have them printed for them, in Spanish of course) and distribute them widely, met with no rebuke from Baltimore. We also recommended (supposedly humorously) that everybody accept invitations of Calles and Cannabal to dinner and pester them by talking about the persecution. I do not see that there was anything so awful in this boxed paragraph. Father Daniel Lord in St. Louis, who is circulating a leaflet "Keep Out of Mexico," wrote us a letter for

---

* By 1934 the Child Labor Amendment had been ratified by thirty-six states. In supporting the Amendment, the *Catholic Worker* opposed the unanimous opinion of New York's bishops, including Patrick Hayes, who believed the Amendment would supplant the role of parents.

"keeping out of Mexico," which he asked us to publish, and we shall do as he requests and print it in the next issue. But our differences of opinion there did not seem to disturb him or the people in Baltimore to any great extent.

Lastly, as to the article of Donald Powell, of Washington, on the popular attitude toward having a baby which is expressed by the non-Catholic element, and as we know many middle-class Catholics not well grounded in their religion, in the words which are the title of the article, "We can't afford a baby." This article is the beginning of a regular campaign which we wish to carry on which is constructive and which we believe will do a great deal of good. In the interests of Catholic motherhood, we wish to point out all that is being done to give free, or reasonably cheap care to mothers in the way of clinics and hospitals, prenatal and post-natal care. We, of course, wish to call attention to the attitude of pride which prevents so many women from taking advantage of the opportunities offered them of this care. We call attention to the need of it and even to the lack of recognition of this problem and lack of constructive work done along these lines, so perhaps that is what antagonizes. You cannot campaign for such things as baby clinics and maternity wards without revealing the fact that there is a dearth of such conveniences for Catholic women who are forced to go to city clinics where they are often handed out birth control information and advised, even commanded, to make use of it.

We are not going into the subject of birth control at all as a matter of fact. We are not going to mention rhythm or however you spell it at all. We are going to endeavor to do a constructive piece of work by building up a public opinion amongst doctors and mothers and associations of women, for recognition of the need for more and better babies.

We are already receiving fine letters of cooperation from these groups.

I do hope that this explanation will satisfy you and convince you that we are not just trying to be controversial and that we have seriously considered these things, even prayerfully considered them. If you knew the number of Masses offered each month, if you know how we invoke the Holy Spirit over each page we write, over each letter we write as a matter of fact. After all, we realize overwhelmingly our responsibilities in getting out a paper which has a circulation of 65,000. And we do pray God unceasingly to guard and guide us.

The late Monsignor Chidwick, when at the request of the Cardinal he passed on the good word that His Eminence was pleased at our good work, spoke seriously to us on avoiding injustice to the rich in our attempt to be just to the poor. He also said that undoubtedly we would make mistakes, but that the thing was not to persist in them.

He encouraged us much, God bless him.

As I understood you to have said, it was not necessary for us to submit every article written, but only those having to do with matters of faith and dogma. Father McSorley has not the time to read each thing as it goes into the paper, I know. We consult him before each move we make, and discuss articles with him beforehand. He has been a kind and patient advisor.

If you wish me to come up to see you at any time, I shall be pleased to whenever you say.

Your fellow worker in Christ's Kingdom,

TO A DOMINICAN SISTER

JUNE 24, 1935

Dear Sister Thomas Aquinas [O'Neill]:

I was so glad to get your letter about Peter [Maurin]. He certainly is stimulating and we would be lost without him. It is he who is responsible for all the things that are done around here.

I am sorry to say [Tamar] Teresa said nothing at all about

her Confirmation except that she could remember all the fruits of the Holy Ghost and that if she tried real hard she could remember the gifts.

Since I left you I have been reading both the books you gave me with deep enjoyment. They are the kind of books that I shall always keep right by me and, since you addressed one of them especially to Teresa, I am taking special pains to talk to her about it since she is not old enough yet to read it. I have always had a great devotion to the Holy Ghost anyway, and that is why I appreciate so much having the Forgotten Paraclete.

Again, thank you very much and I do feel that you are a very dear friend.

TO THE NEW YORK POLICE COMMISSIONER

Dorothy and other Catholic Workers were among the demonstrators who protested the docking of the Bremen, *a German liner, on the Upper West Side. Among the crowd were many communists. When one of them climbed up and tore down the swastika flag he was shot in the leg, thus provoking a riot on the dock. At a subsequent demonstration Dorothy was a witness to further police violence.*

JULY 1935

As an editor of the *Catholic Worker* and a member of the Friends of Catholic Germany, I was present at the demonstration of the Communists both at the sailing of the Bremen on Friday night and in front of the police station on 47th St.

I am writing to protest against the unexampled brutality of a few of the police on that occasion. As a rule the patience of the police is to be commended, but on this occasion when they were endeavoring with success to hold back the crowd, someone came out on the steps of the station and ordered the police to "wade in and clear them out."

I was sitting on the steps of Unity Hall, a building a few doors from the station with a Catholic girl from Marquette

College, Milwaukee [Nina Polcyn] when two men dragged another man up the steps by the side of us, knocking me over in their haste, and in the darkness of the doorway, one man held the victim while the other began smashing his face in.

I called to the policeman on the sidewalk in front of me and one rushed up the steps. When he saw what was taking place, he came down, making no attempt to interfere. The others stood there and when I continued to protest they merely say, "You can't prove nothing by us. We didn't see anything." And even as they said this, the two men administered a final blow to their screaming victim and then hurled him down the street and made their way back to the station house. Since no one else was allowed to pass, I can only assume that they were plainclothesmen.

As Catholics we too feel called upon to protest against the Nazi persecution of Catholics and Jews by demonstration and distribution of literature. We feel that we would be neglecting our duty as Catholics if we did not do this. The Bishops of the Catholic Church have stated that many of the social aims of the Communists are Christian aims and should be worked for by Christians. We feel that Communism is gaining in this country, because Christian people do not protest against injustice as they do.

We oppose Communism on the grounds that it aims to establish atheism as a state religion, aims to abolish private property, and seeks a violent revolution.

Social justice is a part of Christ's teaching and we must work for that. We abhor the violent tactics advocated by Communists and it is for that reason that we protest the violent tactics employed by the police.

If the police do not set an example of law and order they are unwittingly aligning themselves with un-Christian forces.

The tactics pursued by the police the other night were Nazi tactics and a shame and disgrace to the U.S.

Well could the Communists turn to us, knowing us to be Catholics and sneer, "Where is your brotherly love?"

Patience on the part of the police is a more effective weapon as you well know. Bloody violence such as I witnessed merely serves to water the ground for Communism.

You know that saying, "The blood of the martyrs is the seed of the Church." The same holds good for Communists. Opposing them by violence will merely add recruits to their cause. By upholding peace and justice you take away from their grievance and block their attempts to precipitate violence.

We feel that the police need to be reminded that it is not *Communists* they are fighting, but *Communism*. Bishop Landries has said that "every creature is a kind of sacrament, a visible sign that contains a fragment of the idea of God."

Communists, inasmuch as they are creatures of God, are our brothers. These are the ideas which the *Catholic Worker* with its 100,000 readers is upholding.

TO CATHERINE DE HUECK

In reply to an appeal from Catherine, Dorothy promised some financial assistance, however little. She used the occasion to discuss her trials with one of the guests, Mr. Breen, whose angry tirades and racist jibes were a constant torment.

JULY 1935

It is with a very heavy heart that I am writing to you. We are so broke, and we have such heavier expenses in the summer that right now things look hopeless. But of course we must not be hopeless. Yesterday I told Miss McKenna about your plight and another friend of mine, and we are all going around collecting quarters for you. We have given ourselves two weeks to try to raise some money and we can't tell how much it may be. It may be only twenty-five. But we will send what we can if you can wait two weeks. The very fact that it is for your Don Bosco house makes us feel responsible. So let's all pray like mad and see what turns up. Maybe you will get it up there, or maybe we will get something here for you.

We ourselves are going on very short rations, eating two meals a day and slim ones at that in order to feed the children and adults that come to us for help. We have gotten the garden commune, the rent of which is guaranteed for the summer, but the food we must gather together for ourselves. Just this morning I put on the ferry three kids and three adults, all very much in need of sun and good food for a while. Here we sit at table twenty at a time, and down there it is about fifteen during the week and thirty for the weekend. And I dream of and figure about food continually. I made a pilgrimage to St. Joseph last week to tell him to take care of us all this summer. We have no money to get out our July edition, and we are planning to make it a summer one coming out about the twentieth of the month.

You know even when we put an appeal in the paper, we sometimes get nothing. God allows these desperate times I am sure because it is necessary for us. After all we are talking to the insecure, to the poverty-stricken, so why should we have less worries and more security than they. We too have to be harassed, to fret, to figure and eventually to lay it all at the feet of God. What He wants done, He will manage for us. If it is His will that we should be hungry, all right, and if it is His will that we should be evicted, all right. These things only happen for some good reason, so don't worry. We are harassed too, yet really we do not worry. It is a trouble, but one that God sends us, so that in our soul we can take it peacefully, even though our human mind goes scampering around trying to figure what to do. God will show us a way out.

Will you please pray real hard for a Mr. Breen who is at the present moment my greatest and most miserable worry? The very fact of my asking you now and your prayers the minute you get this (stop right at this point and say a Memorare!) will help me now in my sore distress I know. There is no time with God and he will see the prayer you will make in a couple of days and help now. Isn't that a helpful thought? Anyway, Mr. Breen is at present downstairs, with his clothes hanging off him, cursing and swearing and raving at us all. I am at my wits end. He has been with us for the last year, and just suddenly this last week has gone to pieces. He would not stay with us, not caring for "kikes and dingos," as he says, so we've been paying for a room around the corner and he has spent his days with us. Now his landlady has put him out, and he still refuses to stay with us. We don't know what to do. He sits at the lower window like a Cerberus and growls and curses at everyone who comes in for a bite of food or for some clothing. He hates us all, he hates this place, he says he is going to die, yet he won't have the Sacraments, etc. He won't bathe, he won't dress. I have to ask one of the men to button him up. He is going to sit right there. He won't go to a hospital. He won't be comforted.

And he, after all, is Christ. "Inasmuch as yet have done it unto the least of these," you know. It's the hardest problem we have yet.

I know that if we send him to a hospital, he will, with his present temper and shoutings and cursings, land in the psychopathic ward. Can you imagine Christ in the psychopathic ward?

We need prayers, you see, so please pray, and ask each and every member of your household to immediately say a Memorare. Please do this for Mr. Breen. The other trouble of yours, gigantic as it is, seems simple in comparison. We'll take two weeks to gather together funds, as I said, and we'll send on what we can.

I'd love to be seeing you, and all your works right now. Have courage. The more trouble you have, the more miserably you seem to be getting along, the more worth the whole thing is in the sight of God. If you had it all easy, if you took pleasure in it, it would not be worth much. And even if to you it seems to be going badly, that doesn't mean a thing. You don't really know what you are accomplishing. God makes it hard for you because you are strong and can stand it really. You are privileged. You know how a symphony, the best in the world, sounds like nothing if you yourself are tired and not in the mood for it, and yet that doesn't detract from the perfection of the work. It's the same with our work. We have no way of judging it, so it's no use trying.

Lots of love, darling.

Dorothy

JULY 17, 1935

Here is a bit of money which I would advise you to spend for food rather than the plumbing bill. The plumbing bill I would stick under the statue of St. Joseph, and I'd advise the rest of you to start saying the thirty days prayer to St. Joseph which never fails. And add appeals to Don Bosco too.

We've been getting our grocery bills which amount to seventy-five a week paid, in the most miraculous fashion due to St. Joseph. Also I think, because we are all fasting from meat which saves some, and does make meals rather tasteless, but is a necessary step. It is a united front with the Communists who have a meat strike that we can enter into most wholeheartedly.

The paper is going to press tomorrow night so I must sit and toil over some stories. And it's muggy, the flies swarm all over the place, I have poison ivy on my feet and in general life is a discomfort. However, there is so much work to be done that one is kept in an anesthetized condition.

Love from us all, darling, D. Day.

TO FATHER HANS REINHOLD

Fr. Reinhold, whom Dorothy met at a Catholic Charities convention in New York, was the port chaplain in Hamburg, Germany. In reply to his questions about escaping from Nazi Germany, she urged him instead to stay at his post, come what may. In the end, he did flee Hitler and settled in New York, where he joined Dorothy and the Catholic Worker in their support for striking seamen. When his political activities drew criticism from the archdiocese, he moved out West.

AUGUST 12, 1935

I have been ill and that is why I did not write you immediately upon receiving your letter of July 4. If you are banished from port-towns, can't you work elsewhere for the time being? It is true that the general feeling here in America is unsympathetic to other nationalities. Also, the people feel that a priest should stay in his own country, on the battlefield, as it were, rather than go away somewhere else and leave the people priestless. Also, that he should continue work under obedience to his bishop, even though he runs great risk. I have no sympathy for the nationalistic attitude of Americans but with the instinctive feeling of the rank and file that the priest should stay in his own storm-tossed country I do sympathize. On all sides the Communists are calling attention to their martyrs. To Thaelmann, for instance, and to Dimitroff, who has been rewarded for his brave stand at his trial by being made head of the Third International. His defense of himself has been published in pamphlet form and has a wide circulation here. On the Catholic side Cardinal Fahlhauber has become an outstanding figure here on account of his fearlessness. Can't you stay in Germany rather than in Switzerland?

You ask me in your letter whether I can see any point in your going back and I answer your question, though it may have been a rhetorical one, by saying, "Yes," and believe me I have considered this prayerfully before writing. We love you very dearly here and would love to have you with us but my whole feeling is to advise you to remain in Germany, come what may. It is your own country and the eyes of the world are on Catholics there.

Do write to us again when you can as we shall always be anxiously awaiting news of you.

I am writing your name in my Missal so that I shall not fail to remember you daily in Mass. Please do pray for us too and excuse my presumption in freely expressing my feelings. If I do not know what I am talking about please excuse me.

TO AN ANGRY SUBSCRIBER [MacAlan Gardner]

Dorothy learned not to entrust Mr. Breen with acknowledging contributions.

SEPTEMBER 30, 1935

Your letter certainly was a scorcher, and I can't say as I blame you. And now I shall have to write in great detail to you in order to make peace.

It's this way: our office here is made up of the lame, the halt, and the blind, mentally as well as physically. And it was one of them lame, halt, and blind ones that answered you on the pious and snippy card. Let me tell you about him. He is our cross, specially sent by God, so we treasure him. He is sixty-five years old, an ex-newspaper man who used to work on the Boston, Washington and New York papers, lunched with Coolidge, and so forth. He got out of a job when the old *World* went under, landed in the Municipal Lodging House where he slept in the largest bedroom in the world, 1,700 men there, and eventually found his way to us. He has been with us for the past year. All summer he has been sick, having had two strokes, and he had to be nursed like a baby.

And he's not just a nice sweet old man by any means. He's a hellion. He roars at us from morning to night and doesn't agree with a single stand we take. Occasionally, when he is bellowing for some work to do, we give him letters to acknowledge, and yours went to him with the note just to acknowledge and to say that we were writing later. But he didn't give the letter back,—it was placed in the file, and hence you got no other answer. The reason we could not answer at once was that some of us were away, on different fronts.

I'm sure if you met Mr. Breen you would understand his temperament. He begins the day by howling that breakfast is late, that he has to sit down at the same table with a "kike" and a "nigger," that the young up-start intellectuals around the office are a bunch of fools, etc. He takes his morning paper when he has finished with all of us and goes on to public characters, excoriating them until he is on the verge of a stroke.

And then other days he is mild and sweet and patient under his afflictions (because he does suffer abominably with a lame leg). His pride suffers at his dependent condition. But you do have to admire the large and impersonal way in which he complains.

Every now and then he greets someone who comes for shoes or food with the pleasant "We haven't any, and if we had we wouldn't give it to you," and we have to watch him and, when this happens, chase God's ambassadors down the street and bring them back.

There's really nothing we could do about it. We can't put him in a home—there is no place but the city home on Welfare Island and they'd kill him there. He's living with us, and he'll probably die with us, so that's that.

What got him in your letter was your allusion to the *Daily Worker.* He sees red when Communists are mentioned. In fact, I'm sure he thinks we are all Communists.

So all this having been explained—and you have put us to a lot of trouble by your own letter which was as bitter as hell—we can get down to answering some of your questions. But really, you know, you were most ready to lose faith in everything we stood for and to think us a bunch of pious hypocrites. Why didn't you send back the postal with something brief and snappy,—such as, "What the hell!" We all felt quite miserable to think of you out there in a rage against us, and we really felt our guilt too.

Anyway, please excuse us, for we do indeed regard your letter with great seriousness and would be delighted with your cooperation.

In the first place there is not much chance of starting a branch of the paper yet out West. We try to make the paper national in scope. Out in Milwaukee and up in Toronto, where we have groups cooperating with us, they put in mimeographed sheets bearing their own news and problems. That is, of course, if they are not going contrary to the spirit of the paper. In Boston, there is a headquarters which the branch of the Campion Propaganda Committee has taken over and they handle the paper and try to follow the program of study and action we advocate. The main work is the work of propaganda and combining it with works of mercy. That's how the early Christians won over Rome,—by combining the two. I understand that during the dock strike [of 1934] Catholic women fed the strikers? It would have been good to have passed out copies of the paper then to set forth the teachings of the Church as to workers' rights, etc. If we had had someone like you on our lists, we would have appealed to him to help us in that work.

The great work which is to be done is to change public opinion, to indoctrinate, to set small groups to work here and there in different cities who will live a life of sacrifice, typifying the Catholic idea of personal responsibility. Numbers and organizations are not important. We are just beginning after all. But one person can do a tremendous amount of boring from within, in his office, factory, neighborhood, parish, and among his daily acquaintances and associates. For instance, we have one lone man in Butte, Montana, distributing the paper to the men as they come from the mines. The trouble they have to combat there is extreme nationalism (their all-American plan) and also the modified socialism which tends towards fascism which the workers are getting interested in.

I cannot go into much detail as to our Farming Commune idea which is the one we advocate. What we are doing is trying to put our ideas *immediately* into practice, that is to live them. And at that we have not really started to do it yet. We take in the homeless,—we try to make this office, this house we have, a center of Catholic Action, a half-way house where people can exchange ideas, where we can hold forums, where we can perform the works of mercy. But it is only a half-way house, a step towards our ideal. Four-fifths of the Catholic population are in cities. They have to get back to the land. And when we take the

Catholic Worker and the whole crowd and get out on a farm and build up a community there, a place big enough where anyone can come and add himself to it,—then we will be making a real step.

And it isn't that we wish to isolate ourselves. The monasteries during the Dark Ages were centers where Catholic thought grew and was disseminated. The monasteries do not influence their surroundings now and change them. They adapt themselves to their surroundings.

From such a center we could send out missionaries of labor to wherever there was labor trouble or fascism brewing. We could send out these workers to live with the people in factory towns, in lodging houses,—to talk to them, to counteract the work of the Communists. They are working in just such a small way, sending out a few here and there, and their influence is everywhere felt.

During this last summer fellows from Missouri, Wisconsin, and Boston came down and spent some weeks with us to find out what we were trying to do, and then went back to try to do what they could in their own communities.

If you are ever considering coming East, hitch-hiking or what have you, the house is yours. But we are at present not at all saints and you will see just as much conflict (witness Mr. Breen) amongst us as there is anywhere. Sometimes I think that these large fierce battles the devil stages are being fought out around here in a small way, epitomizing the struggles which are going on in the world and teaching us most practically how to continue the fight.

We are just in the throes of our beginnings—probably we always shall be. But if we can interest people like you even to the extent of writing us such an infuriated letter, it's a good thing and we are not going to get discouraged.

I ask you again, fellow-worker in Christ, to forgive our seeming complacency. We were really all overcome by your letter, and the recriminations fell on my bowed head for let-

ting Mr. Breen answer even by postal by way of acknowledge-
ment.*

Sincerely yours in Christ

TO GERTRUDE BURKE

Miss Gertrude Burke had inherited several buildings on the Lower East Side, one of which, 115 Mott St., she offered to the Catholic Worker. Though Dorothy initially questioned its suitability, she eventually accepted the offer. It would serve as home for the CW for the next fifteen years.

1935

After a great deal of meditation and prayer, and a second visit to the house at 115 Mott Street, I sit down finally to write to you about it. I do hope that you will excuse all these delays, but you know how it is in summer, especially if one has family responsibilities.

In the first place, pledging ourselves to poverty as we do, I do not see how we could put ourselves in the position of landlords collecting rents. Even aside from our work, there is my own natural inadaptability for such a role. I would be ending up letting everyone live rent free in the place if they claimed they were too poor to pay. You see what a bad businesswoman I am.

In the second place, the entire front house is occupied, all but one little two-room apartment in the rear. There is no place for an office, let alone for living quarters for the staff which would take up four apartments, aside from the office. The house in the rear would only do for a house of hospitality if it were entirely renovated and cleaned,—and then only if we were all located in front so that we would be on hand to look after it. For as it is, it is a fire trap, with old-fashioned fire escapes which [should]

---

* Mr. Breen remained a part of the Catholic Worker family until his death in 1939. Dorothy recounted his story in *Loaves and Fishes*.

have been condemned long since, with their straight up and down ladders which are of no use to women and children. There are two families with children living on the top floor now. The lower floors are damp and airless, and from the holes I saw in the halls, and according to the young Italian girl who showed us around, rat ridden.

I am indeed most grateful for your very evident desire to help us, but to accept this help we should have to sacrifice principle which of course cannot be done.

I do appreciate, too, your position. You are in possession of property which in reality brings you nothing and which you cannot get rid of by sale. No one is buying property these days, except the city when they want to raze undesirable dwellings and build new ones.

There is nothing that I can see to do about it. We do indeed need a house for our manifold activities, but it seems to me better to go on paying the rent we do, and to help our girls by putting them in a place where there is heat and hot water and private, comfortable bath, where they can regain health and self respect and so be more fitted to meet the world.

I want to thank you again for all your cooperation and consistent kindness and remembrance of us. I should like very much to meet you some time and thank you personally for your kind offers.

Your fellow worker in Christ's kingdom,

TO DAN IRWIN [*a fellow Catholic Worker*]

ST. LOUIS, 2/1/36

I'm writing at Father Lord's office in St. Louis, on this swell typewriter, a great comfort. The weather is still awful, five below, and the trains, mostly excursion, are so hot that one itches all over. Then too, I'm traveling mostly at night, to get places on time, and sitting up is an agony. My back is still lame, and I comfort myself that this misery and fatigue can be offered up as penance for self-love and self-will. Do all you pray, as hard as St. Catherine of Siena (who sweat enough, remember, to bathe the cardinals) that we get our bills paid, that we get the farming commune, and that I don't collapse by the wayside. I really feel fine; my discomforts are only external and so good for me. As a matter of fact, I feel guilty at being so warm and well fed when I know the office back home is like a dank tomb and the meals anything but appetizing and sufficient.

TO STANLEY VISHNEWSKI

Stanley Vishnewski was one of the earliest and most faithful members of the Catholic Worker family. He arrived in the summer of 1934, a "seventeen-year-old Lithuanian boy from the Williamsburg section of Brooklyn," and remained until his death in 1979 (although, according to his longest-running joke, he had not yet decided whether he planned to stay). Given Stanley's relative youth, Dorothy naturally assumed a maternal attitude—advising him on his reading, his social activities, and his efforts at self-improvement.

WEDNESDAY, FEBRUARY 12 [1936]
MOUNT ST. SCHOLASTICA COLLEGE, ATCHISON, KANSAS

When you wrote and talked of listening to "Carmen," I felt so homesick I could have wept. How I am looking forward to hearing an opera when I get back.

Thanks very much for writing to me and giving me all the news of your doings. Is your family in need that you have to look for employment, and what kind of a job are you looking for? I thought that you were going down to the farming commune and work and study there, so that eventually you can be sent out as a lay apostle? If you are looking for a job merely to buy books, that is gluttonous of you, since you can get books at the library and there are plenty of books around the office such as the *Catholic Encyclopedia* which you have not yet read.

I hope you are being a worker as well as a scholar. Last time I went away I told you to study hard and you have been doing that, I notice, very consistently. Sometimes you may think that I scold you unnecessarily, but it is because I want you to make progress, and I want you too to set a good example to Francis. The example of each one of us is so very important, and we are of help to each other when we are doing right.

You know how very fond I am of you, Stanley, and the reason I scold is because I have great hopes for you and the work you are to do in the future in the Catholic Worker movement. But do not be afraid of being the least, and doing the little things around the place. Look how Peter works, how he is always looking for things that he can do. Please do try to be as industrious as possible and if you are leaving the office late in the evening, set an example by cleaning up the two offices before you go. Even though you are only around a couple of nights a week, it makes a difference, and we cannot stress too much this idea of personal responsibility (paying no attention to what the other fellow does or does not do) but doing everything we see to do ourselves. After all, we are doing it first of all for God, and then for each other.

Please pray for me,—write my name down in your Mass book so that you won't forget ever. Pray for me personally that I don't faint by the way, and pray for all the Catholic Workers, and pray hard, with fervor and intensity, like St. Catherine of Siena did, who sweat so much over prayer that she could have bathed the cardinals in it.

My love to you and all of the fellow-workers, Dorothy

TO A PRIEST REGARDING A LABOR BOYCOTT

At the time of this letter, the Catholic Worker *was supporting workers in a dispute with the Borden Milk Company.*

MARCH 16, 1936

Dear Father [Peter] Aikens,

Thank you for sending us the letter from Borden's. We are also very glad to see the effectiveness of our boycott as testified by the huge advertisements run by the company in the *Brooklyn Tablet* and the Catholic News. The fact that the company were put to such expense to defend themselves shows evidence that many of our readers evinced their Christian solidarity by writing to the company. . . .

Of course it is very easy for them to attack our credibility by saying we are "neither sanctioned nor approved" by the diocese.

The only reply that we can make to that is that a lay paper such as ours dealing with controversial matters such as these cannot be "approved" by the diocese. The Chancellor of our diocese told me personally that in regards to politics and economics we had absolute liberty to express ourselves, but that in articles having to do with the faith, we should submit them to an approved advisor. Both Peter Maurin and I have spoken before many bishops who have individually approved of our work. We are members of the Catholic Press Association which means that there is no objection to us as a Catholic paper from this diocese. No one can obtain membership in that organization if the chancery office "objects" to the paper. Our beloved Cardinal has certainly given us every freedom to continue our work in the face of continued adverse criticism over the space of the last three years sent in to him and to the chancery office.

TO CATHERINE DE HUECK

Catherine visited New York in February 1936 and was displeased with conditions at the Catholic Worker. The house, in her opinion, was dirty and disorderly, and she was disturbed by the lack of rules and the presence of too many "hangers on." She discussed her concerns with Fr. McSorley, the CW's spiritual advisor, and recorded, in her *diary, his agreement that "the work is wonderful but that [Dorothy] has no organizing ability at all." As Catherine observed, "It is funny how good people can get it wrong."* When Dorothy caught wind of these concerns she requested clarification.*

MAY 11, 1936

I saw Father McSorley last week and he told me to write to you and to ask you to tell me the same things that you told him by way of criticism of the Catholic Worker.

He asked me whether you had written and said that at your visit to him you had said that you were going to write. I told him that I had heard from you but that you had not said much about your visit here. I didn't answer your last letter right away for I thought you had not left Ottawa and I would not have been able to reach you. Do not worry about us going completely to the farm. Our House of Hospitality will continue in the city and also our Roundtable discussions. We are all comfortably settled at Mott Street and the place looks beautiful with $100 worth of paint on it. We have so much space now that we can be more clean and orderly.

We are broke now with not a penny in the bank. Do write to us soon. I love hearing from you and please excuse me being such a poor correspondent. Please pray for us as we pray for you.

In reply, Catherine repeated her criticism directly to Dorothy. This was summarized in an attitude she said she had heard widely: "It is a wonderful work, evidently blessed by God, but why, since all things that belong to God are clean, orderly, and well defined, is there such a lackadaisical attitude toward those little things that matter so much?" She urged Dorothy to observe the need for cleanliness, for rules of life, better organization, and "more hierarchy."

---

* For these and other remarks by Catherine de Hueck, see Robert Wild, ed., *Comrades Stumbling Along: The Friendship of Catherine de Hueck Doherty and Dorothy Day as Revealed through Their Letters* (New York: St. Paul's, 2009).

MAY 30, 1936

You know how much I appreciate your letter of criticisms and how I understand the spirit in which the letter was written. I'm glad you wrote. I realize myself, and often with a rather hopeless sense of not being able to do anything about it, how things were. I am happy to report that many things are now changed. For one thing, the woman that donated the use of the house also bought a hundred dollars worth of paint and plaster and the whole house on Mott Street and the store is bright and shining throughout. It gets untidy—you should see it today with the paper being mailed out! Also it is now full of striking seamen, and many of our gang have to sleep on the floor in the offices. And thirty people have to be fed in a small room, and all the cooking has to be done on a three-burner plate. We are always hard up for equipment. But I was thanking God at Mass this morning for the opportunity He sends us of helping. Even though taking in so many people makes disorder. Four of the seamen are sticking around this morning to help us and as you can imagine there is a lot of conversation and indoctrination going on all the time. . . .

Another thing I always bear in mind is that the devil is constantly busy around a place like this trying to set people against each other. The only thing to do is to plough through all difficulties regardless.

Pray for us all—I know you do, as we do for you,

Catherine wrote again on July 17, now expressing her own discouragement. "Dorothy," she wrote, "how do you awaken Catholics? How do you bring them to the realization of their eternal destiny? How can you put into those sleepy heads and indifferent hearts the understanding that souls are being killed all around them, souls for whom God died!" She acknowledged that "at the end of a day I feel like such a worthless, such a lazy servant." In her dejection she turned to Dorothy for advice, though with some guilt: "It wouldn't do, would it, that the darkness in my soul should blot the sunshine out in yours, so pray for me."

AUGUST 9, 1936

After my month's absence in Washington and Pittsburgh, I return to find your letter, and I was glad to hear from you even though your letter sounded sad. But I'm sure you felt better after writing it. One always does. You sounded, too, so discouraged and you know as well as I do that discouragement is a temptation of the devil. Why should we try to see results? It is enough to keep on in the face of what looks to be defeat. We certainly have enough examples in the lives of the saints to help us. Not to speak of that greatest of failures (to the eyes of the world) of Christ on the cross. Why look for response? After all, we can only do what lies in our power and leave all the rest to God, and He will attend to it. You do not know yourself what you are doing, how far-reaching your influence is. I have heard people speak of you in different parts of the country. Why should you expect to see results in the shape of Houses of Friendship? Perhaps you are arousing in them instead the sense of personal responsibility. After all, God often lets us start doing one thing and many of the results we accomplish are incalculably far-reaching, splendid in their own way, but quite different from what we expected. Let us think only in terms of our own selves and God and not worry about anyone else.

Just had a long blast from Father Sullivan in which he bawls hell out of me and tells me that those who are holding up the procession (meaning me and Peter) ought to get off the road,— that he had wanted to follow a St. Joan, but that she would not get in the saddle, etc.

These are some of the things that are hard to bear. I do know exactly what I am doing. I know that Peter is a leader worthy to be followed. And no such blast is going to deter me from the program which we have mapped out for ourselves. Even if there is lack of unity amongst us, I just go straight ahead, doing the best I can with the very poor human material God sends. Just look at the kind of disciples He chose for Himself, and how

little they understood Him, how they wanted a temporal kingdom and thought all was lost until the Descent of the Holy Ghost
enlightened them. Why should we expect to be anything else but
unprofitable servants? We simply have to leave things in God's
hands. Get hold of *Abandonment to Divine Providence* by [Jean-
Pierre de] Caussade and comfort yourself with that. It's done more
to help me these past years than any other spiritual writer. In fact
I could get along on the New Testament, the *Imitation [of Christ]*
and Caussade for a long time and I am a pig about books. Spiritual reading is the oil that keeps the lamp burning, as you know.

It is late and I must get to bed. Six hours sleep is all I've been
getting lately and it isn't enough.

Pray for us. Love, Dorothy

*Catherine replied on August 17, noting that her discouragement was
caused by the seeming indifference of Catholics. "I always seem to visu-
alize what would happen to this world if Catholics were awake, I mean
wide awake, and if, instead of being the Church Dormant, we were the
Church Militant. It is not so much discouragement as a sort of feeling
of terrific odds against one, in which the children of light seem to lose
out to the children of darkness."*

NOVEMBER 16, 1936

Just today a priest called up and wanted to know if you were in
jail and I told him if you were, better people had been there before you. St. Peter, for instance. If you are in jail, you must be
very happy.

Your last letter just after you had received approval and all
the misery that goes with it was very understandable. Every
now and then I too am faced by this sense of being caught.

I was talking to a psychopathic ward doctor who said, "People
who were intensely religious were that way because they were
so aggressive and were trying to square things with their conscience." I am sure that you are one of those people who are unhappy unless you have a difficult fight on your hands.

I almost laughed when I heard from this priest this morning but from several others who dropped in last week that you were being followed and suspected of not only Communism but racketeering and general thievery.

I am sorry that I did not write to you before but we have been having a few troubles and things to do around here which kept me from the mail. Do write soon and let me know what jail you are in and I will write letters as will the others around here.

Love to you from all of us.

Catherine wrote on November 25 with shocking news: Friendship House was being closed down by order of the Archbishop of Toronto. The causes were several: suspicions that Catherine was "a Communist boring from within," that she had absconded with funds, that she was an immoral, unworthy character, etc. "Can the CW afford to associate with me?" she asked. "It is for you to say."

12/36

Got your last two letters and cannot really make head or tail of the whole thing. If they are closing Friendship Houses, it is really disastrous. I thought they were only taking them away from you and handing them over to an order to run. That is bad enough, of course, but it is the kind of thing which is always happening in the history of works such as ours. I'm always expecting I'll be asked to leave the work for the good of the cause, and I'm more or less prepared for it. All the kind of gossip and rumors that have gone around about you, have gone around about me too these last years. I'm supposed to be an immoral woman, with illegitimate children, a drunkard, a racketeer, running an expensive apartment on the side, with money in several banks, owning property, in the pay of Moscow, etc. etc. And if outside rumors were not enough, the same kind of stuff comes from the inside, so from month to month, I'm supposed to be in love with this one or that, and so it goes. When men and women are working together, there is always this kind of trash going on. I do not concern myself with it. Sometimes it gets your goat when it comes from within the organization, but the stuff that comes from outside never bothered me. Due to my past life, I am indeed open to criticism, so when the dirt begins to fly it is to be expected.

I should think you would feel privileged and happy to be sharing in some of our Lord's sufferings and above all not surprised as though it were something entirely unexpected. What in the world do you expect? The very fact that there is all this obstruction and hindrance and trouble shows the work must be succeeding beyond your wildest hopes, otherwise the devil would not be putting so many hindrances in the way and trying to break down your morale. For that is surely what is being done. When you write in such terms as "I have fallen a hundred times to our Lord's three," I wonder at you. I wish to goodness I were up there to talk to you. You will think I am cold and unsympathetic, but really darling, I am not at all. I have been thinking of you constantly for the past week. I would hold your head up through it all and if you are deprived of any work to do, abandon yourself completely to divine providence, try to keep to ordinary routine as much as possible, and leave things in God's hands to work out.

If you are deprived completely of a means of earning a living and have no money for rent or food, I would quite simply throw myself on their charity, in your humility be a charge to them, instead of a person who has been taking a charge off the shoulders of others. But I would not flee from the scene of strife and persecution. I'd stay right there and face them out. Besides you are making a decision right in the heat of things which is never good. What does Nicholai say to all this? Cannot he advise you? How come when you have the approval of the Archbishop such as the letter you sent, they turn and close Friendship House?

I really do not understand your leaving the scene where you have been doing such great work. Write to me again.

As you know you are always welcome to come to us though I think you would not be especially happy here because our technique, our seeming anarchy which is a result of our extreme effort to practice personalism along with communitarianism, would drive you crazy. From your very criticism last year, I know how hard it would be for you to put up with our way of doing things. The house is jammed now,—we are always sacrificing efficiency in order to put in an extra bed or serve more people. I myself am sleeping in the back office, my folding cot jammed in between a desk and a pile of papers. You would have to share a room with a girl who is recovering from an operation for tumor on the brain and a woman whom we got out of a psychopathic ward at Bellevue. There does not seem to me much prospect of a rest for you and you say you are very tired. The rest of the staff are just as jammed. Peter shares his room with a convert Jew and the other boys are crammed four in a room with sailors and unemployed. We have twenty-four rooms, but we never have enough room and never will. God seems to want to keep us in just that kind of poverty which means no privacy, cold, stinks, dirt (for you always feel dirty what with washing with cold water and having to go to the public baths).

If you need a rest you had better go up to the nuns of the Atonement, where you can be comfortable and quiet for a time. Or as I said before, stay on where you are for a little while.

I purposely make this letter frank and sane as possible, because you are in such a state of mind. But at the same time, if you do not believe you have our love and sympathy, you are lacking in faith in us. We most truly believe, though, that the devil makes all this hullabaloo just when work is accomplishing the most good, so for that you should be most happy.

One consequence of the closing of Friendship House in Toronto was Catherine's decision, on the suggestion of Father John LaFarge, a

Jesuit priest prominent in the cause of interracial progress, to open a Friendship House in Harlem.

TO DOM VIRGIL MICHEL

Father Michel was a Benedictine monk from St. John's Abbey in Collegeville, Minnesota, and one of the most prominent figures in the liturgical movement. Dorothy was a deep admirer of his work.

1936

Thank you very much for both your kind letters and please excuse me for not answering them both. We are certainly glad of your friendly criticism and will do our very best to work as Christians (this as members of the Mystical Body) and with love rather than animosity.

I regret your fears about moving headquarters into Easton [*site of the new Catholic Worker farm*]. I wish you had taken this up with me before you left so that I could have reassured you. Our propaganda headquarters is still going to be in New York, but Frank O'Donnell and Dan Irwin will have charge of the office in Easton receiving all mail, filling orders and carrying on the work with the school and parish in that city. I shall not be away more than a week out of every month and that week will be devoted to the apostolate of letter writing as Father Lord called it, which is certainly an important part of the work. Such work can be done down there more properly and quickly.

There are articles I must write and things I must do and there is more opportunity for that kind of thing there. Here in New York we are seeing people from morning until night, there are meetings and demonstrations and such activities which must be carried on. I realize the importance of this and don't think that we are deserting the city. The afternoon you mentioned in your letter I had to go down to see Mr. Moody in Wall Street and even so I managed to see six or seven priests during the day and many of those you mentioned as being in the office were still there when I got back. But even so it is important for me and the others to be there. Still you must admit that it is also important to go out into the fields among the steel workers. The very importance of our work lies in the fact that we have this real contact so of course there will be many times when people will complain of coming down to see us and not finding us in. It always concerns me very much when some woman tells me she has been to the office three or four times and never found me there.

We do indeed realize our responsibilities and are not trying to shirk them but the work in Easton must be built up as that is a big part of our program. I have talked these matters over with Father McSorley our spiritual advisor and he agrees with this move which is just a part of our growth.

The one thing I do not agree with you at all about was your feeling that perhaps "each one is willing to let the other one assume the burden of assistance in the general work." We are blessed in the number of fellow workers who come to us and those who shirk are in some way the lame, the halt, and the blind and need to be cared for with love. I can see many ways in which we fall down and I see these defects and faults so clearly that sometimes it is very hard not to give way to discouragement and become critical and desolate. Just because I do not point criticism but feel that it is better to let people recognize their mistakes and rectify them doesn't mean that I do not see where things are wrong.

We all need to watch ourselves constantly. Please continue to help us by your prayers and pray that the Christian Front, Liturgy and Sociology and the Catholic Worker and the newest development, The Catholic Student, progress helpfully. I am very careful at this time to do nothing without the advice of Father McSorley, our approved advisor, so there will be as much united front as he sees fit. He has been in touch with the work since the beginning and thank God that we have a priest who is on hand always to tell us what sides to take.

TO DONALD POWELL

FRIDAY [JAN 15, 1937]

Just to be repentant and show you how bad I feel at your rebuke, I'll write by hand. I have to anyway, as I am in bed and cannot balance a typewriter. I am in bed this afternoon both to rest and because the office is too full to hold one more.

We are very comfortable here at Mott Street and it breaks my heart to have to move. We may get a stay for six months.

We have all of the back house which is divided up into two-room apartments. Miss Clemens of Kentucky, the Sorbonne, and Columbia Univ—formerly headmistress of a school, 60 years old, and now on her uppers, shares my apartment, or rather I share hers. She is delightfully frivolous, takes just a drop of liquor before going to bed, smokes, likes comfort, and has made the place most cozy with an open grate where she sits with her feet in the air, taking spiritual reading.

We also share the room with rats. An old grandfather one comes and sits in front of the fire at night. He also walks across my feet to get up on the window sill to explore the tidbits of food Miss Clemens likes to keep there. Some of the time I sleep with my light on all night to discourage him. For the last few nights we have a reluctant cat staying with us, who offends my sense of smell.

The rats don't like her either. She caught one small one last night and tossed it around the room a bit before I opened the door for her to get out. I was so stiffened with horror even in my sleep that my neck is stiff this morning. Rats, the consciousness of them, make me sleep with a certain rigidity. I tell you all this with a certain enjoyment, because really rats are such a small trouble compared to some of the others which are going on. The others are big fights with the powers that be, ship-owners, priests and lay people who are convinced I'm a Communist. The biggest fight of all is with Father McSorley, who is supposed to be our spiritual advisor, and wants me to publish a statement, defying them all, and inviting them to stop the work if they want to, just to prove I'm an obedient child of the Church. I believe in paying no attention to attacks, but just proceeding, not trying to defend ourselves unless we are directly asked to.

I would like to see you. What do you have to go on benders for when you might be paying us a call? Peter is in Washington now, wandering around somewhere heckling people. He wandered out of here, and I haven't the slightest idea where to reach him. He will return in a week. I am coming down there for Brother Joachim [Benson's] ordination on February 11 and will be there for the afternoon of the 10th, the eleventh and the 12th. I'll be seeing you then. You are dear to always be helping us. You won't let me thank you then, so I must do it now.

Sincerely and affectionately in Christ, Dorothy

TO JOHN BROPHY [*national director of the CIO*]

SEPTEMBER 20, 1937

I hope this letter reaches you soon and that you will not think me presumptuous in writing it. You know the real interest the Catholic Worker has in you and your activities. I consider you a brave man, ready in your integrity to sacrifice popularity in maintaining your position as a Catholic in the labor movement. I can't tell you how much I admired your speech that last time I saw you in New York at the Hippodrome.

This week I have been speaking around Detroit before Catholic groups and also to the auto workers. I spoke over the radio station for them and also upheld the cause of the CIO on the Catholic hour yesterday afternoon.

One of the men was outlining to me the organization for the Ford drive. Certainly the plan to carry on as in a political campaign, working from the outside as well as from within, with house to house canvassing and a thorough education program, is a very good one.

Certainly we must keep in mind the patience necessary for this work. But patience is a hard word, meaning suffering, and people are naturally impatient. The thing to remember is that about half the Ford workers are pretty thoroughly indoctrinated with the idea that [Henry] Ford is a great man, a self made man, and their individualistic ideas are maintained by the press and radio and pulpit.

Certainly at the head of the drive a man is needed who will be of such experience in the labor movement, and of such integrity that he can hold up his hand amid a storm of adverse publicity.

Some of the men I talked to suggested the possibility of two men heading that drive—you and [Walter] Reuther. Of the two, I most certainly hope that they put you in and no matter what your personal inclination. I hope you try to take it over.

TO JOE ZARRELLA

Joe Zarrella joined the Catholic Worker in 1935 after coming upon volunteers handing out copies of the paper in a May Day parade. He went on to become a mainstay of the movement. Dorothy put him in charge of managing the house during her travels, or when she was visiting the CW farm in Easton, Pennsylvania.

EASTON FARM, JUNE 13, 1938

It is beautiful here. I scrubbed the outhouse and kitchen this morning. I tell you to let you know I was sharing your labors. I never see you at your manual labors in the morning without wishing to take a hand. There is room for me to do it all right out here.

The grass is mowed all around the house—a real lawn. Tamar's house. I had peas from the garden today—fresh strawberries, cherries, etc. Also onions and radishes.

The dead tree by our little cabin got struck by lightning Sunday. Tell Gerry [Griffin]. Tell him also to come out soon if he wishes. Mr. O'Connell works along but very glumly. He scarcely speaks to me because when he comes at me with a grim look in his eyes, I say, "Come, Tamar, let us pick strawberries." I am paying Gerry back for not being a lightning rod for me. Tell him I'm sorry I groused at him. I've had peace and rest starting off with one day's headache.

PITTSBURGH, JULY 10, 1938

Too hot to sleep so letterwriting. Glad the letter came from the Leslies for my and Tamar's fare. Funny how people will give money for one thing and not another. They are Protestants. I figure $75 is enough for round trips so use $75 of that money for gas bill or coffee or bread. Cut out apple butter first if necessary. It is heartbreaking—our finances. I've been worrying about you all, whether you are all not pretty young to take it. Whether bitterness and scornfulness is not liable to be the outcome of the struggle. However, your letter sounds cheerful. You have the appeal by now. Not very good. I'll be praying hard and get the gang on it. This terribly hot weather, almost a hundred, makes people indifferent and lethargic.

ANTIGONISH, NOVA SCOTIA, AUGUST 15, 1938

Naturally I am worried to death at not hearing from you. I've been here from the tenth to the eighteenth and not one word from Mott Street. I heard so often in Pittsburgh, and now no word, so I can only conclude that there is trouble that you are trying to keep from me. I'd much rather hear than not hear.

Got an anonymous letter, very nasty, dated Brooklyn as one might know, threatening my ruin and saying that a move was underway to have our books examined. Usual charges of the leaders living in comfort and the workers around the place going hungry. Calling us a bunch of racketeers. Fr. [Ignatius] Cox of Fordham is up here and also threatening us. Says he has been receiving many letters daily in regard to us. There certainly is a widespread move again to have our blood. If there is need for me to come back send a night letter. I'd hate to miss the tour, as Fr. Coady has kept me busy around here speaking so though I've seen something of the handicrafts, I have not seen the study groups or coopers and credit unions.* Also the miners and steel workers want me to speak to them next week.

After all, troubles have accumulated before and praying will do more even than my being there. I'm doing that hard, so that I'm sweating at it. The letter from Brooklyn warned me to come home immediately and meet my fate which is one reason I wish to continue the tour in faith and be home a week from Sunday.

TO DONALD POWELL

Responding to Powell's news of his impending marriage.

SEPT 4, 1938

Your news in a way makes me very happy and in a way is distressing. If she is not baptized you cannot be married by a priest. Will she be baptized? Excuse me for being so personal but after all we are old friends, if only by correspondence. When is the date? Do let me know so I can offer up my Mass for you that morning.

We are being investigated—much opposition. It does great harm to the group because people can get so self-righteous and complacent under unjust criticism. Sometimes I think it would do us all good to be suppressed. Maybe then we'd turn into real bums and lay apostles. Pray for us, please.

In Christ, Dorothy

---

* Father Moses Michael Coady organized the Antigonish Movement, a network of cooperatives in Nova Scotia. Dorothy described their work in the September 1938 issue of the *CW*.

P.S. I'm so glad you're getting married. I wish God hadn't put the finger on me. Of course I queered things for myself pretty thoroughly in the past. This is the only thing He can do with me. But a home and a companion is just about the nearest one gets to happiness in this world. I'm all for appreciating the natural joys. It's damn ungrateful not to.

TO EDWARD BREEN

In her book Loaves and Fishes, *Dorothy described Mr. Breen, a former newspaperman who settled at the Catholic Worker in his seventies, as "someone we will not soon forget." He had appeared one day at the Worker, sat down without a word, and proceeded to answer a tray of letters. (He was exceptionally proud of his calligraphy.) His task complete, he had announced his plan to stay. Stay, he did, until his death in 1939. In the meantime, his apoplectic temper and open racism were a constant irritant in the community. Nevertheless, for all his open contempt for other members of the household, he held Dorothy in the highest esteem. In a letter addressed to "Dearest, fairest, Miss Day," he proclaimed: "Breen is all yours. You have been a great mother to this old fool, a dear sister and a too easy boss. No person nor clique can take from me the sweet assurance of your kind deeds and fine thoughts." Though she often corrected him for his "roarings," Dorothy made it a special spiritual discipline to treat Breen with love and patience.*

UNDATED (OCTOBER 1938?)

Dear Mr. Breen:

This is but a note to tell you to be good and to be happy even though it means a great effort of will. I know you haven't been feeling well, you poor dear, but take care of yourself, and try to keep calm and peaceable in mind, and you will make me happy. I know things become very hard and disagreeable at times, but just offer it up for my intention. And right now we've all got to be praying hard for funds, so remember that on your hard worked rosary too.

You ask John Curran if there is anything you need in the way of pills, laundry, paper, cigarettes, magazines, etc. etc. Your wants are so few, you so seldom complain—you are getting to resemble Peter [Maurin] in your detachment in regard to material goods. I do admire the gallant indifference to material discomforts and surroundings.

I have brought down a raft of letters to answers—the apostolate of letter writing is just as important as seeing people. Also I have two articles to write, the priests to visit down here, a speech to make at the Parent Teachers meeting, a picnic of the parochial school children here at the farm, etc. So I shall be busy for two weeks. I must do some heavy praying too, and I shall remember you, as you remember me.

In reply, Mr. Breen wrote: "As long as I live I shall always be proud of having had you as my boss and my friend. Your little glimpses into my mind on personal responsibility a few days ago remade me and I have, thank you, ceased to hate people as I was wont to."

TO THE COMMISSIONER OF HEALTH [*City of New York*]

DEC 10, 1938

On the advice of Mr. Strach, assistant to Mr. Hodson, I am writing to let you know of the predicament we are in and to ask your intercession.

Due to the fundamental principles which underlie the work we are doing this letter must be rather long, so I beg your patience.

For the past two years, the CATHOLIC WORKER has been feeding from 1,000 to 1,500 men every morning through a breadline at the office of the paper, 115 Mott Street. Through twenty other houses in other cities throughout the country, similar lines are maintained, some being fed three times a day. The desperate condition of transients, uncared for either by federal or state relief, makes this necessary.

The Catholic Worker does this work for a number of reasons, though seemingly it is quite outside the province of a labor publication such as ours. In the first place, we are urging upon the Church the necessity of its bearing the burden imposed upon it by Christ Himself, to feed the hungry. He said, "Inasmuch as you do it unto one of the least of these, you do it unto Me."

Also, according to canon law, every bishopric is obliged to maintain a hospice to care for the needy and the pilgrim. In these days this is not being done. Men are not merely mouths to be fed and bodies to be sheltered, but are creatures of body and soul, and we maintain that it first belongs to the Church to care for them and that only in times of national emergency should the state bear so gigantic a burden as it is doing today.

Not only as Catholics but as patriotic Americans who love our country, we feel the necessity of personally being responsible to do something for those who come to us. We cannot say to the needy who flock to the offices of a paper dealing with labor and the need to rebuild the social order: "Go, be thou filled," and hand them literature instead of bread. We have to see personally that we give them something to satisfy their immediate needs, whether it is food, clothing, or shelter.

To put it in round figures (the way charities estimate their works), we have provided 49,275 nights lodging these last three years; 1,095,000 breakfasts of bread and jam and coffee; 131,400 lunches and suppers.

These are figures for New York City alone. If we continued this turnstile method of estimating what we, a group of insignificant lay people, have been able to accomplish, and counted the numbers fed in twenty other centers, the figures would be tremendous.

We are doing this because of a feeling of personal responsibility; and we are also doing it as an example of what could be accomplished by the hospices which we advocate as part of our program of relief and rehabilitation (providing work by maintaining workshops for mutual aid, taking care of religious needs, and educating towards a land movement).

In connection with our land program we have started three communal farms outside of New York, Boston, and Detroit, and two others are being started outside St. Louis and Milwaukee. Here by giving men or families one acre and helping them make a start, we hope to settle people and thus aid transients in this way. The farms are from seventy to 150 acres.

All this work we have been able to do in 5 years not only with the aid of the paper, which brings in sales at one cent a copy, $1,200 monthly, but with the aid of friends and with the money we ourselves earn at outside employment, writing, lecturing, and ordinary jobs. We believe with St. Paul that, though the laborer is worthy of his hire, it is necessary to sacrifice, to work ourselves to put our program into effect.

There are thousands working in this movement throughout the country and it has the support of many bishops and priests as well as laypeople.

And now the Health Department is trying to stop this work which we are doing! On receipt of an anonymous letter a year ago (not from our Italian neighbors because they sympathize in the work), investigators began calling on us every few weeks. We made many changes but each time additional demands were made upon us. We have tried to be reasonable, to do everything which we could. But the fact remains that in an old tenement such as we inhabit, the use of which is donated by one of our readers, it is impossible to make some of the changes required by the Health Department. The latest requirement is to put a wash basin with hot and cold running water in a toilet which is too small to contain it and to sterilize the cups between using, cups which are at present washed with hot running water, just as they are in all drug-store restaurants for instance.

Ours is an old-law tenement, cold water, unheated. We who work and live here are perfectly willing to undergo the hardships which such a life entails. We are not only sharing to some extent the poverty of those around us, but the poverty of Christ, and we feel ourselves privileged. We ourselves bathe at the public baths (which by the way are closed until August next!) or at the homes of friends or in old-fashioned wash tubs. We have a hot water heater in the store where we serve the coffee and the water can be taken from there in basins to wash one's hands. But this does not satisfy the Health Department's requirements, as we of course understand.

Be assured that we do appreciate the need for the regulations of the Health Department and all it is trying to do in a city so gigantic as this. But at the same time we know that these requirements are not being met within restaurants throughout the city and that if letters of complaint were sent in by our friends and readers, the Health Department would have to hire an army to investigate, if they really, as they claim, follow up every complaint.

Day before yesterday the investigator came again and said that the permit which the Department claims it is necessary for us to have will be refused. Which means, I suppose, that our line will be shut down. Of course we do not intend to stop. We will start again just as often as we are stopped. We believe it to be a grave injustice not only to the transients but to the old and crippled in the neighboring lodging houses who find it impossible to get down to South Ferry or 25th Street. Also it is a grave injustice to the work we are trying to do. It will cause grave scandal and the organized protest of our readers will be an embarrassment which we wish to spare the city, especially since we recognize how much good is being done here in New York. This city has more mercy and charity towards the poor than any other in the United States and we realize that nowhere else is such care taken of local homeless men. At the same time there are always grounds for criticism of treatment and facilities provided.

We do not intend to have our work stopped. We will organize protests and bring out the fact recognized by you also that the "spirit quickeneth while the letter killeth."

TO THE EDITOR OF THE *CENTRAL CALIFORNIA REGISTER*

JANUARY 17, 1939

Enclosed is a copy of a statement we made in the Catholic Worker in regard to sit-down strikes in Michigan. I suppose you have seen the statement made by Attorney General Murphy recently that accused the sit-down strikes of being illegal. That does not necessarily mean that it is immoral. I was scandalized to find on my speaking trips throughout the country that many of our Catholic lay people think in terms of sin when they hear the world immoral. They picture men and women locked up in a factory, night and day, for weeks on end, dancing and carousing. It seems a shame that they should take so stupid an attitude.

Father John M. Maguire of St. Victor's College says that the sit-down strike is not morally wrong. Also Father Jerome Hannon, Assistant Chancellor of the Pittsburgh diocese in an article in *Ecclesiastical Review* in July, 1937. Both theologians indicated that its use can be justified. Of course, practically every strike is condemned as unjust by the employers and they use every means in their power to convince the people that the strikes have violated the condition of a just strike. So it seems to me we must be very careful in judging. As St. Louis said, "We must always be on the side of the worker until he is proven wrong."

TO MARY FRECON

Mary Frecon was a member of the Blessed Martin de Porres CW House in Harrisburg, Pennsylvania. She worked in a predominantly black section of town.

JANUARY 17, 1939

As soon as the terrible Christmas rush was over and we could breath again, we all of us around here began worrying about you, wondering why we had not heard from you this long time, and now I feel very guilty, hearing how sick you have been, that I did not sit down and write to you before.

I often say around here to our own crowd that we are so careless of each other, that while we are saving the world one of our nearest and dearest is liable to die under our noses. We all send our love to you and pray that you are completely recovered.

Your letter has us all tremendously interested and we are using parts of it in the next issue of the paper. I don't care what [others] think about the place. The poorer it is the better, and the more hopeless it is the better. You go right on where you are and don't worry about working someplace else until you yourself see fit. The Communists say that the work among children is of tremendous importance. Through the children you reach the parents. You are doing one of the hardest jobs there is because it is seemingly hopeless, but God bless you for it. I am sure that your letter we publish will inspire many.

TO MARY DURNIN

Mary Durnin was a good friend whom Dorothy met in her travels through the Midwest.

CALIFORNIA, MARCH 27, 1939

The migrant situation gets worse and worse out here. I'll be visiting all the camps before I get back, the ditch camps, farm camps, and federal camps. I'm also invited to speak down in Arizona where the cotton situation is horrible. Also San Antonio. So you might as well tell everyone I shall not be back before the middle of June.

No one has a solution for these problems but the Catholic

Worker. I say that with no presumption. But the only decent suggestions are on paper, but we have the men and women willing to start at the bottom, with voluntary poverty, and really begin. And it is that that counts, not waiting for the government or someone else to do it. Our beginnings are infinitesimal but God can take the mustard seed and make it grow. It is the weak ones who confound the wise.

TO CATHERINE DE HUECK

EASTER TUESDAY, 1939

Just a tiny note to say I love you and God bless you and thank you for remembering me on your retreat. Everywhere I go I hear how mightily you have been working, tearing around the country and speaking and everywhere arousing people to new energy and love. I don't think you will ever know how much you are accomplishing. Not only in Harlem, where those children will never be the same again, but among the people you meet around the country.

Please pray for us all. We had one death last week; Mr. Breen is very feeble and needs much nursing; and I have had toothaches. So unimportant a suffering, but so irksome.

We are going to get out a great May Day issue with pictures and all—sort of a Memorial Day affair. So what about a little summary of your work?

I want to be seeing you soon. Can't we run off by ourselves, meet half way, the way my sister and I do, so we will both be free of our respective families for a few hours? You know, I often think with joy of that first visit we had together in that nice large apartment of yours in Toronto. We really had time to talk, and space to talk in. You and I need a lot of space, and when we get to heaven we'll put in our bid for mansions where we can stretch. I always think of you with love and sympathy in that one room filled with books and people, bulging with talk. Not enough room. God bless you and pray for me.

TO ADE BETHUNE

Ade Bethune (1914–2002) entered the CW movement when, as a young art student, she took the initiative of sending in some drawings of saints to illustrate the rather drab and text-heavy newspaper. Dorothy was captivated by her work and asked for more. She also asked her to design the paper's distinctive masthead: Christ standing before the Cross, his arms embracing two workers—one black and one white—their hands joined in solidarity. Her work fundamentally defined the paper's aesthetic tone for years to come.

JULY 17 [1939]

Rushed as you are it is a shame to burden you with more work. But Sheed and Ward would like your jacket for the book [*House of Hospitality*], ash can or tenement, or as you suggest, spreading over the back of the book where you see the title and author. Like *Grapes of Wrath* for instance. Also like that, with the name over the scene like illustration enclosed. [*Sketch of a book jacket.*]

Fr. [Joseph] Woods left yesterday and Fr. Palmer arrived today. God bless them both for their help. You will probably take me to task for lecturing Fr. Woods. He talked about you a great deal and I was rigorous about the duty of religious to be withdrawn and not dependent upon people for stimulus. He disagreed with me insisting it was right to take natural good as it came along and friendship was a good thing so get as much of it as you can. My argument was that if you didn't limit your desires for this good thing and practice *agere contra*, the Lord would take care of it for you and deprive you by withdrawing it and not by distance but by a loss of taste for it. My feeling was that he was talking altogether too much about it, always waiting and waiting for times for conversation and then these four-hour conversations would be all about the one subject. Perhaps I exaggerate. But you get my meaning. I was quite worn out after my trip and these long conversations which amounted to the self-probing of Father's soul exhausted me completely. I had to finally tell him quite abruptly that I did not want to talk about it any longer, so then he talked about Benedictinism. I have not been well—just fatigue from speaking every day several times for a month—and I am afraid I was not as patient as I should be.

I do feel though, that because you, Ade, are strong and good and beautiful, people are going to cling to you and lean on you and try to sap your youth and strength. It is awfully hard to protect oneself and you are so generous in every way. So forgive me for talking about this to Father Woods.

TO JOE ZARRELLA

Dorothy wrote from Florida, where she was visiting her ailing mother.

FLORIDA, THURS, DEC 7 [1939]

Just a note to say mother is better, but not out of bed yet. She refuses to come north, prefers to die down here. Can't say I blame her. She is so surrounded by friends, then Cousin Kate is a nurse and tho she does live on an island, there are telephone connections for the convenience of the Coast Guard and we can get in touch easily.

Mother and Aunt Jenny are so delighted that we are going to be here for Christmas, and Tamar will have a real family holiday.

I have been reading the Little Office every day, also the New Testament, also the *Imitation of Christ*. There is a chapter there on too much idle conversation which I took to heart. When I come back you will find me a most silent, disciplined, organized person after my thirty-day retreat and vacation. Maybe! I am wondering whether I ought not to give up my trip west after this long stay away. Oh dear, I wish there were signs from Heaven. I dream every night, sleeping ten hours a night, it's no wonder, of breadlines, the Cleveland unemployed, of strikes, of wars. During the day I sit and crochet and visit with the family (they won't let you read much), make meals, wash a few dishes, sun myself and rest. I am really enjoying myself.

10 p.m. Mother is listening to Bing Crosby and Aunt Jenny is knitting. Just now the paper came. Thanks ever so much. Again too much long stuff. I may be in a dull state of mind generally, but it seems to me there is a sameness about recent issues—lack of freshness in writing, omission of many aspects of the national scene. Perhaps a change of makeup would help. Perhaps editing out long stuff. One long article a month is enough. Perhaps I am just stale and rundown. Anyway, I know I'll feel a lot better when I come back. Tomorrow early to Mass and I remember you all then and many times a day. Love to all of you.

POSTMARKED DEC 11, 1939

Mother had another slight attack. She is very weak and has to stay in bed. I am having a really good rest, preparing meals for three, reading, sleeping, eating. Mother really needs me and I am so glad to be here and really useful too. Her condition is natural at her age the doctor said. No immediate danger but she must be careful.

As I read over the paper, I think it is pretty good. That lawyer's letter is splendid. The truce of God story is first rate. We might better have omitted the political article on bills against civil liberties, but otherwise the paper is good. The subheads are striking as to type and double line, etc.

DECEMBER 31, 1939

On a trip you never have a moment, you are at the disposal of others every minute, your devotional life is of convent-like regularity,—and the work grows. I could settle down as comfortably in the House of Hospitality and more or less follow my own will, see people when I feel like it, etc. This way I do as I'm told.

Peter [Maurin] certainly is indefatigable. He is surely sowing the seeds and there will be results one day, if not in our time then in the next generation. I feel the same about all our group, they are all feeble and faltering, but somehow they keep going. The Brothers in Pensacola are the same way, working with very little, but their very presence and their persistence means so much. And our example leads others to go out and do it better. We can't see the results and should not expect to. When it gets down to it we can just remember St. John's words, when he was dying, "My little children, love one another." At least we can all work towards doing that. And it takes some work.

Dear Joe, when I think of you even, I have such a warm feeling of thanksgiving and joy at all you do, how much of the burden you bear. God bless you and love you and strengthen you. Please don't change or get tired. I can travel with a light heart because of you.

PART III
Called to Be Saints
1940–1949

Within two years of its founding, the Catholic Worker had reached a circulation of 150,000. Seminaries and churches around the country ordered bundles, while zealous young people sold the paper on the street. There turned out to be quite a large audience eager for a paper addressing social issues from a Catholic perspective. But this popularity abruptly waned in 1936 when, in response to the Spanish Civil War, Dorothy declared her pacifist position. Her stand provoked outrage from both friends on the Left and fellow Catholics, who viewed Gen. Franco's cause as a crusade against godless atheism.

With the outbreak of World War II, Dorothy's commitment to gospel nonviolence faced an even more terrible test. Orders for the paper plummeted. Many of the houses closed, as young men enlisted in the armed forces or, in smaller numbers, went to prison or work camps for conscientious objectors.

Dorothy, meanwhile, had embarked on a serious intensification of her spiritual life, inspired by a series of retreats with Fr. John Hugo, a priest from Pittsburgh, who became a close spiritual advisor. Hugo presented the Christian life as an ongoing call to conversion, *a matter of stripping off the old person and putting on Christ. In a way, this challenge to spiritual heroism was what had initially attracted her to Catholicism; it was a message she had been seeking ever since her conversion.*

Still, the ordinary challenges of Catholic Worker life went on. Dorothy pursued an unsuccessful plan to establish a retreat house for alcoholic priests. At one point she took a leave from the Worker to focus more on prayer. Her daughter Tamar was growing up, and Dorothy struggled with the changing responsibilities of motherhood.

In these years, as the ideal of unconditional love seemed ever more folly in the eyes of the world, as the message of the Catholic Worker was widely dismissed as irrelevant, and as the clouds of fear and hatred spread across the globe, Dorothy took comfort in the supernatural folly of the Cross.

TO STANLEY VISHNEWSKI

Dorothy began the year with a trip to the West Coast.

SPOKANE, WASHINGTON, [JAN 28] 1940

The rain pours down, the distant mountains are covered with mist, one sunny day is succeeded by six rainy days. I have been wet ever since I left home, it seems to me. But just the same, spring is with us out here. You can see the buds on the trees, and you can hear spring in the sound of the birds.

Here is my program. Every day I get up at six and Mass is at six thirty. Breakfast at quarter past seven, and every day about, a different house or convent. Meetings every morning, afternoon, and evening. This morning I speak at the Good Shepherd house at nine, then catch a ten-thirty bus and go out to Pullman where Washington State College is, get there at twelve-thirty, get back here at seven-thirty to speak again. Tomorrow four meetings and I'll take the train for Seattle at ten, spend two days there and go on to Portland again for four days and then to California. The reason I am so long in the Northwest is because there is tremendous interest in the work, among the workers and students. I have spoken to longshoremen and lumberwokers and various other groups in each city. Besides, this is the first time I've ever been up here. Perhaps it will be the last, who knows?

I do not know when I will get home. Surely it is my duty to visit the other houses. After all, they are our Catholic Worker houses, and it is up to us to get around and visit them. I can scarcely consider Mott Street my home any more. And the world in the unsettled state it is, we may ourselves be engaged in war, the paper may be suppressed, and then we would all settle quietly in concentration camps or jails.

Coming from Portland to Spokane by bus the other day, it was terrifying. We were high up on mountainsides, looking down on the threat of the Columbia River. Then we'd be tearing along the riverside, and then up we'd go again, around hairpin turns that made you hold your breath. The Columbia River highway is famous as a beauty spot. Then we went through wild desert and waste lands, all rock and sage brush as far as the eye could see. Then through farming lands, where the wheat farms are four thousand acres each! Doesn't it make our farm look sick? But these people are being ruined by their greed, by their speculation. I met one woman whose husband was ruined by the collapse in the price of wheat. And they were raising everything they needed too, but could not keep up with taxes. Have you read "How Much Land Does a Man Need?" by Tolstoi? It is a short story and you ought to get hold of it.

This is a happy Lent as I am held strictly to routine, doing the same things every day, doing as I am told with no time to be slothful or to do my own will. Mass every morning, time for spiritual reading while traveling.

Hope you are remembering me daily in your prayer. Write to Gerry and ask him to forward to you *In the Footsteps of St. Francis*. It is a wonderful book and we can all learn so much by it. To be simple as little children, to live in the presence of God, to love God in his creatures, to do away with all suspicion, anger, contention and lack of brotherly love, to do the little things each day as well as we can and to start in all over again each morning, refreshing ourselves, steeling our wills,—this is all we need to keep in mind.

TO CATHERINE DE HUECK

FEBRUARY 1, 1940

As "lifter-up" I do think the Little Office of the Blessed Virgin is about the best thing possible. If you go at it briskly and with great energy you can get through it in three quarters of an hour, but it is nicer to spread it out through the day. There is a very good edition by Fathers Callan and McHugh with copious notes, and I think the translation of the hymn is very beautiful. Bits of it keep running through your mind, and verses keep popping up that seem to be an answer to many situations. I know that it is constantly lifting me out of trouble, so do get hold of this particular edition.

We will dash off together when I get back and sit down and eat herring and drink tea.

Much, much love, Dorothy

TO JOE ZARRELLA

In her extensive travels, Dorothy tried to keep in touch through letters home. Some felt her place was in New York. But she felt strongly that the Worker was a movement, and that she needed to get out and survey the various houses, to report on conditions, to spread the word, and inspire others to action.

PORTLAND, OREGON, FEBRUARY 24, 1940

Here I am covering a lot of meetings and meeting all the priests and union leaders. Right now I am waiting to go to a meeting of the Timber and Wood Workers, CIO which broke off from the

Brotherhood of Carpenters which included the lumber workers up here. They have three fourths of the men now. The situation is difficult in the northwest. Plenty of Communism in Seattle but not much here.

Tell Bill [Callahan] he will have to hold off a bit for copy [for the paper]. And to please not to come out until he gets it. I am so booked up for meetings that I have to count on doing all the writing next Friday. That will mean I will cover everything up here in Seattle and Portland and there is some very interesting stuff. Instead of including it all in "Day by Day," I'll write a number of shorts. Bill wrote saying he had expected copy before this. Where does he get that idea? He knows how dilatory I am about getting copy in. He is attributing to me virtues I do not possess. But truly, with four meetings a day, and so many people to see in between, there has not been a day free to write.

I feel well, the weather is overcast and drizzly but not cold. I get slightly convulsed with nervous indigestion what with so much speaking, but in general things are going along all right. I wept a bit over O'Connell and felt like hell for a day, but we will just leave it in the hands of God. I'm glad you wrote me about it. We only pray about our troubles if they worry us, so don't be afraid of worrying me. I can do a lot of praying, even though I'm not there to help. God bless you all. I do miss you, I miss even the weather. I miss the pleasure of groaning and lamenting with you over the weather. I thought the other day that the being deprived of poverty, as one is on these trips, is a hardship. I feel like a fish out of water, going from convent to convent, being fed sumptuously, sitting in state with six nuns standing by to converse, which results in the nervous indigestion too.

Thank you for all you are doing, the weight you are carrying.

3/5/40

I am glad Peter [Maurin] is on his trip. He does enjoy getting around in speaking. Where is he now? Have you any forwarding address? And I wonder where the rumors get around that he is in opposition to me and my way of working and that is why these trips. Jim O'Connor wrote that he would not have returned to the work had it not been for my letter in the paper to him. As for his project—building up troubadours of God—I'm all for it. I wish we had more apostles on the bum, and if we don't raise 'em up, the persecution will. Peter's ideas are bound to bear fruit. He is a great teacher and one can see the results of his talks everywhere. Some of course do not understand, but that doesn't matter. I hate to see any indication of your being impatient with him. Gerry wrote to me from the farm about that book, *In the Footsteps of St. Francis*, and recalled the danger of our becoming Brother Eliases instead of St. Francises, in our order, efficiency, trying to get things done, etc. There is always that danger. We must contain ourselves in patience, remembering each morning that our main job is to love God and to serve Him and if we don't get things done due to interruptions, well, it cannot be helped, and God will take care of what we leave undone. But a tranquil spirit is important. St. Teresa says that God cannot rest in an unquiet heart. I have to remember that many times during the day.

What if everything goes to rack and ruin? We can only do what we can to make order, but in the long run it's ourselves we have to look after. So daily Mass, and *meditation*, and spiritual reading. What about an extra fifteen minutes after Mass? It will help and the house will not fall apart. You may be distracted, you may be in a frenzy about the work to do, you may want to get to the post office, but the very effort of will holding you there is a prayer. Of course getting to bed early is essential. At least at twelve, and many times we can make it earlier. If you get to an eight o'clock [Mass] you can still have your fifteen minutes. But you can't have it at Mary [Johnson's]. I know we give scandal and arouse irritation by being up there so much. We just have to be careful. It is just criticism when it takes us away from our work in the morning. As for the evenings, that is another matter. I do feel that we have often been criticized and justly too, however.

Here I write a letter of chiding, when my heart is filled with love and sympathy for you in your tremendous job of keeping things going. But you understand.

THURSDAY MARCH 14, 1940

Finally I can get down to writing a letter. Yesterday I spoke five times and it left me with a stiff neck and back. Why it would do that I don't know. But I feel as though I had been chopping wood or doing a heavy day's work. Aside from the stiffness I feel fine. No headaches, thank God, and that is always what I dread. The work is going along fine. I am certainly glad I came out, and I think the best thing for the work. Peter is so right about the need of some to go about the country.

I am convinced that I should visit each of the houses for two days on the way back. I still have San Francisco, Pasadena, Sacramento, Oakland, Berkeley, Los Angeles, here in the West. I'll try to be through here by the first, but am not sure I can make it. I leave here tomorrow morning for San Francisco. I'm in despair at the lack of time. When one comes so far, it is best to stick it out and not rush. It costs so much to get out here that one must take advantage of it. And I always hate so to start out on a trip, that I might better make it thorough while I am on the road.

As for the houses,—this is our work. I started so many of them. I owe it to them to spend some time with them. There is no reason why I should be in New York all the time. Which means I should go to St. Louis, Chicago, Milwaukee, Minneapolis, Detroit, Toledo, Cleveland, Akron, Pittsburgh, Buffalo, Rochester, etc., on the way home.

All of this is so that you can assure me that I can go ahead and take the time that I need. I am sure that things are going all right in New York. I am sure that they do not go any better when I am there. No one place should depend on me. If they do, it is not right. So please in your next letter, let me know if you feel equal to the burden of carrying on there.

I feel assured that though we know nothing of the results of such constant speaking engagements, that even though the CW may never see them, countless people are aroused in new ideas, a sense of responsibility, to new works, to renewed effort, because of hearing about the CW and the basic ideas of our work. At so many of the meetings there are groups of people who have heard me speak time and again. When they hear that I am to be in town for other engagements, they come to all the meetings, over and over again. I have covered non-Catholic groups, Protestant colleges, labor groups, as well as so many Catholic groups.

We have to do the work most needed, that's all. Try to adjust ourselves to it, take it as happily as possible, etc. I'm afraid I'm not very good at bearing my fatigue. When I get up in the morning I go around groaning and grumbling and aching all over. And I've been told I look snappish at people when they throng around me telling me how wonderful the book is, the work is. I've got to learn to smile sweetly and love my neighbor. The thing that bothers me is that so often a pile of women flock around me and keep others who have something to say away. Like yesterday at Reed College, non-sectarian, first rate, where I wanted to get in touch with the students after the meeting. I had to ask the women, half a dozen of them, to go outside and wait in their car, so as to give me a chance to speak to the fellows who have questions to ask about the work. Those are some of the little things that irritate you. Club women and social workers, etc.

SAN FRANCISCO, MARCH 1940

Oh dear, so many problems. Oh yes, Kate told me it was said around there I was not coming back. Do tell her June fifteenth, or some such date, just to quiet her. I would pay no attention to this, but I find the rumor really went around that Peter had left the work for good, but only came back because I pleaded with him in the columns of the paper to come. Jim O'C says that in his letter too. It is what people would like to think. Also Minna Berger told me that the rumor went around after I was here last time that I was out drinking and seen to take nine whiskeys. Lord, Lord! I've never touched a drop outside of the Johnson household for years and years and years.

Monday I go out to see three seamen in San Quentin, in the afternoon to visit Harry Bridges [*leader of the longshoremen's union*]. With the work going along so splendidly here, and widespread interest, it would be criminal for me to hasten. The transient situation, the labor situation, the hordes of friends we have here now that we did not have last time—all make it necessary. I am so happy things are so progressing. We must work while we can for the night cometh when no man can work. The sun is shining on us now, at least out here, so continue praying for me. I am keeping well and so full of joy the way things are going.

4 APRIL 1940

The enthusiasm is great and most encouraging. I realize how necessary it is to travel around, but it is so hard being away from home. Even your letter sounded cold and distant and I feel as though people resented my being away and traveling. (Not you—but all who doubt, etc.). Gerry didn't write and from the bitter note on which he ended I can see it is because we omitted the April issue and because I am away, and because I let Bill write the editorial. It hurts so to see these feelings persisting. And they all land on me. Forgive me for complaining, but I get blue being so far away. I ought not to complain out here where it is so beautiful, with a huge bouquet of flowers on my table that I picked myself today, calla lilies and lilacs and roses. The room is sweet with them.

I worry about you all, working so hard, struggling so, suffering with the cold and fatigue and many visitors. And yet, think of all the young people who have no work to do, no mission in life, or if they have jobs, ugly routine office jobs with no future, no purpose, no freedom. It is one's free will that brings one to the work. We should certainly all of us consider ourselves privileged.

Sometimes when you get very tired, why don't you go home and sleep the clock around. That is what I'd like to do right now.

Much love and how I wish I were there to talk to you instead of write.

In Christ the migrant, Dorothy

LOS ANGELES, APRIL 22, 1940

It is important that we try to stick together and be loyal to each other and try to see each other's good points. God knows, living together we can see each other's bad points and weaknesses quick enough. We can be under no delusions. But we can never have enough mutual love.

I know I can trust you to see that visitors are properly taken care of, that people are treated with consideration. I know you sometimes get impatient, but I know too you are sorry for it. I know as long as you are getting to daily communion, God will take care of any mistake you make. I feel more at ease on this trip, than ever before about the house.

I'll write the appeal tomorrow and mail it on to you, and I'll be seeing Miss Gage this week or next and appeal to her too. Somehow we'll make out, we always have. It is a fearful struggle but we will manage somehow. Thank God there will be enough money to pay the installment on the farm. Do start a picket line to St. Joseph again immediately. It is hard to write the appeal, away from you all as I am, deprived of poverty, you might say. I feel so much happier when I am at home—it is so much harder to see poverty when one is not living with it. It is a constant ache in the heart.

My articles for the May issue are not so hot. I have great difficulty in writing. Please pray for me, for speaking and writing. People are so hard and indifferent, one feels imprisoned.

I miss Tamar terribly, it's like a toothache. But we had December together anyway. Much much love to all of you at Mott Street. And God bless you Joe, for all you do.

TO AN ENGLISH CATHOLIC WORKER
While war raged in Europe, Dorothy maintained her pacifist stand.

TUCSON, ARIZONA, MAY 3, 1940

Dear Bob [Walsh]:

Please don't expect me to answer all your questions. Besides, you wrote on January 25, and you have probably forgotten the very questions you asked.

Every night in all the houses we offer up prayers for peace, and I know that all of us in New York think most especially of you and the work that you are trying to do there.

We still hold, in spite of Norway and Denmark, that nonviolent resistance is the only sane solution, and that we have to continue to make our voice heard until we are finally silenced— and even then, in jail or concentration camp, still to express ourselves. These ideas have been expressed far better than we can by Father [Franziskus] Stratmann. If there are not some who still hold this ideal, still speak in terms of the counsels of perfection, the ideal will be lost.

I do not see why we must accept the inevitability of war. It was only in the last century that slavery was done away with here in this country, and I suppose that everybody thought it was inevitable, something to be accepted, before that time. If we are working towards peace, we must look with hope that in a future generation we will do away with war. You know with how great suffering and how great prayer we are trying to hold up these ideas.

I do not believe in being isolationist. I believe that we must hold ourselves in readiness to help with all our resources exhausted nations. I think we should pray for a peace without victory, as the Holy Father advised in the last war when they suppressed his encyclical.

The other day in Los Angeles I met an English actor by the name of Noble who said, as Churchill did, that it was madness for us to have entered the last war. His point of view was probably different. What he said was that there would have been a peace without victory had the United States not entered, and there would not have been the resultant bitterness and spirit of retaliation afterwards.

I am glad that there is still so much freedom of expression in England and that you are able to continue working.

Do write when you can. And give my love to all.

TO BILL GAUCHAT
Bill Gauchat was a founder of the Cleveland Catholic Worker. In light of the world crisis, Dorothy felt it was crucial that leaders of the movement attend CW retreats and focus on the "primacy of the spiritual."

JULY 13, 1940

The retreat is at Easton, August 30, Friday night. We'd like everyone to be there Friday night, and the retreat will be Saturday and Sunday and Monday discussion. Father [Paul Hanly] Furfey will give it—you know him of course. You must make it, of course. We all feel that the retreat last fall blessed the work all during this year. It marked changes for everyone and I could see them at the various houses.

What did you do with the appeal we sent in regard to the war? Some of the groups sent them back signed. We were in Washington the past two days testifying at the Senate Military Affairs Hearing [*about the military draft*], and they listened with great respect to our point of view and there was good opportunity to put over some personalist propaganda. Monsignor Barry O'Toole also testified, and Monsignor [Michael] Ready for the National Catholic Welfare Conference asking exemption for seminarians if the draft goes through, but failing to see the necessity for it.

God bless you. I'm longing for us all to get together again. God willing I'll start out again this fall and visit all the houses in the Middle West. There have been many problems of late.

TO PETER MAURIN

It was Peter Maurin who inspired Dorothy to found the Catholic Worker in 1933. She revered him as the true founder of the movement, her mentor and teacher. But having supplied "the ideas" behind the movement, Peter was content to remain in the background, traveling, working on the farm, speaking where invited, propagating his ideas through recital of his "Easy Essays." Dorothy wrote with great affection about his holiness and his loveable eccentricities. Among other things, he was evidently hopeless about schedules, finances, or anything of a practical nature. It is little wonder that no other letters from Dorothy to Peter have survived.

JULY 18, 1940

Dear Peter,

Arthur Sheehan says that Sarah Wingate Taylor wants you to speak at the Islanders Colony, Clark's Island, August eighth and ninth. Will you drop Arthur a line at Upton if you want to go up? Tell somebody to send a postal for you, or get a penny postal yourself and let him know. You are terrible about correspondence, hence these minute directions.

Everybody says the school has been going along fine, except that you have worked them to death. Father Woods will be able to stay down the entire summer; his prior has given him permission. He will be back on Friday. Will has left and has gone home to live with his family. The children have been down at the camp at Staten Island for almost two weeks, and aside from three of them having poison ivy, everything seems to be alright. Tell Tamar and Janette that they, of course, can stay where they choose. If they don't want to go to Staten Island, it's perfectly all right.

Much love to them all, and to yourself.

P.S. Give the ten dollars to Arthur for the necessary staples, and give Tamar twenty-five cents for her mice.

TO ALL THE CATHOLIC WORKER HOUSES

In light of the war in Europe, Dorothy sent a letter to all the CW houses reiterating the pacifist position of the Catholic Worker *and insisting that those communities that suppressed the paper should disaffiliate themselves from the movement. It was the only time Dorothy ever issued such a diktat. The response was mixed.*

AUGUST 10, 1940

Dear Fellow Worker,

Since we are the only Catholic group in the country opposed to war as a means of "saving Christianity and democracy," since we have gone on record again and again in the columns of the *Catholic Worker* opposing modern war, we would be glad to have our readers register with us their position as conscientious objectors to conscription and to war.

We know that there are those who are members of Catholic Worker groups throughout the country who do not stand with us on this issue. We have not been able to change their views through what we have written in the paper, in letters, or personal conversation. They wish still to be associated with us, to perform the corporal works of mercy. In such cases they will still distribute the paper (and, since they are called Catholic Worker groups, it is their duty to do so). In other cases, they take it upon themselves to suppress the paper and hinder its circulation. In these cases, we feel it to be necessary that they disassociate themselves from the Catholic Worker movement and not use the name of a movement with which they now are in such fundamental disagreement.

Our workers have taken it upon themselves to try to follow the counsels of perfection. They accept the assistance of others and their cooperation in so far as they can give it. Many can only go part of the way, what with family obligations, health considerations, even a different point of view. If they wish to work with us, we are glad and thankful to have them, but they cannot be said to be representing the Catholic Worker position. Sometimes there are only one or two at a House of Hospitality who follow the position of the paper. Perhaps in some cases there are none, but a group are associated together to feed the hungry, clothe the naked, shelter the harborless in a House of Hospitality.

Perhaps it would be better in these cases for the Houses to disassociate themselves from the Catholic Worker movement. They can continue as settlements for the works of mercy, but not as Catholic Worker units.

There are several reasons for this move. If you wish to continue the work without hindrance from the Government after the conscription law shall have been passed you will have to do this. Even after you have disassociated yourself you are liable to have this trouble so that if you disagree with us, you had better make your position clear now.

This means of course that you will not accept papers which you do not intend to use. We are in need of all our papers—we must pay to have them printed, so it would only be fair for you to notify us not to send the papers, or for you to send them back if they already have been sent.

We have been consistent in our position, so there is no reason to suppose that we are going to change our stand in subsequent issues of the paper. There is no reason why we should not be associated together as friends and fellow workers, but there is every reason for not continuing to use the Catholic Worker name.

This letter is being sent to all the groups, and we wish you would take it up with your group and talk it over. Perhaps in some cases the leadership in the Houses do not follow our position but there are members of the group who do. If these latter will send in their names so that we can get in touch with them, so that we can send them literature, so that they can be registered with us in time of trouble, we will appreciate this forethought.

We are sending under separate cover a Pacifist Handbook which contains a good deal of necessary information for conscientious objectors. Those who desire other copies, please let us know. We intend to get out a short pamphlet ourselves, stating our position.

Please get in touch with us immediately, before the next issue of the paper goes to press.

Sincerely in Christ,

Dorothy Day

TO JOHN COGLEY

John Cogley was one of the leaders of the Chicago Catholic Worker and a prominent dissenter on the question of pacifism. Ultimately he left the movement to serve in the army. Later he would become an editor of Commonweal *and a distinguished liberal Catholic journalist.*

[UNDATED 1940]

Regardless of differences of opinion on war and conscription we all bet you will not fail to come to retreat [at Easton].

Meant to write but ten thousand visitors prevented. Everyone will be much hurt. You are bone of our bone, and flesh of our flesh, not bone of contention.

Love,

Dorothy

TO JOE ZARRELLA

Meanwhile, divisions and tensions were surfacing at the Easton farm.

OCTOBER 12, 1940

Do excuse if I was cranky when you were in town. I must try to be more patient. Got another letter from the relief people down there about the Buleys and their complaints of not being one of the gang, and needing a stove, etc. It's no use talking, we do not do our share unless we can make them feel more a part of things. That is the one thing we can do for them. Instead of having plans and blueprints we have the actual people, the kind nobody wants, that the government will not help, the kind that are always being passed on. We've got to try to make the start of a Christian community and loving people because they are other Christs, and pray to be able to love them, and see Christ in them. Five years, and have we even a start of a Christian community? They are all good, but pagan rather than Christian. So it is up to Larry [Heaney] and you, it puts you on the spot. Of course I am not forgetting Ruth Anne [Heaney] and the help she is giving the kids. Janet was in making some sour remarks and I was upholding the farm and our ideas at a great rate this afternoon. I've asked Dwight [Larrowe] to come in and I'm going to start him off making plans for a workable farming commune, presupposing we had the money, and then we can start praying for the money.

Sometimes I think things should be more desperately hard, or more easy. If people were down to rock bottom, would they help each other more, or would it be, "Let the devil take the hindmost"? Things are hard down there, and more monotonous than they are in town, I know. So I do think we should plan as much as we can, despite the lack of faith and the suspicion of the others. After all we can look around and see two farms, stock, buildings, all a great deal for us little ones to have gotten so far. And the Lord will not cease to take care of us.

TO STANLEY VISHNEWSKI

NOVEMBER 21, 1940

Got your letter this morning and hasten to write encouragement. I must get you Caussade's *Abandonment to Divine Providence* to read which will convince you that God has need of you being right where you are. Dryness and lack of recollection can be good signs too, you know. God usually gives comfort to weak souls who need encouragement and when they have progressed somewhat and He thinks they are strong enough to bear it, He permits this dryness. If you are faithful to your morning and evening prayers, and make your morning offering, and carry your rosary in your pocket so that you will remember to say even a part of it every day, you will be getting along fine. If you have to force yourself to pray, those prayers are of far more account with God than any prayers which bring comfort with them. That act of will is *very* important.

I cannot tell you how much we depend on you, Stanley, so be cheered. You are very important to us. The very times when you think that no progress is being made are usually the best.

TO THE BUFFALO CATHOLIC WORKER

[UNDATED 1940]

Marjorie gave me your letter to read and I am so glad that you are all hanging on. Until people do have all these problems and suffering the work is really not getting underway. In so many cases everybody has a grand time getting everything started, everything goes so smoothly, the men are all so nice, everybody cooperates, and then life settles down to a dead, ugly monotony of meals and lodging and nothing at all seems to be done or done right and we seem rather to be contributing to people's delinquencies rather than helping them; and that of course is the charge that is made always against us.

You can look at all the men at all the houses and see them as pretty rotten. That, of course, is the way we should see things; to see men as but dust; from the human point of view that is perfectly true, and we should have to have a dictator with an iron hand getting them regimented and whipped into line and making them do what they should do.

But from the standpoint of the supernatural they are a little less than the angels and if we could only keep that attitude towards them! When we are in love with people we see all the best that there is in them and understand very clearly their failures and their lapses. But the love continues strong and works wonders.

I often think that our Lord must have been terribly bored with the disciples very often, humanly speaking. Certainly he wasn't picking out brilliant, accomplished, pleasing personalities with whom to live. Isn't it in today's epistle where the mother of James and John wanted the best place for her two sons? So even the relatives were hanging on to see what they could get out of the situation. He certainly had to get away from them every now and then and do a lot of praying.

If we could only keep this early fervor and enthusiasm about people.

A friend of mine, Mrs. Livingston, was telling me about a story she read in *The Saturday Evening Post* of all places a year or so ago in which a young girl is wildly in love with a wastrel until later on when this had been broken up and she had been married for a year to a man of good solid character, she ran into her former love again.

She confessed to her husband that she had been afraid of meeting him for fear some of the old glamour remained, and she said to him: "Now I can see him as he is." And her husband, who must have been a man of great discernment, said to her very sadly: "Perhaps it was before that you were seeing him as he really is." Or as he was meant to be, which is what he wanted to bring out.

This story brings out the idea of the kind of love we ought to have for people, a love which sees their value, and sees them as God intended them to be, rather than seeing them as they are outwardly.

They say that a mystic is someone who is in love with God, again using that comparison as the kind of love we should feel. This is one of the most absorbing problems of all the work, this relationship we have to all those around us, the tie that holds us all around the country together.

I have said over and over again that Catholics have more faith in God than they have in man and that is the trouble with religion. It is a transferring of our hopes from earth to heaven and from man to God to such an extent that we turn to pie in the sky and forget that we are all members of the Mystical Body of Christ right here on this earth.

It is one of the good things about the Communist heresy that they have seen this aspect of the truth, this necessity for recognizing human dignity and the nobility and grandeur of man, man who is a little less than the angels, who has been placed "over the work of His hands with all things set under his feet." That psalm certainly paints a magnificent picture of what man is "that God should be mindful of him." And we have got to think of every man on the breadline and every man living in the house in that way.

It is a terrible struggle and it will go on all through our lives and perhaps we won't see any fruit of this vision, any material- ization of this vision, let us say, immediately around us. Every- body is going to condemn us for wasting our time on drunks and bums and people who don't respond in any way to these ideas.

Don't blame the situation you have in Buffalo on the lack of leadership in the house. Down in Baltimore they have three fools for Christ who are living right in the House. They are expressing these ideas, having rosary in the evening, spiritual reading at meals, carrying hospitality to folly, in general carrying the teaching of Christ to an extreme so that they are a scandal to the neighborhood and to the city.

You can't blame the police for raiding them and you can't blame the good respectable Catholics for being scandalized. Certainly we can't say that the Baltimore house is what a house should be but they are expressing an idea and calling attention to a need, and eventually they will start houses of hospitality in all the poor sections and the parishes will wake up to their responsibilities.

When you are feeling especially bad you ought to take time off to visit a few of the other houses. I just got a letter this morning from a sister who said she found the Philadelphia house best of them all.

Physically, it is, and I always enjoy visiting there and certainly the fellows at the head of it are a wonderful crowd but they go just so far and no farther. They limit the number of people in the house, they never have more than fifteen or so and their breadlines also are short. The house has been repainted and cleaned and painted constantly and to such an extent that they even admit they do not want anybody in the house who can't contribute to the building up of it. And later on when it is all finished they will go ahead and take in more. But by that time it will be so beautiful they will be afraid to take in more and will find some excuse like the building department or the fire department or health department to limit their hospitality again.

I really am not condemning them because everyone's temperament is different and God is working through all these people, and they are doing exactly what He wants them to do. I think He probably wants this house to be a beautiful example so as to encourage others to work along these lines. He uses people's temperaments whether they are cautious or reckless.

And we should be only too delighted that there is such an infinite variety in His creatures, human beings as well as plain animals. Down at the farm the other day we were meditating on the delightful differences between the earth worm and the goats. And the infinite variety of joyous and beautiful things there were around us. Well, we ought to rejoice in people's different temperaments too and not want them to be all alike. God forbid!

TO CATHERINE DE HUECK

In many of her talks, Catherine de Hueck liked to recount the story of a night spent at the Catholic Worker when Dorothy supposedly shared her bed with a syphilitic homeless woman. According to Catherine's account, Dorothy said, "Catherine, you are of little faith. This is Christ come to us for a place to sleep. He will take care of me." Reports of this story never failed to irritate Dorothy. "I can't even sleep with my daughter," she retorted, "she wiggles too much!"

FRIDAY AFTER ASH WEDNESDAY [1941?]

No, I cannot say that I remember the incident. I only know this, that though I have slept on the floor I have never shared my bed. I know that most assuredly, so when you tell the tale that I took a syphilitic into bed with me, you make me out one of those creatures fanatical and quite lacking in common sense and there have been actually reactions against us and the work because of this story. The Church is noted for common sense! She first segregated the lepers. You will have the board of health down on us all if you continue to repeat this story, so please, please! Your generous, Russian exuberance in defending us often delights me, but I must confess this story got under my skin. I shall continue to deny it as I hear it. But I do love you, my dear, and always shall. Only you're too damn humble. You worry too much about your own humanness which makes you so charming and so *effective*. I have never suffered from the complete lack of privacy to which you have submitted yourself this last year. It is good to urge each other on to virtue, but remember, we are comrades stumbling along, not saints, drifting along in ecstasies.

I'm dying to see your new paper. We are so broke, I wonder if we are not on the verge of complete annihilation. Then we will go down to the farm and cultivate our gardens. Pray for us, darling.

In Christ, Dorothy

TO GERRY GRIFFIN

Dorothy described Gerry Griffin, who came to work at the Catholic Worker in the late 1930s, as "an irascible, hard-working young man who endeared himself to me by loving Dostoevsky." He was in charge of the house of hospitality until 1943, when he went overseas to serve with the American Field Service. In this letter she refers to plans for an upcoming retreat with Father John Hugo, an event that would mark a significant milestone in her spiritual journey.

DAVENPORT, IOWA, JUNE 18, 1941

Here I am in your beloved state, the best state in the union, where there is no poverty, where, if people work hard they get on in the world, where there is no need for Catholic Workers and why don't we stay home where we came from. Anyway, that is the way some of the dear old priests here feel about me, and I'm homesick, and wonder why no mail.

The reason I may be late in getting home is a few more speaking engagements which I ought to take on account of the money, if they intend to pay me. Which means I'll be stopping at Clinton, Iowa, Sinsinawa, Wis., Milwaukee, Chicago, Detroit, etc.

And especially I may not get home, because I intend to make Fr. Lacouture's eight-day retreat (complete silence, but not bread and water), which Father Hugo is giving July 3-11 at St. Anthony's orphanage, outside Pittsburgh at Oakmont, Pa. He is the

Father Hugo who wrote on the controversy with Father [Paul Hanly] Furfey on our land page and who, I discover, is another follower of the *doctrine*. I spent the day with him at Pittsburgh, and am so happy that now any of us who wish can make the eight-day retreat. Hereafter anyone who wishes to join us will have to go and make it as a sort of novitiate. Not that they cannot turn heels just the same, but it will be a good start, and if they get it, it's something to go on. Of course there are those amongst us who consider we've got it all already (that what Arthur [Sheehan] said), but I think that that is a most dangerous attitude of mind. Some of Brother Matthew's friends said piously that just being around a CW house was like making a retreat. I told them they were all luxuriating in poverty and piety and being very precious, and that I was afraid eventually many of us would be damned into hell for our complacence. . . .

If Fr. Roy's superiors don't want him to give the retreat, Father Hugo will give it and I'm sure everyone will like him. He is about Fr. Rice's age, and nothing namby-pamby about him. He rigged up a telephone system in an invalid girl's room in Pittsburgh and gave her a conference of an hour every night for a month. So far about fourteen are going to be in on this one, and I'm wishing you or Joe, or both of you could meet me there. It would be a real rest for your souls. This should be a real renewal, a new beginning, a renewal of the inner man, and God knows we all need it. Father Rice says he doesn't want to take it because he hears everyone comes out a changed man, and he does not want to change. I think he'll take it eventually. Fr. Hugo is a classmate of his.

In other words, I am completely sold on this retreat business. I think it will cure all ills, settle all problems, bind up all wounds, strengthen us, enlighten us, and in other words make us happy.

I send my love to you, all of you. . . . I know how you appreciate this general love, so I send it especially to you, a special brand of Iowa love. I love each of you for particular things, so don't read this dourly and say "love, love love." Blessed Sebastian Valpre says, "He who really loves God never uses the word enough."

TO A PRIEST CRITIC, *on the use of force and spiritual means*

EVE OF THE FEAST OF ST. JAMES [JULY 24, 1941?]

When I got back to New York and found you had been to see us and I had missed you, I felt badly indeed. There is not a day goes by that we do not think of the English group and pray for them. We cannot in any way feel divided, in spite of differences of opinion as to war. We feel however that we must go on expressing ourselves in the paper as we have done from the very beginning as to the use of armed forces under modern conditions. We have had trouble all through the Spanish war, and our position has been brought up again and again in the labor movement, in our opposition to the acceptance of class war techniques and terminology. It is very hard to discuss these things right now without arousing antagonism, but as long as our country is not yet at war, we feel we must do everything possible to spread these ideas. Probably if we were at war we would be suppressed.

It is undoubtedly true that we fail again and again in expressing ourselves correctly, but we do trust that the Bishops will not allow us to fall into any error without calling it to our attention. Cardinal Hayes said once that we would without doubt make mistakes but that the thing was not to persist in them.

As for the united strength of the Catholic Worker body, there are of course differences of opinion among us here in the United States and although that has caused grief, I do not think that it has "jeopardized the strength of the CW movement" as you put it. Mr. [Frank] Sheed seems to think that I am imposing personal opinions on all our houses and farms and cells and individuals associated with us, but I do assure you that articulate, or inarticulate, no matter how clumsy we are in expressing ourselves, there is a great sense of unity among us.

We look upon the striving toward perfection as a precept, a basic precept, an essential law of Christianity and for ourselves we must refuse to bear arms against our enemies. If we could only write enough about the love of God and the love of our neighbor for the love of God, we would not need to mention conscription or conscientious objection in the columns of *The Catholic Worker*. Certainly I do believe as we progress ourselves in the love of God and the use of the spiritual means to reach our brothers, we will not need to speak against the use of force. More and more people will be drawn to the love of God and neighbor and will find it impossible to throw a hand grenade or operate a machine gun.

As it is however, we are stumbling along falteringly. Please pray for us and excuse our clumsiness and stupidities.

Of course from the natural standpoint, our obligations to others, our fellow workers, our hungry wives and children, if we are workers, might lead us to argue that we are justified in not turning the other cheek; that all other means have been used, that a "certain amount of goods is necessary for a man to lead a good life," and so we justify our resort to the use of force in strikes, in civil war. The same of course, from the natural standpoint, in regard to international wars. When we are speaking of the state, I understand of course, that one cannot argue from the supernatural standpoint. The state is for the temporal welfare of its people and there is no such thing as a Christian state to use the Christian means of love, of prayer and penance.

It is natural for the state to have armies, navies, air forces. But God works with a Gideon, a David, a Moses with his arms held out in prayer.

Thank God our spiritual leaders are calling to the mind of the people the use of spiritual means. In Montreal they are calling for a black fast on Fridays. The Ladies of the Grail and the thousands of groups organized by them, pray with arms outstretched. Prayer and sacrifice, prayer and penance, prayer and fasting, these are the means emphasized by our Holy Father, by our bishops.

If lay people would only listen. If we only had a proper estimate of that virtue of obedience and listened to and obeyed the Holy Father, there would be no need for armies. Twenty million people (there are twenty million Catholics in the U.S.) praying, fasting! Why, for *ten* just men, God saved a city! To deny the efficacy of prayer against Hitler is to deny the power of grace.

This emphasis on the supernatural of course puts a tremendous burden on the conscientious objector. Having abjured the use of natural means against an enemy, he is under obligation to use the means he professes to believe in. And God help us, lest in saving others, we ourselves are lost. If St. Paul worried thus, what a great obligation we are under, in undertaking this work.

Please pray for us, Father, and be assured that there are many among us who do indeed join with you most intensely in prayer. May God keep you safe from harm.

TO JOHN CORT

John Cort, a fresh graduate from Harvard College and a recent convert to Catholicism, joined the Catholic Worker in 1936. His interests ultimately gravitated to the labor struggle and he left the movement to help found the Association of Catholic Trade Unionists. At the time of this letter he was recuperating from a bout of tuberculosis.

AUGUST 4, 1941

We are all very much grieved to hear that you have to give up your work for the time being and mobilize yourself again.

I am invited to meet your friend Harry Bridges this afternoon at a cocktail party. It is not to be a press conference like the last, to which I did not go though invited. I am going up there, though I don't want to, as it is a chance to bring once again some of these ideas to people who, of course, are not particularly interested in this point of view that we stress. It is an extremely difficult thing to do always and results are in God's hands. Of course we are misunderstood, and by good people like you, but I am sure the bishops are glad that we take this embarrassing job upon ourselves. Somebody has to carry on the tradition of being a fool for Christ's sake and the A.C.T.U. is entirely too reasonable. Natural reason, not right reason.

This is not to start a controversy, but just to tell you I still love you and get better quickly.

TO TAMAR

Dorothy's daughter had grown up in the Catholic Worker—sometimes at boarding schools, often in the care of others. "She was, of course, everything to me," Dorothy wrote in The Long Loneliness. *But they were often apart. Encouraging Tamar's interest in crafts, Dorothy sent her to a special high school in Montreal that offered training in spinning and weaving. Tamar, for her part, loved the Catholic Worker. But there were difficulties in being the daughter of such a revered and public figure—particularly one who was so often away from home. Taking after her father, Tamar was fascinated by biology and natural history, much more likely to enjoy a book about insects than* The Devout Life *by St. Francis de Sales.*

[NOVEMBER 5, 1941]
YWCA WEDNESDAY NIGHT 8:30
Dearest Tamar,

I'm writing this from the YWCA where I'm staying overnight. When you rent a room at the YW you never know whether you will get a single room or one with two roommates like I have tonight. One is an older woman and the other a young girl who is working at her first job. I told her I had just left you and she told me her mother had just left her two days ago. They live two hundred miles away and this is her first job and her first time away from home. So you are better off than she is, as she is working at a pokey old stenographer's job in the city, whereas you are preparing for a delightful work in the country.

You must write or I will be anxious about you. Let me know if you are homesick, if you need anything, and write every Sunday. Everyone will be writing you so you be sure and write me. Be a good girl—if you feel blue, say the Stations. It is the best cure. They say that making the Stations gives you courage and fortitude. And say the rosary every night. Shall I send your missal? *The Devout Life* by Francis de Sales? Any other book? Let me know if you sleep well, etc.

Much much love, darling.

Your mother

TO ALL THE CATHOLIC WORKER HOUSES

The Japanese attack on Pearl Harbor on December 7, 1941, brought America into the Second World War. Dorothy sent this letter to all the Catholic Worker communities and published it in the January 1942 issue of the Catholic Worker.

[DECEMBER 1941]

Dear Fellow Workers in Christ,

Lord God, merciful God, our Father, shall we keep silent, or shall we speak? And if we speak, what shall we say?

I am sitting here in the church on Mott Street writing this in your presence. Out on the streets it is quiet, but you are there too, in the Chinese, in the Italians, these neighbors we love. We love them because they are our brothers, as Christ is our Brother and God our Father.

But we have forgotten so much. We have all forgotten. And how can we know unless you tell us. "For whoever calls upon the name of the Lord shall be saved." How then are they to call upon Him in whom they have not believed? But how are they to believe Him whom they have not heard? And how are they to hear, if no one preaches? And how are men to preach unless they be sent? As it is written, "How beautiful are the feet of those who preach the gospel of peace." (Romans X)

Seventy-five thousand *Catholic Workers* go out every month. What shall we print? We can print still what the Holy Father is saying, when he speaks of total war, of mitigating the horrors of war, when he speaks of cities of refuge, of feeding Europe. . . .

We will print the words of Christ who is with us always, even to the end of the world. "Love your enemies, do good to those who hate you, and pray for those who persecute and calumniate you, so that you may be children of your Father in heaven, who makes His sun to rise on the good and the evil, and sends rain on the just and unjust."

We are at war, a declared war, with Japan, Germany and Italy. But still we can repeat Christ's words, each day, holding them close in our hearts, each month printing them in the paper. In times past, Europe has been a battlefield. But let us remember St. Francis, who spoke of peace and we will remind our readers of him, too, so they will not forget.

In the *Catholic Worker* we will quote our Pope, our saints, our priests. We will go on printing the articles which remind us today that we are all "called to be saints," that we are other Christs, reminding us of the priesthood of the laity.

We are still pacifists. Our manifesto is the Sermon on the Mount, which means that we will try to be peacemakers. Speaking for many of our conscientious objectors, we will not participate in armed warfare or in making munitions, or by buying government bonds to prosecute the war, or in urging others to these efforts.

But neither will we be carping in our criticism. We love our country and we love our President. We have been the only country in the world where men of all nations have taken refuge from oppression. We recognize that while in the order of intention we have tried to stand for peace, for love of our brother, in the order of execution we have failed as Americans in living up to our principles.

We will try daily, hourly, to pray for an end to the war, such an end, to quote Father Orchard, "as would manifest to all the world, that it was brought about by divine action, rather than by military might or diplomatic negotiation, which men and nations would then only attribute to their power or sagacity." . . .

Let us add, that unless we combine this prayer with almsgiving, in giving to the least of God's children, and fasting in order that we may help feed the hungry, and penance in recognition of our share in the guilt, our prayer may become empty words.

Our works of mercy may take us into the midst of war. As editor of the *Catholic Worker*, I would urge our friends and associates to care for the sick and the wounded, to the growing of food for the hungry, to the continuance of all our works of mercy in our houses and on our farms. We understand, of course, that there is and that there will be great differences of opinion even among our own groups as to how much collaboration we can have with the government in times like these. There are differences more profound and there will be many continuing to work with us from necessity, or from choice, who do not agree with us as to our position on war, conscientious objection, etc. But we beg that there will be mutual charity and forbearance among us all.

This letter, sent to all our Houses of Hospitality and to all our farms, and being printed in the January issue of the paper, is to state our position in this most difficult time.

Because of our refusal to assist in the prosecution of war and our insistence that our collaboration be one for peace, we may find ourselves in difficulties. But we trust in the generosity and understanding of our government and our friends, to permit us to continue, to use our paper to "preach Christ crucified."

May the Blessed Mary, Mother of love, of faith, of knowledge and of hope, pray for us.

TO DWIGHT LARROWE

Dwight Larrowe, a member of the New York Worker community, was initially a leader among the conscientious objectors. But later, much to Dorothy's disappointment, he changed his mind and joined the army. After the war he became a Trappist.

FEB 12, 1942

I think we should spend much more time in trying to understand the point of view of our opponents and the point of view of our friends who do not go all the way with us. In view of St. Thomas' teachings on a just war, and in view of all that has been written on the subject—although that is not as much as it should be—it is not surprising that we do not find priests out and out pacifists.

Msgr. O'Toole was very sorry when I saw him and begs us to please stick to the counsels [of perfection] as the basis of our objections. He says that there we are all on perfectly safe grounds, and have an unassailable position. It is when we start arguing foreign policy and the question of justice and injustice that we arouse great antagonism. We all know, too, that often our tone is far from charitable, and certainly the way we speak of our President and the President's wife is far from respectful.

He called our attention to the fact that he stresses participation in war, opposing participation in war rather than opposing war. On this point he has been accused of quibbling, but the fact is the statement of the law defines conscientious objectors as objecting to the participation in war, rather than as objecting to war. So we must remember this definition in the law.

Later on he will write us another article—a discreet one, he said—but right now he is going to let the matter rest. He is in very much the same position as priests interested in the labor movement who are belabored by both labor and capital. And we are all very fond of him, and do not want him to be so belabored on the one hand by the C.O.'s and on the other hand by his confreres at the C.U.—not to speak of the FBI men who accuse him of a lack of patriotism.

Arthur [Sheehan] has been telling me all about the hospital project in Chicago [*alternative service for C.O.s*] and Gerry [Griffin] has been going around wringing his hands and saying, "I hope they won't turn it down!" You know how we feel about the works of mercy, and how anxious we are that the Catholic C.O.s should give an example of selfless service in wartime. I certainly hope that they will get the number that is wished—and that is twenty. The experience will be invaluable, as undoubtedly we are going to have a plague before we are through. From the human standpoint, of course, it does not sound too inviting, but I do hope and pray that the boys will take advantage of this opportunity and not wait for something else. If they turn down these opportunities that come to us, it will be disastrous for the Catholic C.O. movement, but if we set an example, Catholic C.O.s will begin increasing by the hundreds throughout the country.

I will put in a couple of extra hours in church with the intention that as many as possible will volunteer.

TO BISHOP FRANCIS A. McINTYRE, *New York Chancery*

At the time of this letter Bishop McIntyre was an auxiliary bishop of New York. Dorothy had known him since the time of her conversion when he was a young monsignor working in the chancery office. Later, as Cardinal Archbishop of Los Angeles, he would become a notorious scourge of Catholic liberals and modernizing priests and nuns. But despite his reactionary positions, he always retained a soft spot for Dorothy Day, and she for him.

This is the first of a long series of letters concerning Dorothy's desire to establish a retreat house for recovering alcoholic priests. The plan never got off the ground—perhaps due to skepticism about entrusting such a project to a laywoman; perhaps also because of questions about her collaborators, Fathers Pacifique Roy and Clarence Duffy. Both had encountered criticism—Roy, for the rigorism of his retreats, and Duffy, an Irish priest, because of his activism in the labor cause.

MARCH 6, 1942

I wish to lay before you some ideas and I trust you will not think we are presumptuous. Since we are down here on the Bowery practically, we are always bound to have many such situations arise [alcoholic priests]. I can think of a half-dozen cases now and our priest here in the neighborhood says there are many more. If this diocese could only support a farm, rather far off, in the country, so that the men would not be next door to temptation as they are in Stirling [N.J.—*site of a treatment center for priests established by the Missionary Servants of the Most Holy Trinity*], a great step forward would be made. There would be plenty of work to do, building up the place, raising food and animals, building up a library for study. We have a most dear friend, Father Pacifique Roy, Josephite, right now in a parish in Baltimore, who is most anxious to be released for just this work which is very dear to his heart.* For two years now he has talked to me about it. He could be released, especially if another diocese accepted him for this work. If you got the necessary permissions, and if there was property belonging to the diocese which would be suitable, we would undertake the responsibility of getting the work underway. You know how we feel about voluntary poverty and manual labor, and with these as a basis, much could be done.

Father Roy is one of the most saintly priests I have ever met, and just conversing with him is like having a spiritual conference. He has been my spiritual adviser since I met him in August 1940. He has a great practical knowledge, too, and visiting

---

* Father Roy, a French Canadian Josephite priest, was one of Dorothy's closest spiritual advisors. She described his saintly life in *The Long Loneliness* and the story of his death in *Loaves and Fishes*. She credited him with introducing her to a favorite line from St. Ignatius: "Love is an exchange of gifts."

his parish I have seen his work for the Negroes and the school children. With his own hands and with the help of some derelict men from our Baltimore house, he has dug out a basement, installed a dozen showers, toilets, locker rooms, heating plant, etc., a work which would cost thousands if the labor had had to be paid for. These skills along many lines (he has built shrines, stage settings, etc.) would be most handy in teaching the men he would be caring for, and all doctors call attention to the great therapeutic power of all such manual labor.

He is a French Canadian, and he reminds me a little of Peter Maurin, with his enthusiasm and fervor. If he starts talking to you, he is quite likely to hold you for three hours, regardless of all other work to be done.

Father Clarence Duffy, whom you will remember, is still with us, but his troubles are not those of the others.* He has won the respect of all these last years by his integrity, his patience, his humility and constant work in the way of reading, writing, discussing, sowing the seeds that will have their results in the Catholic rural life movement in America. (For a man interested in community living, he is the most rugged individualist I have ever met!) But of course much of such work must be done alone. He lives in a little apartment around the corner from us, says Mass daily at St. Francis Church, and lives a quiet life of work, very much by himself. He is much the opposite of Father Roy, in that he thinks practically only of the material aspect of the work and finds it difficult to talk or write of the spiritual aspects. But he would work well with Father Roy.

I do wish I could have a chance to talk to you more about this work, or that you would send for Father Roy and talk to him.

Meanwhile, since our work consists so much of the works of mercy, we must of course accept any case that comes to us, but

* Father Clarence Duffy was an Irish priest who lived with the CW off and on since the 1930s.

yet with a very sad sense that in such cases as these we are most inadequate and are able to do little.

TO FATHER JOHN HUGO

Dorothy's introduction to Fr. Hugo, a young priest from Pittsburgh, was among the most important encounters of her life. After attending one of his retreats in Oakmont, Pennsylvania, she adopted him as a close spiritual advisor. Fr. Hugo's strong emphasis on holiness as the defining goal of Christian life struck a chord with Dorothy, and in some ways it powerfully realigned her spiritual outlook. His rigorism, his stress on sacrifice and on loving God before all other things, appealed to her instinct for the heroic. A typical Hugo saying was, "The best thing to do with the best of things is to give them up." Though Dorothy urged all members of the Catholic Worker to attend his retreats, they were not universally popular. Here she is addressing Fr. Hugo about her scheme for a retreat house for alcoholic priests.

MARCH 18, 1942

Father Roy was here Monday and Tuesday after having to give a day of recollection at Paterson on Sunday. He went to see Bishop McIntyre and was received very favorably and was asked to draw up a plan. The Bishop also asked where these retreats were being given for priests, so will you let me know at once the date of the retreat for priests to be given at Pittsburgh, so that I may let him know. I also want to get two priests who are with us on for it, although they both have jobs now.

Here is a copy of the letter that I sent to Bishop McIntyre. He asked Father Roy to draw up a plan, and Father Roy asked me and I am asking you. Are you any good at drawing up plans that bishops would approve of—I mean on paper?

We all send our love and be assured we are praying for you most vigorously.

TO BISHOP McINTYRE

MARCH 20, 1942

Thank you very much for your letter of March 14. We are very happy to do anything that we can, and we are most anxious to help Father Roy get the work established that has been his dream for many years, so please do not speak of this as a difficulty for us.

It is hard for Father Roy to draw up a plan for the retreat house about which I wrote you. In my letter I notice I speak of the place as "a farm," rather than a retreat house, but according to Father Roy's ideas the place would be a house of penance where they would begin their work by an eight-day retreat. It would be called "The Retreat House of Jesus, the Worker." There is a retreat house by this name in Quebec.

From fifty to one hundred acres would be sufficient. The house could be a plain one, there could be more building done later in order that there might be private cells. These are all Father's Roy's ideas that he asked me to explain to you. He wishes to impress upon them the great good that they could do, more than ever before, because they have suffered themselves. He wishes them to understand that on coming out it will be to work only for the very poor, and that they will come out to the slums and not to comfortable rectories.

Since voluntary poverty is accepted and the providence of God depended upon, there will be no specific charges made, and any bishops can send anyone there to be taken care of. The house will be supported by voluntary contributions. There will be sufficient land to grow most of the food consumed.

The Sermon on the Mount will be the constitution of the new association, if this is what God intends to come out of such a work.

It is hard for me to write such letters as these to you, because they are probably filled also with "inexactitude of expression"! The enclosure about a basketball game which I am sending to

you is just to illustrate a point about Father Roy. Here he is dealing with the most controversial matter, a question of race. Our
House of Hospitality in Baltimore was closed by a court injunc-
tion because all our neighbors objected so much to our taking
in Negroes and white men in the same house. During the two
years of its existence, the young men who were in charge of the
house were brought into court quite a few times, because of
the bitterness of the feeling about the race question. And here is
Father Roy having an interracial basketball game! There have
been others in the past, and it is quite taken for granted. It is
because he deals with such matters from a supernatural rather
than a natural angle that he is able to accomplish such wonders.

All of these ideas that I have been expressing are Father
Roy's. You told him that you would be interested in seeing a
plan, but it is very hard to draw up anything formally. Such work
as this would have to grow by itself. It could begin so very simply.
All that would be needed would be a piece of property with a
house on it far enough away from a town to insure privacy. It
would also mean accepting Father Roy in this diocese, and his
release from his order.

Please excuse me for taking up so much of your time.

TO JOE ZARRELLA

EVE OF ASCENSION [MAY 1942]

I met a saint at Santa Barbara—a Catherine Sullivan, who fasts
until three every day and works hard and gives all her money to
the poor. She has worked as a migrant, and now has settled in
S.B. It is a beautiful place, the mission is wonderful, but the prosperity everywhere jars. Catherine was a godsend. And she is not
one of the simple ones. She is a very intelligent woman, capable,
quiet, and hard working.

San Francisco is sparkling, prosperous, gay and festive. Market
Street is thronged with soldiers, sailors, all having a good time.

The streets have army cars, army trucks, jeeps, and all the boys are gay. All the boys are on their way to Australia from here. This is the shipping out place. The movie houses have crowds in front of them, restaurants are full, people throng the shops. There's an alarm every day, and an air raid warning going this minute. I don't know the difference between the two. People stand around and gape. Not too much traffic due to tires but they have street cars and cable cars here, lots of fun. War is wonderful! The boys are having a good time, seeing life, and everybody frankly is enlisting for war work right at home, nice jobs in the commissary department.

I was invited to speak at a meeting of Young Christian Workers last night and after I had finished talking like a Jeremiah of racism and poverty and housing and industrialism and the seeds of war and sat down, Fr. said, "And now what shall we do about that dance on Friday night?" and without further ado everyone discussed whom to invite. I don't wonder Jeremiah was flung down into the slimy pit for his prophesying. That's what's going to happen to me. It won't be the government but our own.

God bless all of you. Pray for me. In Christ, Dorothy

TO PRESIDENT FRANKLIN D. ROOSEVELT

Dorothy wrote the president on behalf of Odell Waller, a black share-cropper convicted of killing his white landlord over a financial dispute. The case attracted national attention and went all the way to the Supreme Court. Despite five reprieves, as well as support from prominent figures such as Eleanor Roosevelt, John Dewey, and Pearl Buck, Waller was ultimately executed on July 2, 1942.

JUNE 23, 1942

Dear Mr. President,

I am writing to you in regard to Odell Waller, condemned to die July 2. Certainly, if you do not intervene yourself, nothing further can be done to save him. It is not a question of guilt so much as of degree. It certainly has been proved without question that he was not tried by a jury of his peers. He did not have an unprejudiced trial. It was not possible on account of the poll tax which disenfranchises so many.

We have been writing about this case in the CATHOLIC WORKER for many months, enlisting the support of others throughout the country who have done what they could to see that justice was done.

The case right now has tremendous significance. We all know that you and your administration have done perhaps more than any other president to call attention to the condition of the Negro in this country and the poor sharecropper and tenant farmer. We realize the tremendous problem that lies before you in dealing with such issues.

Right now throughout the country there is such bitterness among the Negroes toward the Whites. I have noticed it on a recent trip I have made to the West Coast and back, visiting the houses of hospitality which are part of the Catholic Worker movement.

The recent meeting at Madison Square Garden, called by A. Philip Randolph, President of the Brotherhood of Sleeping Car Porters, and attended by 18,000 Negroes, showed plainly the feeling which is growing more and more strong each day among these black brothers of ours. It was a good meeting and a restrained meeting but the feeling was there and it was impossible not to see it.

We beg you to intervene for Odell Waller, whose mother appeared at that meeting the other night, and by your clemency to show that there is a recognition in this country that we are together sons of God and brothers in Christ, and we are aiming indeed towards a Christian democracy. We pray for you daily in these most terrible times.

Respectfully yours,
Dorothy Day, Editor
The Catholic Worker

TO BISHOP McINTYRE

Dorothy's plan for a retreat house for priests was making little progress.

JULY 30TH, 1942

It is now more than three months since I wrote you last in regard to Father Roy of Baltimore and his idea in regard to a house of penance for priests and a retreat house for the poor. During these months the work of planning has gone steadily on.

What we need to have, of course, is a farm, of about 150 to 200 acres, with a house on it, preferably with a few buildings. A place of this sort would give work to the men who were there, a work of farming, gardening, caring for animals (rabbits, chickens, goats, sheep, pigs, as well as cows and horses), carpentry, shoemaking, bookbinding, machine work—indeed many crafts besides farming could be set up just as they are in Benedictine monasteries.

The natural foundation of the work would be manual labor and voluntary poverty. The supernatural foundation would be the retreat which would begin the work, the day of recollection which would continue it, the hours of praying. And it is not just one retreat, but a series of retreats, conferences, studies, which dig out the sand and supply the rock foundation of the new building, the new life. The work would be the putting off of the old man and the putting on the new. The "dying" would begin at once, and the "living" too. And while this work was going on, the work of giving retreats to the poor, the very poor, would be prepared and would take place. The very sufferings, the degradation undergone by these "other Christs" would make them more ready, would prepare them more thoroughly, for this work of serving Christ in His Poor. The very fact that these two works would be combined—the work of taking care of priests in trouble, and the work of building up a retreat house for the very poor—would serve to bless the project. It would be emphasized from the first that those entering must abide by the rules of the foundation and must never expect to be sent back to comfortable rectories, in comfortable parishes, to a life too hard, paradoxically enough, for them to keep their balance.

It is Father Roy, of course, who has been released from his work by his superiors and given leave of absence to get this work underway, so the planning continued at a great rate.

I am hoping, of course, that he will be accepted by this diocese and that you will somehow find a place for the work to start. I am hoping this because it is the right place. New York is so vast a place that many of the priests from all over the country find their way here and descend to the sordid anonymity of the Bowery. It is a large diocese and I am sure there must be some place out in the country where there is available land and buildings, just enough to make a start.

There are many anxious to participate in this work and contribute to it in one way or another, but I am convinced that Father Roy has the supernatural point of view, the experience, the practice, to enable him to find others with his same fervor, and where he seems to fail, to accept with patience the crosses. Whenever there is talk of imprudence, of folly, I can only think of the "folly of the Cross" St. Paul tells us of. The folly of the Cross, abandonment to divine providence, these are the proper beginning for any kind of work.

All this of course, sounds tremendously ambitious and presumptuous from the natural point of view. And if in my freedom in expressing myself, I am presumptuous, I do beg to be forgiven.

My connection with all this is because Fr. Roy is my spiritual advisor, and because he has commissioned me to do this writing to you. Also because here in our Catholic Worker house, we are constantly running into this problem.

The more we work along material lines (and we are still feeding about fourteen hundred a day, and our two houses in New York are full and the farm is bulging) the more I am convinced that without the spiritual foundation which those retreats give the work is hopeless. From a material standpoint, the work is foolishness, quite contrary to common sense. The state could do it better and also, from the Hitler point of view, the degraded poor could be sterilized or liquidated. From the natural point of view, the degraded poor with whom we come in contact are scarcely worth anything. From the supernatural point of view, in such ones we see Christ Himself, and so the work is transformed and love makes it easy. Also we recognize that whereas man is but dust, he is also by baptism a son of God, and the idea of building up a retreat house for the degraded poor is something so necessary, that without such an aim this work is most incomplete. It is to be hoped that in many dioceses there will be such houses.

It may be argued—houses, run by fallen priests, or reclaimed priests—for the poor? They will be scandalized. But the poor are far more scandalized by the comfortable rectories, the cars, the golf, the radios, the theater, the vacations in Florida, yes, even the drinking of the respectable priest. How can their hearts help but go out to these poor men who have suffered so deeply, who have fallen from so high an estate, who are struggling too intensely to rise and serve God?

Father Roy is most anxious to see the Archbishop and you to talk over these ideas, and it is in preparation for such a meeting that I am sending you this letter.

Your servant in Christ, Dorothy Day

TO TAMAR

One of Dorothy's concerns about Tamar was her growing attraction to David Hennessy, a young man thirteen years her senior who was living at the Catholic Worker farm.

MONDAY [AUGUST 30, 1942]

Did you read *Song of Bernadette* yet? I am trying to get it. I hope too you are helping John with the potatoes and Marjorie with the canning. You know, I suppose, that I strongly disapprove of the way you are sitting around all summer, doing nothing, not even weeding your garden. When I come out next week, after the paper comes out, and still find you not helping others, but always sitting around with Dave, I'm thinking seriously of bringing you into town. I had hoped when Marjorie got out there you'd spend more time with her, but she says you do not. This protest on my part has nothing to do with Dave. As far as I know him, he is perfectly all right, but my protest is the way you are wasting your time and devoting yourself exclusively to him. You know yourself you should have regard for my wishes, even my orders on this subject.

It just occurred to me that you really might not know how I feel about it and that is why I am expressing myself now.

TO GERRY GRIFFIN

Gerry Griffin spent most of the war in the Middle East and North Africa as an ambulance driver with the American Field Service. Dorothy wrote him regularly—long, newsy letters about CW life. A frequent topic was her concern about the relationship between Tamar and David Hennessy.

NOVEMBER 24, 1942

It is a rainy day, and the place looks filthy. Jack is playing with ACCO correspondence. Dwight and Arthur just had a fight. Jay is over getting supper at Maryhouse. Anne got married to Jon last Saturday. Miss Clemens told Miss Weiss she had gotten rid of two ex-nuns and would get rid of the third. Peter is still in Chicago. . . .

Mrs. Johnson just came in to answer the telephone—Mrs. Strumpendarrie offering five dollars to buy a turkey for Thanksgiving day after tomorrow. Joe and Alice [Zarrella] come in regularly Sat. nights to play cards with the Johnsons. Joe got his call, went to the AFS and does not know whether he is taken. I sent you the last issue of the paper, come to think of it, with all the news. My Day by Day was addressed to you ... A filling just came out of my tooth. Damn. I will have to go back to the dentist. Stanley is going once a week. Tamar is happy at Ade's, but *he* [David Hennessy] writes to her every day and special delivery on Sundays. I'm going up there again to speak at New London Sunday and I shall see her and exact a promise from her that she will not marry until she is eighteen. She is happy there, happier than she has ever been in school, but he keeps after her. Damn again.

I visited the camp last week [*Camp Stoddard, the CW-sponsored camp for conscientious objectors*] and Hossag and I talked of Dostoevsky and love and loneliness. The latter, he said, came from reading Thomas Wolfe. We had a free-for-all meeting, and I told them what I thought of them, but also what I thought of the world significance of their actions. [Camp] Warner is much harder to get to than Stoddard. On the way home the train was filled with Dartmouth students going to a Dartmouth-Columbia game, and others for the Yale-Harvard. Many girls. We were crammed in, there was much drinking, it was disgusting. Give me busses. Give me the Bowery.

DECEMBER 8, 1942

Arthur [Sheehan, wrote] a book review on cooperatives, a book by Fr. Leo Ward, about Nova Scotia, in which I am referred to as a *little* woman. About as correct as most of the things that are said. And oh, yes, David Gordon, in his *Catholic International*, refers to me in reviewing Harry Sylvester's book. He says that I went social gospelling with him around the country in his Chevrolet recently and wrote about it in the paper in my oleaginous prose!

How I miss you and Joe [Zarrella]! I find myself groaning inside about the good old days. I miss you terribly, with all your dour ways. I always felt you and Joe needed me, and didn't mind my bossy ways. You never made me feel in the way, and now I go around like a lost soul, like Peter. But how good it is for me, and how much I have. I shall indeed get the Peter [Mauirin] book done, and lots of other writing besides.

I've worried a lot about Tamar this summer and fall, but she seems so happy with Ade, I'm pretty content about her. She is staying right there with her, no vacations, and she loves it, though she pretends to rebel. Every day she gets a letter from Dave [Hennessy] at the farm. He has taken to drinking, according to Helen Gott, so I do hope that blows over. Have I told you some of these things before? And does it all sound trivial in the midst of conflicts as you are? You know yourself how we are conscious always of what is going on, how oppressed in spirit we are, how we fill in with our imaginations all the things that are happening, that might happen to you.

That being said, I'll go on with trivialities. . . .

MIAMI, JAN. 21, 1943

Glad you were forced into talking on the CW. Isn't it hard? I usually weave my talk around Peter's personality, and then the abstract stuff on personalism and communitarianism go over better. The more you see of the world the more it seems hopeless that Christianity will work, enforce order, brotherly love. The more obscure seems our mission! What are we doing? What for? Who are we to do it? And how strangely the work grows up, here, there, and everywhere. Personalism isolates you in this mad world; and considering your own nothingness and God's beauty and glory and majesty and loving kindness, studying to know Him, to love Him, to worship Him, and love others in Him starts us off in the communitarian end of it.

We accumulate others around us in trying to love God and keep His commandments, and then even though you begin as a Father of the Desert you end up as a Communitarian. But my ten years experience teaches me that to continue to be a personalist, it is a good idea to keep the Desert Father in mind. Dwell in a cell, solitary, look to oneself, and judge not others, see no beams in others' eyes, see God everywhere, and Christ our brother everywhere.

Whenever I get confused I think of the beginning questions of the catechism, and life becomes simple again. I've had such a delightful six weeks down here, reading Caussade's *Abandonment* and the Desert Fathers. A large number [of the Desert Fathers] fled to the desert to escape military service and the women to escape dishonor.

When I read these books I realize that we are still plunging ahead through thickets of misunderstanding and paganism and that we are beating a path and not making much headway. Certainly, our farms, our houses, while they are rallying centers for thought, have also proven to be battlefields.

Did I tell you that Tamar sent me a hand-printed (quill and India ink on good paper) chapter of Eric Gill's *Christianity and the Machine Age*, and bound in white sail cloth. Very beautiful. The David influence. I wish she had made the Sermon on the Mount, but later for that.

He writes to her every day, damn it, and she replies, and they are laying all their plans to get married as soon as she is eighteen. And here she is seventeen in March. Do pray she gets over it for he drinks, and certainly doesn't like work, and boasts of being a dreamer, not a worker. Can you imagine Tamar leading a life like Helen's? She is always falling for the underdog. Thank God for Ade. Tamar loves it up there. They are always busy, and she has a pet white rat, which she has named David, and a canary, and rabbits, and come this spring there will be a garden to take care of. She knits, spins, cards wool from our old ram, letters, draws, sews, poses at the art association there at Newport for which she gets five dollars every two weeks, so that according to Ade's budget she is practically self-supporting.

Tamar enjoys the whole atmosphere. It is poverty, asceticism, a Christian life and using the good things at hand. And living and learning how to manage as the Bethunes do is wonderful training for her. But when I think of how every time I came down to the farm all summer, I found her just sitting out with Dave, on the grass, under the trellis, just sitting, sitting, sitting— I realize that she can relapse into the slothful type of person very easily. You see I am giving you all the gossip.

I feel sorry for anyone coming in on the CW now. How did it all come about? What is it all for? And no matter how much you may try to talk, to explain, it seems impossible. People hear what they want to hear, and understand what is in them to understand, no more. You and Joe and I certainly had a long tranquil period together there—things did get on well. And even if it all falls apart, there is the paper to come back to, and wherever we have a headquarters there will be people dropping in and sleeping on the floor and eating what the neighbors bring in.

And it will be the same in other cities, where our readers feel impelled to follow suit. Right now, sixteen houses are open, sixteen were closed. I don't care if they all close. Let the bishops start the hospices in their empty old buildings after the war. Let us practice charity and poverty as much as we are able, wherever we happen to be. The world always will be in a mess, and always was, as St. Teresa say. As long as we keep charity in our hearts to each other and peace and joy. In spite of hell and high water, as my mother says. Coming from sea people as she does, her grandfather was captain of a whaling vessel in Plymouth and his three brothers were lost at sea, her speech sometimes has a nautical flavor.

Lots of love, Gerry, and I am so glad you are happy. We are too, and we will be waiting for you to take over when you come back.

TO NINA POLCYN

Following her graduation from Marquette University, Nina Polcyn spent the summer of 1935 at the CW. (Among other things, she was Dorothy's companion in protesting the Bremen, *a ship sailing under the Nazi flag.) Returning to Milwaukee, she co-founded Holy Family CW House in 1937. Later she moved to Chicago, where she founded St. Benet's Catholic bookstore. She was one of Dorothy's closest and life-long friends.*

ST. SCHOLASTICA, FEB 10 1943

Hope you got my so brief note congratulating you. How are things coming now? What are you doing? Are you still as happy as you were when you wrote that good long letter on Nov. 20? Certainly we know our vocation if we are happy in our work. "Necessity" and "impulse" and "attraction" are the 3 signs, Caussade says, of the will of God.

I'm leaving day after tomorrow and will make 10 stops thru the South on the way home. These visits to remote missions always cheer me. It is so much like our work—in its littleness; we have to make so many acts of faith and hope to keep going, to keep our charity alive.

Did you realize Fr. [John] Hugo has changed his stand on war completely and thanks us for showing him the "light"?

Do write soon. Love to all. In Christ, Dorothy

TO GERRY GRIFFIN

MAY 14, 1943

Got one of my periodic lectures; Sappé said that I was sarcastic. Michael Kovalak said I was too rough and frightened people away, etc. The usual stuff, but I wonder if I am getting sour and bitter. Hope not. First John Curran blamed me for using womanly wiles, then these young ones blame me for being too sarcastic. But you know how it is. One expects much of them. There are no saints, damn it. I can't put my head on their shoulders, as Mrs. Buley said. Do you remember? What we all want are people to look up to, to admire, to respect, to imitate. What we want are saints, so when we fall down we blame each other. However, the Lord's developing saints in His own way, and keeps them from being attractive so that we will not lean on them, will not "put our heads on their shoulders" but on His.

Got a good letter from Tamar. I'm happy that she is so happy, but I miss her. Maybe she will take a nursing course in N.Y. next year and be with me. Hope so. I miss you too.

TO TAMAR

After her time in Montreal, Tamar spent a year studying arts and crafts with Ade Bethune in Newport, Rhode Island. She later considered this one of the happiest years of her life. But at this point Dorothy determined that she should attend an agricultural school on Long Island to prepare herself for a farming life. Though Tamar—with Ade's support—was inclined to finish high school in Rhode Island, Dorothy was quite certain she knew what was best.

JUNE 1943

Under separate cover I'm sending you that farm school catalogue, with various parts of it underlined. Do not lose it. Read it, and ponder the idea of whether you want the agricultural school or the nursing. You probably will have to have four years high school for the nursing. As for this school, with the training you have so far had I'm sure you could register for this fall, or next if you so wish. If you waited until the following fall you would have to go to high school up there, and to me the idea is not so good. Remember that it was quite a wrench to me to take you out of high school so for you to go back and take a good deal of unnecessary work in order to get some of the necessary, seems foolish.

I don't think you are too young for Farmingdale, though the average age for beginners is eighteen. If you show these requirements to Miss Murphy, and get your credits from Immaculata, you can make up this summer what is necessary to have completed two years of high school. That and your Canada experience, and your seven years of vacation farm background, not to speak of your experience with Ade this last year in homemaking, gardening, animal husbandry (to put it technically), will be sufficient for you to start this fall, Sept 28. I have sent for an application blank for you to fill out.

I have marked various parts of the catalogue for you to read especially. You would have to take the straight first year course, then choose the next year some of the things you are most interested in such as beekeeping, poultry, orchards, forestry, or what not.

If you wish to go to this school, I see no reason for you to wait another year, or to spend that year going to high school, if Farmingdale will take you. The career I think you should be fitting yourself for is farming, whether on one of the farming communes or on a farm where you are working and earning a salary. I do firmly believe that young women should have a dowry and a hope chest, and be prepared to help their husbands as much as possible.

Do drop me a line at once and let me know what you think. The general consensus of opinion is that you are a docile creature and easily led, but I do know also that you know what you want very decidedly. And I think what you want is farming and country life more than nursing and city life. You can take a first aid course at Farmingdale and you can easily take a course in practical nursing at the Ballard school (a six-months course) some time in the future if you so wish, which will fit you to take invalids or children on your farm to help support it if you need to.

You had better register for English, physics, math and what else you need this summer, even before you get your credits. You didn't finish geometry and you have not had chemistry or physics, have you?

Maybe I'll be running up to see you before I leave for Washington. I'd like to talk this over with you and get it settled. So I may come up soon. Write at once please about it.

Love, Dorothy

TO ADE BETHUNE

JUNE 30, 1943

I sent Tamar a catalogue of the Agricultural Institute in Long Island (not far from my brother's house) and explained about her credits and entering in the fall. I'd rather she'd do that than go back to high school. There is no particular reason for her to wait another year if after a personal interview they will take her. It would be good for her to graduate from such a school (she might be able to make up credits there) start working and earning her living and saving capital to get started on a farming commune after. After all she will be 19-20 before she is through.

What do you think of all this? It will be a wrench for both of us not to be having that feeling of being a part of the de Bethune family. Tamar has never been so happy but as your mother said, she's apt to get in a rut and get a bit spoiled for the rigorous life. She'll be much on her own at the Institute and perhaps part of her expenses she can earn the second year. Her father will help a good deal. It was sweet of you to say she was a help. I know she is, but I know too that every extra person is more work and more expense—also a great distraction from work.

You have such an abounding generosity that you give of yourself constantly to others and there is truth probably in what your dear mother says about your own work. That's one of the things I love about you most—your readiness to give up your work itself for the sake of others. But your genius God gave you is a treasure and your work is so far-reaching you'll never know yourself the great good it does. So I can understand your mother getting a bit worried at times.

TO TAMAR

Though Dorothy stressed that the final decision regarding farm school belonged to Tamar, there was little doubt of what she felt was the right decision.

JULY 6, 1943

Dearest Tamar,—

I'm not going to come up until August first. Then you can come down here for a week's visit. Mother is looking forward to seeing you, also Della, and we'll probably have some picnics and a swim together. Also we can visit that agricultural school, and you can make up your own mind.

I must say after prayer and fasting I'm all in favor of the idea if they will take you with what credits you have.

Due to the war, and its continuance, such schools may not go on—after all, much of their male registration is cut out. This is a small school too, and I'd hate to have you miss it. They have beginner's chemistry there and physics, and they also have courses in English. They have a great variety of students, even those with no high school at all. And they are of all ages.

I know you are happy at Ade's but you cannot be a child all your life, and I disagree with her idea that high school will help you. I do not think it will. I also think you are more mature than she and her mother think. I have seen you for seventeen years to their one, and I do think that no matter how mistaken mothers may be, they do know their daughters a little better than others. My two brothers went one year to high school and were practically illiterate when they launched themselves into the world. Now one is the editor of the *Journal American* here and the other speaks four languages and has been a foreign correspondent for twenty years. This high school business is the bunk. I'd only make the concession of another year, if you actually have to have it. Otherwise I think you can get what you need at Farmingdale.

In the long run however it is up to you. If you wish to stay at Ade's another year, you are welcome to. I know that they both love you dearly and feel that they have a great deal to offer, as they no doubt have.

However, you be thinking of it yourself. I am anxious to hear from you about it. If you don't want to settle anything until after we see each other, let it go at that. Perhaps that will be better.

Much love, darling.

Dorothy

JULY 15, 1943

Dearest Tamar,

I was afraid I would not hear from you before I left so telephoned last night only to miss you. I'm glad you were walking down to the water. It refreshed me just to think of it. Right now, Thurs. morning, I am lying in bed, waiting for a headache to wear off so I can take the train to Baltimore to visit our c.o.'s there at the mental hospital. It is fearfully hot and it is cool up here, lying around in a kimono. I hate to move. Got your letter this morning.

Your writing continues atrocious in spite of a year's association with Ade. Has she given you up as a pupil, and is that why she wishes you to go to high school? You are surely able to spend a little more of your time practicing writing. I feel rather hurt about it. Ade fails to teach you and then calls you illiterate and begins talking about high school. I am still opposed to the high school idea. You can get chemistry, physics and English, which you do not like, at Farmingdale.

However, I leave you to make up your mind, after you have visited Farmingdale and see what they have to offer. That is the special reason why I want you go come back with me. We will plan on coming, straight from Upton, as I do not wish to be too long away. So please bring some city clothes with you—a tailored dress or a suit and blouses.

Much love, darling.

TO FELLOW CATHOLIC WORKERS

During a retreat in July 1943, Dorothy determined to take a leave from the Catholic Worker. In her journal, she wrote, "I no longer feel I can save my soul by this work; no, more, I am in danger of losing it. . . . The world is too much with me in the Catholic Worker. The world is suffering and dying. I am not suffering and dying in the CW, I am writing and talking about it." She shared this information in a circular letter to the Catholic Worker houses. Later, in the September issue of the paper, she announced her plan.

JULY 28, 1943

This has been my third retreat at Oakmont, Pa., and now having made it the three times I begin to understand, I begin to get the full impact. There were six full days in complete silence. My resolution was confirmed and strengthened that this retreat is the foundation for all our activity. Without it we do not know what the Folly of the Cross means.

For a long time now I have talked about the Fathers of the Desert. For a long time I have threatened to get away and be one. This retreat has confirmed me in my conviction to seek God in prayer and poverty and work, leaving the Catholic Worker and manifold activities to the very competent staff hereabouts. Peter [Maurin] and Arthur [Sheehan] will select the material for the paper. Dave Mason and Fr. Duffy will get it out. I will no longer be directly connected with the Catholic Worker. This may seem at first glance a startling decision to have come to. It was only arrived at after prayer and fasting, and after having made these three retreats.

I shall still continue to write a Day by Day column for the paper. I shall wish to keep in touch with all of you in this way. But I won't be answering mail—I won't be seeing people—I won't be engaged in the multiplicity of occupations as now. After a year of prayer and study, hard work and fasting, the retreat house idea may develop. We hope too to have monthly days of recollection this coming year. Of those you will have news in the Day by Day column.

This separation cannot be made until the middle of September what with the men's retreats. Meanwhile, there is the Aug. and Sept. issues of the paper to get out.

In Christ, Dorothy

TO ADE BETHUNE

JULY 28, 1943

Thanks for your two letters. Of course, enjoying the great silence of the retreat, I could not answer. Also I had to think. As far as I can see, you are right and Tamar should stay with you another year. This decision I have come to without really consulting her. She has not committed herself one way or the other in her letters, or rather notes. Since she has not made a retreat (I really should have taken her on mine) Fr. Hugo suggests that I take her out to the Ladies of the Grail in Chicago for that two-week course of theirs, "The Grain of Wheat" or "The Harvest." The former begins Sunday (so we would leave right after the outing and arrive a few days late for the two-week course), and the other is in September, so that Tamar would be late in registering for school. However, she could make that up. I have some other most momentous issues to discuss with you also when I see you. Looking forward to Sunday.

With love, Dorothy

MONDAY AFTER ASSUMPTION, AUGUST 1943

About Tamar. It is absolutely decided that she is to go to the Grail retreat which means we must leave N.Y. Sept. 7, in order to travel by bus and get there in time. It takes three weeks, the retreat and course. The School at Farmingdale opens on October 11 this year. Mabel Egan is also going there, so Tamar would room with her. She has sent in her credits and references and has to await a personal interview. When we went out there to see the place they said undoubtedly they would take her for one term to see if she could keep up with the work. She would not be able to graduate without her high school credits, but she would have the course. I do not think much of degrees or graduating.

It is too bad about the garden and about the harvest. And I am sorry too to seem to go so against your plans. But the suggestion of high school was the thunderbolt which started the whole thing off. Also, the apprentice idea is rather out isn't it, since there are no apprentices, what with your illness?

Tamar has gained immeasurably by her stay with you. And as for me,—I'm sure you know how deeply grateful I am, and how I shall always love you and your mother for all you've done.

Love, Dorothy.

TO FATHER HARVEY EGAN

Fr. Egan spent time at the Catholic Worker in the late 1930s while still a seminarian. He was an ardent supporter of the Hugo retreats, and he remained close to Dorothy for many years. At this time Dorothy was preparing to take a year's leave of absence from the Catholic Worker.

AUGUST 19, 1943, ST. JOHN EUDES

Thank you for your very good letter. Fr. Farina wrote right after and he had made a novena of Masses so that the Holy Spirit would enlighten him as to whether it was God's will for me to leave and the answer, he writes very assuredly, is yes. So I can have no doubts whatever.

The work is in a healthier state than it has ever been. More unity, peace, and concord. Every night the rosary and Compline; every day a number of them making their hour. No railers, no scoffers, no detractors. Deo gratias. Also, everyone takes it as perfectly natural that I should make this move. They see it as a step ahead, and a good thing for the work. At first it hurt a little, that no one should think of it as a great sacrifice on my part. They all rejoiced as though I were choosing a rest, as though I were taking a well-earned vacation. And the work is the dearest thing in life to me, aside from my daughter. To give it up has cost me many a sleepless night. Not that I have hesitated, but I really have suffered.

When people say, "Without you the movement will fold," I know that they are all wrong, that they know very little about the work or the people concerned. It is filled with little saints, hidden saints, who have been keeping it going with their hard work and their prayers. It is of tremendous importance and immensely blessed by God. Don't you suppose I realize that it is the only paper—the only Catholic paper—crying "Peace, Peace." The only one which calls for the works of mercy—the Folly of the Cross—as a program. It is because it is doing so much, and because it means so much that God has called upon me to prune it and to prune it that it may bear much fruit. And that pruning takes me out of it,—only to work more actively, in prayer, to hold up its arms (because their work is prayer) by my prayers.

You are dears, all of you, to suggest first to send me helpers and then to invite me to a "cave" out there. But I must be near my mother, who is 73 and who needs me, and who will even come to stay with me for a month or so at a time. My being a hermit will not be very luxurious in the way of silence and solitude. There are family responsibilities of course which I cannot side-step, nor do I wish to. I'm the only link the family have with the Church, with the faith. But this move will mean getting out of public life, getting away from leadership, stepping down and being the least, serving, praying, being subject, rather than wielding authority. It was as I knelt in front of the statue of the Blessed Mother that the message came to me to leave the work. She lived a hidden life. That's what women ought to do.

I have expressed myself over and over in the CW. Everyone knows what my point of view is. It is not as though I were trying to get out of facing an issue. For ten years I have written and edited, and spoken, and been on committees, and multiplied my occupations, and all over the world women are doing the same, on one or another side of the question. On the one hand are the Waacs and Waves, and on the other are the reformer women, like myself, the protestors. It is about time that women chose the better part, and lived the Mary life, and by that I mean the Blessed Mother life, which must have been a combination of Mary-Martha in the quietest way imaginable. Isn't it beautiful to think of? You are cultivating just such vocations out there. Countless women who will work quietly, and hiddenly, and prayerfully.

I have come also to the conclusion, these last years, that we must ever put the family first. All our work hereabouts is because some family is shirking responsibility or has made it hard for father or son to stay within the bounds of the family. We should hang on to each other now that all the world is being torn apart. I had long since given up my family and my father used to reproach me, saying that charity began at home. Now I see my mother, my sister, and my two brothers more often, remembering that the family is the unit of society.

I forgot to say also that I will not stop writing, unless I get some intimation that that is what God wants me to do. I'll write the Peter [Maurin] book,—it needs a good going over—articles for magazines, and columns for the CW to push the retreat movement, and days of recollection. After all, I leave only in order to pray for more saints, more leaders, more workers, more slaves of Mary to take care of the tremendous needs after the war. And to use those weapons of the spirit which we have been talking so much about.

I look forward to seeing all of you, if God wills.

Your fellow worker in Christ, through Mary, Dorothy

Dorothy's year away from the CW lasted only six months. Much of that time was spent living in a Dominican convent in Farmingdale where she could be near her daughter. Tamar, by this time, had revealed her desire to marry David Hennessy. Despite misgivings, Dorothy

gave her consent, provided that Tamar await her 18th birthday. The
wedding took place on April 19, 1944.

TO GERRY GRIFFIN

MARCH 14, 1944

Now Tamar comes to me and wishes to be married next month,
now that she is eighteen, and she wants to live in the Buley
house with Dave. They will whitewash, scrub, clapboard it, etc.
You can imagine what a state it is in.

I'm glad Tamar is going to marry into poverty and farm life.
They have been seeing each other once a month all winter when
she went in to have her teeth fixed, and when they sprung the
date on me, I was surprised but not too much so. Having been
with Tamar steadily since last August, I can see she knows her
own mind. And the fact that he has lived there at the farm two
years in poverty and loneliness and is willing to accept the land
and hard work is all in his favor.

He is working this winter with a slate roofer so there will be
a little income. He may grow into a Mr. Breen, Mr. O'Connell
type, gruff and howling, but Tamar loves him, so what can I say.
In the morning I am happy for her that her life is going to begin
there on the farm, and by evening I am morose and worrying.
Periods of transition are hard.

I'm praying for you daily, and I do not forget, so please remember I am hanging on to you. Will you come back on fur-
lough or for good? The CW certainly has no record for CO's.
Practically all have capitulated except John Doebele and Jim
Rogan. There are a number of absolutists and paying the penalty,
influenced by our stand. I am saddened at times by the whole
thing and at the failure of us all. You have chosen no easy way of
course. But at that it is easier than jail. The greatest temptation
of all is to fling yourself into death, and into sin, to share the
misery of one's brothers. Do you remember that was the

paragraph that Broun and Peglar fought about in my first book. It is a temptation with me all my life. On the one hand to be with one's brothers, and on the other to be a hermit. It is a very subtle temptation, a choosing between man and God. Meditate on these things. God help us all. Much love to you, my dear. I'm not supposed to be writing letters. I'm supposed to be a hermit. But here I am succumbing to the temptation. Pray for me too. God bless you always and keep you safe.

TO THE CHANCELLOR OF THE PHILADELPHIA ARCHDIOCESE

Dorothy continued to advocate for Fr. Roy's retreat house.

FEAST OF ST. JEROME, SEPT 20, 1944

Our dear friend, Father Roy, a Josephite, has arrived for a visit and it is in regard to him that I beg your favor. He has been released by his superior for an indefinite period to do a special work. He has his faculties and is in good standing. There is no question about that. Bishop McIntyre and Archbishop Spellman of New York both know him, or of him, and of the work which he is setting out to do, and they are much interested in it. It is too bad our farm is not in their diocese, but I am afraid that I am one of these ignorant converts who have gone rashly ahead, without sufficient knowledge of procedure, and acquired houses and farms without first going to the chancery office of the diocese in which we are locating. Perhaps it is because we have had so much encouragement from bishops that it has made us seem to be presumptuous, but we did not mean to be, and we have gone ahead, not wishing to bother too much the chancellors and bishops about work which we had undertaken on our own responsibility and for which we were financially responsible. But this was when our work had to do with the corporal works of mercy, rather than spiritual. Feeding the hungry, clothing the naked, sheltering the harborless—this was so plainly work for lay people, for single people, for families, for all Christians, that it was foolish to think of asking permission.

But now that it comes to the spiritual works of mercy, and priests are involved, we must keep in touch with you, let you know what we are doing, who is here, and asking you each time for faculties.

We do not presume to try to work with priests who are in trouble, but it had been quite by accident that in many of our houses and farms people have brought them to us, and it has been hard to know what to do. On some occasions there have been as many as ten in all our houses.

Fr. Roy, on the other hand, has been released to undertake a work for these men. He is gathering, little by little, a group of priests who will together undertake to start a retreat house for them, a place which will be conducted as a second novitiate. We have talked quite a few times with Bishop McIntyre about this and he believes that an order should of course carry on this work. If Fr. Roy is able to gather a few priests together, they may be able to start such an association, so that the work will have the continuity as Bishop McIntyre says. He has not committed himself as to whether or not this group will be accepted in the New York archdiocese, nor can there be anything definite said until after the war, perhaps.

All of this may sound very novel and strange to you, but the idea flows out of eleven years of experience in building up the lay apostolate in poverty, and housing and feeding tens of thousands of men and women on our breadlines. During the Depression we had over a thousand a day in New York alone, and goodness knows how many altogether in all our houses.

Because of the very vastness of the work, we are forced to go far deeper in attacking the root of the problem. God has supported us in work which both state and organized charity could have done far more effectively, and efficiently, doubtless in order to show that He wishes us all to be personally responsible for our brothers.

Fr. Roy will be in Philadelphia the next weekend and will come to see you. Thanking you for your patience.

Gratefully in Christ

TO FATHER HARVEY EGAN

SEPTEMBER 27, 1944

God bless you for your letter which we will publish on the front page in the next issue of the paper. Underneath it, I shall carry the news item that Fr. Joseph Meenan, St. Stephen's Church, Pittsburgh diocese, has turned in his registration card, feeling that cooperating with a government order which he has come to consider wrong, was a mistake in the first place, and that he wishes to repair that mistake as best he can. Or something of that sort. Are there any of your group who are going to turn in their registration cards? I shall be delighted to print a list of priests, and would be more than grateful if a little statement came with it.

God be praised, I am deluged with many troubles and anxieties, and the work proceeds with the utmost of difficulties. At least 75% of the CW movement is against me, personally, and my feathers are torn out one by one. I always had too natural a love for people, and the Lord, I do thank Him for it, is taking care of it for me. Doesn't it give one a feeling of safety to know that He will take care of those things which we omit through pride and self love and blindness.

The first retreat at Maryfarm was magnificent. Only fifteen, but it went beautifully, and it was a taste of heaven on earth. No wonder the devil is busy trying to prevent it. And in addition to the retreat house, there is the paper to get out, an appeal to write because the bills, after my year of retreat, have piled up. The printing bill alone is three thousand! I wonder they let us print another issue. You see, we misappropriate funds, spending what comes in for subs, for food, for the house, etc. Oh dear! St. Joseph has a nice tangle to straighten out.

TO STANLEY VISHNEWSKI

FEAST OF ST. DIDACUS, NOV 13 1944

I just heard that you were taken ill and operated on! And in my absence. Why did you not wait until I got back? I hope you did not suffer too much and that you are recovering quickly and they are taking good care of you.

Stanley, I have a wonderful plan for Mott Street. You know that Italian bakery around the corner. I want to rent it, and have the girls set up a headquarters there to bake bread for the line. It will be a center of discussion, of knitting, and sewing, and indoctrination, a place where the women visitors can go and learn more of the things they can do to help the movement. It will be a sample of home, a sample of the farm, a sample of the soul of woman. What fun!

Well, I have to go to an assembly, so enough now. God bless you and keep you. Take good care of yourself. Let what sun there is bake you, eat plenty of oatmeal and drink plenty of milk, and sleep twelve hours a night. You will be moving mountains when I get back. Thank God for everything, as your Franciscan friend Fr. Mooney says.

Move love, your mother in Christ, Dorothy

TO GERRY GRIFFIN

DECEMBER 6, 1944

I have come to the conclusion that I have had so much natural love in my life for people that God is now proving me. He is pruning down my natural love so that I may have more supernatural love. And the love which comes out of this daily dying is real and true and enduring. When I really learn to love, then all these contradictions will cease. I do truly realize that other people see all my faults more clearly and they are quite rightly irritated by me.

Living around the CW is more like living in a refugee camp than ever. In town we remain dirty, but the work goes on. We have put quite a few thousand into the farm in the way of a new roof, new flooring, windows and doors. You will love it. It is so beautiful down there now. Dave Hennessy goes around saying everything changes and everything remains the same, so do not worry. Though you may not recapture old joys, you will come back with such a maturity of experience and appreciation of home and God knows we need you so that you will have no time to think, you will just have to work. But as I go over things the three days a week I am in, I can see you running around cursing and shouting. Pray for fortitude and patience now to contain yourself. You'll need it.

TO DONALD POWELL

FEAST OF SAINT THOMAS [DECEMBER 21, 1944]
Thanks from the bottom of my heart. It was good to hear from you again. I had wondered and wondered how you were. I have a sense of delicacy about writing to old friends, because often in war time, they are friends no longer. Funny.

About my year. I made up my mind that women need to be active. That such a year should be spent in hard work in a hospital say, not off in a convent, on one's own. However, I was following direction. Also, being near Tamar and settling my own mind as to the question of her marriage. She is very happy, and her husband is a good one. A 4F. Loves poverty and the land. My other decisions were that things must go on as they are. It's our job, the houses, farms, manual labor, poverty. A simple program and one to last a lifetime. We can always go into it deeper and deeper.

Your apartment sounds like hell. You are the one who is living in poverty. We have space and privacy in our slums, even if we are cold and dirty a good part of the time. And that may be our own sloth. Middle class people certainly have a hard time. Why don't you find a nice cozy slum to live in with a backyard for the two kids? They sound wonderful.

I love my son-in-law. His father works for the Veteran's Bureau too in Washington. The name is Hennessy and they live in the southeast part of town. Seven sisters. Tamar's father had seven sisters too, and she wants a boy! Such optimism. The son-in-law loves poverty, country, animals, and books. Tamar is lucky.

Wish you could get up on one of our retreats at Easton. The place is beginning to look swell. Besides you should be looking over your future home.

TO CLAUDE McKAY

Claude McKay was a Jamaican-born poet and writer who became one of the central figures of the Harlem Renaissance. Drawn to communism in his youth, he became disillusioned after a trip to the Soviet Union and later embraced Catholicism.

NOVEMBER 2, 1945

Thank you for your good letter. I was thinking of St. Paul's Chapter 12 to the Romans; and his idea that some minister and some prophesy. We all have different parts, in the Mystical Body of Christ. Some teach and some rule, some serve humbly; he brings that out several times in his Epistles.

It was also in the First Corinthians, chapter 12, verse 14 on; it seems to me that this clarifies the idea that society cannot be leveled—that we all have different functions and should respect each other's work and each other's persons. I think you and I are thinking different things when we are talking about fighting Communism. I am afraid I did not make myself clear concerning the part of Mr. [Louis] Budenz but I feel that in his going to college, a typical bourgeois college, filled with race and class prejudice, in fact, if not in theory he fails the workers and that he is not opposing Communism with anything positive.*

When people are standing up for our present rotten system, they are being worse than Communists, it seems to me. There is so much positive work to be done that I hate to see people wasting time in this way. I am not arguing for any common front with the Communists—with our voluntary poverty, our works of mercy, the decentralists movement, our fighting of the industrial system, our opposition to war and revolution— it seems to me our position is clear.

Certainly I agree with you that the class war is a horrible war that goes on in our midst all the time. And when I am talking about St. Paul's ideas of vocations, I am not upholding any class ideas—that it is just that if a man has a vocation to be a teacher, he should be a teacher. I don't see how anyone can say that we are endorsing the Communists.

TO GERRY GRIFFIN

Griffin returned from the war in July 1945 and once more resumed responsibility for managing the CW house. Dorothy placed great confidence in him. But differences in their temperaments, and differing approaches to leadership of the movement, steadily clouded their relationship.

DECEMBER 3, 1945

I hope you are feeling better. Marge said you were having general misery with your stomach. If you could survive British cooking and then suffer under CW's, I'm surprised. Or is it just working at Mott St.? Lou said he and Joe were sure you were never coming back. Kay also said you were not (while you were in England). You make me wonder about you so much. Not only now, but

---

* Louis Budenz was a high-ranking member of the Communist Party. In 1945, he left the Party, embraced Catholicism, and dedicated himself to combating communism.

always. You are a hard man to live with you know, but I do love you, Gerry, and am so glad you are back. But you give me the feeling at times that you hate my guts, as the saying goes—that I get on your nerves terribly.

It is hard to talk to you too and I suppose it will be increasingly hard over the years if we stick together. You are like Forster, and my brother Sam, in a way, both of whom love me and hate me and cannot talk to me. It baffles me. Again, I feel like giving up and going away, and just leaving the work. Throughout the history of the CW I've just been ruining it and wrecking it, according to a goodly faction. Any collaboration, any growth, any deepening of the work has been looked upon as ruining it and all the old timers look back on the carefree Bohemian days with nostalgia.

But with the world in famine and pestilence unless we deepen our spiritual life and call into play spiritual weapons, the rest is worth nothing. As I've been repeating until you're all sick of it. But then you give the impression that the Grail, the Retreat—these are outside influences, and that you are irked by them. It's all the Church, and we have got to use the means God sends us. It might have been Legion of Mary, Holy Name, Catholic Action, Jocism, etc. But we are merely working with those who will work with us, help us, etc. What other priests besides these retreat priests have so helped us with time, money (even just to be associated with us), serving tables, etc.

But then I remember you were nauseated by Ade's and my speechifying that night years ago. I guess you are just an Irishman and I must put up with you. Anyway, I do love you. God bless you.

TO FATHER HARVEY EGAN

MAY 29, 1946

You are indeed being tried right sore. And I have not written because I am being tried sore—illnesses in the family, Tamar ill, please do say a prayer for me. No, better I should beg you to offer up a Mass of Thanksgiving for me. I guess the Lord is permitting you to be greatly tempted. So do not dream of ever giving up. How are we to learn if we are not taught and who is to teach us if not you and the likes of you. God will take care of all mistakes. I cannot imagine what you are talking about when you speak of grave harm to souls. God just would not permit it. Do not doubt it. I have heard nothing, I was afraid my criticism hurt you, discouraged you.

Fine gratitude I showed when you came those thousands of miles in a blizzard and gave a retreat to a peculiarly conglomerate crowd. But not having any thanks from men, think what your reward must be in Heaven. What is dangerous is your present state of mind,—a temptation of the devil. So I beg you to rejoice in your afflictions, tell our Lady she cannot possibly allow you to dishonor her Son in any way, and go ahead. You are her slave, she will have to take care of you.

About the retreat, I wish you would give the same retreat but with one conference a day about the Blessed Mother as a preparation for the feast of the Assumption. I am 48 and so often feel I can talk like a mother to young priests like you, and I do think that first you expect too much and too quickly, and then you get discouraged. Please do not. Just go on sowing, or even just ploughing up, and the crop will come. God bless you. You are one of our dear, dear friends and I could not bear to think of your giving up.

In our Lady's household,

Your fellow servant, Dorothy

TO CLAUDE McKAY

Matters at the Easton Farm had reached a crisis point. While Dorothy had wished to refashion the farm as a retreat center, some of the resident families rebelled against her authority. Dorothy finally resolved to abandon the farm to these families and to move on. Her worries

were compounded by the feeling that Tamar's family was siding with
the dissenters. (David Hennessy by this time made no secret of his
strong distaste for the CW.)

20 DECEMBER 1946, EMBER FRIDAY

A happy and holy Christmas season. Do please forgive me for
not writing. A multitude of troubles has been descending upon
me these last months and I was able only to do what I had to. The
families at the farm have long been in revolt against the retreat
house there, including my daughter's, and they made it so hard
that we had to just move out, turning the farm over to them.
Now we are looking for a new place.

It has kept me pretty heartsick because for a second time I
have had to give up family. A grandmother is just as intent and
attached to her grandchildren, even more so, than a mother. So
I have been doing some severe penance for the sins of my past
life—for rejecting children in my radical days.

Fr. Roy has tumor on the brain and has lost his memory. His
mind is much confused. We are surrounded by people with
mental illnesses, two drug addicts, 3 pregnant women, one the
wife of an addict, another with a disappearing husband.

Do you read Dostoevsky? I love his religious spirit. Just came
across his *Diary of a Writer* with a series of essays about the Slavo-
philes and Westerners—atheism and religion.

My brother, a red-baiter and anti-Semite, is being held in a
concentration camp in the American zone in Germany a year
and a half now without trial. He is mistreated, according to a
chaplain who has just returned. Say a prayer for him, please. He
is at least sincere, and risked his neck. As an American he is entitled to a trial and sentence.*

---

* Dorothy's older brother Donald was a journalist stationed in Finland. During the war, his identification with the Finns and their sufferings under the
Russians, combined with his own anti-Semitism, turned his sympathies to the
German cause. He fled Finland for Germany and after the war he was detained
as a Nazi collaborator.

Dorothy refers below to the impairment of both Peter Maurin and Fr. Roy. Maurin, after suffering a stroke, had announced that he was "no longer able to think." As for Fr. Roy, Dorothy believed that he was a "victim soul," someone who had voluntarily assumed the sufferings of others to relieve their pain. In any case, Roy's impairment signaled the end of her plan to establish a retreat house for alcoholic priests.

FEBRUARY 8, 1947

Yes, Peter has lost his memory—his mind—Fr. Roy the use and control of his body, and I have lost my family—daughter and grandchildren. We all have to die—if we don't put off the old man to put on the new, it is done for us. That is a consolation at least—that God will purify us in spite of ourselves. It's a price to pay in this work—a work not to be undertaken lightly. If the Communists in their Gospel of force pay with their lives, we also have to lay down our lives for our brethren—if we are trying to oppose love to force it has got to mean something. Think about this when you are suffering and pray for me too. It will all probably get worse before it gets better.

TO THE DEAN OF THE DIOCESE OF ALLENTOWN, PENNSYLVANIA

Dorothy describes her intention to sever ties with the CW farm at Easton, Pennsylvania.

FEBRUARY 20, 1947

Dear Msgr. [Leo G.] Fink,

I wish I could come to see you and talk with you instead of trying to write a letter, and I wish too, that I had been at the farm while you were there, so that I could explain to you some of our great difficulties. I understand that you were from the country, and so were pretty well disgusted at our general inefficiency.

I do not want to excuse myself, but in justice to the work, I feel that I should write to you to try to tell you that we do realize our great failures in living up to the things we profess. It is talk, of course, that we try to do too much of, on many occasions.

The very workers that God sends us are the lame, halt, and the blind from the leaders down to the very least. We work with poor human tools, as well as insufficient funds. Most of the people who come to us have no skills and our best farmer is a former seaman. Maryfarm is certainly a failure and always has been a failure and we are humbly conscious of the great generosity of the diocese in permitting us to have retreats there. Little by little, however, it has become impossible for us to work there and now we are moving out. We have failed completely in either bringing about a change of attitude in the people who were there or in coping with the situation as it stood. We could no longer stand the strain and so have moved completely, leaving the place to the four families who are there, and a couple of single people who choose to remain.

It seems to me that in dealing with the terrible problems of today in our paper, we have them exemplified in our mistakes. We write about insanity and the care of the mentally ill and we have three or four of them amongst us. At one time last winter there were six. Many an agency sends those to us whom they cannot handle themselves and some we have cared for amongst us and three we have had to place in mental hospitals. We talk of the need of the family, the need of holy families, and the peculiar heresy of the family springs up amongst us. If we are guilty of presumption in writing of the clergy and the laity in the "Church and Work," immediately we see the failure of such presumption amongst those who have come to us, either for help or to help others. If we write about squatters, even jokingly, we suddenly have squatters with us who cannot be disposed of because of theirs or their family's need. There is never a situation comes up that does not have to be dealt with firsthand. We have to suffer for every mistake we make, but, of course, that does not keep us from going on making them.

The stone house you referred to in your telegram will indeed be used for a Christ house. We had thought we were using it for that when we were housing retreatants. Now it has been rented by a dispossessed family in the neighborhood. The upper farm has been turned over to the three families who are there. We will no longer have any connection with the farm at Easton.

I am writing a letter to this effect to the Chancery Office, but as you are a dean of the diocese, I am also notifying you.

I am indeed sorry for the times that we have given you offense, and I do beg you to forgive us the mistakes that we have to pay for in our failures.

TO DONALD POWELL

By this time Tamar and her family had moved to a farm in West Virginia.

MAY 1947

Wish you could get out of the city on an acre, have chicks, goats, room. Yes, Peter [Maurin] is still Petering more than ever. He has sowed all, but remains an inspiration to us all. Takes the eye of faith to see it often, to the young people who keep coming. Shows the validity of the appeal, youth keeps flocking.

Tamar and Dave got a place at Berkeley Springs for $1,200 and have a decrepit house, but 70 acres. Goats and chickens of course. Dave tries to live on what he sells of books, mail order, so pickings are lean.* They burn only wood, no electric, no washing machine, ice, carry water, etc., but I do hope they stick it through. There is real poverty, but liberty of spirit. Dave likes his beer and wine, but fortunately cannot afford too much of it, just enough to celebrate on feast days. Thank God Tamar is a sober soul. We have too much of the other on the line; even

---

* David Hennessy operated a mail-order business in books on Distributism (the works of Chesterton, Belloc, Gill, and such writers).

among our married, life is often made a hell. Do pray for us all. Nervous breakdowns, jails, drink, illness, sudden death—it's the lot of us all these disordered days. But I am not really discouraged. I think we are going straight along the appointed way for us, the only way for us. I never expected anything else, but the others did.

TO GERRY GRIFFIN

Dorothy's relationship with Gerry Griffin had reached a breaking point. After this letter he departed the Worker in bitterness. Later, when he proposed to return, she asked him not to.

[UNDATED, 1947]

I could curse and tear my hair out whenever I read one of your letters. As a matter of fact I never wanted to read it at all, but not to would be the equivalent of hanging up on the phone.

I want to accuse you of being anti-female and anti-clerical. Without knowing it you have been pretty well poisoned by the anti-Day elements around the Catholic Worker. I've seen it coming a long time. Whatever move I made would be combated. Subconsciously you'd like me to sit back and never do anything else. You don't really want women to help in the work; you don't mind them hanging around—it gives you a chance to be contemptuous—but you don't see any room for women in the work. You've come back with the idea firmly fixed in your head that the Grail and the clergy (through the retreat) have taken over. You want a chaplain on the farm, but you'd like him to be an automaton, deaf and dumb and no trouble, so you won't have to speak to him or work with him.

I am not content with just feeding people, just throwing them some food, clothing and lodging. I love them enough to want them to be happy. I want them to come and make retreats to be straightened out, because it is the only thing that ever will help them. The house on the island will be a house of hospitality for women, but run decently, with prayers, and singing and retreats. And it will be the first of many, I hope. I certainly don't ever again want to run the little sample of hells we had around here in the way of groups of women.

No, you are honest and conscientious and careful about money and will not spend money as the Coddingtons and Bill did. You will bury yourself in work, too. You will not eat your bread idle . But you have a fiendish pride that will be your ruin. It just happens to take another form. With all the false meekness of your letter, you show plainly enough how wrong you think I am. "I hope you know what you are doing." I see more clearly than ever before what I am doing.

I have tried to show my trust for you and confidence in you by turning over the trusteeship to the farm, by turning the paper over to you. But in your childishness, instead of doing the work on hand with your whole heart today, you have brooded around about bishops and cardinals and $15,000. Men hate change. I suppose what it really is, I, a woman, have taken to moving all the furniture just when you had a job on your hands, and you resent it.

I guess we just cannot work together. In that interval when you were home and going away, I kissed you goodbye those mornings when I woke you up, because I felt that you were lonely, that you were suffering here, and that you were going away again. You didn't want to go, and yet you didn't want to stay. Nothing is ever the same again, as we always find out. The desire that it should be is surely an adolescent one.

I told you before, that night we came home from the opera, that you should look around and find something that you liked to do. I think you are superlatively good at this work, but you are foolish enough to expect happiness. You can't take the Cross. So since you cannot take it, you might as well go. Certainly I can't stand these scenes, these glum and glouring moods. You asked me once if I wanted you to go. Of course I do not. But if it is for your happiness, if you can find some work abroad or at home that you like, I'd be glad to see you go. Your contentment in works shows your vocation for it, and you certainly are anything but content.

As for me, I'd love nothing better than to get out of it altogether in my selfishness and desire to settle down with Tamar and the children. But I feel there are certain things I must do before I settle down, and if I get them started I can truly stop.

I should be used to men failing me. I've had to bring up a child alone, and I've certainly seen more than my share of the gross and selfish in men. I've had many men love me but few protect me. As a matter of fact the love I've had has been hate too. It's better to have that purgatory here than later. I've wanted human love too much,

Do not be sorry for yourself nor emphasize your poverty. When you go to something else, surely you should take an outfit and some money. Only pride will keep you from it. You are rich in that. As for me, I am not sorry for myself either. I get what I deserve and I get what help I deserve. But if I were not convinced that I were right, and that this work had to be done, I surely would be most unhappy over such a letter as yours.

Love, Dorothy

TO AN INQUIRER

Dorothy received many letters requesting advice about how to open or operate a house of hospitality. This reply was published in the January 1948 issue of the Catholic Worker.

JANUARY 1948

Dear Fellow Worker in Christ:

Unless the seed fall into the ground and die, itself remaineth alone. But if it die it bringeth forth much fruit. So I don't expect any success in anything we are trying to do, either in getting out a paper, running houses of hospitality or farming groups, or retreat houses on the land. I expect that everything we do to be attended with human conflicts, and the suffering that goes with it, and that this suffering will water the seed to make it grow in the future. I expect that all our natural love for each other which is so warming and so encouraging and so much a reward of this kind of work and living, will be killed, put to death painfully by gossip, intrigue, suspicion, distrust, etc., and that this painful dying to self and the longing for the love of others will be rewarded by a tremendous increase of supernatural love amongst us all. I expect the most dangerous of sins cropping up amongst us, whether of sensuality or pride it does not matter, but that the struggle will go on to such an extent that God will not let it hinder the work but that the work will go on, because that work is our suffering and our sanctification. So rejoice in failures, rejoice in suffering! . . .

One of the reasons we have so many helpers I suppose is that we put up with each other, though criticism is rife, and I sometimes think I am living amongst a bunch of anarchists, so vehemently do all accept Peter Maurin's writings and conversations on personal responsibility and "being what you want the other fellow to be" (and St. Augustine's "Love God and do as you will"), all of which is interpreted as meaning "I am on my own," though living in a community of people. It is thus in a House, and thus on the Farms, which makes us like large headstrong families of vociferous people. We do keep more or less of a rule on the farm. We behave like a family in the House in town. People come to meals on time and try to get to bed at a reasonable hour, and it is generally recognized that daily Mass and communion are fundamental to the work. . . .

What are we trying to do? We are trying to get to heaven, all of us. We are trying to lead a good life. We are trying to talk about and write about the Sermon on the Mount, the Beatitudes, the social principles of the Church, and it is most astounding, the things that happen when you start trying to live this way. To perform the works of mercy becomes a dangerous practice. Our Baltimore House was closed as a public nuisance because we took in Negroes as well as whites. The boys were arrested and thrown in jail overnight and accused of running a disorderly house. The opposition to feeding the hungry and clothing the naked is unceasing. There is much talk of the worthy and the unworthy poor, the futility of such panaceas. And yet our Lord himself gave us these jobs to do in his picture of the last Judgment, and as Fr. Furfey said once, we are not excused for ignorance. It is a good thing to live from day to day and from hour to hour. . . .

One of the reasons we have so much help is it is voluntary and there is no "boss." Of course I have the right to say who cannot be head of a house, and the groups accept my authority there. But at the same time, I can pass a judgment and say "So and so does not represent the movement," and so and so will go right on representing the movement, and there are quite a few who believe themselves to be the only surviving Catholic Workers. Oh yes, our movement is full of generals, and full of Pecksniffs to such an extent that the air positively reeks with piety and smugness and self righteousness at times and I wonder people do not flee from us in disgust. I keep taking vows of holy silence to escape it, but I reek of it too. Alas. It is so easy to talk, and so hard to do. It is so easy to love people in theory. But anyway, we do hang on to those principles that each should be the least, should take the least place, that each should take less, so that others can have more, that each should regard himself as the worst. And then we go ahead and fall seven times daily, and seven times seven. . . .

We are convinced that the world can be saved only by a return to these ideas: voluntary poverty, manual labor, works of mercy, hospitality. They are fundamental. They are more important than getting out a paper, than lecturing, than writing books. And yet we have to do those things because we must give a reason, as St. Peter says, for the faith that is in us. ("And our faith must be tried as tho by fire," an old teaching.) . . .

Peter Maurin emphasized the primacy of the spiritual, the correlation of the spiritual and the material, translating these ideas into actual living today, whether in the city or the country, in shop, office, field, factory or workshop, as Kropotkin says.

With these war years we have come to emphasize more our opposition to the use of force, the necessity of sanctity, of aiming at perfection, at a spiritual renewal while undertaking the making of a new social order. Hence our emphasis on retreats.

To answer a few of your questions:

Help. We get helpers because we first of all do the work ourselves, scrubbing, cleaning, cooking, etc. If we have to do it alone, all right, but usually people walk in the door and seeing you enjoying yourself at such tasks as washing windows, they ask to help. . . . The dignity of labor, the joy of it, the penance of it, a philosophy of labor—all these things are matters of discussion while we actually work.

Leaders. We have no committees. Wherever in our houses we have had them they do not work. The person in charge of the house, living in the house, working there, is father and mother of the group. The Benedictine ideal, not the idea of majority rule. The leader may make mistakes, but he can repair them. He has to stand a lot of criticism, and keep going; or leave, or step down and let another take his place. People could take turns, but in general it is best to have one leader to take responsibilities and make decisions. We are absolutely opposed to committees. Personal responsibility, "littleness" are points too important to the work to be neglected. They are the very basis.

Money. Here where we get out the paper, we list what money comes in, we card catalogue it, because we send out the paper and have a mailing list. In the other houses what comes in is paid out for the bills by the head of the house and his authority and integrity is not questioned. If it is, he just bears it, unjust accusation and insinuation. If he is in charge, he receives contributions, pays the bills, and keeps no books any more than the average family does. There is never enough to worry about.

Relation to the Hierarchy. We do not feel that we need

permission from the clergy or bishops to start a house to practice the works of mercy. If they do not like it, they can tell us to stop and we will gladly do so. But asking them to approve *before* any work is done is like asking them to assume a certain amount of responsibility for us. We are the gutter sweepers of the diocese, the head of our Detroit house said once.

TO AMMON HENNACY

Ammon Hennacy (1893–1970), who at this time entered the Catholic Worker stage, brought with him a uniquely American brand of social activism. Imprisoned as a conscientious objector during World War I, his reading of the Bible had inspired him to embrace a form of Christian anarchism. Afterward he dedicated himself to living out his convictions with as much consistency and courage as he could muster—and he had vast reserves of both. He stood for the "One Man Revolution," the idea that each person could change the world by beginning with himself or herself. He began writing for the CW about his "life at hard labor" while living in the Southwest. When he finally met Dorothy Day, he felt that he had discovered his true soul-mate. To be sure, his feelings were not entirely platonic. Although the first pages of this early letter are missing, it is clear that Dorothy felt it necessary, from the start, to establish the boundaries of their relationship.

[C. JANUARY 1949]

[*2 pages missing*]

. . . a dear friend it is different. I feel you have a right. But not him. I kissed Dave Mason goodbye when he left. I felt so sorry for him, his temperament is so unfortunate—he just cannot work with others. But I certainly would never think of kissing Tom or Bob. I think older women must be pretty careful. There are so many silly ones, they degrade love. I have a great love for you of comradeship but sex does not enter into it. When one is celibate, one is celibate. There is no playing around with sex. I've always felt that way. I always felt one should go whole hog or not at all. But what an expression to use! It is "whole hog"—the liberal attitude to sex. Lenin had the right idea, in his letters to Rosa Luxemburg.

Oh, I will be so glad to see you—we will talk our heads off—but don't work me too hard. I have not your ferocious energy,

Love in Christ, Dorothy

Dorothy refers below to a brief marriage that followed her breakup with Lionel Moise and before she met Forster Batterham. She had never written about this episode, and she was surprised that Ammon somehow knew the story.

FEB 13 [1949]

Got some poems from Curtis Zahn who said you told him I had been married to Berkeley Tobey. How did you know that and where did you get your information? I often wonder how much of my past life is known by our friends and fellow workers and how much is gossip and how much true? Not that it matters. Womanly curiosity on my part.

As for this contact business—I would not have mentioned it but you brought it up first. My publisher, John Chambers, has the same way of kissing one on meeting and although I always return his greeting it makes me uneasy. I guess I take these things too seriously.

Funny—I went into this business in my book I'm writing—the reserve of the Anglo Saxon—I cannot help myself. I always feel I must crawl into my shell inside. I always was that way. The expression is not nice—but I believed in whole hog or not at all. I never did believe in playing around, dallying, going in for kissing and embracing unless I really meant something serious and ultimate. And I feel the same way now. I am a celibate by choice and intend so to remain, which is not surprising since I am 52 in Nov. I am glad I turned to God in my youth with all my ardor and energy. Fr. Hugo said once, quoting some saint, "The best thing to do with the best of things is to give them back to God." It is in that spirit that priests and nuns take vows of celibacy. Not because they are giving up something evil but something good and beautiful. But you got an idea of all this in my book *On Pilgrimage*.

I love to hear of what you are doing, your good useful life of hard labor. Hope you get the bread. It seems silly—such a mailing price. But that is a communion.

TO FRANCIS CARDINAL SPELLMAN

Cardinal Spellman, the Archbishop of New York, was the most powerful prelate of his time—the "American Pope." When the largely Catholic cemetery workers employed by the Archdiocese went on strike he took it personally. Charging them with acting under the influence of Communist agitators, Spellman arranged for Catholic seminarians to cross the picket line and dig the graves. He was "proud," he proclaimed, "to be a strikebreaker." In this light, Dorothy's decision to align herself publicly with the striking workers was a fairly significant act of defiance.

MARCH 4, 1949

Dear Cardinal Spellman,—

I am deeply grieved to see the reports in the papers last night and this morning, of your leading Dunwoodie seminarians into Calvary cemetery, past picket lines, to "break the strike," as all the papers say. Of course you know that a group of our associates at the Catholic Worker office in New York have been helping the strikers, both in providing food for their families, and in picketing. We understand that from the very beginning of the strike, there had been Communist offers of help which the strikers rejected. Instead they came to us, knowing that we were Catholic, thinking that in some way we could aid them. They have come to our meetings and to our discussions, and we know them and know that there is no Communist influence among them, that they are all Catholics. Their union is solidly Catholic.

I am writing to you because this strike, though small, is a terribly significant one in a way. Instead of people being able to say of us "See how they love one another," and "Behold, how good and how pleasant it is for brethren to dwell together in unity," now "we have become a reproach to our neighbors, an object of derision and mockery to those about us."

It is not just the issue of wages and hours as I can see from the conversation which our workers have had with the men. It is a question of their dignity as men, their dignity as workers, and the right to have a union of their own, and a right to talk over their grievances. Regardless of what the board of trustees can afford to pay, the wage is small compared to the wealth of the men represented on the board of trustees. But I do not wish to compare "horizontally," as Msgr. [Edward M.] Betowski used to warn us against in his conferences. Regardless of rich and poor, the class antagonism which exists between the well-to-do, those who live on Park Avenue and Madison Avenue, and those who dig the graves in the cemetery, the issue is always one of the dignity of the workers. It is a world issue.

As you know, we are pacifist. I remember talking to you about our position some years ago, pointing out that our position was that of pacifism in all wars, class war, race war, civil war, international war, world war. Living among the workers, in the slums, we have seen evidences of all these wars. Now finally we have what we never thought we would have among us, another sample of war, the bitterest, the saddest of all, the antagonisms between worker and Church, between the laity and the cleric. It is shocking to think of, and heartbreaking to witness.

These men are all Catholic. You are the outstanding Cardinal of the Church in America, a diplomat, a confidant and advisor of Pope and President. You are a Prince in the Church, and a great man in the eyes of the world, and these your opponents are all little men, hard-working, day laborers, hard-handed and hard-headed men, filled with their grievances, an accumulation of their grievances. They have wanted to talk to you, they have wanted to appeal to you. They felt that surely their Cardinal would not be against them.

And oh, I do beg you so, with all my heart, to go to them, as a father to his children. It is easier for the great to give in than the poor. They are hungry men, their only weapon has been their labor, which they have sold for a means of livelihood, to feed themselves and their families. They have indeed labored with the sweat of their brows, not lived off the sweat of anyone else. They have truly worked, they have been poor, they are suffering now. Any union organizer will tell you that it is not easy to get men out on strike and it is not easy to keep them out on strike. But the grievance has grown, the anger has grown here.

If there were only some way to reach peace. I am sure that the only way is for you to go to them. You have been known to walk the streets among your people, and to call on the poor parishes in person, alone and unattended. Why cannot you go to the union, ask for the leaders, tell them that as members of the Mystical Body, all members are needed and useful and that we should not quarrel together, that you will meet their demands, be their servant as Christ was the servant of His disciples, washing their feet.

[*Though the rest of this text is missing, Dorothy elaborated publicly on her position in the April 1949 issue of the* CW.]

TO FRITZ EICHENBERG

Fritz Eichenberg, a German-born artist and convert to Quakerism, was one of the great wood engravers of the twentieth century. He achieved fame for his illustration of literary classics by Dostoevsky, Tolstoy, and the Brontes. After their meeting at a Quaker retreat, Dorothy asked Eichenberg if he would contribute some of his work to the Catholic Worker. *This was the beginning of a deep friendship. It also marked a permanent transformation of the visual appearance of the paper. Eichenberg's illustrations—such as his "Christ of the Bread-*

line," or his "Labor Cross"—*were an artistic expression of the spirituality otherwise communicated through words. For his part, Eichenberg
recognized in the Catholic Worker the deepest expression of his own
moral vision. In this initial letter, Dorothy shares news of the death of
Peter Maurin, co-founder of the Catholic Worker, on May 15, 1949.
Eichenberg responded with drawings of Maurin.*

MAY 1949

Peter Maurin died Sunday, was buried Wednesday and Thursday a.m. your beautiful gift came and I wept over it. I was so
moved with joy. We will have them for our next issue in which
we write of Peter. They are exactly right, and how can we ever
express our gratitude? The others feel as I do.

In Christ, Dorothy Day

TO HELENE ISWOLSKY

*Helene Iswolsky was the daughter of the last czarist ambassador to
France. After immigrating to New York, she became a writer and scholar.
She also founded a circle called "The Third Hour" to promote dialogue
among Catholic, Protestant, and Orthodox intellectuals. Dorothy was
drawn into this circle and she and Helene became close friends. In
later years, before her death, Helene would come to live at the Catholic
Worker farm.*

JULY 5, 1949

Thank you for your good letter. It was a very bad time indeed
for you at the time of Peter's funeral and I am so sorry that you
have been overworked. We are talking about Peter so much
and really, in a way, expecting so much from him. He had been
sick for so long and now I have somewhat a feeling as though he
had gone off on a trip and is very busy about the apostolate. He
used to leave to go off on three- to five-month journeys and
we would be getting repercussions of his visits all over the
country.

Do try to rest this summer. I am a little afraid that the Dominicans regard us with suspicion and very much feel that we are verging on heresy. I don't think our ideas are so much mentioned in European journals as our stress on the corporal works of mercy. Doubtless the retreat "heresy" or the pacifism "heresy" or the anarchist "heresy." At any rate they pay pretty close attention to us at the Chancery Office so we feel safe here. Also as Peter used to say, "It causes to think."

TO TAMAR

The Hennessys were growing restless in West Virginia, but Dorothy discouraged them from moving north.

2 AUGUST 1949

Thank God the heat has broken a little. But it is still muggy. The paper went to press yesterday and arrived this morning and I'm air-mailing one this afternoon. I am trying the various ways of reaching you. I get all your letters all right, unless you send them to the farm and they have to be forwarded.

You do worry me with talk of [moving to] Washington. I wouldn't mind your going to the city if you hung on to the farm. Just rent in town, and see what it is like. Oh dear. I do know how lonely you are, but I do assure you that a mother with small babies is always lonely. She is really in isolation. Even Marge [Hughes] here doesn't see too much of anyone. Days pass without people dropping in, and here she is right next door. But of course, just the consciousness of people being near is a comfort. And also you can have too much company, as I remember down on Huguenot.

There is a real polio epidemic here, cases increasing every day. The papers keep warning everyone to keep their children out of crowds and not to let them get over-tired. Marge is worried of course. The noise is terrific with all the windows open. But I will have a couple of days in the country this week, and all next week with you God willing. So be prepared for my arrival. Kill a fatted chicken. I'm dying to see you. I'll bring some records along, if it is the last thing I do. I have a most beautiful symphony of Tchaikovsky and I'll get some folk songs.

AUGUST 14, 1949, VIGIL OF THE ASSUMPTION

I always hate to leave you so much. You and yours are the dearest things in the world to me, as you well know, and I suffer with your sufferings, and am lonely with you, and worn out with you, etc., altogether too much. After all, it is silly to try to carry someone else's cross. I do love you and Dave so much though and would give anything to see you settled better. The one thing I was trying to say when I was leaving you was that wherever you go, people will be immersed in their own problems and may seem unfriendly, but you yourselves must be friendly too. I love that quotation from St. John of the Cross, "Where there is no love, put love, and you take out love." It really works.

You love other people, and they love you. Your friendliness evokes theirs. You always give the impression of being an independent soul.

I'll be praying for a place for you, and a job for David, and that you will be all settled before the baby comes. Do write often and tell me how things are progressing.

Much much love, Dorothy

TO EMILY COLEMAN

Emily Coleman, a writer and poet, led a colorful life. In her youth in Paris she had served as a secretary to the anarchist Emma Goldman, then moved to New York where she converted to Catholicism, with Jacques Maritain serving as her godfather. She grew close to the Catholic Worker after attending retreats in the late 1940s and for many years wrote a column from Peter Maurin Farm. Though she later moved to England, she eventually returned to spend her last years at the CW farm at Tivoli. There she died of a brain tumor in 1974.

AUGUST 22, 1949

What a horrible job you've got! If you are willing to take a job standing on your feet, why don't you get a job as ward maid in a hospital where you would be far more useful?

Selling dresses, indeed! It may be recreation as well as a rest for mind and soul, but oh, dear, you are catering to woman's vanity and contributing to their delinquency, etc., and in other ways delaying the revolution.

Hope to see you soon.

In Christ, Dorothy

TO TAMAR

Responding to Tamar's complaints about her life, Dorothy wrote with rather startling frankness. This exchange marked a low point in their relationship.

SEPT 10, 1949

I am glad you enjoyed your visit, and it certainly is good of David to be willing to take charge of the children that way so that you can go on visits. I am sitting here drinking a cup of tea because we have run out of coffee and we are so broke I can't go to the store to get it. I had tea on hand so am rather enjoying that.

As for your situation, there is not a place to rent on Staten Island according to newspapers or real estate men, or personal friends whom we have had looking. Your situation cannot be taken care of so quickly or easily. It is just not possible today to move around on account of the complete lack of places to move to. It used to be that people could change apartments or move from town to town, but it is certainly so no more. That is why we keep stressing that the municipal lodging is full of women and children whose husbands have jobs but still they cannot find themselves a home. As you say, you have no money for a down payment on another place. By the time you sold out, paid your debts, moved, there would not be enough left for a down payment. And besides keeping up payments would depend on whether or not Dave could get a job, keep it, and his health.

This place is packed to the doors. There is not even the four rooms here available as the two back rooms have three women in them since the top floor is all taken. Last time you were without David we had the entire four rooms and then you said you would never inflict this on the children again. As for the farm, there are nothing but dormitories, and the carriage house is a freezer in winter. It would be impossible with the children. So you must just settle down and wait.

I am convinced after constant thought on the situation that you will just have to grit your teeth and bear it for a while and see what turns up. Nothing can be settled in a month, so when you say you wish I'd come down, bring you back with me while David settled up, it is impossible. If you do it, or insist upon David doing it, I tell you there is no place here for you. You have no idea what rents are. Also that prices here are double too because the cost of living has gone up.

Frankly, I think David does not want to move at all, and that you are the one who is insisting upon it. You have been talking about a job for him for the past couple of years. I do not think he could find a job or keep up with one if he did. And I do not think it is worth doing, here in the city. Bookshops, yes, but I've inquired about that chain book store business and there are no jobs. Unemployment is increasing everywhere, and young college men are delighted to work for little. So a family man doesn't have a chance.

Many a time in my life I have felt just as trapped as you do, with your children coming and so much hard work. But the fact is that you have a home, even though it is in such shape, and 75 most beautiful acres. You have shelter, and your children are happy there, and you have enough to eat. And all I see around me every day is human misery increasing, breadlines growing longer, unemployment getting worse. Your situation does not look so bad to me as the situations around here. You may think

Marge has it nice and cozy, but she lives in the middle of hell, with four children now cooped up in a dingy apartment shrieking and quarrelling and when they go on the streets or playground in imminent danger. And Joe sitting around doing nothing, not a lick of work, and everyone in the house despising them for eating here, and using their unemployment insurance which still goes on, just for rent and staples. There is not a person in the house who does not say, why doesn't he support his children, what is he doing hanging around? You talk of Catholic Worker families. You will notice that we have no Catholic Worker families except them. Even the families we help are on the relief roles besides. The Catholic Worker families at Easton are grubbing along somehow on their twenty-seven acres. People are lonely wherever they are.

I shall write you very frankly, and if you wish to get mad, very well: you talk about being alone, but I warned you when I was there last, that you find the people around you hateful wherever you are, because you have got in the habit of criticizing them, not loving them yourself, being unforgiving, harping on their defects. It would be the same anywhere. You are bitter and critical and you have admitted it yourself. No matter what one does for you, you are not really grateful, you keep talking of people doing nothing to help you or David. You have been helped ever since your marriage. You have had the fruits of my toil, which has meant not only the thousand dollars you got for your place at Easton (because a good deal of that place was paid for by my *House of Hospitality*) but you got the thousand from the place on Staten Island. You got money for the truck, which was by no means earned by you, or was coming to you, and I spent at least five hundred those months I was with you. You were given your cow. You are given things constantly, books, clothes, and you are not only not thankful, and do not acknowledge them but you complain the more. You ate with the CW at Easton, the CW paid for the feed for your animals, you took from the common store. You have ever since your marriage five years ago been helped and helped and helped. And your whole attitude is that you are never helped. I think that no matter what is done for you, you will be the same and that wherever you are, you will be unhappy and lonely, and disliking people around you.

When you were a little girl you used to try to like people and side with them. I remember you defending Frank O'Donnell and Mr. Breen and Kate Smith when others criticized them.

A few people may have fed you the idea that you were abused and neglected but if I had had to earn my living on a job, you would have been away from me all the time, in school perhaps. As it was, you traveled with me, you have been to Mexico, Hollywood, Florida, Nova Scotia, Atlantic City,—if you begin to count up Newport, Canada, the Grail,—your contacts with people, your privileges, and begin trying to feel grateful instead of feeling abused, it would be very good for your soul.

I remember telling David once, down at Easton, before you married, that your critical attitude must be the result of his companionship—he laughed at you for your tart remarks, your pugnacious spirit, and developed it further. I told him when you were nasty to Miss Clemens that you never used to be that way. Instead of trying to help each other to be better, to be more calm and loving and helpful, you have dragged each other down. And I blame the woman more than the man. I have seen that you nagged at him, did not try to develop his good qualities, did not really help him in his intellectual work either. He has a splendid mind and I am sure more opportunities will open up for him in the future. But meanwhile, neither of you work much. You sit around, you let things run down, you wait for others to help you, you let discouragement make you sour and mean.

I know that any woman with a bunch of kids cannot possibly keep up with things herself, but I do know that you could do much more than you do. Especially in keeping an optimistic spirit, a thankful spirit. I am blaming you for not cheering and encouraging David on, not loving him enough. I know you love each other (and of course you are going to make each other suffer).

You were this way in January when I was down to see you, and in spite of the fact that I had just had an operation and then had a bad cold, you had temper tantrums, throwing things on the floor, letting yourself go. I made up my mind then that I would not come down any more, that I could do nothing for you. I relented, but I have come to the conclusion that I do not help you, but am further spoiling you.

This letter of course is going to make you more angry than ever, but I'd rather have the thing come to a head now than drag out this way for years. I continue to say that I will help you when I can. I will send a girl down to you to help when the baby comes, and hope that she will not be scandalized by your temper and your attitude to the Catholic Worker. As a matter of fact, David is quite capable of taking care of the children and we do not even need to do that. I am only writing this letter because every letter you write gets worse. And I am convinced I do you harm by giving in to you. I have seen it in others, and so I know I make myself guilty too. I am convinced that it is only when you have no alternative will you settle down and buckle to and try yourself to get straightened out. When I have seen your temper, I have felt, God help the children and David. They have already started to side with him, as I saw in the case of Becky when I was cleaning the yard and fixing the window. You will end up by not even getting any help from them.

If I thought I were really helping you, I'd work my fingers to the bone. But I have got to be hard, and it kills me to do so. I just won't write again until you get over it, until you make up your mind to make the best of things, do your share in the marriage and quit complaining.

Love, Dorothy

TO EMILY COLEMAN

SEPTEMBER 17, 1949

I am terribly sorry that I hurt your feelings by what seems to be my lack of understanding. I forget that you are not used to us around here; we, all of us, regard you as an old friend, yet you haven't after all got used to our severe attitudes toward each other. If you had lived around here for one week, you would perhaps get hardened to us.

This whole attitude toward work is something we have been emphasizing for years. I certainly do not take it lightly that you have to go out and try to help support your children and grandchildren.

With much love, Dorothy

P.S. Tamar too is having such a hard time—so lonely for her there. Please pray for us.

PART IV

Bearing Witness

1950–1959

By the 1950s, Dorothy had in large part found her distinctive voice.
Her unapologetic radicalism, her immersion in the world of the poor,
her dedication to peace, and her disciplined life of prayer and sacrament had become for her a seamless garment. With the arrival of
Ammon Hennacy in New York, the Catholic Worker entered a new
era of activism. In these years, Dorothy regularly returned to jail for
her part in annual protests against the city's compulsory civil defense
drills. During a time of Cold War fears, conformism, and the pursuit
of prosperity, the Worker—with a vision rooted in the Sermon on the
Mount—offered a strikingly countercultural witness.

This witness extended, as well, to the cult of success, bigness,
and power. It was in these years that Dorothy applied herself to study
and write about the Little Way of St. Therese of Lisieux. Like the
mystery of Redemption itself, she believed the most important events
in history were hidden in obscurity, the most powerful forces were
disguised in apparent failure.

TO WILLIAM EVERSON

William Everson, who had spent the war years in a camp for conscientious objectors, helped found the Oakland Catholic Worker. Later, in 1951, he would join the Dominicans under the name Brother Antoninus, and achieve wide recognition as one of the "Beat" poets.

APRIL 4, 1950

Thank you a thousand times for the beautifully lettered card. I shall think of you when I use it.

There are always so many things on my mind—I had forgotten about your manuscript. I gave [it] to Fr. Duggan to read because you had written him about Mary [*another member of the Oakland CW*] and told him to pass the letter on to me. I wanted him to read and talk over the article with me, to get his ideas on the subject, tho I know I did say we would not be using it. I am very sorry you were hurt in any way by what you considered deviousness on my part. I mean always to be direct. I had truly wanted to talk over your article with you—and with the idea of the *Commonweal* or *Catholic World* in mind. Also we had wanted more of your poems for the Lenten issue. . . . I am very happy about your going to the Franciscans—there are some wonderful men among them. There is worldliness too—of course, but it seems to me we must keep our eye on the ideal, and away from the faults—a turning to God and away from creatures. I am probably just writing nonsense, being all hollow and a bit tired from Mass. Please pray for us all—we are such faulty creatures, so inadequate for the work we have taken on ourselves. One reason for this fast—it is an opportunity for a bit of penance.* We profess so much and do so little.

Love to you and Mary—I do feel so close to you both.

---

* Dorothy and other Catholic Workers were participating in a week-long Fast for Peace in Washington, D.C., initiated by the Peacemakers.

TO CLARE BOOTH LUCE
Clare Booth Luce, wife of the publishing magnate Henry Luce, was a prominent Catholic laywoman who combined careers in politics and journalism.

MAY 6, 1950

> Mrs. Henry Luce
> The Waldorf-Astoria Hotel

I never did write to thank you for your generous sympathy and telephoning when I was operated upon last year.

I am not sure whether or not you get the paper, but you will see by this issue that we are being forced to buy a house to continue our activities in sheltering the odds and ends of people who come to us. One of the women, a mental case, who stayed with us for some time, said to me once, "A dog can stretch himself and a man can lie on a park bench, but a woman just has to stay up all night." There are so many cases just coming out of mental hospitals or out of Bellevue who have no place to turn and we are sure you will be interested in helping us with this particular work even though you may not be in agreement with many aspects of our program.

The house we are trying to get is the old Paulist convent on West 61st Street and it is a tremendous bargain as real estate goes in New York City. There are two adjoining houses so we can have both men and women together. We already have eight of the $25,000 needed and we have to move in a month, so you see how urgent our need is. Do please help us as much as you can.

Gratefully yours in Christ, Dorothy Day

TO AMMON HENNACY
Ammon made a point of visiting the New York CW from time to time. Dorothy greatly admired his courage and his commitment to principle.

No one, she observed, worked harder, fasted longer, picketed more faithfully than Ammon. But she reproached him for his over-idealized picture of her as well as his habitual anti-clericalism.

MAY 9, 1950

Many times since you left I have been thinking how our crowded lives make us neglect those dear to us. Instead of doing a few things well, we do many things badly. We get so rushed with visitors that we don't think. What I am talking about is that I have felt terribly upset and guilty that I did not give you a contribution to help you on your way back. The trouble with you is that you are so strong no one would think of helping you unless you asked for it. One feels that hunger or abundance, either one or the other, you will take with equanimity and that food means little in your life,—just what you need to keep yourself fit and strong, and that is all. You should not talk about our poverty, when you yourself practice it far more perfectly. You have altogether too high a conception of me, and it embarrasses me terribly when you pull these lines in what you write, about what I am capable of. I am a very weak creature indeed. The only thing is, I can try to do better, and if you keep on praying for me, holding me in prayer in your thoughts, I am bound to do better. So do keep on, my dear.

You say in your account that Fr. Deacy is the only priest friend in New York who is not afraid to be known as a friend of the Worker. If you looked at our files you would find them filled with priests in New York who contribute to the work. Many would write for us if we would let them. We do not like to run the writings of priests because ours is a lay paper, and whenever we start to run the stuff of people like Fr. Hugo, Fr. Chrysostom, Fr. Duffy, etc., they get longer and longer and soon they'd take up half the paper. I am afraid you are always giving the impression to people that we are widely separated from the hierarchy, and we have so many friends among the priests and bishops all over the country. They are not articulate like you and do not have too much opportunity to get out and be an apostle. People are shy, you know, and have different temperaments. I myself always dread getting out on street corners, picketing, or giving out literature. I do it because it is part of my work. I do not feel that it is part of priests' work. As for pacifism, the need is to make public opinion. The priests are confronted with so many do-nothings, that they believe, as Gandhi did, that to kill and be killed is better than cowardice. I do admit that they are blind in regard to the state, and pacifism. But I am convinced if we keep on with our propaganda, more and more will be convinced. Priests are like the majority of laymen on these subjects.

Anyway, I do not believe in slamming them, or giving the impression that we are separate from the clergy. We are all members of the Mystical Body of Christ, and there is a great bond there so we must feel each other's failings as our own. Look how friendly so many of the priests are with you. You will win some of them yet.

I'm sorry we did not have chop suey together. It is again a matter of being rushed. Why didn't you say you would have loved some. We missed a nice opportunity to run out and escape and have it together. I should think more of people's diets. As it is, we all eat what is sent in or set before us. That is one reason we do not take better care of our diets.

Anyway, please excuse me for these corrections. It is the price you will have to pay for greater intimacy with me. If I did not care so much for you, I'd let all these things pass. I promise never to say anything again about you becoming a Catholic. I think I do wrong in that, interfering in any way with people's free will is blasphemy. But still, as friends, when you make what I consider a misstatement, then I feel I must not let it pass. It is like slurs on my Mother.

I am so tired today I can hardly work. City life is bad. The noise, the rush, the heat which is now beginning. If we moved to Staten Island I'd commute and that would mean a long peaceful ferry ride and days of hard labor.

I admire you and love you, Ammon, so do not mind my defense of the Church which is everything to me.

In Christ, Dorothy Day

TO BILL AND DOROTHY GAUCHAT

Dorothy Gauchat met her husband Bill when, as a teenager, she volunteered at the Cleveland Catholic Worker. Over the years she and Dorothy Day became close friends. Among their several children, the Gauchats had a severely handicapped daughter. This experience, in part, steered them toward their special vocation of opening a Catholic Worker–style house for the care of mentally handicapped children.

JUNE 15, 1950

Grand to hear from you, my valiant ones, but I wept over your letter. It is terrible to see a child suffer. I certainly shall remember you also, especially Susie (since I have a Susie myself) in my prayers. I have been remembering her, too. God has some purpose behind everything. I have been so discouraged about the new house, the cost of it, the loss of our appearance of poverty, and the trouble about the farm. Having to work on both angles at once, makes it so hard. Then yesterday Fr. Joachim called, you remember him as the one who gave the 1939 retreat, and he said he had called to console me, to tell me that God was nearest when he seemed farthest away. And it did help too. Also I picked up Acts this morning and read about Barnabas, which means the man of encouragement. I do know that discouragement is the temptation of the devil.

TO AMMON HENNACY

JULY 19, 1950

Your letters are so good. It is wonderful to know too, that if I have to go to jail you will somehow or other keep in touch with me and get letters in to me, and if you cannot, it will not be for your not trying. People are all so busy—it horrifies me to think of people in jail, and their friends and associates on the outside forgetting about them, or at least letting the press of other work crowd them out of their consciousness. I do not write as often as you, but you know that I think of you often and pray for you always. You give me strength, as I said before, and I thank God for you.

Our new house is at 223 Chrystie Street, two doors below Houston. Chrystie St. is a continuation of Second Ave and between Chrystie and Forsyth the whole long street of tenements was torn down and made a park with trees and playgrounds for children. Plenty of benches for mothers and kids. So we face that now instead of another row of tenements.

We will be a bit too comfortable, I'm afraid, oil heat and a few bathrooms. However, we can keep the heat turned down.

I *do* believe in a personal God. I have had too many prayers answered in a direct personal way. Also I believe in praying to the saints, our friends for help. I believe in the resurrection of the body (a glorified body) and life everlasting. That is in the Creed. I'm going to pray to the Little Flower to send you a rose some time just to confound you, so that you will begin to think there is something in this personal business. They are as personal as you and I. Also our Lord Jesus Christ, who is God too, a most personal God, who fed the hungry, healed the sick, and shared the fish on the seashore with Peter.

Keep on praying for me, my dear.

Love, Dorothy

TO WILLIAM EVERSON

FEAST OF ST. PETER'S CHAINS, AUGUST 1, 1950

Thank you for your beautiful letter and the beautiful poem. At this time of war again, it is meet to use a poem like "The Making of the Cross."

It is unbelievably beautiful to me that you two out there can be so abandoned to divine providence, so inert in the hand of God, in the midst of the tumult, even though silent tumult, of poverty and need. To be so surrounded at all times by human beings who are reaching out to you for love and warmth and light is to be surrounded by tumult. I am trying to spend two hours in church every morning before my days begin just to get the strength to go on. And end my days there too. Only these hot nights we sometimes go out and just walk the streets for the breath of air that comes from the bay. It seems to me that you are holding up the work by your prayer. Pray that we learn to pray, that we all learn love of prayer.

Love to all, in Christ, Dorothy

TO A BENEFACTOR [*Katherine McKinnon*]

Dorothy describes a truly anxious time of juggling various real estate transactions. The CW was moving into a new house on Chrystie Street; she had decided to buy a new farm on Staten Island; and meanwhile she faced complications with the sale of the farm in Newburgh.

AUGUST 4 1950

Lately I've been reading Sister Elizabeth of the Holy Trinity and was impressed by the emphasis in her life and writings on prayer and silence and the "praise of glory" in our lives that should make our life here a beginning of heaven. And this reading has been a temptation to me to do no more than I had to in the active line. We had already been hard pressed about getting another place since we were evicted from Mott St. but the Lord took care of that for us, and we have our new home which we will begin to live in September 18. Meanwhile, we are cramped in, doubled up, in half our usual space so that the new owners of Mott Street can start repairs on the rear house.

Last November I had very peaceably begun negotiations to sell the Newburgh farm and buy a property on Staten Island, which is thirty cents carfare away from New York. I paid a thousand dollars down on Staten Island, money which I received from Harper & Bros. for my new book [*The Long Loneliness*]. Then on my return from the West Coast, all hell in the shape of activity began popping. We got our eviction notice here in New York, had to hunt and find a new place, raise thirty thousand dollars for it, and meanwhile go on with the Newburgh transaction. There too was trouble. I was owner, trustee for the Catholic Worker. But I had no legal right, it seems to use the word Trustee. Trustee for what? For the poor? And who are they? Trustee for the names listed on the masthead of the Catholic Worker?

But three priests whose opinion I value highly, urged me go on with the Staten Island place, that no obstacles I mentioned were insuperable, not even the one about too much activity, since what we were working for was for more places for people to come and hear the Word of God, and praise Him.

So this morning, being hard pressed, I asked a sign from the Holy Ghost, as to whether or not I should go on with the purchase, if it was God's will. And I, like the importunate widow, set a limit in my demands of our personal God. I said I wanted a sign by eleven o'clock. At ten-thirty a friend called and said she would contribute two thousand if we could raise the other three needed. The owners offer to take a five percent mortgage if we pay five thousand down. So I am writing to our friends to beg their help. Surely we can find a few in the next week to contribute to this retreat house on Staten Island.

Our Father is a millionaire, of course, but it is His other children who have the purse and who can help us. So I am begging of you even though you have all your obligations out there, in your own diocese and your own retreat house and charities. You have always made me feel your loving interest in our work, so do please help us as much as you can. We only have a week, as the owners have patiently waited since last November as it is, for this sale to be cleared up. If I had not had this so direct sign this morning I would have dropped the whole matter even though it meant losing part if not all of my own original thousand. Do let me hear soon!

Gratefully in Christ

TO AMMON HENNACY

Inspired by Dorothy's example, Ammon began to show an increasing interest in the Catholic Church. For Dorothy, this was literally an answer to prayer. But as Ammon later admitted, the appeal of Catholicism was largely the appeal of Dorothy Day. "If she had operated the Mormon Worker," he noted, "I would have become a Mormon."

AUGUST 16, 1950

I had a lovely visit with my daughter at the ranch. What a terrible tie a family is! We forget everything else except them.

But now I remember the quotation that I wanted to tell you about. It came in the mails this morning from John Doebele, a quotation from Martin Buber:

> Love is the responsibility of an I for a *you*. In this lies the likeness of all who love . . . from the blessedly protected man, whose life is rounded in that of a loved being, to him who is all his life nailed to the cross of the world, and who ventures to bring himself to the dreadful point, to love all men.

Certainly it is a suffering these days with the world situation as it is. It would be so easy just to settle down with Tamar and the kids and write, and get away from all this furor of New York and argument about peace. But now it begins all over again with the war situation what it is. It is really thrilling to read how people are won over little by little. It shows how much can be done by the Gandhi method.

I hope your silence does not mean that you have collapsed from your fast. I am sure that you were able to hold up with your years of discipline behind you. Do take some time out and write an account of your fast and of our picketing.

Much love to you from all of us, Dorothy

P.S. I was so happy to hear that you went to Mass every morning and that you have begun to feel that you understand the Cross. I am going to send you one to wear. Do what your heart teaches you and stop thinking about theology. We must have a long talk about it some time. Father Hugo has written some very fine things about it. If you will take the time to read the books, I will send them on to you. Again, much love.

[C. SEPT 1950]

It is so hard for me to answer your letters because they move me so, and besides I want to be alone when I answer them, so I can think, and not surrounded by so many people as I am so much of the time. Your letters make me love you very much, you are so sincere and one can see the growth in simplicity and humility too. I don't feel in the least worthy of the affection you give me, and your praise. Both Bob [Ludlow] and Irene [Naughton] and I feel that you just don't know us with all our failings. And yet I think you would love us just the same. That is the only kind of love which is worthwhile, that persists even though we may become oppressed by the faults of the others, that sees all the virtues that are there, the Christ in each of us. You are very close to us all. I read bits of your letters to the others and it does them good. You are so strong in the Gandhian technique, which is the Christ technique, to transform others, to change their attitudes, instead of just winning a victory over them. It made your account very stirring. All the little things are so important.

You have great strength, which means that God is giving you much grace because certainly by yourself you could not do all you do. Everyone has a different talent, has different abilities, genius, and yours is of a very particular brand. Not everybody can get out and picket, meet others, fast, work, keep that cheerful, unresentful attitude. Some must be silent, they are born that way, and some must suffer. Many ills do not come through diet, but are mysterious, are sent to try us and strengthen us in other ways. And I think too we help bear the suffering of the world by our own actual sufferings sometimes. Not that we should not be careful of our diet but we cannot impose it on others. Good whole wheat bread, plenty of vegetables and fruits—those one-dish meals that you like so much are wonderful. I like nothing better than to get some pounds of squash and go up to Marge [Hughes's] and have a one-dish meal of squash boiled with garlic and oil, or grapes and cheese. Marge is ill right now, a strep throat, and we are taking care of all her children up at the farm. It is hard too, to be always taking care of people who go on smoking, drinking coffee all day, sitting up too late, not walking, etc, etc., but you have to change people's hearts and minds first before you can do anything, and you can only do that by love and an uncritical attitude and by example. We have enough trouble looking after our own habits without questioning others.

I am a bit afraid of writing too much to you for fear of saying too much or too little. I was so thrilled by your religious experience that third day of your fast. You know I had been praying especially for you, and I was praying particularly that you have an experience of God's personal love,—a feeling that He is a personal God to whom we lift our hearts and minds in adoration, love and supplication. Not to speak of contrition. We have to be sorry to fall so far short of infinite truth, beauty, and love, to be so faithful.

Did you ever read my book, *From Union Square to Rome*? Those last chapters about Holy Communion are answering my brother's objections. I could get you a copy if you want it. I like you to read what I write, because I always write personally, and then you know what I am thinking and feeling.

I am so busy on the book now, going to the library every day to work on it so as to be quiet. We are getting the Staten

Island place too, with its 22 acres where people can come and spend the day in discussions of war and peace, the good life, our faith and its implications.

I would like to impress upon you how I feel about the Church. Of course conscience comes first, but just the same, nothing would ever drive me from the Church. No pronouncement from the Pope or the Bishops, no matter how wrong I thought them, would cause me to leave the Church. I would rather stop the work, keep silent and wait. The spiritual weapons of prayer and sufferings would do more to further any cause than protest and defiance. God writes straight with crooked lines, and arrogance and pride would do more to wreck a cause than any pronouncement from the hierarchy.

Not that I anticipate being stopped, being suppressed by the Church. As a matter of fact, I heard the FBI went to the Chancery office during the war and wanted them to stop us, but they refused. The fact of the matter is that with all their mistakes, all their expediency, all their diplomacy, the churchmen still believe so profoundly in human freedom that there is far more leeway than anyone believes in expressing oneself. Even in making mistakes. Perhaps it is more the laity who have this freedom.

There is the tradition that all reforms come about from the bottom up, from the masses, from the people. All dogma such as that of the Immaculate Conception and the Assumption is first of all believed and accepted by the masses of people before it is pronounced a dogma. It would be the same with war. There would have to be a widespread acceptance of heroic love as a means and we have to do our job of agitating and educating before the bishops would impose burdens on the faithful which they are not prepared to accept. Their own attitude toward the state is wrong; they fear it but they do not oppose it, in word or deed. It is the attitude of persecuted people too often. But the persecution will get worse I am afraid.

Thank God you are not the hopeless sort because things do look pretty hopeless from the human point of view. And I also since I am so busy from morning to night with people, the writing, business, etc. Not to speak of family once in a while. I had a lovely four-day visit with Tamar and they did forward me your letters, and I thank you for them all. I treasure them indeed. Two twenty-one year old boys just came in and want to talk about Gandhi of whom they have just heard. We will loan them *Satyagraha* and while they wait for me and Bob they are reading your article. Remember always, I love you and pray for you and I count on your prayers.

TO WILLIAM EVERSON

OCTOBER 11, 1950
FEAST OF THE MATERNITY OF THE BLESSED VIRGIN MARY

Your poem was too late for October but what a wonderful one for the Nov. issue—the month of the dead. It is an awe-inspiring thing—I am glad you sent it. These days, when we may be pushed into War III—we should all feel on the edge.

God certainly listens to our prayers. Had been ill recently, an operation threatened, and now the doctors say I do not need one yet. However, we all do need proper sleep and quiet and much prayer so do as much as you can. At our new farm—the Peter Maurin Farm—we have a sick priest—he has just been a year in a mental hospital. For his sake we will limit the numbers living here. However our work days meant 40 people last Saturday and our Sundays will be very crowded too.

I am so happy about our new homes, on Chrystie St.—and here at Staten Island. The poverty of Maurin House, Oakland and Maurin House Chicago shames us. We must try for more and more personal detachment. I am so glad you have the press! We need to bring beauty in the midst of ugliness. It honors and glorifies God. To see such beauty from a dung-heap of a slum!

Let us love one another and uphold one another by our prayer.

In Christ, Dorothy

TO MONSIGNOR EDWARD GAFFNEY

Msgr. Gaffney was at this time Dorothy's principal contact at the New York Chancery Office. One day he summoned Dorothy to tell her that the Catholic Worker *would either have to cease publication or change its name. She pondered for some days how to respond to this instruction. Opinions at the CW differed widely. Finally, Dorothy composed this letter. "No one liked it," she noted in her diary.*

JANUARY 28, 1951

FEAST OF ST. THOMAS AQUINAS

(AND WE BEG HIS PRAYERS)

First of all I wish to assure you of our love and respectful obedience to the Church, and our gratitude to this Archdiocese which has so often and so generously defended us from many who attacked us.

I wish too to say that it is because we do not wish to take advantage of such kindness, nor to count on the official protection which the name Catholic brings us, that led me to say the other day that we could change the name rather than cease publication of the *Catholic Worker.*

You very rightly advised me to talk matters over with the staff here and to let you know the results of our conference.

No one of course wishes to change the name. All feel that the *Catholic Worker* has been in existence for eighteen years, since May 1933, under that name, and that this is no time to change it, so late in the day. I am sure no one thinks the Catholic War Veterans (who also use the name Catholic) represent the point of view of the Archdiocese any more than they think the *Catholic Worker* does.

We could very well, however, put a box under our masthead each month (dropping the notice that we are members of the Catholic Press Association) which would publicly point out the fact that the opinions expressed in our journal are those of the writers whose names are signed and are not to be confused as an official point of view, as *the* Catholic point of view. That it is recognized that we are aiming at clarification of thought, always listed as the first plank in Peter Maurin's program.

"We are all ready to receive respectfully and give practical heed and application to all scientific, scholarly criticism and correction of mistakes; to all disciplinary directions as to wrong-doing, and to all theological or spiritual censures of theological spiritual errors."*

But we cannot simply cease the publication of a review which has been built up, with its worldwide circulation of 63,000 over the last 18 years. This would be a grave scandal to our readers and would put into the hands of our enemies, the enemies of the Church, a formidable weapon. I would hate to see such writers as Paul Blanshard, the *Nation*, the *Daily Worker*, and the *New Republic* hastening to our defense.†

I will admit that I personally am at fault in not being more careful as editor and censor. It is my job as publisher and editor and it has always I know been expected of me at the Chancery. I confess that I have not given sufficient time to the matter of the paper, being occupied with so many other cares.

But regardless as to whether or not I am at fault, I and my associates have spent years in a study of the social order working at the same time for a new society within the shell of the old, a communitarian society as opposed to the capitalist, the corporative *order*, as opposed to the corporative state.

Recognition of the clarification we have brought about comes constantly in other reviews and journals published all over the world, Australia, New Zealand, India, Italy, France, Germany, England, Ireland. As I told you before, I could bring you a file of letters and clippings from many authorities, mostly clerical, which would show the value which has been set upon

---

* In what appears to be a later draft of the letter, this paragraph in quotation marks was crossed out, with this note in Dorothy's hand: "No insert needed."
† Paul Blanshard wrote a number of bestselling books based on the thesis that Catholicism was inimical to American democracy.

our work. Issues have been studied which concern the laity and family, most vitally in this way.

As to opposition to the capitalist order, it is no new thing. Besides the quotations which we have used from *L'Osservatore Romano* (which have been a matter of dispute since they were published) there are the writings of Fr. Luigi Sturzo, Fr. Vincent McNabb, Fr. Romano Guardini, and Eric Gill and Hilaire Belloc and G.K. Chesterton, to name but a few.

The Vatican paper warned us recently of regarding Americanism or Communism as the only two alternatives. You are of course familiar with such books as *The Servile State* and *The Restoration of Property* by Belloc, and the statement of Pope Pius XI in *Quadragesimo Anno* that as many as possible of the workers should become owners. The impossibility of this under our present finance capitalist system is clearly shown in Bishop Haas's book on the social order.

We are trying to make the kind of society which doesn't make for war, a society where each is not seeking his own, a functional society in which there will again be a philosophy of work, and not an acquisitive society.

We are trying to change society in a peaceful way by the works of mercy, trying "to make the rich poor and the poor holy," as Eric Gill said.

No one by now can consider us as anything but pacifist in our techniques of changing the social order. It is hard to see why our criticisms of capitalism and labor unions should have aroused such protest.

Perhaps it is the way in which it was said. So again I repeat we will try to be less dogmatic, more persuasive, less irritating, and more winning. But of course it is hard to make these offers. I can reform my own style, but how that of others? God gives people their temperaments, and some are fiery, harsh, dogmatic, and unadorned, too condensed, too uncompromising.

However, the synthesis which we are trying to achieve is appreciated and understood by scholars and workers throughout the country and it is a work which is going to continue whether by us or others in the lay apostolate. We are breaking ground, we are the vanguard. The very fact that we have been attacked as demagogues shows that the *Catholic Worker* has reached a great number of people, even with its emphasis on voluntary poverty (surely not an attractive doctrine for the worker who is suffering so from the high cost of food, and whose only aims usually are to fight through his trade unions for bigger pay and shorter hours). Voluntary poverty, a philosophy of work, an insistence on the holiness of manual labor, the personal responsibility of all to practice in some measure the works of mercy, in other words, the implications of the fact that we are sons of God, all these things are beginning to prove attractive to the poor. And so we are called demagogues.

I do not think it is realized just what the *Catholic Worker* has come to mean in the minds and hearts not only of the poor but of students, young intellectuals, priests and scholars, throughout the country. We can point to many illustrious names as our friends both in this country, in England and in Europe. Attacks made on us will be construed as attacks made on these ideas and a demonstration of the fact (of which the Church is all too often accused) that even thoroughly religious and humble, historico-critical and philosophical research and thought in matters of the social order, even though thoroughly unofficial and preliminary, is not tolerated and is impossible within the Roman Catholic Church. Again I repeat, our tone may often be wrong, our writing obscure, our ideas incomplete, and errors are bound to crop in. But with the proper attitude these things can be overcome.

Human truth has to grow organically, one mind meeting with another mind in the struggle for agreement only to go on to more struggle for more truth. This organic growth is seldom an orderly neat affair. Sin, error, and their various mutilations enter into the picture and make any integration difficult.

But I must not write at any further length. We trust that you understand our desire for obedience and we are confident that you will consider carefully and in the spirit of charity our aims and positions on the development of the Christian social order.

Sincerely in Christ

Dorothy Day

Nothing further was ever said about changing the name of the Catholic Worker.

TO WILLIAM EVERSON

ST. AGATHA, FEB 5, 1951

I have been ill since Dec. practically and hence so remiss with correspondence. Everyone has had something resembling flu and mine affected eyes, ears, teeth—head in general was a most painful affair. And somehow you keep going, ashamed to take to your bed when so many are ill. Did you read the life of Van Gogh—*Lust for Life*? When I read how he lived with the miners and suffered with them I was inspired.

I pray you and Carroll [McKool] remain, live in your poverty and give testimony of your love for the poor. Newman says the love of comfort—no, comfort itself, is the cause of tepidity. Our new house is so much more comfortable than the old that one must pray harder, strip oneself more daily to counteract it. I've been reading the life of Mao Tse-Tung and the story of the Long March in China, and their poverty and incredible hardship and the government they set up in caves, a university too, and their work for the peasants. I will write about it perhaps. But more and more I realize how poverty, sharing, is the link with the masses. And as Jack English wrote, "Sunday is in a way our one remaining religious link with them."

I feel our poverty, whether hidden or public, is our best weapon—our purest protest, our holiest work. So God bless you and confirm you in it, dear brothers in Christ.

Love in Christ, Dorothy

TO AMMON HENNACY

FEB 21 1951

What a dear you are! One is never too old to enjoy a Valentine! Your dates arrived in time for supper last night and were enjoyed by all. And I must remember to thank you too for the little lamp, so gay and light. And the *Arizona Highways*. It is so beautiful it makes us all long to visit you.

It is pouring rain today and the wind howls around the house, which is warm and snug.

My work does not depend on the weather—I can write all day, but Hans the carpenter and others feel limited as to what they can do. I love your letters, every one, with their detail about your life, work, and the people you meet.

Dear Ammon, I do pray for you and beg you to pray for me.

Love, always—in Christ—Dorothy

TO TAMAR

Dorothy's attitude toward Tamar had considerably softened since her previous letter. In the meantime, the Hennessys had moved to West-minster, Baltimore. They would shortly move to Staten Island, living for the first six months on Peter Maurin Farm.

4 MARCH 1951

WRITTEN ON YOUR BIRTHDAY

Helen Crowe came in and she was glowing in her praise of you. She can't get over what an idyllic time she had on her visit last spring. And she agrees with me that yours are the most beautiful children in the world. And you are the most wonderful person. She is always telling me how lucky I am to have such a daughter. She says you are a great person in your own right. And that is the way the Grail feels too. And many another.

Everyone in New York is having flu. The Boston Archdiocese

has been released from fasting on account of it. Pat McManus just called saying she had had it three times in three weeks. I just got rid of one cold two weeks ago, and last night I had a high temperature and pains in all my bones. Today just a bad headache which a fever also leaves. I hate dropping germs around even though David says he believes in God and not in germs.

Paper goes to press tomorrow. I was called to the Chancery Office last month on account of our condemnation of capitalism in Bob [Ludlow's] January article. Of all things. I should think it would have been anything else but that. But if I gave them *Black-friar's* article on capitalism, that whole issue, and *L'Osservatore Romano* stuff, they'd still object. It may be the FBI are putting pressure on them. Anyway, they want to see me again this coming week so my visit is called off on two counts. It's all to the good, all for the best, whatever happens. I am always convinced of that. For our correction and also for our good, even if the work gets suppressed one way or another. It is hard to understand but I am not going to worry about it. Peter [Maurin] is still busy stirring things up in heaven too.

Rain and cold here. Wish I were there with you. And above all I wish you were moved into the town. I'm always in favor of a village economy if one cannot farm well. If you are not a heart and soul farmer, then such days as this are hard on the farm. I am glad you have the radio and electricity anyway. That is some company. I was afraid that pump or the piping would go on the bum during this hard winter.

Much love to all of you and a happy birthday. I bet the children are enjoying it.

TO ADA PIERCE McCORMICK

Ada Pierce McCormick was a writer and community activist in Tucson, Arizona. She founded a nondenominational Little Chapel of All Nations to "promote the God-seeking impulses in mankind."

APRIL 21, 1951

My daughter and the four children are on the train right now coming up from Baltimore. They will stay with us in our barn in our Staten Island place until they get a house they are looking at. They sold their West Virginia place for $1,500 and are buying one for six thousand, a six-room house and four acres, within commuting distance of N.Y. Hope they can get a mortgage. They have to have a $2,000 down payment. I shall be so happy when they are settled near me. They went to W. Va. as a revolt against community and then nearly died of loneliness. They did well at gardening and raising goats and rabbits, chickens, a sheep, and a pig, and got some money, about ten a week from their mail-order books. But with the increase in family, the fifth is now on the way, they realized they had to be near a job.

They are also delighted to be near our S.I. community. Tamar has a loom and a spinning wheel and can teach the girls with us, and they will learn too about the responsibilities of family. Both Dave and Tamar want the basic things, not the luxuries.

As to Social Security, someone said once it was a confession of failure. A Christian employer should be paying his help a living family wage, enough to save on, to educate children, take care of illness and old age. Insurance should not be necessary. But if it is, it should be cooperative, mutual aid, and not the insurance of these big companies. The state is better, since it is now necessary, but the smaller the group, the smaller the unit, the better. Dave got nothing, not even state unemployment insurance. Workers in general have to put up with much injustice and should not let it embitter them, but work to overcome it and better conditions for others. And then too, we must give help and accept help when we need it, with the humility and simplicity of children.

I am in the rather funny position of giving away all I have, royalties, money from speeches, and having no salary, unable to help my child and grandchildren. So I beg from the relatives and am going to borrow from friends without interest and repay them from the royalties which will come from my new book which Harper's is publishing in the fall. Being in such a position is embarrassing at times.

I do thank you for your interest and for your help too. I feel I am a happy woman with all the little ones near me.

TO AMMON HENNACY

MAY 10, 1951

What a joy you are! Pomegranate blossoms, not reproaches. Dates, flowers, and good letters, and all when I needed them most. I was on the last lap of my book. Thank God it is finished now, as far as I am concerned, and handed in. They may turn some of the stuff back to me to be rewritten but I can do no more. I never want to see it again.

Dave Mason working on the *Sun Herald* and now it has folded up. I have a most difficult time with David—he is in love with me, and thinks I allow myself to be deceived and exploited by the staff. Jealous of Bob [Ludlow's] position, he cannot endure Tom [Sullivan] (and the latter is the best man we ever had in charge of finances, house and men). Dave's attitude to me is almost insulting since, if he loves me as he says, he should trust my judgment more. Also, he resents being no longer in charge since the war. But he is a Dr. Jekyll and Hyde character, one day all goodness, and then every few months having spells—(striking men on the line on two occasions for instance), flaring up into violence which is anything but pacifist; on one occasion he told Kichi Harada, our late Japanese guest who was with us for years, that the Japs deserved what they got at Hiroshima! One wonders if he is responsible. Simply incomprehensible, the spirit that gets into people. Community life is a great test. Now, with the younger group, the spirit of work and service gets better and better. Dave Mason never could get reconciled to letting the young ones have responsibility.

What makes me pour out my woes to you at this moment I do not know. I'd tear up the letter but have too many to write in catching up on my correspondence so shall let this go on to you. You will understand. As St. John of the Cross said—where there is no love, put love and you will take out love. The trouble is, if you love people, often they misunderstand.

Pray for us all, and remember my love and respect for you increase always.

God bless you,
Dorothy

TO BILL GAUCHAT

MAY 26, 1951

I hear by telephone last night that I will have to go over the whole book again [*The Long Loneliness*]. Publication will be delayed until February, and I will not make my trip to Detroit and Ohio. My first obligation is my book, and the world is a hard taskmaster, far worse than the poor, I assure you. We get away with a very sloppy job when we are working on the cause, but when you are working for the *New Yorker* or for Harper's you must be very slick and sophisticated, also grammatical! There are also a few fights in connection with dogma. I am trying to be very patient, because it does me good to have to present things not so they are acceptable but so they are *understood*. When writing in haste in the *Worker* one gets away with murder. People take it who agree with you. Others, no.

COLLECTOR, INTERNAL REVENUE
Custom House, New York, 4

Neither Dorothy nor the Catholic Worker ever paid any federal income tax. This led to occasional tussles with the state. In this letter she en-

deavored to explain her position, admitting to her correspondent that her explanation would probably strike him as "insufferable."

[UNDATED 1951]

Dear Mr. McMahon:

I received a notice mailed May 16, to call at Room 627, to see Mr. John Toner about the audit of my 1949 income tax. Due to the fact that I live in community with a group (the Catholic Worker) and whatever I earn is turned in for the common support of that group, I have no personal income, do not keep accounts, and so am unable to report.

My belief in voluntary poverty is fundamental to my pacifism, which pacifism forbids me to pay income tax (so much of which goes for war) even if I had an income.

By your name I presume you are a Catholic and you may consider that no Catholic by religious belief can be a pacifist or refuse to pay income tax. Perhaps you never met Catholics who were conscientious objectors or who held this position. I know that we are pioneers in this field and we hope by our writings and our lives to bring about a more general knowledge of these ideas and a renewal of faith in Christ's teachings in the Sermon on the Mount. Any prosecution of any one of us for breaking laws we do not believe in or paying taxes for war will only serve to bring about further clarification of thought, so we would welcome it. Or rather, I hope I would. I certainly do not want to go to jail, but if some day the "all-encroaching State," as our bishops have termed it, does prosecute me, which it would do if it were legalistic and insistent in its rejection of Christianity, which it isn't, I hope I would be given the grace to endure it and be accounted worthy to suffer for Christ, who loved us and died for us, and who said we should love our enemies. He himself lived for 33 years in an occupied country and did not lift a hand against the oppressor.

You probably will find this letter insufferable, if you have never studied these ideas or considered them. But please forgive me if I sound pietistic. I owe it to my country to give an explanation of my point of view.

You may quote to me, render to Caesar the things that are Caesar's, but St. Hilary commented on that, that the less we had of Caesar, the less we would have to render to him. We try to serve God at the Catholic Worker by serving our brother and that means we have a breadline and feed 500 people daily, and we take into our family, which is the staff of the paper, many people getting out of state and city hospitals, alcoholics, mental cases, and other sick and injured people who are victims of our finance capitalist system which has full employment only in time of war or preparation for war. We saved the State countless thousands of dollars these last 18 years, supporting thousands of people who would otherwise have had to be cared for by the welfare state, which Hilaire Belloc called the Servile State, and which Pope Pius XII calls the providential state.

Yes there is difference of opinion among Catholics. Cardinal Dougherty of Philadelphia opposed conscription. Cardinal Spellman upheld it. Catholics of Germany and Italy fought Catholics of America and France.

I am enclosing some literature—papers containing articles by Father John J. Hugo of the Pittsburgh diocese, "The Immorality of Conscription" and "Catholics Can be Conscientious Objectors." Also a pamphlet, "The Gospel of Peace." The latter has the *imprimatur* of this diocese. It is hard to explain why they gave it unless it means that Catholics are free to debate these questions as the theologians are debating the question of modern war.

I send this all to you because I am a pacifist and because I do not intend to pay income tax. This letter and the literature enclosed explain my absence. I am the mother of so large a family, I am asking you to study this material at your leisure rather than ask for my presence and my explanations in person.

Sincerely yours in Christ our Brother,

Dorothy Day

Editor, *The Catholic Worker*

TO WILLIAM EVERSON

JUNE 5, 1951

Your beautiful book came this morning and it rejoiced my heart. Everything about it, the feel, smell, sight, sound and all over taste of it, the appeal to exterior and interior senses does honor and glory to God who made you. I feel so proud that this was produced at Peter Maurin House in Oakland. For me it was the perfect illustration of the indomitability of the human spirit or I should say it gives a glimpse of Christ in man in all His beauty and loveliness, showing through all the sadness and squalor, the affront to the senses one finds in a Catholic Worker house. I thank you and love you for sending it. God bless you wherever you are and in whatever you want to do.

TO AMMON HENNACY
Beginning on August 6 Ammon fasted one additional day for each year since the dropping of the atomic bomb on Hiroshima.

JULY 18, 1951

I worry about your six-day fast and picketing when you have so little flesh on your bones. Remember, I'll be praying for you—offering the Holy Sacrifice of the Mass for you each morning and receiving Communion, and any special thought will be of you.

And I will write every day so let me know what address then.

We have had great troubles with our priest at P.M. farm last week. Drunk and disorderly. Scandalous behavior. He is in the hospital now. Hope to bring him home tomorrow. 70 x 7. Forgiving 70 x 7.

Stanley V calls us the Order of the Contemptibles! A good name. The despised, the foolish of the earth!

Many people must look on you as foolish but you are wonderful.

NOV 8 1951

There is so much to say, and so hard to get it all down on paper. So much about the mystery of suffering, for instance. Over and over again on my trip I was visiting some stricken family—a child dying or dead, or born an idiot, or crippled, men (3 of them) dying of cancer in their mid-thirties, etc. Not sin, fear, or diet, but a mystery, a sharing in the sufferings of the world.

Today was my birthday. Your dates came a few days ago and we all enjoyed them very much. You are sweet and thoughtful to send them. I'm looking forward to being out in Arizona Jan or Feb. There are a number of places I must stop on the way. Louisville, Memphis, St. Louis (first Augusta, Ga.); anyway it will be a zig-zag trip which will land me in Phoenix. By that time my book will be out. It is not too good but as good as I could write it in all the stress and strain of our work.

You are always idealizing me, when you mention me in letters to others. I am different entirely from you in the way I look at people, my approach to them, my own way of compromising, giving a little here and there—all women go ahead that way. They are like God, who is said to write straight with crooked lines.

I wonder if you understand what I mean. In reality you are much more dogmatic than I. You judge—you say you have a right to judge, "having been thru the mill."

The example you set is tremendous, but I do not feel you have a right to judge as you do. Everyone is so different. The great job is to judge ourselves, to know ourselves, to change ourselves.

Love, Dorothy

DEC 27, 1951

Letters are piled sky high so this is just a note. So many people always to take care of! But thank God Tamar and Dave are now all set in their own little place, small, compact, and though his job only pays $50 a week, they can get by. Dave can't stand Bob Ludlow. One night he said, "Ammon Hennacy's stuff is more Christian than his!" meaning too that you are also almost beyond the pale. He is a follower of Belloc and Chesterton and not a pacifist at all. But he is a distributist, which is on the way to being an anarchist. I'm very fond of him, and he and Tamar are happy.

Love, in Christ,

Dorothy

Dorothy's memoir, The Long Loneliness, *was published in January 1952. It was widely reviewed and attracted attention far beyond Catholic circles, even inspiring a two-part profile in* The New Yorker.

JANUARY 1952

I have been laid low with laryngitis, no voice left me, so it is good to rest. Dwight Macdonald was down to interview me for a profile for the *New Yorker*. He had already gone to all the staff while I was away in Canada. He is nice enough but very muddle headed. No longer a pacifist. POLITICS was a good magazine while it lasted. I got good reviews in the *New York Times* and *Herald Tribune*. Terrible picture in *Newsweek*. I look as though I should be in a mental hospital. Saw no Catholic reviews of my book yet. They sold 7,000 before publication. Tomorrow I speak at an IWO meeting, defense meeting, in N.Y. if my voice allows. If not someone will read my speech.

Yes, I am looking forward to seeing you. Ash Wednesday I will be there for sure, God willing. A friend of mine in San Diego told me of a little convent in the desert, Tapawa, Arizona, where I would love to go stay a bit to write. Also I want to visit the Hopi if I can while I am there. Is that possible? I would like to see them spin and weave. They are the truly poor, getting down to essentials. You too of course. Poor Mike Harrington said he would rather go to a military prison than a federal one with c.o.'s because he felt he could not keep up with their heroic conduct.

That is the way people feel about you. Until they know you, that you truly do not judge others.

I hate being used as a club to beat the Church and the

hierarchy over the head with. I am a loyal Catholic and please God intend to remain one to the end of my days. I have no reservations when I say I mean obedient Catholic. Were they to tell me to stop I would stop. "All things work together for good to them that love God." I believe too in spiritual weapons and the triumph of truth.

I have a hard time getting these ideas into the heads of liberals like Harpers, Sugrue, Macdonald, Eichenberg, etc. I believe Christ's body and blood are present in the sacrament and that I partake of it as truly as I partook of my mother's milk. Eichenberg thought I took it as a symbol. I literally believe, Lord help my unbelief.

Love, Dorothy

FEBRUARY 8, 1952

It is very hard to write this letter. I am writing to Father [George] Dunne too. I cannot make the trip west. It is not just that the first time I started Eric got pneumonia, and the second time Becky [*her grandchildren*]. She is now in the city isolation hospital with a fever of 106, measles and pneumonia. These signs should be enough for me, but I was so afraid of putting my family before God—His work for me—that my heart was torn as to what I should do. So two days ago I asked for a direct sign from the Little Flower [St. Therese of Lisieux] and asked in the form of money to send back to you the $75 since I had already spent it around here on emergencies and was going to get it back from Tom. I asked St. Therese to send it to me yesterday and late last night Chas McCormick came down for the bread for the line bringing my mail, and there was the check in one letter—also a letter immediately after, a very rare picture of the Little Flower, the one we have in our chapel which is named for her and before which I had prayed. So I am sure I should not go out at this time regardless of speaking engagements. I had only 4 counting yours, but they always increase as I go along. Yesterday too was the feast of a saint who got sick each time he started out and well as soon as he turned back.

I am terribly sorry about this. Please do understand, and pray for Becky, who is very, very sick.

Love in Christ,

Dorothy

P.S. I'll send the money on as soon as I get to New York to get a check. I have no checking account now. I appreciate your sacrifice in sending the money, knowing how you worked for every penny of it.

FEB 9, 1952

I certainly feel badly about not coming out but it does seem to me with the children so sick, and Tamar so hard-pressed I must stay home.

The only thing I feel bad about is you. You have boosted this meeting for so long. But if, each time I set out, the Lord pushes me back, there is nothing I can do. Just got your last letter and sure feel bad. But if you can come in the fall we can see each other then.

Every time you hold up Bob [Ludlow] and me as examples of true Christians I squirm. There are plenty, like Dave Dellinger, who are far better than we are. He and Bayard Rustin are the best speakers I ever heard. They are brave and poor, both have been jailed many times.

Bob practically wants to hide when you come, he feels he falls so short of your enthusiastic estimate of him. You say you will now write letters into Chrystie St. to be forwarded. But write to me here, if you still want to write to one who has badly disappointed you.

Aside from you, I am well pleased to stay at home and be silent, and work. I have done enough traveling and talking. Of course writing is not silence.

Seven years ago I took my year off. It is time I stayed in one place.

Today I moved all my things down from Chrystie St.

Love, in Christ, Dorothy

ST. VALENTINE'S DAY, 1952

Your letter made me happy indeed. I felt so badly at breaking engagements but everything indicated it. And in addition to signs and wonders, I lost my voice this past week. I am using fruit juices and praying for the grace to fast completely instead of partially.

I am going to stay quietly here and work at my writing and also begin going over your letters—such a file of them!

As for us seeing each other—could you not visit here this summer? See your family—then come on here for a month. You will do us all good. We can work in the garden together. Have outdoor conferences, a pacifist colloquium in fact. We will advertise your visit a few months in advance so people can plan their vacations to come.

They are distributing the papers on the street—at Fordham, now. Mike Harrington is a whiz. Much youth and energy. Not an absolutist but he prepares people for it. We need all kinds. So please don't say pipsqueak!

Every day I pray for you in our little chapel. We could not be closer if you were beside me. Pray about this fasting business for me.

Love always, In Christ, Dorothy

FEB 1952

You know I save all your letters and they are better than Pepys' diary of his times. They should be published as a running commentary on our times. They surely show a one-man revolution going on.

I'm going to get a batch of them in shape to submit to Harpers. If they are sure they can sell 5,000 of a book, they'd take it.

And with our advertising it, we could surely sell more too. It would include of course all your articles on life at hard labor. The only trouble is this. They charge so much. The alternative would be for us to publish it—sell it at a dollar a copy. The only thing is we never have any money ahead to publish with. We should have gotten Peter's book out again (the plates were destroyed thru a mistake of Dave Mason) but there is never the $1,800 ahead needed for an edition of 5,000. I don't like that stapling and paper binding which makes a book hard to hold either.

The thing about having the big bourgeois firm publish is—they reach every bookstore in the country. They have a large staff of salesmen.

I read your letters, some of them at the table at P.M. farm and everyone likes your articles. Even people who think they disagree are influenced without their knowing it.

I'm certainly looking forward to seeing you. I'm tempted to stay much longer than 2 weeks. I'd like to finish my new book on St. Therese, a short affair (a woman's book). The main point of it being to make people realize their personal responsibility, how everything they do matters. Most young people have such a sense of futility these days—they are paralyzed.

Love, in Christ, Dorothy

TO MONSIGNOR EDWARD GAFFNEY

Msgr. Gaffney authorized the Worker to allow priests to say Mass at the chapel at Peter Maurin Farm on Staten Island. Still, he was less susceptible to Dorothy's intercession on behalf of Fr. Clarence Duffy, an Irish priest and close friend, whose political activities had made him a thorn in the side of the archdiocese.

PENTECOST MONDAY, JUNE 2, 1952

We have been praying for you most specially at St. Teresa's chapel at the Peter Maurin Farm in Staten Island at our daily Masses. We can never forget your goodness to us, your unfailing kindness. When you telephoned during the Christmas holiday, it touched me deeply. Fr. Kiely has been getting on well, Fr. Cordes is much improved in health of mind and body, and we have a full house of 25 people, including a Negro family with eight children. And now Father Duffy is back with us. He showed me his papers, his letters from his bishop, telling him he would have to settle down to ordinary parish work—which he tried to do in Providence, R.I. some time ago, for a period of some months. Then another letter saying that if he did not give up speaking and writing, he would withdraw his celebret. This giving up of activities, he said, he promised to do, but the New York archdiocese wrote him that under no circumstances was he to offer up Mass in this archdiocese. He understands this, and says that he will *go* to Mass at the farm. He does not look at all well and says that the country and gardening will do him good.

As you can well guess, I am writing to beg the great favor of you to intercede for him. I have not worked at this job for nineteen years without realizing more and more that the great and powerful weapon to be used against the powers of darkness is the Holy Sacrifice. I hate to talk or write this way—it sounds like platitudes, but you know what I mean. Some days I feel so completely helpless, so unable to put a pen to paper, to answer a letter, to handle a situation, to do the perfectly ordinary things that make up the day's work. But when I feel the most completely helpless, then the thought that we have the Mass is the greatest comfort in the world. The most we can do for Fr. Duffy and the world around us is to provide a place for him to live and function as a priest and so I am begging you to let him offer up Mass again here.

I think I know in a way what Fr. Duffy suffers from. Being an ex-Communist, I know how great masses of people are with the best intentions in the world trying to work against poverty, against war. We will not talk of the motives of the leaders, the godless atheism of the philosophers of the movement. I can see Fr.'s sense of frustration, his tremendous grief at the horror of war. He is just ten times as sensitive as the rest of us. He sees too, the tremendous numbers of Catholics who have left the church and have gone over to this heresy. He is a shepherd looking for lost sheep. And he cannot see that by becoming wolves ourselves, we are not going to be able to regain them, or overcome the enemy.

Please do not take that great spiritual weapon to draw all men to Christ from his hands. Let him say Mass down here at the Peter Maurin Farm, or at the Newburgh Farm. (By going from one to the other, his restlessness may be helped.)

I only hope and pray he stays here. He is not as young as he once was and he cannot garden with ease as he did at our Easton farm fifteen years ago. I'd hate to see him pick up and start wandering again. He has no money, of course. He is not a man that can be used, otherwise he would have had the money to keep going, to keep traveling. He has his own ideas and they are based on the encyclicals and his trouble is that he has gone into the highways and byways on his own to talk them. We would be so happy to have him stay with us and will do our best to keep him.

Dorothy received a reply from James B. Nash, Vice Chancellor of the Archdiocese: "It will not be possible to extend any further courtesies to Father Clarence Duffy in this jurisdiction. Such courtesies have been consistently abused by Father Duffy in the past. He has persistently refused to be guided by the counsel and directions of his superiors and has in the past invoked the privilege he enjoyed of saying Mass here as an evidence of his good standing as a priest and ecclesiastical approbation of his 'work.' The result has been an enormous amount of scandal and considerable embarrassment to the Church. In view of Father Duffy's record of incorrigibility, I think it advisable that he be encouraged to return to his own diocese in Ireland."

TO AMMON HENNACY

At last, Ammon began making plans to move to the Catholic Worker house in New York. Dorothy was thrilled.

FRIDAY JUNE 28, 1952

Thanks for your June 23 letter with its good news of your getting here in August. I am delighted and yet I worry too. I am afraid you will be suffering too much by the time you get here, from physical exhaustion—I am afraid to put this strain upon you. What about your flying? Are you against it? There are those bargain flights to the Coast for eighty-five dollars and you would be saving on meals and certainly you would be conserving energy. If you stop over for rest you will not get any rest but will be visiting. You can visit on your way back. Wish I could contribute to the fare but royalties have not come in yet, and I have not a penny. Tom [Sullivan] has full charge of the exchequer now and I ask for what I need. It is a good way. We could pay your way back, however, as I'd have the royalties by then. I've ordered them to be sent to Tamar. She will use half (they are trying to pay off their little house) and the other half are turned over to the CW and will be paid out in bills in ten minutes. I've been thinking I'd treat myself to a new rebuilt typewriter.

I'm sure you were not much interested in Bob [Ludlow's] last article, but he is absorbed in the problem of the Eastern churches, and Church unity as a means of beginning to bring about peace. Bob is primarily religious and interested terrifically in religious problems. I am trying to urge him to write more about peace but he has written so much, he feels he has said it over and over. But that is what we have to do. I'll keep at him, however. Also, I suppose he gets tired of the constant heckling. It goes on continually. Instead of finding a support in Mike Harrington, he is upset now about Mike's socialist affiliations. He has become a member of the Socialist Party. Mike seems to put to one side Kropotkin, Tolstoi, etc., and what it really means is he wants activity, getting out on the streets talking, and that means to him immediate action. Trouble is, most of the priests bolster him in this. They say we must live in the world, so we have to accept the state, vote, etc. We have not begun to use our spiritual weapons. If Mike put in an hour at Mass, another hour at prayer during the day, and tried to practice the presence of God, the way of a pilgrim, constant prayer, then he would realize the futility of this activity of his.*

Charles de Foucauld in the spiritual field (he was a monk in the desert) never had a single follower, but he made such an impression on the minds of men by his giving up his soldiering and going off and living with the Arabs on dates and milk and wheat and honey, praying without ceasing, that they never cease to call attention to this way. And you, with your one-man revolution, have done more to point to the spiritual way of manual labor, hard work, care of your fellows, by an immediate practice of the works of mercy, by prayer and fasting, by voluntary poverty—Oh Ammon, you do not know how I wish we had more like you. You too are alone, but you are having your effect.

Enough now. Love, in Christ, Dorothy

TO JACK ENGLISH

Jack English had been a member of the Cleveland Catholic Worker before enlisting in the army during World War II. After spending much of the war as a POW in a Romanian prison camp he returned to the Catholic Worker. When he eventually decided to become a Trappist monk, Dorothy was elated. His was the first religious vocation nourished by the movement, and she embraced him with deep maternal pride. English— Father Charles as he became—joined the Trappist monastery at Conyers,

---

* Michael Harrington, a young man of great intellectual gifts, was part of the CW community at this time. Ultimately his commitment to socialism won out over his Catholic faith and he moved on to other work. His experience at the Worker, however, inspired him to write *The Other America*, an influential exposé of poverty in America.

Georgia. He was evidently a wise and holy man. Unfortunately, he was also a serious alcoholic. As a result, his religious life was fraught with stops and starts and much suffering. Dorothy's letters to him are marked by deep tenderness and affection. Here, in sympathizing with his sufferings, she alludes to the growing strain in Tamar's marriage.

AUGUST 21, 1952

Tom [Sullivan] gave me your letter to read, since I knew about the affair, and for the life of me, I do not understand why you are in such a state now about it. As far as an experience goes, I know that every commandment in the book is broken, when it comes to drink. It all goes together. What really counts is your tremendous striving towards perfection. God has his hand on you, without doubt, and will not let you go. How else could anyone stay as long as you have in a Trappist monastery without special graces? The fearful thing will be if you do not correspond to them. That is the most terrifying line in St. Paul. That warning, that if we do not correspond to the graces we receive, they will be withdrawn from us.

The great wonder is that when we turn from God, He still holds to us so that we do not fall even lower. He has taken care of you with such infinite love, "prevented you with blessings of sweetness," to use the quaint old phrase in the *Imitation*.

Do hold on, from day to day, we need you there so. You are holding us up in ways you do not know. You with your flounderings are preventing others from falling.

What strength there is in going on just from hour to hour, day to day. You don't know anything about it, what is generated by that suffering. Of course you have to suffer to attain love. You may be just within grasp of Something and turn back.

It's like marriage, this going to orders. So many turn back, so many keep starting in again. Marriage, failure, divorce, remarriage and so on. What do we ever learn of love? My poor Tamar is going through a hard time now. Nothing but surliness and violent complaining on the part of David. Steady work, the realization that with children and a home there is never going to be anything but the daily grind, the commuting, the poverty—he is thirty-eight now and it is a critical age.

And Tamar becomes more womanly, more gentle, and grave under it all. I pray daily that they become saints, and I see these things happening under my eyes, and I realize that this is the way God is making them saints. I stay away mostly, only see them once a week, and then not too long. Take the children to the beach for instance. It makes me suffer too.

You have suffered so much, and each one's suffering is different. You have been brave in the past, to endure, and I am praying that you will be brave now and endure. I will be praying for you, and I will try to do some penance for you, I do not know exactly what, but I know that penance is needed as well as prayer. I will pray I have the grace to do penance—I am not very good at it. You know you have our love always. You are part of us around here.

P.S. If you have to leave—you belong here of course. No place else. I told you that before. Love, D.

TO AMMON HENNACY

Ammon arrived in New York in August. During a retreat that month, Dorothy addressed this prayer to God: "I want with a great longing that Ammon become a Catholic, and I ask you this now, here on the eve of the feast of your mother's Immaculate Heart, to soften his heart and convert him now." Her prayers were answered in September when Ammon chose to seek baptism. Dorothy shared her joy in the January 1953 CW: "May he work more wonders than Gregory the Wonderworker."

OCTOBER 9, 1952

Did you get any poison ivy? I did—just a bit on one arm, just enough to remind me of you and that good day of hard work. The way little Eric [Hennessy, *her grandson*] followed you all day! Working together with people in silence brings a far closer feeling than any talk. I suppose I feel that because there is too much talk at the CW.

I know a good deal is necessary but a woman likes to get things done. We could have self-subsisting farms if we spent the same effort in working. Why not both? But talking takes strength too. But it is sad to see people getting soft bodies that will have a hard time enduring persecution. We need to be hardened and strengthened. That is why I pray to fast. God will send the grace and strength in His own good time. Meanwhile, speaking of food I wish I had made that omelet. I made eggplant instead, but I guess you liked it. A woman is born to nourish children and men too.

Love, in Christ, Dorothy

Ammon related that a story about Dorothy had partly inspired his decision to become a Catholic. She had been shocked in church one Sunday, she told him, when the organist played the "Star-Spangled Banner" after Communion. While the rest of the congregation rose to its feet she had dropped to her knees. But she was made uneasy by the suggestion that Ammon's conversion was motivated by hero worship rather than doctrinal conviction.

NOV 1, 1952, ALL SAINTS

About your St. Raphael letter. I did not kneel at the breakfast: I told you they played the Star Spangled Banner after Mass at Church. I knelt *there*. It is certainly easier to kneel in church rather than in a banquet hall behind a table. So you are giving me credit for something I did not do and saying actually you were "jolted into the Church" by that. My shock at their playing and singing it in church, right after the Holy Sacrifice of the Mass was what made me mention it. People do not listen to you, or they hear what they want to hear. Even you, in listening to me. Peter used to say—"People do not listen, they prepare what they are going to say." They hear part, and if that is striking—do not listen to the rest.

I hope you will not be "jolted" out of the Church by my calling this to your attention. It makes me so uneasy when you say you are going to become a Catholic for love of me. When you say you feel spiritually the Church is your home, I feel better.

When you are baptized and receive Holy Communion then we are closer than brother and sister, or husband and wife, because the same blood will flow in your veins and mine, the blood of Christ. But your eyes should be on Christ—not me.

Can you read over the Creed in the Mass in your missal and agree that that is what you believe? That is necessary for reception into the church. When they say it is "reasonable to believe" I find it easy. And St. Anselm said, "I believed, therefore I understood." Faith came before understanding. And faith is a gift of God. It cannot be imparted by any other person. I cannot give it to you. Only God. Maybe my prayers helped.

Love in Christ, Dorothy

TO TAMAR

NOV 19, 1952

Fr. [Marion] Casey baptized Ammon two days ago and he received Holy Communion for the first time yesterday. A great day. His father was brought up a Protestant on a farm in Ohio. But his grandfather was a Catholic from Ireland. So he was only one generation removed. You and I on the other hand have a long history of English Protestantism in back of us. So though he seems like a Midwest Protestant he is more Irish and Catholic.

I leave tomorrow for Fargo, then Spokane, maybe stopping off in Butte. I'm praying your guardian angels to take care of you all. I want to write these two books, the travelogue and the life of the Little Flower. And get enough royalties, if Harper publishes them, to buy a little cottage on the beach. That is my dream. Even if you and the kids just stayed in it summers, just as Forster does his, and David could get to work from there. The bigger dream would be to have a big house by the water some day. It is fun to dream about these things. Do try to put unpleasant thoughts out of your head. You must have to pray about them, otherwise you will get ulcers of the stomach, the way Forster did. Mother used to go in for reading Christian Science and Unity, so as not to think unhealthy thoughts—a right instinct on her part, just as she said she went down town and bought a new hat when she got melancholy. Sometimes there is nothing on this earth we want, and I've been through those times. Neither food nor drink, not a movie or downtown or a new hat, not a book or anything else. Fr. [Louis] Farina calls them tunnels and temptations to discouragement. I always got through them by manual work.

I can remember down on the beach when I was lonely and going through such a time. If I just cleaned the house thoroughly, my mind and soul became more orderly. Even the semblance of order, though I knew the dresser drawers were a mess. Also to take the kids out for a walk. Even if you have no strength to begin with, you get it on the walk. We need to stretch our legs and lungs. Forster used to insist on a walk, a regular Britisher, and it did me good though I never wanted it. A walk to the farm and a taxi back! Just to walk over and have a cup of coffee and look around and home again. Some clothes might have come in. Or you might need a bit of food. Try that. And a book too. Start reading *Kristin [Lavransdatter]* over again, or the *Master of Hestviken.* You read them when you were such a child, you'd get a lot now out of the former. She had a great wisdom, Sigrid Undset. Of course you've read Dickens, otherwise I'd say Dickens and Jane Austen and the Brontes. Just something to pick up at night, and to look forward to during the day.

Hope you don't mind my staying away so long, but a long

trip like this is not only good for me, but I get a lot of work done and get the money too. So pray for me and hang on. Fr. Casey is such a dear friend. He said he was saying a Mass for you this morning. I remember once Fr. McKenna said a Mass for me and cleared up all my troubles at once. A miracle. Not that everything ever does stay cleared up. That's life. Much love darling. I do think you are a wonder and growing all the time, through troubles and vicissitudes too. It is always hard when the babies are all small. You can do so much and have so much too, so many interests.

NOV 26 1952

Just a note as I leave this morning for Seattle. I have been praying to [G. K.] Chesterton and Eric Gill to find David better and more satisfying work and to take special care of him. I hate to think of those long hours of commuting, when the work is not too happy. It would be all right if the job were all right.

Out here they do not want any speeches. They are scared to death of Russia, one would think it just around the corner, just over the hill. Saw Bishop White yesterday and he was vehement in his distrust of the state which is taking over the children. No objection from him on our anarchism and pacifism. A very pleasant visit. But the chief Republican woman in town had circulated that on unimpeachable evidence I was a Communist so the only school would have me was Marycliff.

TO AMMON HENNACY

JANUARY 1953, LAKE PARK, FLA.

I'll bet you are glad I am gone and you can settle down to work, physical and mental. We did not have too much time together, really just a couple of days. If we had gone by bus to Tucson we would have had that time together. You talk about being shy with me. That is because you are only in love with your idea of me, not really me. How can you be when you have really seen so little of me, a few days here and there.

However, I do agree we can appreciate each other, from our writing to each other, from the cause on which we are engaged, the life we truly share with each other.

Always my love, Dorothy

Ammon was busy writing a memoir, Autobiography of a Catholic Anarchist *(later revised as* The Book of Ammon). *Reading his treatment of her, Dorothy felt she must again strenuously discourage his tendency to idealization, if not infatuation.*

MARCH 13, 1953

Send your book all at once, so I can go over it all at once. I'll be happy to go over the whole thing right away, but I'm afraid you'll have to wait two weeks. Tomorrow I speak in Morristown, the next day in Philadelphia, the next in Jersey City. Wednesday I go to Montreal for a week, then Holy Week. David [Hennessy's] youngest sister is getting married March 28, and he and Tamar are going to Washington so I'll take care of the kids Friday, Sat., and Sunday, which means they get to bed at seven and I'll have three long evenings, all to myself to read and work on it.

About your conversion chapter, which I am returning now (that is what you want isn't it?). I loved all but the first four pages of it—your whole writing about me seems to be sentimental, too rapturous, and I do not like it at all. The rest of the chapter is wonderful. But I am afraid I am going to censor what you write about me. I must insist upon this and I am afraid you are going to be displeased about it, but I must. I think, too, I have the right. My life is public enough without this emotional writing. Neither Tom nor Bob liked it at all. And it isn't just modesty or humility or anything like that on my part. I just do not like it. Fritz Eichenberg said you wrote to him and I was mentioned every other line. Mary Thornton wrote to me in shocked accents that you were in love with me.

Young people who are used to looking upon me as a mother are repelled, just as children are repelled in the lack of understanding of the life of their parents. For one thing you are sixty nearly and I 55. A mature age, when calm affection and friendship, deep and sincere, can be respected, but romantic love not. There is something quite sane in this. Such love is associated with youth and the time of mating, and the idea of procreation (the sexual act cannot be considered just alone by itself, but in its last end) and just as Sarah laughed when told by the angel that she would conceive in her old age, so also to the natural mind, the idea of sexual love is out of place at our age. It is next to impossible to write about such love of people in their sixties without either seeming ridiculous or revolting.

I am utterly frank in writing to you this way because I want to prepare you for the fact that I am going to ruthlessly cut out of the book any reference to me along these lines. At our age we should be turning to God, not to each other, the whole direction of our thoughts should be to increase in the love of God. It is only in giving up a thing that you can keep it; it is only by such a sacrifice on your part that your love can be beautiful and holy. So please, please, do not mind if I do this cutting.

I have not written also because I hated to write this way, but it has been bothering me for some time now.

Love always, in Christ, Dorothy

TO EMILY COLEMAN

MARCH 18, 1953

While meditating in church this morning, I thought so much of you, and the quality of love you have, and how much you did for us while you were here. How you went out to people, how you warmed them, how you saw them as God sees them, what an interest you took in each one's spiritual life. Never think I did not appreciate that. It warmed my heart too.

Do come to see us when you can. Fr. would so love to see you, and your being around would buck every one up. Be our spring tonic. Why not come out for a few weeks. Forget what it does to you, how it drains you. You must have stored up a tremendous amount in your cisterns.

TO FRANCIS CARDINAL SPELLMAN, ARCHBISHOP OF NEW YORK

Ethel and Julius Rosenberg, members of the Communist Party, were convicted of espionage for their alleged role in passing atomic secrets to the Soviets. Despite calls for clemency by many people, including Pope Pius XII, they were executed on June 19, 1953. Dorothy had little pull with Cardinal Spellman. Still she appealed to his compassion.

FEAST OF ST. MARGARET OF SCOTLAND, JUNE 10, 1953

Dear Your Eminence:

I am writing this in church, after receiving our Lord, and I am writing with love and with hope. It is easy to hope here in the presence of the Blessed Sacrament, but hard to hope outside.

A young Jew who comes to see us daily told me how his grandmother, when she did her shopping at the East Side markets, met the grandmother of the Rosenberg children, and how she was grieving and mourning. I am a grandmother too, and I too shop for my children, and am concerned with life, sustaining life, and it hurts my heart to think of the situation of this family. So I am writing to you to beg you now, on the eve of their execution next Thursday, to go to see them, to intercede with the President for them, to beg President Eisenhower to change the harsh sentence of death.

So often we are asked to make a proof of our love, of the

reality of our love for our brothers. Love is one word which we all understand, Communist or not. So often it is not possible to reach others who are so far from us, in mind and soul, and to whom it is hard to speak openly. We cannot talk to them, we cannot reason with them, we cannot, above all, bargain with them, offering clemency in return for confession. But we can show love, and everyone understands that.

Jesus, our Way, told us what kind of love His Father has for the sinner,—the folly of love that made the father rush out to embrace the prodigal son. He had no way of knowing whether he repented truly, whether he would not go out 70 times 7 again. Osee was commanded to marry a harlot, and even support her and her lovers. And Jesus from his Cross in utmost yearning asked His Father's forgiveness for those who were taking His life (as so many Communists are taking the lives of priests and prelates today).

Here, in the presence of the Blessed Sacrament, I do beg you not only to pray for the Rosenbergs, but to intercede for them to President Eisenhower. Of course you may say that he has not heeded the Pope, but you are so close to him. You are accessible to him. He knows that heart you have for mothers and children, and that you are not afraid of showing tender love and compassion.

When I saw your picture on Christmas in the daily papers, sitting between soldiers having breakfast with them, I felt like crying, with gratitude, too, that you were there. But love knows no boundaries and our dear Lord told us to love our enemies, so if you would only go that short distance to Sing Sing and make this gesture of love for enemies!

We are so careless of life these days, so profligate of this humanity of ours, that Christ paid so much for. He showed how He loved traitors. By taking on their human nature and dying for them.

He has bought the Rosenbergs with a great price. How much

we should love them. Please, dear Father of us all in this area, erring and faithful alike, please make this hard gesture of love.

Sincerely your servant in Christ,

Dorothy Day

TO EMILY COLEMAN

Dorothy had determined to write a book about her favorite saint, Therese of Lisieux, bringing out the social dimensions of her spirituality, her teaching of the "Little Way."

JULY 6, 1953

It is 4:30 in the morning and I have been awake since 3,—one of those sleepless times. So I decided to get up and work. Every time I sit down to write that book on the Little Flower I am blocked. I just can't seem to get anywhere with it. It is like working on that biography of Peter.* I just am not a biographer. What I write is dull, undistinguished, and I am faced with the humiliating fact that I can write only about *myself*, a damning fact. Of course, it is in relation to the work, about the work, about people, etc. So I wonder if I should not just write as I have been, the story of the poor. Fr. [Harvey] Egan, a dear friend, assures me I should give up trying to write about Therese, but write about the laity, our work, our ideas.

Isn't it funny. Some days the ideas pour out, and other times one cannot write at all.

TO FATHER HARVEY EGAN

Father Egan, a priest in Minnesota, was a good friend to the Worker. Recently he had sent a contingent of women to the Catholic Worker

---

* Dorothy's book about Peter Maurin was never finished. A historian, Francis Sicius, later filled in the gaps in her manuscript and published it as *Peter Maurin: Apostle to the World* (Maryknoll, NY: Orbis Books, 2004).

from Maryhouse, a lay community, for which he served as spiritual director.

FIRST MONDAY IN ADVENT [1953]

I've been sick all this last month so that I could do no writing of letters though I've been intending constantly a thank you letter for all you have done for us in sending us the *women* of Maryhouse. I started to write girls, but they are indeed women, mature, balanced, more normal than any I have ever met. What a joy and a strength to us all. And how I hope our relationship will continue over the years. If only they can keep coming, two by two. Down here at Peter Maurin Farm we now have five priests! Please pray for these lost shepherds.

We did not choose this work, but the Lord seems to put us in it. It is part of the house of hospitality work. There are three at Maryfarm too. How I wish we had two of the women at each place. Here we have two girls, one of 17 and one 30 and both so moody, so emotional, and so undependable. One feels always her responsibility as a leader, and so little that of a "slave." If only this coming year we could grow in true devotion to the Blessed Mother. One of the difficulties with being a slave and trying to serve with silence, and gentleness and sweetness, is that to others one seems to be condoning, overlooking sins, not taking much account of sins, so then the others feel they must take up the slack and show disapproval, speak out and condemn etc. So then there are words and hurt feelings and moods again. What a tremendous need of spiritual formation there is and what a work you have done for twelve women, and how that has spread, we will never know how far.

I have been wanting to write you a long time just to tell you that not once did one of the five ever show anger, suspicion, judgment, impatience in their work. They are unfailingly gentle, courteous, kind, hard working, patient, really making goodness so attractive that without a word people have done better.

What an example to me. I go around saying, "Mary, meek

and humble of heart, make my heart like unto thine." They were the ones, by their example last winter, who plunged me deeper into true devotion. Of course I had been consecrated to Mary ten years ago, I had made my oblation, done my daily readings, conscientiously prayed, but it certainly needs the quiet example to strike home. Thanks to your work, your direction, through Dorothy, Marie, Mildred, Jane and Lucille, I am starting the Marian year with a greater depth of insight into the glories of Mary. And I just felt I had to write and tell you so. They all may depend on you, and you must feel it, but think how far from you they are and how far your influence has extended. I do marvel at it all.

Do pray for me in my present miseries. It is something which will not pass probably for months to come, so I need to be patient. I have the best medical help too.

TO JACK ENGLISH

DEC 31, 1953, FEAST OF ST. WILLIAM

Got your letter this morning and hasten to answer it to assure you of our prayers. Of course I let Tom [Sullivan] read it and he says never a day of his life passes but that he prays for you that you remain there. And I told you, last September, just before I left for the West, that I could see you only in a Trappist monastery.

I have such utter faith in you, Jack, that you are bearing a tremendous burden of temptation for us all, that you are sacrificing for us all. It is as though you are lightening our load so that we can endure here in the world. You surely have a vocation, I know it, and you never could have remained this long, you never could love it as you do.

Interim for lunch. Michael Kovalak is again in a bad state, talking about therapeutic marriages and demanding that I provide him with opportunities to see the Cardinal, otherwise he is going to join the Eastern Orthodox Church so he can marry and be a priest at the same time. He has been all right for a long time, but is not so good now. And Slim is talking to himself from morning to night, right now on the top steps just outside the open window. He is threatening violence too. Madness and drunkenness. Smoky in a terrible state for two weeks but is pulling out of it now so that he can go to his niece's graduation. Yesterday I had to drive the station wagon down for bread and it smelled of vomit and human excrement from the people sleeping in it at night. We spent the day scrubbing out the thing at the farm. Drunkenness and madness and filth and ugliness. A picture of hell. Just contrast that with your life down there.

And it is your prayers, your suffering, your temptations that enable us to bear things cheerfully, to spend hours in the chapel or in church, to keep up physically and mentally, to be happy, even.

Helene Iswolsky said she had some shattering spiritual experiences. Our life is shattering in a physical way, but gleams of spiritual joy come through it all. As I prayed for Fr. Kiely the other day, at 6 a.m. while he was talking drunkenly in the kitchen, I had a tremendous sense that Jesus, in his humanity, was present with us, that greater forces were being brought to play, that compared to this sum total of human weakness, struggled against (and they are all struggling, suffering) there were gigantic forces for good, great currents of grace set loose in the world like a mighty wind to purify and freshen the sin-laden atmosphere. It was like the breath of the sea, these thoughts, I was sure. I was sure we were doing what God wanted. And I am sure too, that you are holding us up, so be valiant.

Do get St. Jerome's letters to read. I'll send them on if you do not have them, otherwise I would not part with them. His letter on virginity tells of his life in the desert and his temptations and struggles. For your delight and refreshment, I am going to send two of my dearest treasures, the *Paradise of the Fathers* and Helen Waddel's translations too. You can give them back some day as they are hard to come by. But they will cheer you in the struggle.

Or maybe nothing will. Maybe you can neither read nor pray but just endure. But hold fast. Of course we are praying for you.

Love always, in Christ—Dorothy

TO AMMON HENNACY

[UNDATED 1953]

Still reading your book. Am on page 298 and am wondering if you had better not end the book with your conversion instead of inserting it before your travels. Certainly I would consider your conversion the climax and to go on with travels an anti-climax, structurally speaking. Also—I am aghast at the number of names you misspell. Of those I know, I mean. So wonder about those I don't know. I am hoping that David Dellinger catches them. When you misspell a name, people begin to question your other facts. Maybe Dave will send the whole manuscript back to you to go over again and correct and check. Frankly, I have so much less time than you do, that I cannot do it. But really it would not hurt to go over the whole thing again. It is very, very long. Much longer than my book. Also you repeat a great deal, because you have collected all your articles, all your tax statements, all your leaflets, and then those books reviews, all of which are very interesting, but they are going to make for a very expensive book.

It is one o'clock and this is the only letter I have been able to get at today down at P.M. Farm. If I lived alone down on a beach, as I would like to, I would get some work done. As it is, I am dealing with live human beings, not soil and plants and words, as you are. I am saying that, not in criticism, but to make you understand, as you surely do, the difficulties of my job. It is, in a way, the difference between a man's work and a woman's work.

The man deals in the realm of the idea and sacrifices every-thing, even human beings, to work it out. A woman gets along as best she can, leading and guiding, taking into account poor weak, human nature, thinking of people as her children, nour-ishing, tending, encouraging, conciliating, trying at least to keep them alive, for while there is life there is hope that among them will be a few heroes and saints.

You will notice my notation on p. 229. These are words of contempt. They are whips, and truly I do not consider a pacifist has any right to use them. Scorn and contempt are part of hatred, they do not bring out the best in man. I would be afraid of using them myself. Example is the best teacher. Love and example—Peter Maurin exemplified that. He always was expecting so much of people.

About the cutting in the last issue. I was not at the printers that day. Tom [Sullivan] cut the article because it was exces-sively long. He told me about it, and as I tell him in the case of my articles, I told him to go ahead. He'd rather you'd write two five-page parts to be continued than to have you write one ten-page article. Sometimes he prints all of mine and sometimes cuts. Anyway, he is makeup man.

In a way you are like Fr. Duffy. When he used to write for us, if we cut three lines out of one of his articles, he'd pick it up and use it the next time. He never wanted one word of his to be lost. Which is nonsense. One of the reasons why I don't mind your repetition is that people have a hard time getting the point. Still, it might have more impact as a book if it were cut down. *One* tax statement. *One* story covering all the picketing over the years, instead of a detailed account of each one, when in the long run they all seem alike. *One* story of irrigating the lands. *One* ac-count of your garden. *One* visit to the Hopi. As it is, it is a diary, a month by month account. Go to any printer yourself out there in Phoenix and ask them how much they would charge to print a book of 400 typewritten pages.

Have you even counted the number of words to a page and

the number of pages? Usually there are three hundred to a page of manuscript material prepared for printer. I am sure yours run about 525 words to a page. Even at 350 pages, 500 words to a page, your book is 175,000 words long and my book *The Long Loneliness*, 96,000.

Our letters certainly are becoming businesslike. I've actually been taking days on this. Meanwhile Fr. K. off again, people sick, mother and child arriving for help, kids raising hell around the house, no sleep last night, and I'm just dead for lack of quiet. I'll finish up in a few days and send it on.

Love, Dorothy

TO A YOUNG MAN

APRIL 4, 1954

Dear David—

Hope you don't mind my answering your letter longhand. We are listening to Beethoven's 9th Symphony—great rest for the soul. As soon as I read your letter I thought—the tragedy there is not the struggle with the parents, but not to have companions in your revolt against life as it is lived today.

When you say you want to love your fellow men you just have to begin at home. Please don't argue with them—it is hard enough your being a Catholic. No one can win others by argument, only by love, and remember as Fr. Zossima said in the *Bros. Karamazov*, "Love in practice is a harsh and dreadful thing compared to love in dreams." It is so easy to love people at a distance—not folks at home. I know how it is. We each of us have been thru it all.

After all, you are being supported by your parents—they are putting you thru school and you owe them love and gratitude. I do think all young people should get off on their own as soon as they can—then they begin to appreciate those at home too. The most Christ-like way is to see Christ in them—just don't see the rest. Love them. It is so hard not to hate those who don't love their brothers—Negroes, Indians, Japanese, Russians—and it sure is silly when we add to the sum total of hate, too.

What is your nationality—it is a strange name—you might be a Nigerian, a Japanese or a Finn for all I can tell. Are you studying music? Do write more.

God bless you always and thank you for your help too.

In Christ, Dorothy

TO FATHER HARVEY EGAN

1954, EASTER WEEK

After three days of rain at the close of Holy Week, we are now rejoicing in beautiful weather. I am with the family at Maryfarm where Marion and Lucille are in tranquil control. All is going well. There are four priests here, three of them most difficult, but at least persisting. The longer I am in the apostolate the more I am sure perseverance and constancy are the two great needs. To be faithful to a work, a family, a husband, a wife, or children, or cause, or penitent. To be even-spirited. To have equanimity, no moodiness, never to be discouraged.

As I have told you before, the Maryhouse women have all that and in addition to loving them and learning from them, I appreciate, too, all that you have done and God bless you for it. There was an article in *Blackfriars* or *The Life of the Spirit* recently which emphasized the need of spiritual direction, or rather spiritual directors,—that great need that exists today, this day of Catholic action. Everybody admits the need but no one wants to do it. On the one hand, in the lay apostolate, in Catholic action, the priest has been warned not to do it all, to stand off and leave it to the layman to act, to speak, etc. and on the other hand, there is no *spiritual* direction.

I have noticed for a long time the lack of willingness on the part of priests to give direction, to be considered spiritual directors. One young priest of the retreat group said: "They do their own will, anyway. They do not take direction after asking for it." Of course. That is where patience is needed, and forgiving 70 times 7. And repeating and repeating and repeating, until people begin to realize how they are following their own will, and not the will of God.

Another young priest, also of the retreat, said women had too sexual an attitude. They were looking for someone to lean on, to take the place of a husband, especially if they were nuns. They wanted too much attention. And he would not give them direction.

Another complains that it was only women who made the retreat, or wanted direction. Scorn of women here. Yet who followed Christ and humbly served him, and stood at the foot of the cross, and afterwards opened up their homes to the apostles and gave the first churches? I become sensitive about this scorn of the laity and scorn of women. Some more war, or seeds of war, in our midst. Conflict between worker and scholar, men and women, priest and laity, etc. All mixed up.

Irene Naughton said once about confession, "If only the priest would say one little thing, reminding us of the love of God, instead of 'Three Our Fathers and three Hail Marys.'"

Fr. Roy used to give unusual penances like reading a certain chapter in the NT or *Imitation*, or do without coffee for a day!

On the other hand, you, in simplicity and vigor, went to town on the business. The women asked for it and got it. All the preparation they did to consecrate themselves to the Blessed Mother; three rosaries, their hour, their little office, the litanies, besides their reverently prepared Holy Communions, confessions, and daily work. It was a formation such as only nuns and sisters have, and which lay people need, if not in a group, as the girls had it, then singly.

Of course this direction flowed over into their material life, too,—being women and pliable, they got direction, too, in regard to their life and work. They lived together, they bought a house, they ate a certain way, they kept certain hours, they devoted themselves to certain works, catechism, literature, visiting in the parish, mimeographing, etc. For a long time they did not work for wages, but worked under your direction and Fr. Herman's, I believe. When they got the little farm, they planted, harvested, canned, kept a cow and chickens, also under your direction. (I remember Dorothy mourning the loss of their cow when you ordered them to cease keeping one.) They have literally followed your direction in everything and then you thought the time had come for them to do without direction. I know that Fr. Chapman says that the function of the spiritual director is to teach the penitent to do without a spiritual director. And I would amend, if they have to. In a way they have to, with you removed to the uttermost part of the diocese. And yet you have continued to give your direction by mail, and more in the matter of material direction than spiritual. For instance, now they have undertaken this debt (under your direction) and now they cannot do any apostolic work until it is paid off. As to a "plan," it is almost impossible to make one.

If you forgive me for saying so,—this idea of their not starting work until the debt is paid off is hard to understand. Their "work" goes on during their job, and their job should always be such that it can be considered an apostolic work. Every morning they have begun. "Now I have begun" is the motto or whatever you may call it of some nursing order of nuns. And Fr. Faber says that people are making spiritual progress if they are always making beginnings.

What if a family did not begin their work of raising a family until they got their debts paid off! People are always in debt and always will be. How many works in the Church are free of debt? Once one is paid off, an expansion in the work is undertaken and more debts are accumulated. The Holy Father said to a community of nuns that they should never hesitate to run up debts in their work for the poor.

When a family buys a house these days it takes a long time

to pay it off. And if sickness comes up or other unforeseen setbacks, they may lose all that they have saved and built up.

In our work here we are clear of debt in the house on Chrystie Street (but pay $600 a year taxes) but we owe four thousand on Maryfarm where we have had so many retreats and sheltered so many transients and taken care of so many sick and dying. Our debts are always there, to butcher and grocer, utilities, etc. But they get paid.

And consider we ourselves are earning our living. If we went out to work we would leave the sick and old and hungry uncared for, correspondence undone, there would be no paper, no clarification of thought. If we paid ourselves a salary, each of us, and then turned it into the work, it would be a madness of bookkeeping and inefficient efficiency. And we would still be appealing for alms, as does every university, hospital, community chest project and so on. When people get a Guggenheim fellowship they consider it an honor, but it is surely an alms, too.

I understand that you want the girls to work for as high a salary as they can get which would mean not apostolic work, but worldly work as efficient secretaries for business executives or advertising agencies, etc, etc. I cannot tell you how wrong I think this concept of work is. One should take joy in one's work and feel that it is worth doing, that it is contributing to the sum total of human needs and happiness. It should in no way be a work which caters to luxury, increases desires, builds up the kind of society which makes for war.

Here are things I feel very definitely. You have asked my opinion and I am going to be frank and open, knowing that you want it so. These are some points of disagreement as to the future, as far as I am concerned.

I do not think the women can work at a job in office, industry, schoolroom, hospital, and put in apostolic work on the side. It is two jobs, not one. If they do two jobs, they should be paid for two jobs. If they are working for one employer, they must give themselves to office, or school, or hospital, and that is a full-time job. They need in addition to eat three meals a day, prepare them, wash up, wash their clothes, clean their house,— all these material things, besides going to Mass, making their hour, praying. I know that you have told them, and others have told them, that they should be able to work a 40-hour week, and work in a parish besides, and the girls have tried to do it. I said a few years ago when I was there that I disagreed absolutely with this and I do more than ever.

When it comes to trusting in God and living on alms, I would like to know what the priests do, the monks, the nuns, all the religious. Of course, they put in a full day of work, but it is considered that the workman is worthy of his hire, and so they get their living, and a very good living it is. They live far better than most laymen. The money for this, all of it, comes from the laity. All right then, let them give their money, but not their lifeblood besides. It is asking too much, more than is asked of any priest or nun, to work at a double job. Those who ask them to do it should be ready to go out and try it. It would be a revelation to work for a year and find out what an all-day typing job, filing job, nursing job, really means, if one is a good worker, and conscientious, and not just a wage slave. The priest workers discovered this, and were drawn so far from their spiritual work that they had to be stopped. They could not do both. The Little Brothers of Jesus, whom I have written about with such approval, earn their living, pray their prayers, but they do no works. They do not work in parishes, start schools, hospitals, or anything else. They just live in the midst of poverty, in poverty, quiet and prayer.

Now if the girls wish to model themselves on the Little Sisters, then let them do this. Work, come home, live their lives of prayer, pay their bills, give what alms they can spare from their own living expenses and paying their debts. But nothing else. About the kind of work. Was it in yesterday's breviary lessons that the kind of work was emphasized? Peter could go to his nets, but not St. Matthew to his tax-gathering. Therefore, St. Gregory said, let a man consider the kind of work he does. Working in a department store, in a tax office, etc., etc., would be out. The work should be good, something in which they can take pride and offer to God. Teaching is good and nursing. It is wonderful that Rose is having that course. But as to stenographic work in the business world, in some business dealing with something the world could well do without,—what a misery. Nursing, teaching, cooking, all these things come naturally to women. But each has not the same vocation, of course. . . .

One thing is sure,—you should go on with the spiritual direction you have given them which shows in their lives so beautifully. Do they not do a great deal by their prayers?

All this is too long, I know. I might better write more frequently and at less length. I am sending a copy of this letter to the girls, so it will be as though we all had this talk together.

We all send loving greetings.

In Mary, Dorothy

TO BRENDAN O'GRADY

Brendan O'Grady was writing a thesis about Peter Maurin. In response to a series of questions, Dorothy provided these answers.

[C. JUNE 1954]

Quite a few friends have written and asked me if they could see your manuscript, but I have not let it out of my hands. I have felt guilty at keeping it so long, but I have been ill, quite a few months, though all right now. Thank God.

Now to take up your questions:

1. Peter Maurin is most truly the founder of the Catholic Worker movement. I would never have had an idea in my head about such work if it had not been for him. I was a journalist, loved to write, but was far better at making criticism of the social order than at offering any constructive

ideas in relation to it. Peter had a program. I tried to follow it, though I confess I thought it very simple at first, not at all a powerful one. One only realizes how little one knows about putting the Beatitudes into effect, of following up on the works of mercy, when one starts to do them. Peter lived what he believed, esteemed poverty and manual labor, and at the same time quoted Lenin, "There can be no revolution without a theory of revolution." Which meant for him that we must read and study and broaden our outlook, enlighten our minds, inflame our hearts, etc. He brought us [Romano] Guardini, Karl Adam, Luigi Sturzo, [Jacques] Maritain, Eric Gill, [Hilaire] Belloc and [G.K.] Chesterton, and he applied all his ideas to the conflicts of the day. In 1933 the *Atlantic Monthly* articles about whether a Catholic could be president were being published, and Peter always pointed out that [Al] Smith would have to be a Catholic first of all, and then an American, that his higher loyalty was to God, and that indeed these loyalties would sometimes conflict. His teaching in regard to the state, state responsibility, state aid as against personal responsibility was decisive and made us put into effect our principles. Read my articles about Peter in a recent issue of the *CW* about his exaltation of the idea of freedom. We never knew what freedom meant before. Yes, he was a leader, a teacher, a founder. I was a journalist, a doer, but without the theory I would have gotten nowhere. I was the active principle in the partnership, I admit, but then women are always the practical ones, the housekeepers.

2. As for Marc Sangnier—Peter was a young man then, and he might have been a hanger-on of the movement as we have so many today.* He might have sold papers on the

---

* Marc Sangnier (1873–1950) was a lay Catholic reformer in France and the founder of Le Sillon, a movement that aimed to reconcile the principles of Catholicism with democracy and social justice. In his youth, Peter Maurin was affiliated with the movement—before it was condemned by the Vatican.

streets, the paper that Sangnier published. He might have just been in on the discussions without being a leader. Knowing Peter, he would be silent, a listener. He always made a great point that people should learn to listen. Peter talked so little about himself that it was hard to get facts from him. He emphasized that he was interested mainly in ideas. I am sure he did not realize at first why I had to talk about Rosie the cow in farm columns in the paper, or tell of our daily life. He wanted straight, serious articles on ideas. But I had almost gotten fired from a newspaper in Chicago for presenting straight stories, when what the editor wanted, especially from a woman, was feature stuff, so I soon learned to write that way. I tried to clothe Peter's ideas so that they would be recognizable, strike home, as it were, so that others would be influenced by them. Writing about old people, relatives, for instance, and the family as the unit of society, made some of our readers recognize the fact that they should care for their own, in spite of difficulties rather than pass them on to an impersonal institution.

3. I do not believe Peter knew Jacques Maritain before the latter came to visit us in New York. M. Maritain came to visit us from the Catholic Center club where he was staying. I first was invited to call upon him there. Then he came and spoke for us. He said our place reminded him of [Charles] Péguy's in Paris. I am not sure how much Maritain appreciated Peter's genius. He always tried to give me the credit, thinking it was modesty and humility on my part. Peter's sureness, his insistence on his ideas, his quaint techniques which you bring out so well, his man-in-the-street tactics I do not think were sympathetic to the Maritains, who are scholars and saints, but I think in an entirely different class. Far more attractive than Peter, who was dirty, ill-clothed, unwashed—a real St. Benedict Joseph Labre in our day

when we put such emphasis on showers, and daily baths and the toilet in general. Peter, by his very ignoring the amenities of life, made us realize that many a young family sold their souls for a mess of pottage (modern plumbing) and had to give up ownership (and responsibility and stability) in order to have the latest home. Peter was hard to take, for us all, I think, in some ways.

4. No, Peter did not know Péguy.* I am sure he was influenced by Péguy's style of writing. He used to quote him often. He never told me he had taken such a style. He just said "it makes to think." He often sort of sang [his essays]—he memorized them as tho they were verse. He answered questions often with one or another of his "essays." And by the way, did I mention in my letter to you that it was my brother John who called them Easy Essays and the name struck. I am sure Peter thought of them as a form of free verse, but I did not, and I am afraid that there I imposed my journalistic will on him. Poor Peter used to say sometimes, "Man proposes but woman disposes."

5. I had heard that St. Augustine wrote in phrased lines. Perhaps Père Gratry. Anyway I never saw any such writings. I was trying, evidently, in those early days to explain why Peter wrote that way. He says that by dividing into phrases people read more easily. Certainly many journalists have done this. It is not out of the ordinary. I never said that [Pierre-Joseph] Proudhon [*an early French anarchist*] wrote this way. I have one book of his, "What is Property?" and also Fr. [Henri] de Lubac wrote his life, *The Unmarxian Socialist*. A great book. I have both. As for influence, I do not think a man admits to influence as much as a woman does.

---

* Charles Péguy (1873–1914) was a French poet who tried to reconcile his Catholic faith with his socialist leanings.

6. Campion Propaganda Committees were started by Tom Coddington, who married Dorothy Weston, one of the editors of the paper. The emphasis was on sociology and liturgy, and the committees had many weekends at a shore place we rented on Staten Island. They took over the picketing of the Mexican consulate and the German consulate, and I allowed this though not in favor of it. It was on the advice of Fr. McSorley who thought we (the Catholic Worker) might get into trouble and thought we should use another name like that of the Campion Propaganda Committee. Sounded too much like Communist tactics to me. But we did it. It did not last long, though it was very popular for a time. They had a good group in Boston and Washington, and the former group started the house there. I have never talked much about them because the leader, Tom, went so completely wrong, one could only consider him mental or possessed. Fr. [Paul Hanly] Furfey was much impressed by the Campions. Dedicated his first book, *Fire on the Earth,* to them. I have always felt he judged us all severely on that. That it was the CW fault somehow that we did not prevent this going astray. He has never been close to us since.

7. No apprentices ever started a house. Local groups, CW readers, interested in the works of mercy started them, called on Peter or me to come and speak, begged and worked and kept them going for years. All were due, those we listed as ours, to Peter Maurin's agitation.

One could go on so indefinitely, to tell all the things which stemmed from the Catholic Worker. It would seem like vainglory. But no one would ever realize how much Peter Maurin is responsible for. I am really surprised at your question—that you did not realize this. As for Peter's influence, many of those who ran the houses argue that they follow Peter, and then they go their own way. But I would say that they find their vocation, their attraction to one or another aspect of the work, and carry it out. People are still arguing as to whether Peter was a pacifist or not and I try to handle this in the article I referred to and which I enclose.

Gratefully in Christ,
Dorothy Day

TO BILL GAUCHAT

JUNE 16, 1954

Just sent you yesterday two terrific tomes to review. Hope you can stand it. Helene Iswolsky thinks very highly of [Pitrim] Sorokin,—says he is one of ten Russians whom Lenin thought so highly of that he let them out of Russia and they are a leaven in the world, and help to keep us in mind of the greatness of the Russian people. [Nicolai] Berdyaev is another, [George P.] Fedotov, who was the editor of that book on Russian spirituality, etc. We must always be seeking concordances, rather than differences—that is the basis of the ecumenical movement, which is part of the peace movement.

I think of you all so often—your sufferings (which Leon Bloy says is the only truly supernatural thing we have to offer to God). God has counted you worthy to suffer. I'm praying for little Colette, and for you all. How I hope you can get a bigger house so you can have discussion groups, a library, a guest-room, a Christ room, etc.—all that will go to make a Christian community. The first and greatest of all communities is the *home*; if things are not right there nothing can make them right. The larger community of families, the parish. Peter's whole emphasis began with the personalist approach, not "they don't do this, they don't do that," pointing out others' lack.

I've just been reading a book on psychiatry, *The Leaven of Love* by a woman psychiatrist [Izette de Forest]; and it is so interesting and often appalling to see what a responsibility parents have for their children's later woes and mistakes.

I'm rambling along because I am awaiting a chiropractor whom Msgr. Fiorentino insists on sending down to me. Had x-rays taken—spine shows trouble. Have to have some suffering in this world, each one of us.

Love to all of you, in Christ,
Dorothy

TO JACK ENGLISH

AUGUST 20, 1954
Dear Frater Charles,—

It was certainly good to get your letter and I wish to reply on the feast of a Cistercian, St. Bernard, to ask your prayers for some ex-Cistercians who are dashing off to try the Little Brothers of Jesus. Pray for them all. If you knew how happy I was to lose workers to religious orders or to marriage! It is those who leave like Irene or Betty Lou who break my heart, for they flounder most unhappily. I do pray for you every day, and I have the prayer card of the Blessed Mother in my missal which reminds me.

My health is generally good now after a complicated operation, benignant, not malign, to use the quaint medical terminology. It was not the hysterectomy but a prolapsis, a polyp and hemorrhoids, most painful and agonizing for weeks. I go into indelicate detail because rumors of cancer go around. People always expect the worst, this is such a vale of tears. My suffering is to be in work and people but I was glad to be accounted worthy to have a little of the physical. It is most important. Job didn't cry out until it was his own flesh that was afflicted. That is human nature.

Pray for us all. We all love you very much and think of you often. How close we are. Your letter, bringing that out, was wonderful spiritual reading for the table here. I'm sending it on to Tom.

Love from us all,
Dorothy

TO FRANCISCO FERNANDEZ
Francisco Fernandez, a Spanish pacifist, often visited the Worker. He was deported to Spain after overstaying his visa.

CHRISTMAS 1954

Thank you for writing and sending me your statements. I wish I had met you before I left. Ammon's letters have been full of mention of you. I do pray for you and beg God to bless you mightily in your struggle for freedom. There are so few who appreciate God's great gift or realize how they slip from manhood if they don't use it to choose the good. Not everyone has the vocation to take a stand, to cry out, as you are doing. The gifts of others may be in other directions. Perhaps God has chosen you to be a reminder—another voice crying in the wilderness today.

Pray for me too, in this pilgrimage of mine.

Sincerely in Christ our brother,

Dorothy Day

TO THE COMMISSIONER OF PRISONS, *Washington, D.C.*
Dorothy wrote on behalf of Morton Sobell, who was convicted along with the Rosenbergs of spying for the Soviets.

DECEMBER 28, 1954

Dear Mr. [James V.] Bennett,—

I beg that you will forgive my presumption in writing to you about a matter which you might well believe to be out of my province. But as a Catholic trying to live an integrated life, as well as an American concerned for issues of freedom and justice, I cannot help feeling myself involved. To visit the prisoner is one of the works of mercy that most of us have no chance of doing. We can feed the hungry, clothe the naked, shelter the harborless, as we on the Catholic Worker have done these past twenty years, making it a matter of personal responsibility first of all, rather than of state responsibility. But we do not visit the prisoner. It is in the light of that particular work of mercy which our Lord commanded us to perform in the 25th chapter of St. Matthew, that I am writing to beg for the transfer (not the release) of Morton Sobell, from Alcatraz to a penitentiary in the East where he can be visited by his wife and children as well as by his lawyer. I understand that there has not yet been a review or an appeal of his case, and his imprisonment such a distance away makes it impossible for his lawyer to see him. So it is not only a work of mercy, but one of plain justice, that a fearless citizen and a Christian should join others in asking for this transfer.

I do not presume to speak as to the innocence or guilt of Morton Sobell. I am just asking for his transfer, because I believe that he is being submitted to cruel and inhuman punishment in his imprisonment on Alcatraz which would seem to be for the special purpose of separating him from any visit from his family or lawyer. I make this appeal knowing full well that any association with his defense committee in this time of unworthy fear and trembling on the part of a great country means being tarred with the same brush as subversive. But our dear Lord whose birthday we have just celebrated was meek and humble of heart and did not disdain the company of publicans and sinners and told us to love our enemies and to do good to those who injure us. It is in His name that I beg you to consider this appeal and arrange for the transfer of Morton Sobell.

TO TAMAR

JANUARY 1955 [ORIGINAL MANGLED]

So immersed in writing that cannot do letters. Only a few chapters [of the book on Therese] left. Have gotten to the last part of her convent . . . the death, then the conclusion. I think it will be good. Hope so. Anyway what a great sense of relief I'll have at getting it done. Poor Fritz Eichenberg said that he never wakes up without having a realization of a heavy weight on him, of unfinished work, the job he is paid in advance to do for Harpers, a child's Bible, illustrated. Thinking of that, I did not bother to ask for an advance as I really should have. That would have clinched the sale of the book. I felt just as much the sword hanging over my head, having promised to write the book. As it is, that Chambers is liable to turn it down, there being no contract signed. Caroline Tate suggests Harcourt.

Had a nice visit with them, and am trying to persuade Allen [Tate] to write for the paper. Along the distributist lines—his name carried much weight. He too is a monarchist, as Dave is, but being a writer, he would be able to make his position more understood, the king as a symbol, so even if he dragged his politics in, it would not be half so against the anarchist position as democracy is, as it is.

How little these things matter, and how important the work each one of us does. Wish you would write. Leonie wrote to Marie, sisters of [St.] Therese, or vice versa, in their letters, "I love to know what you are doing. It may be little in appearance, but I myself am doing little things in my office of procurator, with my pears, my apples, my carrots, my beets and my radishes. But in the eyes of God there are no big things here below, there are but little things, nothings; even the most magnificent deeds are [little in His] sight. But if, from our little deeds, He sees love shine, then . . ." [*text missing*].

Visitors every afternoon. Speaking Friday, Saturday, Sunday. Then I leave next Friday. After I make my big jump and see what my fare is, I'll send some more money to put away for the mortgage. Did Becky ever finish that Lavelle book on the Little Flower? I started to read it to them and she was engrossed in it. How I love them all. It is like a toothache. But I must do my work, and my temptation is to be with you always. Lucky you don't have a big house, I'd move in. It's never any good, an in-law in the house. Enough, I must catch the mailman. I miss you and love you very much as you know, and you are always a comfort to me.

Love, Dorothy

TO FRANCISO FERNANDEZ

APRIL 24, 1955

Tom kindly forwarded your letter to me in Montreal and I just got it the other day and this is the first chance to answer it. It made me so happy. I wept with joy. I love such long letters—they are as good as a visit together, and your descriptions of the services and the priest and the children are beautiful. And the joyful climax to the Holy Week, your receiving the body and blood of our Lord. Now the same blood is flowing in our veins and we are closer than brother and sister—I mean in this way, that we both have the supernatural life of God in us. Now we are truly one—all of us at the CW with a great unity. You are our representative in Spain wherever you are, so keep writing.

The only reason why Peter used the word anarchist was to make people think. He really preferred "personalist." Also he thought we should avoid all political weapons.

I come back to an appalling pile of mail, and after all night on the bus I don't feel up to much. So I'll finish this now and get it off to you quickly.

Again—love from us all. Especially remember us when you come from communion. In Acts, the men at Emmaus knew Christ in the breaking of bread.

After returning to Spain, Fernandez had trouble finding work. Eventually he got a job with a U.S. company building an air and naval base in Spain. Neither Dorothy nor Ammon was happy about this. As Fernandez noted, "They seemed to believe I could be able, if I try, to spread in Franco's Spain the pacifism of the CW. I guess they believe it because they had never lived under a dictatorship."

MAY 14, 1955

We were worried about you and very glad to get your letter. Ammon was shocked, I am afraid, but I certainly can understand how you feel, how close the ties are in a family, and the needs of a mother and father do come first. "Needs" not "wants" are the things to be considered, however. Too many parents make their children sacrifice themselves to working so that they can boast to the neighbors about their children. We have to give up father and mother, son and daughter, over and over again it seems to me. I know that I pray Tamar and Dave and the children will become a holy family, and when I see them beset by trials, then I worry, and it may be those same trials that are contributing to their holiness. Poverty (not destitution) is a blessing. The very fact that your mother had roomers, and a big enough house to rent rooms, makes it appear that it is not destitution but hard work you are worrying about. Even then—it is a blessing when people love to work and work hard. If Ammon's wife had loved him and clung to him, it would not have been so easy for him to take the absolutist position. He knows that. But he is upset and wishes you had gone on teaching—that would have been enough. Anyway, your trial has not yet come up and the bigger and in some ways easier sacrifices may be ahead. God will give you grace for what you have to do. Maybe you will wander the roads begging yet.

All my love, though of course we hope and pray you get on the right course again.

Are you getting to daily Mass and communion? That is nourishment—strength—you will receive inspiration from the Holy Spirit to know what to do. It will be as hard to do that in the face of the opposition to the Church (it is so unusual to see men at daily Mass) as it is to oppose the evils of the State.

TO JACK ENGLISH

Dorothy describes here an audacious act of civil disobedience in which she, Ammon, and other pacifists refused to cooperate with a compulsory civil defense drill in New York City. This was the beginning of an annual protest that led to several stints in jail.

ST. JOHN THE BAPTIST, JUNE 24, 1955

The best time to spend an hour in church is right after the eight-thirty Mass at Nativity. Then there are only a few old ladies, including me. This morning I had so many things on my mind. On June 15, when there was supposed to be a nationwide air raid drill, 28 of us refused to obey orders and sat out in City Hall Park. It was our usual group, War Resisters [League], Peacemakers, Fellowship of Reconciliation, and Ammon, Carol Perry, Pat Rusk, Mary Roberts, Mike Kovalak, Stanley Borowsky, and me from the CW. Also Eileen Fantino, Mary Anne [McCoy] and Helen [Russell]. We were all arrested, and from 2 p.m. on we went from jail to jail, Elizabeth Street, Thirtieth Street, Center Street, and finally we women ended in the Women's House of Detention on Greenwich Avenue.

It was a most wonderful experience of performing the work of mercy of visiting the prisoner, by being ourselves one of them. When I knelt down in that little cell in the women's prison, I thought, this is the closest I shall ever get to a Carmelite monastery. But it was a brief experience, and we were out on bail the next noon, some of us, the bail being set for $1,500 each. The rest had another night. When Bob was arrested, the bail was only $45. They are beginning to take us more seriously, in the peace movement.

Now it is a succession of court cases, and each week we must go sit in court all morning, and watch our poor fellow workers from the Bowery and their parks being lined up. If you are smart enough to plead guilty and say you have a job to go to, you get off. If you are a foreigner or dirty or have no home, they act as though it were a favor to you to send you up for five to ten days. We have got acquainted with judges, lawyers, police, as well as other prisoners. It is a new world, as though we had moved into *Bleak House*, or *Little Dorrit*.

Anyway, even though we intend to plead guilty, the case is still pending and will be continued maybe until fall. I do hope so, what with Tamar having a baby in July. Two things for you to pray about. Another, the sale of the Newburgh farm going through. When we concentrate on Staten Island, we can still have our retreats and days of recollection and it is far more convenient and inexpensive for all. We can charter a bus for fifty dollars and take a load of Chrystie Street out for the day.

So all this is on my mind, and I tell you about it not to distract you but to beg your prayers. I was praying hard this morning about it all, and felt a real sense of joy. Then when I got back to the office, there was Brother Joel's letter and that made me even happier. He says for me to write to you first, as I owe you a letter. But you know you are both in my prayers, as is the whole monastery there. I feel very close to you, and there is no sense of loss, but a great sense of enrichment. God is so good. Our lines are cast in goodly places.

The rosary bell, which you started so many noons ago, has rung, so I must go.

Much love to you of my family there.

In Christ, Dorothy.

Just finished *The Lord* by Guardini. Now reading his on *The Rosary.*

TO SUPPORTERS OF THE CATHOLIC WORKER

Apart from her ongoing protests over civil defense, Dorothy found herself in court on another matter—charged with being a "slum landlord" because of deficiencies in health and safety codes in the Catholic Worker house. Publicity about the affair actually turned to her advantage. After a story about her ordeal appeared in the New York Times the judge softened his tone, and generous supporters, including the poet W. H. Auden, quickly raised the necessary funds for repairs. This letter was addressed to members of Maryhouse in Little Canada, Minnesota.

MARCH 1956, FEAST OF OUR LADY OF SORROWS

There is no time to write to each of you separately, but I want to thank you each one who has written in our trouble and let you know that St. Joseph is good and we are getting the help we need little by little. It is true that it is begging, but the contempt that goes with it, the standing before the judge over and over again, the misrepresentations in the papers, the being accused of being a slum landlord and exploiting the poor, etc, not to speak of my past life being dragged in again and again, all goes with it so it must be pleasing to our Lord. The Chancery got in touch with us with sympathy and sent a priest from the Catholic Charities to offer help if it came to an eviction so that in itself is a great blessing. Fr. Faley continues to suffer—it is cancer, as you doubtless have heard. Two operations so far, and he is in bed and will be some time. He is 69 and has been so healthy all his life.

We are the offscourings of all, poor beggars, and if we went out to take jobs there would be no work done at all. One cannot work in the world and [do this] "on the side." Most of the apostolate is working in the world and very few wish to be considered beggars. I cannot emphasize this enough. As for criticism of our program, you all know how I feel and have always felt. And I love you all so dearly! As dear friends, as loved children, you can be sure of that.

In our Lady's love,
Dorothy

TO JACK ENGLISH

APRIL 5, 1956

Dearest Bro. Charles—

Just got your good letter today and was so happy—it was a ray of peace. All this month has been a torment—Holy Week especially so, so it was a good Lent. One particular brand of suffering—it is hard to be at peace when you see those you love around you wrecking themselves thru drink—Veronica has been drinking all Holy Week and Easter Sunday too so please pray for her. Larry, the painter, fell down stairs and broke eight ribs, piercing his lungs and is just now off the critical list. John Murray is in the hospital too, and so on,—you know the story, the same old story. Remember Tom's head on one of my stories—"Love is to care and not to care"—I just realize the truth of it, but how to care and not to care—to leave all to God. To pray, and be at peace, etc. I just suffer. Of course I pray for you each day, and count on yours.

How I'd love to get away for a few weeks! Maybe later. But I'm still being summoned to court—on making changes in the house. Did you know I was convicted of being a slum landlord last month and fined $250 for operating a firetrap? Yes, there have been all kinds of suffering. But the unjust judge started a wave of publicity and sympathy and we were sent enough money to put in a sprinkler system and are in the midst of other changes. My Therese book is accepted but needs working on.

There is such grief on every side—letters are full of it, and new bomb tests from Russia, England, and U.S. beginning April 15 to last all summer. And our lone voice cries out and it all seems so hopeless. But we can't just sit back. In the twinkling of an eye God can change everything. The Holy Father in his Easter message warns against pessimism.

We all send our love—Dorothy

TO SISTER GENEVIEVE OF ST. TERESA

Sister Genevieve was the religious name of Céline Martin, elder sister of St. Therese of Lisieux. While three of her sisters, including Therese, preceded her in entering the local Carmelite monastery, Céline had delayed her own entry and stayed home to care for their father until his death. It must have been thrilling for Dorothy to address a letter to this living link with her favorite saint and spiritual patron. (She does not mention in her letter, as she does in her book, that when she first read the autobiography of St. Therese she considered it "pious pap.")

APRIL 16, 1956

Dear Sister Genevieve—

Under separate cover you will receive a copy of *The Long Loneliness*, in which you will find some account of the Catholic Worker, which will serve, if you will be so kind as to glance through it, as a sort of introduction. I have hesitated for years to write to you, knowing how full your life must be of correspondence with a world which so loves your little sister St. Therese. I am just one of the many who have written books about her. Because I am a convert and because my autobiography was published by a non-Catholic firm, Harper and Bros., I am anxious to bring her story of the little way to the non-Catholic readers of our country.

My book is finished and I am now rewriting it. I have read Fr. Piat's story of your family (together with most of the other books which have appeared about St. Therese) and her account of the many letters your dear mother and father wrote interests me greatly. Have these letters ever been published in France? I have laid great emphasis on the home life of St. Therese, because of its great importance today. The need to restore the family, the good life of the community of the family, as a beginning in restoring all things in Christ, is a theme of the book I am writing. So I am begging you to let me know if any copies of the letters of your mother and father and sisters have been published or privately printed in France. I should like very much to see the letters and will send the money for them at once, if they have been printed.

Will you please ask the sisters to pray for our work, and for the little book, which frightens me, I feel so completely unworthy of writing it. Begging you to excuse my presumption in writing you and taking up your time.

P.S. The story I am writing is a very simple one, not one of great research or originality. What there is distinctive about it is my personal reaction to the story of Therese, the message of Therese in my own very active life as a Catholic, a journalist, and in a way a social worker. Also I am writing it most specially to reach the non-Catholic.

TO JACK ENGLISH

MAY 18 1956

God bless you always. When I open my missal I see the card you sent of the Blessed Mother a few years ago, and always pray for you.

All the men have kept sober since we moved from Maryfarm. They sure had gotten in a rut of drinking. All of them had found some neighbors for whom to work for drink and it was appalling. Now they are a sober lot and the Staten Island place is a dream. I told them that we'd move again if they got into such a state again.

Otherwise all is quiet, peaceful, etc. We raised $28,000 to do over the whole house according to plans of the housing dept. Did you get the news of my fine of $250? Tom had stalled them off since the fire and when they landed on me it was like a ton of bricks. In this last year I am twice convicted—in the air raid drill (there is a suspended sentence of 6 mos.) and as a slum landlord (and the fine is suspended too). Some day the axe will fall. New laws make it necessary to keep books better, to register with the state because we solicit funds twice a year, and give an accounting each June. Charlie [McCormack] is good to work with—good at business, orderly, and not combative. I've never known such quiet, at home, I mean.

NOVEMBER 28, 1956

Yours is a great suffering—I can see that, and of course we do not pick the particular kind of suffering we want to bear. But thank God you have some little burden of suffering to bear at this time when there is so much of it in the world. You are accounted worthy to suffer. When it dawns on us that this is a little coin the dear God is enriching us with to purchase salvation—our own and others'—it ceases to be suffering. Remember, "Our infirmities were multiplied—afterward we made haste."

I've found that so many times. I was thinking, too, how often and how many of us feel unloved, unwanted, on many and many occasions during our lives—all the misunderstandings there are in families, even between husband and wife. We all want heaven here and now, no patience, no waiting. Don't think I don't understand how you feel, because I have felt the same many a time. How many times I have felt even a wall of hatred and resentment around me—sometimes over little things, and also over the big ones.

The opposition to the work, the idea that I did not understand or interpret Peter correctly. There really is not a soul around the CW who has not been the occasion of suffering. Just recently when we were talking about bringing out another edition of Peter's essays, [I learned of the] group meeting at Agnes's and Betty's to talk over the work a few years ago [and] the suggestion that Mike Harrington be the one to write an introduction was enough to floor me. Mike Harrington, who never knew Peter, who himself is a fallen-away Catholic and a Trotskyist! How fantastic can people get, and this from one's nearest and dearest. There has been many an occasion when I never wanted to see a CW again.

And then some such thought as that of St. John of the Cross would come, "Where there is no love, put love, and you will find love," and makes all right. When it comes down to it, even on the natural plane, it is much happier and more enlivening to love than to be loved.

Of course there would be this postponement in your taking vows! Didn't the same thing happen to the Little Flower? This is no time to consider (most childishly) that nobody wants one, or to use such expressions as hitting the road,—it is a wonderful chance to grow in love. If we were not being pruned, and pruning surely hurts, we would bear no fruit. I'm convinced, with your social conscience, with the contacts that you have had all your life, that a life of prayer and penance is going to save countless souls.

I was thinking this minute of that fellow you met in London [Charles Ashleigh], who was the former editor of the *Moscow News*, whom I also knew in Chicago when he had just gotten out of Leavenworth. Your prayers will reach out to him and to countless others. You are the power house down there, and all of you so close to us and there are so many times I pray to my guardian angel to bear messages to yours for help of one kind or another.

I'm sure that even before you get this all will be going on as before and that you will be even glad of an additional year to prepare for your final vows. After all you will still be gaining the grace of vows. And there is plenty of natural exuberance to be toned down which must many a time and in many ways have intruded on others and made them feel that you are an odd duck amongst monks.

Hang on, Jack, and remember that we all love you and count on you. Also I remember telling you once that with you it would be the Trappists or nothing. I am convinced you are where God wants you and this disappointment is in the nature of a gift. I'm praying for you always and most especially this Advent.

God bless you mightily. With love in Christ, Dorothy

TO THOMAS MERTON

Thomas Merton was a monk in the Trappist Abbey of Gethsemani in Kentucky. In 1948 he had published The Seven Storey Mountain, *an account of his conversion and entry into the monastery. It became a surprise bestseller, making Merton the best-known Catholic spiritual writer in the English-speaking world. Before entering the monastery he had worked with Catherine de Hueck at Friendship House in Harlem, but he never visited the Catholic Worker, and he and Dorothy would never meet. In her letters she always addressed him by his religious name, Father Louis.**

DECEMBER 26, 1956

Dear Fr. Louis,

Alice Catherine tells me that you have offered Christmas Mass for me and the Catholic Worker at the Monastery, and it has made me very happy indeed.

We have had a very beautiful Christmas here, and quite a sober and serious one too. There have been occasions in the past when the entire kitchen force got drunk, which made life complicated, but you must have been holding them up this year, and please continue to do so.

God bless you always. Gratefully in Christ,

Dorothy Day

TO JACK ENGLISH

Dorothy refers to the Pope's Christmas message of December 1956, which outlined the provisions of a just war and stated that if these conditions

---

* An account of the correspondence between Dorothy Day and Thomas Merton, including her letters (edited by William H. Shannon), may be found in Anne Klejment and Nancy L. Roberts, eds., *American Catholic Pacifism: The Influence of Dorothy Day and the Catholic Worker Movement* (Westport, CT: Praeger, 1996). Merton's letters to Dorothy appear in William H. Shannon, ed., *The Hidden Ground of Love* (New York: Farrar Straus & Giroux, 1985).

were met a Catholic citizen could not be a conscientious objector. In her
column in the January 1957 CW *Dorothy responded to this argument*
with her conviction that it was impossible in the modern age for these
conditions to be fulfilled. Meanwhile, her book on St. Therese was lan-
guishing with the publisher.

JAN 26, 1957

It made me happy indeed to get your letter telling me you had
renewed your vows for a year. I'm ashamed not to have answered sooner but a lot of sickness around and much work at
Chrystie St. and the farm. About the Pope's message. We wrote
3 articles on it in the *CW*. I do not know whether you get to see
it. But if you can read the Jan number, do. Of course "I am a
daughter of the Church" and will keep silent when I am told to.
Until then I must continue to write as I do, and emphasize the
supremacy of conscience. It seems to me that that is what Joan
of Arc was canonized for, not because she was the warrior maid
but because she followed her conscience. My *Therese* has been
with Harper since June. Anne Fremantle says it is banal, and
Exman [*editor at Harper*] that it is colorless. I do not know. I
wanted to let the non-Catholic know about her.

Tamar will have her 8th [child] in Aug. She and Dave are
very unsettled about whether or not to go to Vermont. Please
pray for them and ask Fr. Abbot to pray too. I am more attached
to her than to my writing. At least she disturbs me more. So
please pray. And you know I do for you. I was in jail for 5 days
last week [*for civil defense protest*].

FEB 26, 1957

Saw Graham Greene's play, "The Potting Shed," a wonderful
thing on faith. A happy play, and reminded me in many ways of
the spirit of *Labyrinthine Ways* [also known as *The Power and the
Glory*]. Both those writings of his make one feel the power of the
priesthood, and how strong they are in faith. I have always felt
that, realizing how they have to go on and on, giving absolution,

the sacraments, seeing so little change in people apparently. I also saw an Italian and a French film, both beautiful things. Pre-Lenten going out. I am going to try to keep a very quiet and recollected Lent.

Tamar and Dave want still to go to Vermont and I hope he gets some work soon. My brother-in-law [Franklin Spier] is going to give him an introduction to one of the Boni brothers, who published my first terrible book [*The Eleventh Virgin*] which I wrote when I was twenty, who have some kind of a factory there, which has to do with making reading contraptions, or filmed books, or something, I do not know. Even for my own sake, I hope they can go, because Dave wants to be away from the CW, and when they are there, I feel I have to help them when I go to S.I. As it is I only go down two days a week.

I want your prayers and the prayers of the community for three special things. One, a homicidal maniac, as they are called, comes in, escaped from a mental hospital. Gregory Zilboorg says it would be dangerous for him to come to his office again, dangerous for him and his staff, so he sends him back to us! I told him tonight that I would write to the Trappists to pray for him. He has been in and out of hospitals for eleven years, he said. Has no conscience, no moral sense, does not react to alcohol or tranquilizing drugs, he tells me. I wrote the Maryknoll cloister too.

The second is the man sentenced to die. They postponed the carrying out of the sentence yesterday to have another sanity examination. He has written me rational letters, in one of which he said he had aspired to sanctity once, had read the Little Office daily, and been a member of the Third Order of St. Francis. It was drink with him. Hanging around the waterfront and on a party with three men, one of whom repelled him horribly. They were in his home, the last he remembered, and when he came to, the two others were gone, and he concluded, "You know the rest." I feel so strongly, how horrible things we are capable of, once God withdraws his grace from us. I feel we should pray very hard for this man, Francis Xavier Ballem.

The third is worst of all. A woman whose word I trust tells me of hearing of a Black Mass (in Greenwich Village, perhaps). And Roger mentioned a strange priest, crippled, out of the Church, who lives on the same street as Anne Marie Barron. So please pray hard. So many want to lead a life close to God, and aim so high, and scarcely can keep the Commandments, the old law. I feel how dangerous are our prideful aspirations sometimes. Better to be like St. Therese, a little grain of sand. One thing helps us—people think we are fools, the lunatic fringe, and their scorn keeps us down.

I do not let a day pass without praying for you. I reread *Seven Storey Mountain,* and do feel intensely that *that* is your life, that *that* life is for you,—it is your true vocation. We all love you very much and feel closer to you than we ever did before. This life is so short, and God rewards the smallest generosities so greatly. Already, I am sure, you are rewarded mightily. Even if you have to renew your vows from year to year for a while, do not be discouraged. Remember Therese, who had the same experience, and who in fact was never really novice mistress, but just assistant to the novice mistress. What a power she is today. You have all the weapons. We can be so sure of that. You have chosen the better part, in fact the only part for you.

TO CHARLES McCORMACK

Charles McCormack served as the CW business manager. Dorothy wrote these letters from the Women's House of Detention, where she was serving a term of 30 days for her part in the annual protest against the city's compulsory civil defense drills.

Charles McCormack
223 Chrystie Street
New York City 2

JULY 15, 1957

MONDAY NIGHT

No envelopes and so I must address you thus formally. It was so good to get your letter and to see Fr. McCoy and Fr. McCaffrey the same day. I put you and Della on my visiting list but only one visit every 2 weeks. Telephone Della and tell her I'm fine—the time passes quickly. We have plenty of copy for the paper and you and Bob [Steed] can manage perfectly.

There is a good library here so we need nothing. I am put in the laundry, ironing; Deane [Mowrer] cleans part of the roof recreation rooms and Judith [Malina, *a member of the anarchist Living Theater troupe*] the main floor, a lively spot with much coming and going which she likes. She cried all last night but is better tonight. Deane is a bit gloomy but our health is good. Two in a cell but there are 4 of us so we are together but in different corridors. Meals much like the C.W., hardboiled eggs today, meatballs yesterday. Stewed figs, raisins, prunes, apricots. Lights go out at 9 p.m. We get out of our cells at 6:30. Good showers night and morning. Work from 8-11 and 1-3. Recreation on the roof so we get fresh air. Not much inside. I'll have prison pallor when I come out. Hope you can read all this.

I pray for you all daily. Got to Mass Sunday, of course. Twenty-five there. I wrote Tamar. Allotted space and time are up. Love in Christ.

[END OF JULY OR EARLY AUGUST, 1957]

I had written you before but the letter was returned to me. Only 2 a week are allowed and I wrote Tamar twice. Do call and see if she got the letters. Now it seems we can only write to those we list as we come in and I listed you and my sister, because I did not want Tamar to be coming all the way to town and waiting around and this her last month. So many rules. But the time is flying—we have passed the halfway mark. All are well here—Judith is on "diet" and gets an egg and orange and milk for breakfast, etc. She is vegetarian. Yesterday I had another x-ray and cardiograph. They sure take good care of you. I was told not to eat starch! Neither Judith nor Joan has heard from their husbands. But the warden came to see us yesterday and he said he will see what he can do. He seems a very fine person—a Hungarian and a Catholic so he feels the Russian situation keenly. He cannot of course understand our position but showed us the utmost patience and courtesy.

It is very hard to make it clear that we do not want to harass people who are only doing their duty and that although we break one law in order to make our point clear about our refusal to cooperate with psychological warfare, we bend over backward to show our respect for the desire for the common good which most laws are for. Certainly our very works of mercy are to show our sense of responsibility for our brothers and our desire to do our share and more than our share in a realm where the State is not supposed to function except in cases of crisis. Certainly Holy Mother City tries to do right by everyone here,—our physical exams, abundant food, clean cells and linen. Tonight we are even having a show, put on by the girls—song and dance, for which they have been practicing some time. Thank God the heat is past. We can sleep again. It must have been hard for all of you there, you in your tiny airless room. No room on the page for more.

TO MARGE BARONI

Dorothy's friend Marge Baroni worked in the civil rights movement in Mississippi.

NOV 8, 1957

Today is my 60th birthday and I am celebrating it by being in Washington to take part in a prayer vigil before the White House against nuclear weapons testing. There is no time with God and prayer is retroactive. The group here is all denominations. Are you a member of any Third Order? Do you know the

Little Sisters of Jesus of Chas de Foucauld? Have you read *Seeds of the Desert* by [René] Voillaume? Magnificent spiritual reading.

In Christ,
Dorothy Day

TO DOROTHY GAUCHAT

FEB 11, 1958

Your letter finally caught up with me and I am so sorry you are so hard pressed. I am glad you have so many girls in your family and that they are such good help. Look how they reacted last summer when you had a miscarriage.

I have been visiting families all along the way, and there are many tragedies in our midst. While I was in Mexico I talked with a saintly old priest, 80, and all he talked about was the need for suffering, the joy in suffering, and how we had to bear our share, and I just burst into tears, and I told him I found it very hard to take, just to think of all the suffering that might happen to Tamar and the family, for instance. He comforted me by saying God never asked anything of you that he did not give you beforehand. But we sure have to bear our part, each one of us in one form or another. If we could only learn to relax under it. If we could only learn that the only important thing is love, and that we will be judged on love—to keep on loving, and showing that love, and expressing that love, over and over, whether we feel it or not, seventy times seven, to mothers-in-law, to husbands, to children—and to be oblivious of insult, or hurt, or injury—not to see them, not to hear them. It is a hard, hard doctrine. I guess we get what we need in the way of discipline. God can change things in a twinkling of an eye. We have got to pray, to read the Gospel, to get to frequent communion, and not judge, not do anything but love, love, love. A bitter lesson. Where there is no love, put love and you will take out love, St. John of the Cross says.

I am preaching to myself too. One of the girls, Eleanor Corrigan, has had a nervous breakdown in N.Y. and she has always been so critical of me that I had formed the practice, self protective in a way, of ignoring her. I should have been practicing love, expressing love.

Got to rush to church—I'll be remembering Bill. Give him my love, this lovely feast of our Lady.

Dorothy Gauchat's sorrows included her husband Bill's drinking and their daughter's recurrent problem with seizures.

PALM SUNDAY 1958

Certainly you have been overwhelmed with tragedy—going thru the Sorrowful Mysteries as Father Farina would say. Most people are always trying, by divorce, separation, etc, to run back to the joyful, and they never get thru to the glorious.

"Let us suffer if needs be with bitterness," the Little Flower said someplace. Certainly it is a grim thing—trying to grow in love. God is good to be showing you the way. He must have great things in store for you and Bill. He certainly loves you—letting you, leading you in the way of Christ.

I hate to seem to moralize, but you have to say these things. I have to comfort myself this way all the time when things get harder and harder.

TO MARY DURNIN

JUNE 25, 1958

Just got your letter today and hasten to write to you and to apologize for the delay in writing. I can only plead constant troubles that wring my heart. You can be sure that you and yours are in my prayers and Masses. This morning the only gleam of consolation I had was that when God sends all these troubles and sufferings to the families, he is sending just what they need, to prune them down, so that they bear fruit. If I didn't believe that, I'd be unhappy indeed. How he must love you to be so intent on sending what you need, spiritually. If all were going well and smoothly, it would be really dangerous.

I mean this: Tamar is dying of loneliness in Vermont; David cannot find a job; there are no young neighbors with children; her ambitions to farm, to garden, to keep animals are constantly thwarted by lack of money. My sister sends some, but it was for a deep freeze. Now all the materials to pack away in a deep freeze cost money. Feed costs money, to harvest the hay costs money, to get in the wood for the winter costs money. It is easy for a couple to pioneer but as soon as they have children it is terribly hard. What self discipline it all takes. Anyway, I receive unhappy letters from Tamar, and her unhappiness hurts me. And I see so much of it her own fault.

Dorothy Gauchat and her husband are having a fearful time. He has had several heart attacks, he drinks too much and all but goes insane; she has one child which has some form of fits constantly and her brain is deteriorating. Dorothy Willock and her husband live in great tragedy. He is half paralyzed and speaks in such a way as only to be understood by her alone. He cannot work except a little painful writing and all their friends have to support them. She is going to have her twelfth child.

The terrible suffering we all have to go through, to prune and purify our love. I remember Fr. Farina says we must pass through the sorrowful mysteries to get to the glorious and most of us won't, we keep going back, trying to find the joyful again. We want to live in the honeymoon state always.

Anyway we do not know the heinousness of sin. We do not value grace, the most precious thing in the world. We are willful, so strongly willful, that God has to send all these things to us to cut us down, to prune us. We can only thank God He is doing it. And if it is the innocent who are suffering too (although who is without sin?), then we are suffering for the rest of the world, helping to bear the sum total of suffering, helping to expiate. Anyway we should be more thankful for suffering than we are.

I am writing this way, not so much for you, as for myself, to comfort myself too.

I have two women both over 70 who set me such an example of hard work, giving out clothes and washing clothes, and going up and down stairs all day, that I am ashamed ever to complain. So do not take this as a letter of complaint. It is to make you see that I love you, think of you, pray for you and feel that you are bearing your share in the apostolate. I hope you can sell the house and you will if that is what God wants for you.

TO THE WOODCREST BRUDERHOF COMMUNITY
Rifton, New York

The Bruderhof is a modern Anabaptist community founded in Germany in the 1920s by Eberhard Arnold. To escape Hitler, the community moved first to England, then Paraguay, and finally to the United States. Dorothy held them in great esteem, admiring their efforts to live a life of discipleship in community. She responded here to a letter from their elder, Heini Arnold, who had been stung by critical remarks about the Bruderhof in a recent article by Ammon Hennacy.

FEAST DAY OF ST. JOHN THE BAPTIST

AUGUST 29, 1958

Dear Brothers and Sisters at Rifton,

In a way I feel extremely guilty for not reading proof more carefully on Ammon's article. It is my fault when statements like those you speak of come through and are printed. Ammon's faults are certainly on the outside, especially when it comes to controlling the tongue. And of course it betrays an inner attitude of criticism. The Society of Brothers is just not his meat, if one can use these terms. He is such an activist, and feels such a sense of the imminence of the crisis we are in that he feels only the most drastic means will serve *his* purpose at any rate. He feels his vocation as a St. John the Baptist to keep crying out to people never to relax their efforts, to persist in the most strenuous ways by fasting, street distribution of literature and conversations—by picketing, civil disobedience, etc. We have many a controversy around the office you may well be sure, and I have talked for years of the *diversity of vocations*. I can well understand how you have been hurt by the implications—that yours is a safe way of life, that people are cowardly and evading the issue by going to the Bruderhof, that you have siphoned off good workers from other communities, taking over still others and so on. Not only is it inaccurate but it betrays an attitude of criticism. So I am sorry for my part in it by not catching the lines that gave offense and cutting them out.

There are quiet Americans and cocky Americans, and Ammon is one of the latter. He knows that he is a boaster and a braggart—these words he himself has used in connection with himself. But I do know that there is also a humility there that says, "If I, small as I am, can do these things, others ought to be able to do them. I am an ordinary man." And he is indeed very much the typical American, Midwest farm product, pioneer in his own right in this field. Also he takes a good deal of belaboring around here, and in great good nature too.

Of course he justifies himself, as we all do, but he has lived around here for some years now, in community, which is not natural to him, and spending a good deal of time on work which he does not feel is particularly his vocation. But yesterday he met a Buddhist monk in Washington and wrote of how his humility and lack of self-assertion moved him, and made him recognize his faults. Ammon is fasting, you know, and is on his 26th day now, and intends to go on for forty days. I must confess I am dubious about this—although I know Moses and

St. Francis and many others have made it. A friend of mine, a priest in Pittsburgh has just recently fasted for forty days too, but very quietly—not like Ammon.

We had a little sermon Sunday at our parish church on how it was better to suffer affronts than it was to fast, and that any mortification being involuntary is more meritorious than self-imposed austerities. I need to hear this many times. Just yesterday Ammon told Bob Steed who is fasting here for ten days and going on with the work at the same time, to get away from Chrystie Street and all the women there who were worrying about him and trying to give people vitamin pills, and fast for 30 days.

Perhaps he was being humorous, but I felt affronted and insulted too, at first, until I remembered that sermon. Fr. Lallement said to count that day lost in which we did not have some insult handed us. Meaning that such affronts kill the "self" and so we are enabled to put off the "old man" and put on the new.

And of course, what comes from those near and dear always disturbs us the most. Our worst enemies will be those of our own household. Maybe our own emotions—or our brothers and sisters.

The fact is there are two attitudes, one of which is strongly religious, such as yours and ours (though Ammon's article would not seem to reflect this). As a matter of fact in every community there are the "spirituals" and the more practical minded ones (remember St. Francis and Fr. Elias), and these two attitudes will always be at war. It has been that way with us, always two groupings, one side thinking I'm too pious and perhaps reacting too strong the other way.

Have you read *The Way of a Pilgrim* and his Jesus prayer which was the favorite of the Russian peasant? Or *Seeds of the Desert* by Father Voillaume? Both emphasize the humanity of Jesus, our need to ponder and meditate on his life and words.

I won't be able to come to the wedding, though it hurts us to refuse. We are surrounded by troubles, personally and in community too. Baron von Hugel says that at the beginning of each day, think over what you have to do and then cut half of them out.

My love to all of you, and let us make our troubles bring us all closer together.

In Jesus' love,

Dorothy

TO CHICAGO CATHOLIC WORKERS

Dorothy wrote to advise three young men who wished to re-establish a Catholic Worker presence in Chicago.

SEPT 25, 1958

Dear Ed [Morin] and Karl [Meyer] and Al [Lingus],

We were so glad to get your letter but am sorry too to be so late in answering. When it comes to that, I think you are having and are going to have a very hard time, what with one teaching, and the others working or going to school. One cannot count on the men in the house carrying on. The responsibility is too much. They have come to get help, and they are not in a position to give help to others. We have found this in many a house. If it is left to the others, too many are excluded, and Peter Maurin himself, looking as he did like someone from skid row, would be excluded. One cannot expect full-fledged apostles and indoctrinators from those who come in because of their need.

But pray hard, and someone will come along, some ex-Trappist, some dedicated person who is neither working nor going to school and will take over. But then it will not be easy either.

I am glad new houses are starting. God be with you all, and prosper you, and send you the help you need. I do pray that your new archbishop will not be opposed to you. When John Doebele and Jim Rogan and other C.O.'s at St. Alexius Hospital started a house near there, Archbishop Stritch told his priests that he was opposed to the string of houses of hospitality or other centers without his approval. So you see it must be done only personally. It is your home? Then you can perform the works of mercy. But you must beg as for yourselves, in order to share with others. You cannot live in another place and be separate from the house. That is a denial of personalism to begin with. Might as well just have a center for discussion—a Catholic Radical bookshop. There used to be an old bookstore and center called the Radical Bookshop with a little theater attached over on N. Clark in the old days. Geraldine Udell was business manager of *Poetry*, last I heard, and it was her family who ran it.

Let us know how you get on.

Love to all, from us all, in Christ,

Dorothy Day

TO NINA POLCYN

NOV 27, 1958

I feel so close to you always—you know how it is—I can drop in on you, not having seen you for 2 or 3 years, and it is just the same, we are members of a family. It is not just the CW family—it is *the Church*. Thank God for it, institutional and charismatic. I'm reading the Penguin edition of Dorothy Sayers' translation of Dante. Finished the *Inferno*, now on *Purgatory*. The introductions—70 pages long, about the times, the Church, the churchmen, make our troubles seem so picayune. We are in a healthy state.

TO HELENE ISWOLSKY

Helene was on her way to an extended retreat at Combermere, Catherine de Hueck's community in Canada.

JANUARY 23, 1959

You sound so happy, and I am so glad you are there and know that you are going to get a great deal of work done on the memoirs. I know how refreshed I feel in that northern clime. Tamar's place is always white and beautiful too. I had a good visit with her and she is well.

Give Catherine my love, and tell her I think she is wonderful with her order and her peace. Some of these days I will come up for a good rest, but now while the day is with us I must work. She understands. I am staying at the Jeanne d'Arc residence for indigents and aged females, fifty cents a night. Very comfortable and orderly, the lights are out at ten each night. I am getting some sleep. But we are finding little apartments across the street soon, and a loft for the men who are now all in flophouses. But all are cooperating, and we are really happy to be out of that dirt and confusion of Chrystie Street, with the demolition going on.

Much love to you, darling, and when you are rested work hard so that when you return you will come to the beach to rest and gaze out at the water there.

TO DEANE MARY MOWRER

Deane Mary Mowrer, a highly sensitive and educated woman, joined the Catholic Worker community in the 1950s. Already suffering from failing eyesight, she would soon succumb to total blindness. This did not stop her from courting arrest for her part in the civil defense drills.

APRIL 5, 1959

Got your good letter and this is no answer, just a note. It certainly is discouraging, this homelessness. I certainly have been counting on your moving over near to us, and eating your meals at the CW and certainly we could manage the rent. I would advise you to do nothing, however, until we do get two more apartments. We must redouble prayers to St. Joseph, the home-finder. I feel, ominously, that this *not* finding a place right away must mean that we are slated for six months in jail. By now you have heard from Ammon that the date is set, one-thirty, April 17. I must say my stomach turns upside down at the thought. However, we will be having the prayers of many to sustain us. Pope John says that no one is so abandoned as the prisoner. We will be truly poor as far as we can be. Of course they may be tired of us and not even arrest us. But I have a feeling that the CD [civil defense] people love all that publicity, the very thing we cringe from. I wonder how many of us there will be.

This flu I have had (a temperature for eight days) left me feeling very depressed indeed, and very vague in the head. If anyone asked me what I was doing it for (the CD demonstration) I'd have to say I didn't know. I cannot put two thoughts together, let alone write an appeal. Sickness is terrible. We cannot do enough of visiting the sick too. When we are out and free again, I will ask you to make it a special work (and I will try to share it) visiting one person who is sick each day.

TO DONALD POWELL

Dorothy comments on a biography of Eugene O'Neill, Part of a Long Story, *written by O'Neill's second wife, Agnes [Boulton] O'Neill. Reading the book brought back memories of the winter of 1918 when Dorothy had kept company with the melancholy playwright.*

APRIL 9, 1959

Thanks and God bless you. Yes, Agnes has sent me a copy of the book and came to see me. She is married again and living down on the Jersey shore, and her husband is a fisherman, I believe. When I think how I used to sing Frankie and Johnnie, I bravely lift my voice in singing the *O Salutaris* and *Tantum Ergo*!

No, I don't look back on those days as full of glamour. I always had a New England conscience, and while I loved the East Side and the Jewish intellectuals and the labor movement, I was dragged into Village life for a time, originally by Mike Gold who had a play on at the Provincetown, and that is where I met Gene [O'Neill]. That was one winter, three short months in my life,

from the time I got out of jail on Thanksgiving day in the suffrage days, until the death of Louis Holliday, which shocked me
so (it sent Gene up to Provincetown the same day) that I went
into training as a nurse at King's County Hospital. There are a
couple of years in my life after I left the hospital that I don't go
into. I pointed out in my *From Union Square to Rome* and *The Long
Loneliness* that I was not making a confession of my sins, nor
pretending to tell all.*

My work in the labor field, and with the radical group was
very much in accordance with my conscience—that is why I still
love them all. It is all a question of means and ends.

As for today,—with such movements as the Little Brothers
of Jesus and the Little Sisters (they are out near the Catholic University too and you ought to go see them to write a story about
them for the CW) and with the worker priests (we see some of
the seamen priests—they are not suppressed by any manner of
means), and the tremendous writing going on—it seems to me
these are exciting times we are living in.

The older I get, the more I meet people, the more convinced
I am that we must only work on ourselves, to grow in grace.
The only thing we can do about people is to love them, to find
things to love in them, even when they read the *Daily News* and
spend all their time at television. They don't really. And the *Daily
News* gave us one of the best write-ups we ever had, so while min-

---

* In *The Long Loneliness* Dorothy described her friendship with O'Neill in the
winter of 1918, how he recited to her "The Hound of Heaven," and how "many
a morning after sitting all night in taverns or coming from balls at Webster
Hall" she ducked into St. Joseph's Church in the Village for an early morning
Mass. She also alluded to "a succession of incidents and the tragic aspect of life
in general" which began to overwhelm her so that she "could no longer endure
the life I was leading." One of these unnamed incidents was the death of Louis
Holliday, a friend of O'Neill, who committed suicide before a horrified gathering of friends at a Village saloon. In despair after being jilted by his fiancée,
Holliday downed a vial of heroin and immediately lapsed into unconscious-
ness. While the other witnesses, including O'Neill, fled the scene, Dorothy held
the dying man in her arms. The next day, she walked away from the Village
scene, O'Neill, and a life she "could no longer endure," and soon thereafter
went into training as a nurse at Kings County Hospital.

imizing what we are able to accomplish, at least they attempted to set forth our point of view.

Next week we demonstrate again, stick our necks out, protest, say no, carry out into the street some of the Pope's words, taken out of context of course, such as "War is murder and suicide." (It would naturally follow from that, that it is forbidden us.)

We will be arrested again, in jail again, maybe for a day, maybe for a month or six months. It is not easy. I just have to remember that I am visiting the prisoner, the last work of mercy and the hardest to perform. Do pray for us. Ammon, Deane Mowrer, and I of the CW will go. Charles Butterworth was just arrested the other day for harboring a fugitive, a deserter. He is out on $1,500 bail! Isn't it astounding, how they try to make informers of us all. The world and its ways are quite the opposite of the world of the Sermon on the Mount.

My Therese book was turned down by Harpers, just not good enough. Not my style, according to them. Writing is a chore, but I too must keep at it, to bear witness to what I believe, and also to make some money for Tamar. Families need to help each other.

TO CHARLES BUTTERWORTH

Charles Butterworth, a graduate of Harvard Law School, joined the CW community and came to serve as business manager. For years it bothered him that he had not been to jail. The opportunity arrived when some FBI men came to the CW looking for an army deserter. Charles found the man in the kitchen and told him about the visitors. The deserter escaped out the back way and Charles was arrested.

JUNE 10, 1959

"Thou lovest justice and hateth iniquity, wherefore God, thy God, has anointed thee with the oil of gladness above thy companions."

May this be true of you this day.

Standing before a judge, appearing in court, is harder than

a jail sentence. Whatever happens, I know God has you close to him. As for me, I know you were right to do exactly as you did, and do not worry about the overtones and exactitude of expression of what has already taken place. God takes care of everything, and rights our mistakes, makes straight our paths.

This morning at six I was reading St. John's passion and when Jesus was brought before Pilate, he was "asked about his disciples and his doctrine."

He certainly answered nothing about his disciples,—he just said he had been preaching openly.

Our lives are open to all. We belong to a Kingdom not of this world, tho we are in it. May you be a constant reminder, a witness, of this other Kingdom, this glorious and beautiful Kingdom where we are willing and obedient and joyful subjects.

Remember St. Catherine of Siena said, "All the way to Heaven is heaven, because He said, 'I am the Way.'"

So may heaven be in your heart this day. We love you very much, and as for me, you have done so much to make me happy since you came to us, that mine is a very grateful love.

In Jesus caritas, Dorothy

TO THOMAS MERTON

Merton had written to Dorothy on July 9 to support her civil defense protests: "I am deeply touched by your witness for peace. You are very right in going at it along the lines of [Gandhian] Satyagraha. I see no other way. . . . Now it is no longer a question of who is right, but who is at least not criminal. . . . So don't worry about whether or not in every point you are perfectly right. . . . You are right before God as far as you can go and you are fighting for a truth that is clear enough and important enough. What more can anybody do?"

What with jail and a sudden attack of arthritis, I neglected to write to thank you both for your letter and for the gifts you sent to the CW crowd [*a consignment of "sweet-smelling and -tasting toothpaste"*]. I remember too with gratitude the copies of *Seven Storey Mountain* you sent some years ago. Will you please pray for Charles Butterworth, one of our staff, who will be sentenced next Wednesday in a federal court for harboring a deserter here at CW and helping him to escape. We have done this before, giving the men the time to make up their own minds; one returned to the army and the other took his sentence. Charles pleaded guilty and we don't know what the penalty is. It may be mandatory. Bob Steed may also have to go since he admitted to the FBI that he tore up his draft cards as a protest against conscription. He was at Gethsemani for 18 months. So I beg your prayers for both of them.

July 25 I am off to Montreal to make a retreat with those interested in the spiritual family of Charles de Foucauld. I am trying to join either the secular institute or the association. But am not sure they will have me. I would go on with my work at the CW of course.

We are all intensely grateful to you for all your writings and it delights me especially to see them in bus stations and drugstores as I travel about the country.

Gratefully in Christ, Dorothy Day

JUNE 20, 1959

I enclose a letter to cheer your heart and to keep you writing. Your books are regarded as treasures around the CW and keep circulating. One of the editors even made a pilgrimage to your old home on Long Island. Do pray for him, as he is in a sad state of indecision about everything, idleness and melancholy which are hard to combat. The sense of futility is the curse of our time among the young. God bless you always in your work which has done so much for all of us.

TO KARL MEYER

Karl Meyer became part of the Catholic Worker movement in 1957 when he heard about the civil defense protesters in City Hall Park and impulsively hopped in a cab to join them. Only 20 at the time, he went to jail for thirty days. It was the beginning of a lifetime of service in the cause of peace, and he was frequently arrested for other protests, while also running a CW house in Chicago. Dorothy held him in the highest esteem and even hoped he might one day take over as editor of the paper.

At the time of this letter, Meyer and Ammon Hennacy were in prison for trespassing at a nuclear weapons base in Omaha, Nebraska.

AUGUST 23, 1959

In a way your letter was very disquieting, you seemed so overcome by failure and defeat. You seem much under the influence of Peguy. I have been quoting that for years. "'Where are the others?' God will say," and I do believe that we have to work for others. But we are sowing the seed and it is up to Him to bring the increase. It is all in His hands, and we must keep ourselves in peace, first of all. That is where peace begins. He is our peace. When I was on my "vacation" in April [*in jail*], I read some of Tolstoy's stories and in several of them he preached the moral that God will attend to everything, and we must abandon ourselves to Him. I do wish you would write more personal letters— how things are going, how long you are in quarantine, what work you are doing, who your companions are. In Tolstoy's *Resurrection* he told of how the intellectuals ignored the other prisoners around them, though they thought they were working for them, to save them. Anyway, be happy, like the youths in the fiery furnace and praise God, and He will attend to everything. I'll write often. Hope you got my last letter.

P.S. Charles de Foucauld died a complete failure—no one followed him. He was killed in the desert in 1916. René Bazin wrote his life in 1922. Père Voillaume read it in the seminary and in

1933 started his Little Brothers and now there are 600 of them, trusting to voluntary poverty, silence, prayer, the hidden life of Nazareth, and their spiritual influence is enormous. Who knows but that God will save the city with ten just men.

I do not believe in mass movements. Read the Old and New Testaments. The Scripture is the Word.

TO AMMON HENNACY

AUGUST 28, 1959

Got a good account from Francis, very detailed, of the Omaha incident and we will print it in the paper. I wrote him thanks. He is very good indeed. If you are in Sandstone, you are right near Fr. Casey. If in Missouri, I hope you can help Karl [Meyer] who seems to have been hoping for another Montgomery. You got letters from half a dozen friends asking for clarification of thought and they get the paper so they will understand when you do not write. I am sending this letter care of the United States Marshal begging him to forward it to you, and I am sure he will.

When I left you on Sunday I went down to South Bend to the Liturgical Conference, and met many of our priest friends there from all over the country and many of them asked after you. To arouse the conscience, that is our job. Julian Pleasants says that missiles are outmoded as are all nuclear weapons. What comes next is nerve gas to paralyze the enemy for a few days or weeks until the opposing forces can take over, with no loss of life or property. It sounds like science fiction. I met an Indian priest at Notre Dame who was engaged in chemical research and he pulled the usual stuff about defending ourselves. I talked to him about Gandhi and [Vinoba] Bhave.

While you are in, I will go out on my speaking trip to the West Coast to deliver your message as well as the complete message of the Catholic Worker, which takes in a whole way of living, with the poor, with the works of mercy, with manual labor, with hospitality and life on the land. Your message has grooved you deep and narrow like the Grand Canyon, but my message is as broad as the plains or the sea or the desert. That is the way with women, to spread out and take in everything.

Much love to you from us all. In Jesus the worker, Dorothy

TO THOMAS MERTON

DECEMBER 23, 1959

A very happy New Year to you and may you be faithful unto death.

My constant prayer is for final perseverance—to go on as I am trusting always the Lord Himself will take me by the hair of the head like Habakkuk and set me where he wants me.

In Jesus' love, Dorothy Day

In reply, Merton noted "Perseverance—yes, more and more one sees that it is the great thing. But there is a thing that must not be overlooked. Perseverance is not hanging on to some course which we have set our minds to, and refusing to let go." Perseverance, he noted, sometimes means "not hanging on but letting go. That of course is terrible. But as you say so rightly, it is a question of His hanging on to us, by the hair of the head, that is from on top and beyond, where we cannot see or reach."

PART V

Prayer and Protest

1960–1969

The 1960s were a time of tumultuous change and protest. Dorothy was fully engaged in the issues of that decade, whether traveling to Cuba to observe the Revolution or to Rome to lend support to the peace lobby at Vatican II. As protests mounted against the war in Vietnam, she played an active role, publicly aligning herself with young men—including many from the Catholic Worker—who burned their draft cards.

And yet, while she supported these efforts on behalf of peace and social justice, she was disturbed by a sense of nihilism and a general spirit of rebellion against all authority and traditional moral codes. Many were questioning the "relevance" of such undramatic efforts as the Works of Mercy. They rejected the personalist revolution of Peter Maurin, rejecting, too, the faith that was the basis of her radical vision, and questioning the sacrifices that were the bedrock of her own vocation.

In the midst of so much violence in the world, and so many fears and doubts, she continued to believe that nothing was more hopeful or relevant than the Gospel.

TO THOMAS MERTON

JANUARY 22, 1960

Your beautiful and profound essay on [Boris] Pasternak kept me awake from midnight until four in the morning, thinking about it. I am using the final paragraph in my "On Pilgrimage" this coming month. It was very exciting, all of it, and I thank you for writing it, and for sending us a copy. I carried it along with me on my trip west (I am visiting the Indians, the Hutterites, and the Doukhobors too). I have been taking care of a cancer patient who just died a week before Ammon was released from Sandstone, so after her very happy death (she was baptized the night before she died) I set out on a three-months' trip which I had been postponing eight months.* I get time to read while traveling and am reading Anne Freemantle's *Desert Calling* right now. Very good indeed. Did I tell you I am a postulant in the Jesus Caritas Fraternity of the Charles de Foucauld family? Please pray for me and may God bless you always.

In His love, Dorothy

TO BOB STEED

Bob Steed was a Catholic convert who spent some time with the Trappists in Kentucky before "gravitating to the Worker," first in Memphis and then in New York. Dorothy put him in charge of editing the paper.

THURSDAY, MARCH 11, 1960

The paper was splendid—a fine piece of work—your editorial perfect. The makeup—every article was extra fine. You have

---

* Ammon Hennacy served six months in Sandstone prison for trespassing on a missile base in Omaha, Nebraska. The cancer patient in question was Forster Batterham's long-time companion, Nanette, whom Dorothy cared for during the last months of her life. The story of this particular work of mercy is recounted in *The Duty of Delight: The Diaries of Dorothy Day* (Image Books, 2011), pp. 274–94.

great gifts as writer and editor. Ammon's article was much better writing than usual—lots of humor too. [William] Horvath has a real poetic gift—the first paragraphs of his article, I mean. Poems good—Deane's good—all interesting. It's wonderful to be sitting in a train reading it leisurely and feeling how well the work is being carried on.

But please, Bob, if your fasting gets too much, be humble, give it up. It is good to aim high, but it will show you have no pride if you have to mitigate your fast.

Anyway, you did wonders with the paper—best issue in months.

TO DEANE MARY MOWRER

APRIL 7, 1960, ON A BUS IN OKLAHOMA

You do not know how welcome your letters have been. What a very real apostolate letter writing is I realize as I travel around and see how people welcome mail, and news of family. Perhaps that is the great appeal of those of our readers who do not agree but love us. The paper is a letter from "home."

I am writing this in a bus in Tulsa going on to Joplin when I change for Fayetteville. It is beautiful weather—sunny—warm, no wind. Flowers springing up but trees and fields are bare yet. It is a comfort to me to know you are in S.I. for a few days or the weekend. No matter what the weather it is beautiful there.

Tonight I will be sitting out on a porch in a little house in a little town in Arkansas. Traveling in a bus is like traveling with a slum always with you.

Forsythia is all in bloom everywhere. I am always surprised people don't plan more for the future like flowering shrubs, fruit trees, and berries. I'd like to put some in around the beach bungalow in spite of highway, dogs, kids, etc. Tamar says, "Plant enough and some will surely survive."

I saw Ammon in Los Angeles. He is as hoarse as a crow

from talking. Seems much worried about Karl [Meyer] and my attitude of obedience to authority and is worrying again about air raid drill, if we should be told to obey by Chancery Office.

We have made our protest for 5 years and certainly I would obey "if He should slay me yet would I trust in Him."

The Church means everything to me. It is Christ Himself. I know I could not be asked to do anything against my conscience. Obedience in this confuses Ammon as much as our disobedience in what seems to most people a gesture toward saving life, confuses others. Ammon wants to fight *Church* and State. Just another fighting Irishman.

A demonstration of obedience in this would bring about a more sympathetic examination by theologians of the problem of Church teaching about war.

However, I do not think anything will happen. So we will go thru arrest and imprisonment as usual. The shock is always the same whether it is for 1 day or 30.*

TO KARL MEYER

APRIL 26, 1960

Got your letter this morning [from Cook County Jail] and am certainly sorry to see them pull this psychiatric stuff. Last year they asked Ammon if he had ever been in a mental hospital. They use this approach as a threat, to frighten people or to punish them. I have seen it done before. One of our men was in a t.b. hospital and protested some injustice, and they immediately transferred him to Bellevue mental ward, from which place we had to extricate him.

---

* In 1960 the annual compulsory air raid drill in New York attracted several hundred protestors, of whom only a token number—Dorothy not among them—were arrested. By the next year over 2,000 protestors defied the law and the drills were subsequently discontinued.

I have notified Dr. Karl Stern of Montreal to come to my rescue if anything like that happens to me.

I took the liberty of leaving out a few paragraphs of your last letter in preparing it for copy. For instance, were you there when someone sneered at the chaplain and at the Sacred Host, as you said? It was not at all clear. I do not believe that any prisoner at Mass would make such a remark to the chaplain "as he distributed Communion." So I just cut it out.

I cannot tell you how brave and courageous I think your stand is, and how hard it is to go it alone. I should think it is understandable that you wish to share Eroseanna [Robinson's] imprisonment [*for tax resistance*] in this way. The saints in the church used to go out to ransom the captive and give themselves in the place of the others.

This whole matter of war is so serious that the Holy Father says that it is the first concern of us all, this work for peace. So you are doing as he says, making it your whole life, your whole concern.

It was just last night that I got back from my trip, and antiwar sentiment is spreading all through the country, a real demand on the part of the people for peace. Students are protesting against ROTC and just a few years ago it was one lone student, Donald Reed, who was brave enough to stand out against [ROTC at] Loyola in California.

TO DIXIE MacMASTER

Dorothy was powerfully attracted to the spirituality of Charles de Foucauld (1858–1916), a French aristocrat and military officer who determined, after his conversion, to emulate the "hidden life" of Jesus of Nazareth. He lived as a hermit in North Africa until his martyrdom in 1916. Many years later a number of congregations were inspired by his spirituality, particularly the Little Brothers and the Little Sisters of Jesus. Dorothy attended several retreats in Montreal to explore the possibility of affiliating with them in some way. Ultimately, she decided against anything formal. But it was on one of these retreats that she befriended Dixie MacMaster, a member of Benedict Labre House in Montreal, who bravely struggled to live by the spirit of Brother Charles despite severe physical handicaps. She and Dorothy became devoted correspondents. Their letters often centered on the vision of Foucauld, exhorting one another to deeper faithfulness in prayer and contemplation.

MAY 18, 1960

I have been in a state about writing you about the JC [Jesus Caritas] Fraternity since Holy Week when I made a retreat at a Benedictine monastery. During my retreat I came to the conclusion I did not belong to the women's secular institute but rather to the Secular Fraternity which has such close ties with that wonderful group of young priests in Brooklyn who belong to the priests' union. Ever since our last retreat and my meeting with Margot [Poncet] I have felt that I do not belong there, and have hesitated to write you and disturb you. I am too American in spirit, and I do think the Fraternity is distinctly French, not universal. Not only [that] Margot showed no understanding, but also no willingness to understand. Her distaste for the men on our breadline, for our destitute quarters, was openly expressed. "Surely these men could find work if they tried." The new house at Lourdes is not for the poor but for the comfortably off. I do not mean to be harsh, tho I sound so. I have hesitated to write for this long time because of my love for you. I truly am not resentful of her refusal to listen or to understand at our retreat in Montreal. It was a little opportunity to practice abjection. The Fraternity is just not for me. I will return to the Benedictines where I was before—an oblate—, and when they released me before they kindly said they would always consider me a member of their family. I can still attend meetings of the Secular Fraternity in Brooklyn, and be close to all of you, even closer.

I am sorry if this gives you pain, but I received two sure

graces and lights during my retreat Holy Week, not to be convinced this is what I wish to do. I will always treasure the memory of our simple reunions (not the retreat one, perhaps. It truly
made me feel I did not belong).

This decision of mine will probably be a relief to both Margot and Fr. Voillaume [*founder of the Little Brothers of Jesus*].

Right now we are in the unpopular position of being on the
side of the Revolution in Cuba and that too would be an embarrassment to Margot in all her South American contacts.

So I will not be at the retreat but will try to see you soon—
for a day's visit anyway. There is no one else in Canada [who]
means as much to me as you, my dear sister in Christ.

My heartfelt love to you and yours—Dorothy

TO KARL MEYER

JUNE 3, 1960

This is just a brief note between articles I am supposed to write,
to let you know how completely I am with you, and how happy
I am at your position on the Church. When we were in court
and listened to the young people [*arrested for the civil defense protest*] making speeches to the judge before they were sentenced
to their five days, I thought then how good it was that these
young students were coming along, rising up, to give a voice to
the natural good that is in every human heart, the desire for
peace and justice. Older ones like Ammon and me should do
everything in our power to bring along the new speakers and
writers and publicize what they are doing and leave it to them to
restore hope and faith to the world. The students throughout the
world are making their voices heard.

Just this morning on the radio there was a story of the Japanese students rioting all over Japan protesting the visit of Eisenhower and the imminence of a Japanese American alliance. It is
wonderful to see the protest against our air bases all over the

world. Look at the Mass in time of war, and the promises then that God will be with us when we stay at home on our own soil. I ran across it in an old military pamphlet missal used during the war, which came in with a lot of junk. How right the Church always is—and it is the churchmen who are the cross on which Christ is crucified. But we are to love them and respect them, not fight them. Ammon is too Irish, too class-warish, and too Protestant! It is all part of his very lively and all too human spirit, of course, which is so attractive to the young. I feel that he draws people a long ways, but I feel that you will draw them even further. So God bless you in all your undertakings.

I am glad you work so closely with the whole peace movement, but what differentiates us is our insistence on the works of mercy and the green revolution,* the attempt to practice it now in no matter how small a way by voluntary poverty. The one thing I do not like is their listing Jesus, Gandhi, [Vinoba] Bhave, Tolstoy, Thoreau, all in a breath. As high as the heavens are above the earth, so high is Jesus at whose name every knee should bow. It hurts me each time they do it and I protest it. I won't sign any petition or letter which contains such juxtaposition.

TO THOMAS MERTON

JUNE 4, 1960

An attack of arthritis and flu the last few weeks leaves me full of sloth. It is a good time to stay at the beach house where rain has driven people away. Aside from a disturbed family for whom I beg your prayers, and two ex-seamen puttering around fixing screens, I am alone. To be with eight people is to be alone at the CW. One of the men, Hugh Madden, was five years a brother at Gethsemani. "Disturbed" or a saint, who can tell? Both probably.

---

* The "green revolution," as opposed to the "red" or communist revolution, was the term Peter Maurin applied to his program for radical social change.

The family is most truly disorderly, deserted by the father. The last child by another man. The children already proclaiming loss of faith, bitterness. They are 10 to 16. The last still a baby, so the mother cannot work as she did before, and that is why they are with us. I tell you these things, so you will most specially pray for them. I used to write the old abbot [Frederic] Dunne about my problems.

My own son-in-law, tho strong in faith, has many problems mental and physical and Tamar is having her 9th child in late July. I will be with her for a few weeks then.

Did you ever read "The Friend of the Family" by Dostoevsky? We have one such friend on Peter Maurin Farm this last year. Also many an "Honest Thief" in town. Dostoevsky is spiritual reading for me.

Anyway, I am begging your prayers and be assured I pray for you as I hope you do for me. I am often full of fears about my final perseverance.

Merton replied: "We should in a way fear for our perseverance because there is a big hole in us, an abyss, and we have to fall through it into emptiness, but the Lord will catch us." Because of the prayers of the poor, he noted, "You are the richest woman in America spiritually. . . . You cannot fail even if you try to." He also expressed doubts about the value of his writing on safe subjects like meditation and monastic studies, and speculated whether, in light of pressures from the censors in his order, he should contemplate changing "his situation." "Why," he wrote, "this awful silence and apathy on the part of Catholics, clergy, hierarchy, lay people on this terrible issue [nuclear war] on which the very continued existence of the human race depends?"

TO THE TREASURER, CITY OF NEW YORK

The City of New York had seized the Catholic Worker property on Chrystie St. with the intention of building a 2nd Ave. subway. When the City sent a check to cover interest on their payment, Dorothy seized

on this opportunity to make a point about money lending at interest.
Her letter to the City Treasurer was published in the September 1960
issue of the paper under the title, "This Money Is Not Ours."

JULY 1960

Dear Sir:

We are returning to you a check for $3,579.39 which represents interest on the $68,700 which we were awarded by the city as payment for the property at 223 Chrystie Street which we owned and lived in for almost ten years, and used as a community for the poor. We did not voluntarily give up the property—it was taken from us by right of eminent domain for the extension of the subway which the city deemed necessary. We had to wait almost a year and a half for the money owed us, although the city permitted us to receive two-thirds of the assessed valuation of the property in advance so that we could relocate. Property owning having been made impossible for us by city regulations, we are now renting and continuing our work.

We are returning the interest on the money we have recently received because we do not believe in "money lending" at interest. As Catholics, we are acquainted with the early teaching of the Church. All the early councils forbade it, declaring it reprehensible to make money by lending it out at interest. Canon law of the Middle Ages forbade it and in various decrees ordered that profit so obtained was to be restored. In the Christian emphasis on the duty of charity, we are commanded to lend gratuitously, to give freely, even in the case of confiscation, as in our own case—not to resist but to accept cheerfully.

We do not believe in the profit system, and so we cannot take profit or interest on our money. People who take a materialistic view of human service wish to make a profit but we are trying to do our duty by our service without wages to our brothers as Jesus commanded in the Gospel (Matthew 25). Lending money at interest is deemed by one Franciscan as the principal scourge of civilization. Eric Gill, the English artist and writer, calls usury and war the two great problems of our time.

Since we have dealt with these problems in every issue of the *Catholic Worker* since 1933—man's freedom, war and peace, man and the state, man and his work—and since Scripture says that the love of money is the root of all evil, we are taking this opportunity to live in practice of this belief and make a gesture of overcoming that love of money by returning to you the interest.

Insofar as our money paid for services for the common good, and aid to the poor, we should be very happy to allow you to use not only our money without interest, but also our work, the Works of Mercy, which we all perform here at the headquarters of the *Catholic Worker* without other salary or recompense than our daily food and lodging, clothes, and incidental expenses.

Insofar as the use of our money paid for the time being for salaries for judges who have condemned us and others to jail, and for the politicians who appointed them, and for prisons, and the execution chamber at Sing Sing, and for the executioner's salary, we can only protest the use of our money and turn with utter horror from taking interest on it.

Please also be assured that we are not judging individuals, but are trying to make a judgment on *the system* under which we live and with which we admit that we ourselves compromise daily in many small ways, but which we try and wish to withdraw from as much as possible.

Sincerely yours,
Dorothy Day, Editor

TO THOMAS MERTON

OCTOBER 10, 1960

It was good to get your book [*Disputed Questions*] and I thank you for having sent it to me. I had read the [Boris] Pasternak affair in *Thought* and was much impressed with it, and quoted from it both during a speaking trip and in the paper. And I am fascinated by St. John Climacus.

One of the things which bothers me mightily is the bitterness and criticism of angry young men. Do pray for them and all such. Sometimes I try to tell myself, finding myself too critical, "they are prophets crying out in this time." But there are too many of them. Around a place like the Catholic Worker there are always too many, too much of the rebellious spirit. From the last year we have had with us a youngish woman, brilliant mentally, but destructive in all her criticism, and almost blind, covered with rashes and sores, crying out constantly against her fate. To me she epitomizes rebellion. She always has someone devoted to her, bringing her all the latest drugs and also liquor. Ammon Hennacy hates all medicine and has never taken any. He says my arthritis is because I am stiff-necked and advocates fasting for every ailment. He is a continual faster, a vegetarian, and doing without all food every Friday all day. One Lent he fasted as the Moslems do, another he fasted completely all Lent, for 46 days. He is truly a prophet in many ways. But he sure makes us all feel guilty and mediocre.

But all this rebellion makes me long for obedience, hunger and thirst for it, as a woman does for a husband whom she can esteem and who will direct her. Women especially cry out against their terrible freedom. But trying to be obedient and also personally responsible, responsive to the calls made upon one, means we are overburdened.

Every night we say the rosary and Compline in our little chapel over the barn, heavy with the smell of the cow downstairs (one can hear her chewing her cud) and we have a bulletin board there with names of those who ask prayers. Yours is there. There are half a dozen old men, several earnest young ones, an old woman from the Bowery, a former teacher with one eye, a mother of an illegitimate child, and so on. We all say the rosary, only six remain for Compline. Do pray for us too. Your writing has reached many, many people and started them on their way. Be assured of that. It is the work God wants of you, no matter how much you want to run away from it. Like the Curé of Ars. God bless you always.

TO JACK ENGLISH

OCTOBER 15, 1960

Ammon is going to Utah in January, longing for manual labor and more poverty. Nostalgia for the past. But we can't go home again, and I am sure he will be lonesome. I will miss him and I fear for him out there. If the bishop tells him to close his storefront, which he is going to name after Joe Hill, he will not do it, and then I will have to take his name off the paper, and he will be on his own. He does seem to long for a knock-down and drag-out fight with some bishop just to show he is free. He cannot get it into his head that he *is* free.

Which reminds me that Walter Winchell mentioned me this morning to point out the great freedom in the church, citing Joe McCarthy and Gene McCarthy, *Brooklyn Tablet* and *Commonweal*, me and someone else, I cannot remember.

TO BOB STEED

NOVEMBER 6, 1960

We are all very happy you finally wrote. I chose some paragraphs from [your letter] for the paper so as to give news of your progress. Do keep up the letters and I think you can trust my discretion not to include in printed stories anything which may offend. It gave a very good picture of your travels. I am glad you are going to Ireland. I cut out your crack about the Irish. They have the best drama and some of the best writing in the English language, not to speak of ballads, poetry, etc. And a long theory of political struggle, some of it right down our alley. No use see-ing the too obvious faults. Every race has them. So do not be a racist. I agree with you about the English. I too could settle down with them and live there forever. When I was there, I took interminable bus rides, looking up places mentioned in Dickens and de Quincey. I only traveled around London, however. Today there is news of youth riots in London. Wonder if you were there for the "rumble." Do keep a little diary. Buy one, jot down in it at night. I know you will forget a tremendous lot if you do not take a few notes. It does not have to be discursive. Just jot down. Like Pepys.

TO FRITZ EICHENBERG

In this and subsequent letters, Dorothy refers to Ammon Hennacy's short-lived engagement to Mary Lathrop, a young art student and recent convert, who had lately joined the Worker. Ammon was preparing to leave New York and head out for Salt Lake City to start his own house of hospitality.

DEC 1960

I think of you very often indeed, but I am a firm believer that holidays are for children, and that adults should keep as quiet as possible. But I do love letters, enjoy getting them, and so I am writing you this little one, just to say we all love you, and that your work in the *Catholic Worker* has rejoiced more hearts than you can know, and that many write in to us to tell us these things, and then we are truly so overburdened that we do not save the letters to send on to you, and we should. But Ammon and Walter [Kerell], who do so much of the mail, do not save let-ters, and no matter how many times I protest, they go right on ahead in their own efficient way, and I, who am a hoarder like most women, and who want to save such records, am frustrated. So please accept my apologies and my assurances that your work is much loved indeed. You should feel most encouraged.

And what you have given of yourself these last years at Pratt can never be estimated. Students do not forget great men. Years later, some words, some attitudes come back to them, and they understand, when in the present they do not seem to. How much patience we need. This sounds like a sermon, but I know the deep sadness of your nature, and how you grieve with those who grieve. Your vocation, in a way.

News about Ammon. He is going to marry Mary Lathrop, who is of course much younger, but Ammon himself is so young. Everyone in the office thinks that they are so much alike, and they have been such constant companions this last year, that they are not surprised. It is only those who do not know him, and her, who will be taken aback. They will be married after the next air raid drill.

TO DIXIE MacMASTER

DEC 5, 1960

The day I got back from Boston and the days before I went were so full of calamity. Four phone calls from Chicago, Washington, Canada, and New York, asking me to take care of mentally and emotionally and physically disturbed people! And we are always so full. The Jesus Prayer keeps me from impatience and sadness, knowing that He can do all things, and remembering too how the Little Flower said that one had to learn to say *no* so kindly that the other went away satisfied just the same. It is the part of humility to say *no* very often. But my heart aches with the need for more houses of hospitality. One of the reasons for travel is to get families and parishes to see this need. The very bishops' statement last week about personal responsibility points to it.

One of the things people do not understand about the work and that is that people come to us because of their need and their disabilities, and so many [of those who] are in charge, even the associate editors, are difficult people and it is hard for them to keep up with the work. I have never had a secretary, for instance, and it is so difficult to get letters done, in addition to my writing. The people who have volunteered to help take half the time of dictation, if not more, to tell me their troubles and I am in a state of complete exhaustion at the end because I have been trying to do two things at once, care for correspondence and listen sympathetically to them. It is too much and I end by doing it myself, and getting half the amount done.

Here is the latest trouble to pray over: Ammon wants to marry—he is 67—Mary Lathrop, who is 27. He is overcome by loneliness really. And overactive and over-susceptible to affection. I feel very badly about this, feeling we have failed him. But I find myself judging him too,—so please pray about this. Mary is a fine girl who admires him greatly, really loves him, and wants to be his secretary, companion, nurse, etc, and since his mother is vigorous at 85, Ammon is liable to be as long-lived. She is going on my trip with me, which may have some delaying tactic. They will wait a year to see and let us hope she changes [her mind]. I have seen too many young women in love with one man after another. Mary is another example of someone who comes to us. A Catholic for one year. She sees Ammon's faults too, but desires to "immolate" herself. O dear!

It is a good thing I have no secretary and have to write tiny notes to people or I would be always pouring out my troubles which is not so good. Holy silence is the thing. But you are my novice mistress and I must tell you everything. I love to, anyway.

Your little sister, in Jesus caritas, Dorothy

TO FRANCISCO FERNANDEZ

DEC 21, 1960

Here is news for you. Ammon is going to get married at the mature age of 67 to a girl of 27, who is much like him in temperament. It seems strange to everyone else, but to those who know him, his loneliness, and his affectionate disposition, it does not seem strange all. Here is a girl who will picket with him, work in the fields with him out west, and sell papers on the streets, and so on. She is well educated, a convert of one year, and admires and loves him very much. We never know what God has in store for us. So do pray for him and for Mary Lathrop.

TO A MARYKNOLL PRIEST

[UNDATED 1961]

Certainly Maryknoll has been a wonderful friend to the Catholic Worker over the years, and I suppose we have always had friends and defenders and those who opposed us from the very beginning.

Yes, I do agree with you that we bend over backward in trying to explain Ammon, whom I often accuse of being still half-Protestant. But the CW is made up of those God sends, and the so-called leaders are also the lame, the halt, and the blind. I should not quote that as Deane thinks I am alluding to her and her increasing blindness. But what I mean is that God uses very faulty instruments for His work, so that what is accomplished, and I am sure that great things are and have been accomplished, cannot be laid to us, to our good work, but only to our good will. As for making an "ass" of yourself, wonderful. We are all supposed to be fools for Christ.

TO DIXIE MacMASTER

JAN 10, 1961

I am reading Acts now with a little study guide. And as we travel Mary [Lathrop] reads to me from the Book of Kings. We are still on the first book and it is very stirring. She is an intelligent companion and almost too exalted with joy over her conversion.

She will be good for Ammon, because he is not devout, and I can see she always will be. She certainly affords me daily occasions of examination of conscience. Like community, one is made well aware of one's faults. I can see in myself the impatience of age at the effervescence of youth—the desire always to instruct—the pettiness of mind on my part which leads me to try to check her "glorious thoughts" and try to either elucidate them for her, which is not at all necessary, or to tell her how often her insights have been seen before and are not at all great discoveries—you know the sort of thing.

Anyway, at the end of this trip I shall be more patient and more silent, I hope. One certainly learns a lot, being shut in on long drives with someone who is intellectually mature and a good companion, but emotionally immature and unrestrained. It is exhausting for me and a torture for her. She says she can understand how Ammon felt in solitary confinement! The trouble is, she is very strong and needs hard physical labor. She needs to be put behind a plough. But she is good, and helpful, saves me steps, takes dictation, runs the errands, and I am deeply grateful I have her.

My On Pilgrimages will be but a skeleton of the book we are writing. When we are not traveling, we try to put in three hours a day at it. So you see—I get to Holy Mass and Communion, do my reading and meditating, but again I miss my hour, several times a week, or make it badly with distractions, or worse, just really fall asleep there to awaken greatly refreshed! God is so good to us. What a privilege to belong to the Jesus Caritas!

I am beginning to keep accounts carefully, which is good discipline. In the last three months of 1960, as far as I can see from my diary, I made $240 from speaking at small meetings, and $250 from one large meeting at a non-Catholic college which always pay better just as secular magazines do. Newman Clubs pay ten or fifteen at State universities, and Catholic colleges pay $40 or $50 if you are invited. If you "just happen to be in town" on another engagement, and they ask you to speak, they often pay very little, $10 or $15, which is robbing the poor, really, and not fair. But if you profess poverty, you are kept in poverty, and do not have a chance to be proud at "earning" money. The Lord likes to keep us poor. Isn't it wonderful?

TO DEANE MARY MOWRER

JAN 28, 1961, FRIDAY, ST. JOHN CHRYSOSTOM

We are in New Orleans and it is so cold we have two or three heaters on, all the gas heaters on, and the sun has not shown since we got here. But it was 65 on the way down and we cannot complain of the weather. It is beautiful to see the green and the flowers here and there really is a feeling of spring.

Twice now, three times in this trip, people have said they owed their vocations to hearing me speak—and it makes me feel sure that going around this way is the right thing to do. I am getting a certain amount of writing done. If I dictate direct to the machine, Mary [Lathrop] can do it. If I hand her work to copy, she finds a million other things to do. Ammon was a good boss—kept her at work. He writes her every day—but she tells me she does not want to marry him, but she knows if she sees him he will "pressure" her into it. One cannot get away from listening to troubles.

I feel we are rich in young people right now. God keep them all and increase their zeal and wisdom. "Let no one despise their youth."

FEBRUARY 11, 1961

I am doing quite a lot of writing—getting much material. Sent 2 articles to *Commonweal* which they may not take. Writing another now on a new movement among the Mexicans—a retreat movement.

Mary does not really want to marry Ammon—was "pressured into it." Anyway this trip—beautiful weather and all—is a great penance in a way too. I can only consider it a work of mercy I am performing—and do it with all patience. As I go on living with Mary, I can only see disaster for both her and Ammon. I really fear he will be on his way out of the Church, his desire is so strong to be a lone wolf, he and Mary against the world. His letters to her, which he wants her to share with me, are fantastic. He considers himself, Mary, and Jack Baker, an elite, and includes me because I am editor. No one else in the CW is important. His arrogance—his desire to fight the world *and* the church are a madness. All the applause he gets feeds this. He has such great personal charm that people are deceived. I cannot tell you how I am worrying about this. Usually a trip is a great relaxation from responsibility, but this is hard. Trying to figure out what to do. Ammon cannot believe Mary is not *in love*. He thinks in turn that I am pressuring her. He is announcing everywhere his approaching marriage and Mary keeps thinking and saying "I will have to go thru with it!"

So please pray hard over this. I do not like to write a cheerless letter, but there is no one else I can write to about this.

Much love to you, about this, that you are there to pray and to suffer.

In His love, Dorothy

MARCH 11, 1961

Got your good letter telling about the [Allen] Ginsberg meeting, and I certainly was happy to hear about their coming to visit at the farm. There certainly is a ferment going on. Everywhere I go, the paper and its various approaches make a tremendous appeal to them. It warms the heart. I sent the clipping on to Ammon, but he does not see what we mean. He is the one track mind and what gives him his strength is that concentration on his mission. I guess there is never any changing him and we have to put up with him as he is. As for me, if poverty is the cause of war, it seems to me we have to concentrate on the problems of the poor as the most basic way to attack the problem.

I know I am cheered no end to think of all the young ones taking over.

You are doing a wonderful job—that monthly [farm] column—and it is sure to build up a widespread interest in the farm and our discussions there this summer. It will be nice, sitting out in the grove and hearing talks, stretching our minds, taking the large view, the long view.

TO KARL MEYER

MARCH 11, 1961

At the same time as your letter, a long one came from Tom Cornell about the CNVA [Community for Nonviolent Action] and it is so good I'll probably print it too. Though I would rather have you write a monthly one. What about your getting a passport after your jail sentences. I suppose you can, but there may be some delays. It is a wonderful idea, your getting to Russia, and I hope you make it. Looking over your letter again I can see you sent another copy to the Editors. So I hope it got in. I hope you do not think me too highhanded putting your name on the masthead as I did without consulting you. Ammon may have told you, but he wants his name taken off—there are too many editors, he says, and he prefers to be the one-man revolution. So that is all right too. He has always been the personalist rather than the communitarian.

TO ALLEN GINSBERG

Allen Ginsberg, the famous Beat poet, visited the Catholic Worker from time to time. He wrote Dorothy to see if the Catholic Worker farm might take in Lafcadio Orlovsky, the brother of his longtime companion Peter Orlovsky.

TUCSON, ARIZ., MARCH 16, 1961

I can only answer you sketchily because when I am traveling like this I cannot be answering for the responses of those at home. After all, I am not such a boss that I can say, "Take this nice kid and let him stay at the farm." They are the ones who would be responsible and have to in a way take care of him, and be responsible for him. There is only dormitory space, and a bunch of people all of whom have such troubles of their own, mental and physical, that one could not count on their being kind always, harried as they are by their own sufferings. Living all together through a long cold spring, they have cabin fever.

If I sound uncooperative, I am terribly sorry, but after all, you must understand that I cannot tell other people to extend hospitality. If I were there, I would say yes, let us give it a try, and we can see how he gets along. But I cannot from a distance order people to take in someone to share their lives. I am not an abbess. One of the hardest things, for me, is for people to pass the buck like this when I am away, saying, "Wait till Dorothy gets back," or "write to her." It's just a dishonest way of getting out from under, and not incurring the disapproval of others by saying "no." They keep their reputation, and let me be the one to suffer recriminations.

Phoning me won't do any good. Why don't you go down to the farm and put it up to them frankly. Have a roundtable discussion with Ralph, Ed Forand, Jean Walsh, and Deane Mowrer. They are the responsible ones. You've caught them in the midst of moving in town, and already responsible for a gang of almost a hundred people, in town and out, and I don't wonder they were "a little worried you were going to dump a psychiatric problem on them," while you go footloose and fancy free around the world. And as for how sweet and dear Lafcadio is, of course he is Christ himself, and what you do unto him you do unto Christ himself. That applies first to his brother and then to his neighbor.

I don't know why you put a halo on Death. I'm all for Life, myself—this life and the next. But maybe you are thinking of St. Francis's Sister Death, giving up your life in order to save it, dying to self in order to put on the new man, and so on.

I suppose it is dying daily to keep Lafcadio with you.

Sincerely in Christ, Dorothy

TO DEANE MARY MOWRER
Deane was steadily descending into blindness.

SAN DIEGO, FEAST OF ST. GABRIEL. MARCH 25, 1961

I speak now on one night stands for the next two weeks. The last of Holy Week I will try to spend in a little Benedictine monastery near Los Angeles, I do not know quite where, but they are exiles, from behind the iron curtain, so they say, and very poor.

I do pray for you each day, that you be strong in spirit to accept and use your terrible cross—such limitation of vision. I am so thankful you have the books on records, and community, bad as it is sometimes. We want so much, you and I, and are so impatient. We want perfect community, for instance, and complete sobriety among our fellow workers, and perfect understanding, and we are all so different and find our intoxication in such different ways,—music, books, etc. The poverty that is left to us is just that,—to have as companions people who are so disturbed, who drink, who go contrary to us. I miss you all. Give my love to all, and special love for yourself. (I had a sty on my eye, from strain, driving into the sun, dust storms, and realized more what you go through all the time. My special cross is lameness, and constant pain in my knee. A very little cross compared to most.)

TO CHARLES BUTTERWORTH

ALMA COLLEGE, APRIL 12, 1961

I sit luxuriously in an enclosed garden, a fountain outside, and write a few letters while I wait dinner. A priest, Jesuit, just brought me coffee and tonight I speak to 150 of them. I will come straight home but it hardly looks like I'd make it for the CD drill. However I'll try. Steady driving alone should qualify me for a cross country truck driver's job.

Della wrote about Lily [Burke, *Forster's sister*]—tumor on the brain. Do pray for her. To think anyone would deliberately turn from God. Forster told Tamar she was in a hospital where there was none of that nonsense about a future life. Della retorted that Jews believe in the one God too.

There was an earthquake here the other night. The worst, the local paper said, since 1906 [*in San Francisco*], which I was in. This college is on a hill right over the [San] Andreas fault, whatever that is, but it is the seat of earthquakes here.

I have been having wonderful meetings, here in the valley—and with the poor too. The worst and the best out here.

Because of the lettuce strike, the bracero priests were removed. Where I stayed in Tracy there were 6 bracero camps down the road on every corner, and no Mass on Sunday for thousands of men. Tragic situation, worse than [Edward R.] Murrow pictured. But organizing goes on. I got up at 4 the other morning to go to the slave market on Skid Row to see the shape-up with one of the union organizers. But the hierarchy has much to answer for. They have eyes and see not. And ears only for the growers.

I hate to think of Ammon going to work on Mary [Lathrop] again. She wants the religious life. Do have a Mass said. He thinks you and I are the "pious people" who "pressured" her into rejecting him. I do feel badly about this, and am glad Ammon will be out West.

Every moment is so taken up I find it hard to get a moment to write. Please pray for me and I do for you—that we may all grow in the love of God.

Pray for Lily too that she will not die without faith. I have always been so fond of her. She was my one real friend in all the sisters of the Batterham family.

TO KARL MEYER

JULY 2, 1961

Jack Baker and Jean Morton went on Freedom Walk to New London. Both back now. Ross Hoffman, who was with me at Koinonia, cooking there, is in New London, now cooking on the farm they have some miles away. He says that in their search for freedom all the young ones, 20 years, etc., are discussing and demanding sexual freedom. The Catholic position should be clear-cut but Jack does not see it. He is living with a girl on the East Side. Ammon set the example by living with Mary. They think perhaps they are early apostles, early virgins after a fashion, living and working together. Ammon says he will treat Mary like a father until he can marry her. She keeps asserting she wants to go into a convent when she can find one which will have her. I get very good letters from them from Salt Lake City where they are now picking cherries daily for their living. Want to start a house soon.

Ammon is looking for a head-on collision with the bishop. He has written to him, asking for an appointment, announcing his intention of opening a house and picketing and fasting August 6, and if the bishop does not approve he will put on the sign, the literature, and on the house, "without the bishop's approval." This announcement to the bishop, he thinks, is in the Gandhian tradition; seems to me more like defiance and pressure. Compelling the bishop to acknowledge him or deny him. Mary keeps telling him he wants to pressure her into marrying him, and he insists it is the pious people, me and Charles Butterworth, who are pressuring her not to. Poor Ammon—please do pray for him. In a way we are glad Mary is there to take care of him.

Mary Lathrop remained with Ammon for some months in Salt Lake City, assisting him with the house of hospitality he had named after Joe Hill (the famous IWW labor organizer and martyr). As Dorothy related the story in Loaves and Fishes, *the relationship eventually ended with Mary's decision to return to New York. "She, who was a most devout convert, had fought with Ammon daily over his anticlericalism. So it should not have come as a surprise. But for Ammon it was a shock and he was deeply hurt. He blamed me (because Mary regarded me as her mother). . . . " In a real sense, this marked a parting of the ways between Ammon and Dorothy, though he remained affiliated with the CW and continued to write for the paper.*

In 1965 Dorothy was disappointed by his decision to reject Catholicism and to marry outside the Church. In her diary she wrote, "He has left the Church not for conscience sake but for the romantic, sentimental reasons, because of vanity." Nevertheless, she continued to honor his courage, his faithfulness to conscience, and his perseverance in the pursuit of peace. "Ammon was basically a romantic Irishman," she wrote, "and never lost that sense of drama, that love of life, tragic though its outcome so often was." Believing as she did that being in love "is a reflection of the love God has for each and every one of us," she wrote, "I am glad that this kind of love illumined the last seven years of Ammon's life."*

TO JACK ENGLISH

Dorothy wrote from Perkinsville, Vermont, where she was staying with Tamar in her new home. By this time it was clear that David Hennessy had serious problems, quite apart from his drinking. He and Tamar eventually separated.

---

* Ammon Hennacy would die on January 14, 1970, after suffering a heart attack on a picket line, protesting the impending execution of two criminals. Dorothy hastened to attend his funeral.

SUNDAY, AUG 13, 1961, PERKINSVILLE, VT.

Thank you for your good letters. I save them all and read over your suggestions as to what to read. Someday I would like to publish a book of spiritual correspondence but of course I cannot use any of your letters unless you get permission. Anyway your letters are a comfort to me.

Tamar's husband had to go to the State mental hospital last week. Do pray for him. They are so crowded, you wonder how much care patients get. But we have seen good results. I wrote Karl Stern. He may know someone there. David had been suffering so long, crying "Won't someone help me before I do something terrible." What anguish!

I am here at Tamar's for a week—leaving tomorrow for N.Y. The children (9) are all well, thank God, and all help. Tamar is better. Had stomach trouble—ulcers threatening last winter. She will have to get State aid. She and David believe in it and I do too for emergency measure—my relatives won't help—do not believe in large families and he has only one unmarried sister who supports the mother. They think I should support Tamar and her family but you know how little authors get.

Harper's is taking my next book, *Loaves and Fishes*. Maybe I'll get an advance and clear off Tamar's debts—*The New Yorker* had a wonderful article on Melville and Stephen Crane and how little they got. Melville wrote nothing that last 19 years and worked for $4 a day to support his family.

We as usual are in a hubbub of youthful demonstrations—peace, freedom rides, etc. Our questioning of the social order does not lead to much support—and we are afflicted with too many mentally afflicted also.

TO THOMAS MERTON

By the 1960s Thomas Merton had come to feel that his monastic vocation required a prophetic engagement with the social problems of the day—peace, racism, the threat of nuclear war. While struggling with the censors of his order, he began sending poems and essays to the Catholic Worker, including a mordant dirge in the voice of a death camp commandant, which ended with the line: "Do not think yourself better because you burn up friends and enemies with long-range missiles without ever seeing what you have done." Jim Forest, whom Dorothy mentions, had recently joined the CW after being discharged from the Navy as a conscientious objector. Dorothy set him to editing the paper.

AUGUST 15, 1961—FEAST OF THE ASSUMPTION

I am terribly sorry about that poem ["Chant to be used in Processions around a Site with Furnaces"]. It was snatched from my hands so fast, and before I knew it, it was at the printers, since we were just going to press. All you said in relation to it was: "Here is a gruesome poem for you." And when I read "for you," I thought it was for the paper you meant it. I am indeed sorry for the sake of your friend on the West Coast [Lawrence Ferlinghetti].

Our young friend, Jim Forest, is starting out on a bicycle tour in New England. I imagine to think things over about his vocation. He wrote to ask if he could visit St. John's Abbey, and when the abbot heard he was a c.o. he wrote it was better for him not to come. At Spencer [Massachusetts, Trappist monastery] there was also no room. Our position is more unpopular than ever, with recurring crises. We certainly need prayers. Also I have had personal news: my son-in-law has had to go to the state mental hospital. He is in bad condition for some time and my daughter has endured a great deal. She has nine children and a heavy burden of work on the farm in which they all share.

Just looked at your letter again, and it did not say "for you." So again the dear Lord has to right our mistakes.

About nuclear warfare: Juliana of Norwich said the worst has already happened and been repaired. Nothing worse can ever befall us. On a day like this, the feast of the Assumption, Heaven seems very near. Our Lady, body and soul in Heaven; our Lord, body and soul in Heaven—it makes Heaven a reality for us earthbound creatures. Hope I am not being incoherent. We have had a long day, many visitors, many Puerto Rican children here on the farm. One can't think, which is just as well. Just work. Greetings from us all.

With love in Christ, Dorothy

TO FRITZ EICHENBERG

SEPTEMBER 27, 1961

Ammon just called to tell me that he had heard from you and that you have a picture of Tolstoi which we can use in the November issue of the CW. You are certainly good to us. For some time I have been meaning to write you and beg your forgiveness for my remissness in so many ways. I take your friendship so much for granted, I assume that you understand and that you know our problems, but I suddenly got awful qualms and thought how presumptuous I was, especially in connection with the new Peter Maurin reprint, which the Academy Guild Press is doing out in California and which is using your wonderful work to illustrate it. And here I did not write you anything about it, or ask your permission to use them, and the publisher also did not write to you, I suppose assuming that I did it. These are illustrations which we have used in the paper, and I do not even know which ones he is using. I do know that St. Michael is on the cover. The book is called *The Green Revolution: Easy Essays on Catholic Radicalism by Peter Maurin*. It is due to come out in October or November.

I think of you often with love and with prayers.

TO WILLIAM READY

William Ready was director of libraries at Marquette University in Milwaukee, which would become the repository of the Dorothy Day–Catholic Worker archives.

JAN 26, 1962

Do you remember how a few years ago you asked me to make use of the Marquette Univ. Library for our archives? Do you still wish us to do this? We have nine files of letters, half of which should be thrown out but there is so much work to do around the Catholic Worker it is hard to see when we could get at it. I set one of our editors at the task and found him throwing out a letter from a Trappist abbot about a visit he made with Fritz Eichenberg, the artist, to Pope Pius XII. What would you do with them? Store them as is, in your vast library?

FEB 11, OUR LADY OF LOURDES, 62

What a dear cordial note, God bless you. Thank you for the gift too. But what a bill we'll have from the cartage company. We will send them collect, then, if you don't mind—railway express, and if it is too much you tell us and we'll make good.

I'll go to the farm tomorrow and get the work underway. I'll come in the late summer or fall and we can talk about it then. You seemed to have plenty of space. I can spend a week in Milwaukee and thin down the collection.

TO WILLIAM MILLER

William Miller was a historian at Marquette University and later at the University of Florida in Tallahassee. He would go on to write a history of the Catholic Worker, A Harsh and Dreadful Love. *(Though Dorothy hoped he would also write a biography of Peter Maurin, he instead would write a biography of her, published after her death.)*

[MARCH OR APRIL 1962]

I find I am making a retreat in Minnesota July 5-11 and will be stopping by Marquette either before or after, whichever is more convenient for you and for Dr. Ready (are you a doctor too?).

I wrote to him about your using the papers. I have 3 boxes

of them still, one especially important one about the Houses of Hospitality. It is good someone objective is going to undertake a history. There are so many in the movement who deserve credit besides Peter and me,—it will be good to talk to you about it.

TO AN OLD FRIEND, *regarding her daughter*

The 1960s came early to the Catholic Worker. Most features of the counter-culture were familiar to Dorothy long before the rest of the country took notice. Despite her radicalism, Dorothy was quite conservative when it came to questions of sexual morality and other forms of personal expression. She addressed some of these concerns in a letter to an old friend of the CW whose daughter had come to New York.

For Dorothy, the last straw came when Ed Sanders (poet, musician, and proto-hippie) published a mimeographed journal, "F— You: A Magazine of the Arts," in which he mischievously credited the Catholic Worker *for the use of its mimeograph machine. Dorothy retaliated by banishing Sanders and expelling several young people from the community.*

APRIL 9, 1962

I have been wanting to write to you these last months, but it is very hard to do, and besides I could not see what you could do except pray. Ever since Ellen came to New York, she has been on her own, and since she was eighteen and [I] remembered the time of my own youth when I also went to live on the East Side and earn my own living, I kept hesitating.

She got herself a little apartment. She came in mornings to help very often, but it always disturbed me that she gravitated to the "beat" class at once, as though it were an irresistible attraction. There was a couple of fellows from San Francisco who had wandered in, a tall good-looking Negro confessing to taking marijuana, the other a Zen addict, and we asked the two of them to leave.

But Ellen had already formed a friendship with them, as

well as with a whole group who reversed all standards, turning night into day, clinging together, a dozen of them to the extent that they all began sharing apartments, girls and men. Many non-Catholics of course.

When Charles Butterworth and Ed Forand spoke to them about this, there was indignant talk about our infringing upon their freedom. I insisted that we no longer pay the rent of the apartments they were using, nor [let them] eat with us, as certainly people do not support the Catholic Worker to support a group of young ones who live from hand to mouth, do not work except that they consider the Peace Movement work. I had felt Ellen to be an exception to the others because she was working and supporting herself, but when we became strict she sided, of course, with all the others and took many of them in.

There were as many as a dozen sleeping in her little two-room place, and then finally the landlord padlocked the place and they went over to the West Side, I understand, which I take it means some loft in the Village. The worst thing that happened was the publication of a twelve-page (or thereabouts) "literary magazine" edited by Ed Sanders, which had an obscene title, "F . . . You!" and containing poetry which was pornographic, though they would not consider it so. Every other word was vulgar or obscene. Every four-letter word appearing in *Lady Chatterley's Lover, Tropic of Cancer*, appeared in this, and at the end, the statement was that much of this had been typed and prepared for mimeographing at the Catholic Worker office.

Sanders has a diabolic sense of humor, and his aim was to affront us as much as he could. Some of the writers say they did not write the things attributed to them in the paper. Hundreds of this little magazine have been circulated and it outdid *Howl* of Ginsberg and the others. It would have been a case for prosecution if it had been caught being sent through the mails. I have been able to make no contact with Ellen at all, neither when she came two summers ago, nor when we drove up together from N.Y. and I had my grandchildren with me. Of course she is determined to go her own way. But I think she is planning to hitchhike to San Francisco, which is the home of the "beats."

"The corruption of the best is the worst" and these young people come from good families, have good education, and have been given every advantage. Sometimes I don't wonder the Communists wipe out the so-called intellectuals and Lenin had to write to Rosa Luxemburg of the bourgeois morality of the young. This whole crowd goes to extreme in sex and drugs and then flatter themselves they are at least not perverts.

One of the Quakers said it was the fault of the peace movement perhaps for having such a sense of urgency. The kids are almost hysterically afraid underneath and want to eat, drink, and be merry because they feel death is so close. Also it is a complete rebellion against authority, natural and supernatural, even against the body and its needs, its natural functions of childbearing. It can only be a hatred of sex that leads them to talk as they do and be so explicit about the sex function and the sex organs, as instruments of pleasure. It is just so pinpointed in all their writings and they consider this freedom from prudery.

This is not reverence for life, this certainly is not natural love for family, for husband and wife, for child. It is a great denial and is more resembling nihilism than the revolution which they think they are furthering.

I realize that you can do nothing. I realize too that you must be very unhappy, just as I was when I saw Tamar so set on marrying at eighteen someone who was not capable of supporting her and who has finally cracked up under the strain, and has left her and is living near his family. I know you can't stop her any more than I could stop her. Parents have to let their children find their way, and God brings good out of evil. We grow by pruning and it hurts.

But I did feel that I had to write to you because I love and admire you, just as I was grateful to those who helped me with Tamar. I am praying hard myself and hope you do not think I am unduly pessimistic nor intrusive.

TO WILLIAM READY

MAY 22, 1962

I'm having a fearful attack of cold feet at having sent you our files, what with so many personal letters from people in them. I am wondering if you could hold them—and not let them be used until I can come and help go over them a bit. There are boxes to come for the last ten years. A fearful pile.

TO THOMAS MERTON

Merton had written Dorothy praising the Catholic Worker, the "Beats," and others who were rebelling against the culture of death. Dorothy was not flattered by this association.

JUNE 4, 1962

I am writing to beg prayers from you and your novices for Deane Mowrer, one of our editors, who is undergoing a most serious operation today on her one remaining eye, hoping to save the sight of it. She is blind now, but they hope that if the membrane is removed from the back of the eye, she may have some little sight left. There is one chance in a thousand, the doctor says. He is a great specialist and she is getting the best of care, as the poor do in this city when it comes to medical aid. It is the middle class who have the hardest time for medical services.

And of course I want to thank you from my heart for the articles you have written and which have been so widely reprinted all over the country. You have been the first voice among the theologians since Fr. Hugo and his companions in the Second World War.

Of course I understand from your "letters" which Elbert Sisson let me see on my recent visit to Washington that you are not a pacifist and that you are speaking in terms of modern war.* This may draw the Catholic layman further along the way of peace.

I am sending the letter you wrote me to Fr. Hugo, since, in a way, it seems to concern the whole controversy concerning nature and grace and I thought that he would be interested. He is a very busy parish priest now, with a large school but he might have time to clarify for me some of the points you made in your letter.

Your letters charmed me: there was such a variety of interests, such a richness in them, all of which goes to increase our knowledge and love of God. I am going, I hope, to Brazil this summer to visit the Grail and the Papal Volunteers with whom they are working. My book *The Long Loneliness* is translated into Portuguese by Aimee Amorosa Lima and I shall be very happy to meet her and her so famous family.

We have had visits from a dozen Brazilians connected with unions and the Young Christian Workers who came to our place in New York on a number of occasions. I am looking forward to my trip and this week must get my passport with the amended pledge that I will defend the Constitution according to my conscience or as far as my conscience permits. I will not be going until late July, so I do hope to hear from you. I would most appreciate it if you would put me on your mailing list, for any material which I would keep confidential but which I would like to show our other editors for our own information and enlightenment.

I do assure you that we are not "beats." Charles Butterworth is a Harvard Law School graduate and a convert. He formerly practiced law in Philadelphia and is [35]. Ed Forand is a former marine, reconverted by Fr. Hugo when he was in a

---

* Dorothy refers to a collection of "Cold War Letters," written in 1961–62, which Merton addressed to various theologians, writers, and peace activists (including herself). Because of censorship by the Trappist order of his writings on social topics, Merton chose to distribute the manuscript in mimeographed form. (See Thomas Merton, *Cold War Letters* [Maryknoll: Orbis Books, 2006]).

veteran's hospital in Butler, PA. Walter Kerell is a convert, a lover of music and painting. Judy Gregory is a Radcliffe graduate, and her father is the head of the Law Department of the University of Virginia. She is getting her Ph.D. on Simone Weil and Personalism. Anne Marie Stokes works with non-government agencies at the U.N., teaches French to support herself, and uses her apartment to take care of some of our worst problems in an emergency. Bob Steed supports himself by a night watchman's job and helps edit the paper. Martin Corbin works with the *Liberation* staff and lives with his wife and children at the print shop which supports the Glen Gardner community, and so on and so on.

I say all this because in your letters you associate us with "beats," of whom there have been, thank God, but a few and they a fly-by-night crew who despised and ignored the poor around us and scandalized them by their dress and morals. I am afraid I am uncharitable about the intellectual who shoulders his way in to eat before the men on the line who have done the hard work of the world, and who moves in on the few men in one of the apartments and tries to edge them out with their beer parties and women. They can sleep on park benches as far as I am concerned. Unfortunately we are left with the women who are pregnant for whom I beg your prayers. We have two girls with babies, and three expecting, on the farm now. As far as I am concerned, I must look on these things as a woman, and therefore much concerned with the flesh and with what goes to sustain it. Sin is sin and the sentimental makes a mystique of it.

Actually I am not just talking about the recent upsurge of beats that plagues the pacifist movement in England as well as in the U.S. I am talking about the war between the worker and the scholar that Peter Maurin said had to be overcome by the workers becoming scholars and the scholars workers. But enough of this. It is boiling hot, the work piles up and I must get at it.

TO EMILY COLEMAN

JUNE 9, 1962

Have you my two books, *The Long Loneliness* and *Therese*? If you do not, I will send them to you.

I am having another book out, a history of Peter and the CW, to which I cannot do justice. What I shall do from now on is concentrate on diaries, and perhaps some day we will have enough money to print them ourselves, just to further the movement! I saw the trunk full of Thoreau's diaries and became ambitious.

Are you writing? What? I am always writing. Also I am no longer a member of the secular institute, in formation, but of the secular fraternity, purely lay, of Charles de Foucauld. We meet monthly, keep certain rules, and I give two hours to the study of scripture a day! This sounds gluttonous, doesn't it. But I am soon 65 and lame with arthritis, so I must curtail walking and engagements. Not that I don't go around speaking. I spoke at 40 colleges and schools since Jan. and next month, God willing, I go to Brazil to write about the papal volunteers. One can take a modified oath now, to defend the constitution as far as one's conscience permits, on the passport.

TO THOMAS MERTON

JULY 23, 1962

Thank you for your good letter and above all for the prayers, "spiritual direction," and paper about the English mystics. I read the latter aloud to Deane Mowrer this afternoon while we sat on the beach. It was her birthday—and it was so very, very good, it colored the whole day for us. She is completely blind now, so do keep praying for her. She has an unhappy temperament and a rebellious one. I'm praying she will get to writing more—she can type (touch system), has a tape recorder, record players, FM set, talking books, etc, but lives in misery. So do pray.

I'm trying to get a visa to Cuba. If I get it from our State Dept. I'll wait till Sept.—it will take that long to get one: the inefficiency of bureaucracy. I want to see the collective farms, the educational system, the condition of religion.

AUGUST 23, 1962

Dear Father Merton,

Do not fear, your material will get to Brazil, because I am surely going in April with Hildegard Goss-Mayr and her husband [Jean], in a way as a team, a peace team, to speak of Christian nonviolence throughout South America. I am waiting for them, because I have much to learn from them both. Her husband, whom I met for the first time last spring, on their way to South Africa, was a prisoner of war in the Second World War, and then worked with the priest workers and is committed to the peace position. There is much work to be done, so much to hope from people themselves who want work and land and bread.

Another reason I postponed my trip to Brazil is because my application for a visa to Cuba was granted by our State Department and I also received one from Havana, through the Czechoslovakian Embassy in Washington which is handling their affairs. My boat sails on Sept. 5th, the Gaudalupe, and there is a chapel and a priest on board, and think of it, while I am on the boat I am under Spanish law and will be confronted with pictures of Franco no doubt! I have met the ambassadors to the United Nations, Dr. Garcia and Dr. Premelles and their wives, and they are going back to Cuba this Friday to get prepared or briefed for the next session of the General Council, or whatever it is, of the United Nations. So I will see them there. Also I have contacts with others.

Will you please pray for me while I am there, that the U.S. planes do not bomb nor saboteurs blow up buildings, set fire to cane fields, etc. etc., as the *New York Times* says they are doing daily. William Worthy, the correspondent for the *Afro-American*, says I am quite likely to be shot by a counter-revolutionary so that the blame may be laid to the Castro forces. After all, the revolution is still going on. So there is danger.

It is very heartening to see the reaction to your articles. They are being reprinted here and there, and as a matter of fact, we ourselves can reprint them too now and again. Nothing in our paper is copyrighted and we are only too delighted to see our stuff picked up and published all over.

As for Pax, I am afraid that the main reason it was formed was to take care of the fearful souls who do not wish to be associated with the Catholic Worker. I do not know what will come of it. Jim Forest has the push but not the stuff, as Peter Maurin would say. He jumps from this to that, and when he married out of the Church and insisted marriage had to do with two people and the priest was but a witness, not needed in his case, one realized how little down-to-earth knowledge he had of the sacraments, of the life of grace, of the tremendous teaching of the Church. Now the marriage has been solemnicized but the girl has publicly stated she made promises she did not intend to keep, and that she intends to have no more children, etc. etc. and that, in a nutshell, is why I am so cool to Pax. Actually [he] is the only one in it with any drive. He is so young and works so hard, but at the same time he is so undependable. So pray for them both.

Dorothy never traveled to Brazil. She did, however, travel to Cuba in September 1962, a trip she described in several articles in the CW.

NOVEMBER 12, 1962

This morning one of the two lovely girls who share the women's apartment with 2 old ladies of 78 and a half-mad Jewish convert of 30, and me, 65,—said: "Thank God for Thomas Merton." That was because of the *T. Merton Reader* which I keep on my desk there and we share. Also I say it for your essay on "Virginity" which I have not yet read and which is going the rounds.

The girls had just been going on a peace march the night before, and there had been singing and a play, and the peace walk up to Central Park and the beauty of the fall night, and [they] were so happy, so full of joy, of love of all that is beautiful. But I, like a grandmother, fret and pray. The crowd they are with are drug addicts, perverts, and so mixed up morally—so promiscuous!—that I am always fearing for their safety. So do pray for them all, hold them fast, all of them, in your prayers, that they wake out of this fascination which leads to torment.

And those in this peace crowd do not hesitate to have abortions.

I keep thinking of the first psalm.

Thank you for your letters, your goodness to us all.

I am just back from Cuba, Mexico, etc. and now much desk work to do. Your prayers hold us up. God bless you.

TO DIXIE MacMASTER

DEC 7, 1962

I'm so sorry my first article on Cuba afflicted you as it did. "You seemed truly to be enjoying the sensation you knew your words would create." To be very frank—I think you are imputing motives to me which are false. You are judging on the basis of one article of the series. Also, I am trying to find all the good—the concordances, which we are supposed to find with our opponents. I was happy and probably showed it in my articles, that it was even better there, in Cuba, than I expected. But you have not even waited for my other articles in your haste to condemn me. I must confess to being hurt by your words which I quoted above. I have no time to defend myself. I would not answer at all except that I had been so convinced of your friendship and understanding (not necessarily agreement). I am just home, visited Tamar for Thanksgiving—and here at home there are deaths, illnesses, many serious problems to attend to. So I will consider I owe you another letter later. Give my love to your dear suffering mother and all your family.

TO EUGENE EXMAN, *editor at Harper & Row*
Harper & Row had rejected Dorothy's book on St. Therese of Lisieux, finding it pious and banal. The publisher was eager, however, to publish a sequel to The Long Loneliness. *The result was* Loaves and Fishes, *the story of the Catholic Worker movement. Dorothy was not at all happy with Harper's handling of the book—particularly the work of an outside editor who was assigned to the project.*

DEC 27, 1962

I have written to Mr. Sammis about my dissatisfaction with his handling of *Loaves and Fishes*, and with his handling of me in relation to the book. Mr. Sammis has made not only changes in the wording of my book which do not convey my meaning, but he has also written in transition paragraphs at the beginning of chapters, rewritten paragraphs and has concluded with an entirely new last chapter, written by himself, giving his impressions of our work today and of the young people engaged in this work.

I was given the manuscript about ten days ago and read it through over a weekend crossing out entire paragraphs and indicating parts which must revert to my own writing and pointing out particulars in the last chapter which make me refuse to accept it. Mr. Sammis has hired another editor, Wm. C. to assist him and when I was on my way to the train I asked Mr. Parker to come get the manuscript. Mr. Sammis came also, objecting to my objections, and saying the manuscript had to immediately go to the printers, that your schedule was "very tight." I was making a train and told him I would insist on many changes. He said they could be made on proofs. That he could make arrangements so that we would not have to pay for these changes. This is nonsense, and I must insist that the book be held up until it is restored to some measure of its former meaning.

I did not object to three chapters being omitted, not to writing additional chapters, but the thing is a hodge-podge now and I must register my complete dissatisfaction. I am after all an editor myself and a writer of experience and this experience with Mr. A. and Mr. Sammis has all the way through been a strange one. Mr. Sammis announced to me that he had been handed the job of editing my book; then the contract was sent to me in which Mr. Sammis was to receive 25% of my royalties, which I foolishly signed; and then this slashing job of editing and rewriting began.

I regret very much that you have never had to read my work and that I have been handed over to men of so little understanding as Mr. A. and Mr. Sammis. I hope that you will have time to see me when I return from Chicago around the tenth of January.

Sincerely yours, Dorothy Day

TO JACK ENGLISH

JAN 19, 1963

It was so good to hear from you and to get your good long letter. Marge read it too, and she said too how she enjoyed it, a rich, good letter. And thank you with all my heart for your gift. I am determined to stay home for the next two months, aside from a weekend in Boston, to see Deane, our blind friend, and try to catch up on my mail.

Think of it, we got a donation of $100 from the present apostolic delegate to the U.S. $250 from Bishop Buddy, even a $25 gift from the Bishop in Puerto Rico. I take it as an indication that the hierarchy wish the laity to step out and get moving and not keep trying to drag them into public issues! We have been getting plenty of attacks too, you can be sure. Birchites, of course, and diocesan papers, to such an extent that *Ave Maria*, at Notre Dame, defended me in an editorial. The only favorable one I have seen. If it is not attacks, it is silence.

What cheers me no end is a letter I got from Cuba today from one of the Catholic families I visited. They are all begging me to come back next fall for a visit. "Your visit was to me a great grace and I think many others have been greatly influenced by talking to you." The two messages I brought them were the need to find concordances (the truth comes from the Holy Spirit always no matter from whose lips) and to keep working for the poor, because we will find Him there. Not to worry about work being not the organized work for the church, but just the works of mercy; and to practice faithfully the Christian life in the home. Fr. Matteo said the devil would leave all the churches standing if he could get prayer out of the home. They had been suffering from guilty feelings,—made to feel they were traitors by staying and not emigrating. But there is a goodly body of middle class Catholics there, as many at daily Mass as we ever see, even a downtown church filled at noon. And to evidence their faith by joy and fearlessness. Papers do not seem to get through (sometimes six months later) so my friend asked me to send her clippings in a letter which would reach her. I brought in a lot of books—Mounier's *Be Not Afraid*, also.

Everyone should know by now how we feel about the use of force on either side. But the revolution is an accomplished fact, and the problem is how to live there, and how to influence others. The grace of God can do everything. I insisted that those Latin American countries are going to have a different kind of communism. Where is our faith? I do hope to go back.

TO DIXIE MacMASTER

2/26/63

What tribulations! The Lord has accounted you "worthy to suffer." "Our tribulations were multiplied—afterward we made haste." Wish I could remember what psalm that last comes from.

New translations make tracing difficult. But be comforted anyway. You are doing the hardest work of all, the spiritual work of suffering. Worth far more than my active life.

I have been invited also to the Dominican Republic, where much work is being done by the apostolic delegate and priests for the poor. So I must continue my Spanish which is coming along very well. It grieves me much to miss all my friends in Montreal but it must be. So please understand and pray for me. I pray for you daily, you and yours. We are close indeed.

One weekend I went to Boston (Candlemas) to Deane's school for the blind where I was invited to speak. We all went to a party at the Paulist Church for the feast, and there I saw the Little Sisters too and Celia Hubbard of the Botolph group. It is all or nothing with them, as one can well see and never question. And so it is with our vocation to the CW. It is our work in the world and claims all our strength. God has put us in our vocation and we cannot go out of it. Much love to you and yours.

TO THOMAS MERTON

MARCH 17, 1963

I had the best of intentions to write to you before Ash Wednesday but at least you will have this letter by Easter Sunday. Thank you for your loving kindness to us. I enjoy all the things you send—when I can hang on to them. Your Selections from the Desert Fathers [*Wisdom from the Desert*] has already disappeared, books being convenient to walk off with, but I do thank you very much for sending them to me and little by little the books themselves will be reviewed. Jim Forest has one for the next issue.

Poor Jean [Forest] came to make a retreat with us for the first Sunday of Lent and excuse my critical attitude but the priest was duller than ditch water and actually put people to sleep. In our small chapel it was quite obvious. Do pray for her. I was touched that she wanted to come. [Jean and Jim Forest] have a beautiful baby and I am very happy for them.

I want your prayers too for Ellen who is the one who said, "Thank God for Thomas Merton." She has contracted a civil marriage and had a miscarriage last month and is not too well now. She is a beautiful young girl and the daughter of one of our old Catholic Worker families. And since there are, I can think of this moment, five or six others married outside the Church who are the next generation Catholic Workers I do beg your prayers for them. However, Father Joseph Wood referred me to the book of Osee as comfort in such circumstances.

I have a few friends who are always worrying about your leaving the monastery but from the letters of yours that I read I am sure you will hold fast. I myself pray for final perseverance most fervently having seen one holy old priest suddenly elope with a parishioner. I feel that anything can happen to anybody at any time. But it does irritate me to hear these woeful predictions. As for your writing so much, I am very glad you do. I am sure it is a gift of God and you are just as likely to dry up and not be able to write anything later on, so might as well do all you can now.

P.S. I am probably going to Rome April 16 with a group from Women Strike for Peace who are foolishly expecting to get an audience [with the pope]. I told them it will probably be with 500 other people but a pilgrimage is a pilgrimage and if we can call attention to all the things the Pope has been saying about peace, that in itself is good. We can send our message of thanks to him and if you have any suggestions to offer and if you by any chance get this letter at once instead of having to wait until Easter, do write and let me know what you think.

Responding to her frequent references to perseverance, Merton wrote: "It seems to me that I am almost bound to stay here even for the worst motives, let alone the best. . . . If people are fussing about my being as

they think somewhere other than here, that is their affair. I am here
and unless the Lord pulls me out by the hair of the head (and there is
no hair left) I will probably remain here, as far as I know. I have no
other plans."

TO PRESIDENT JOHN F. KENNEDY
The White House

[TELEGRAM COPY, UNDATED JUNE 1963]

In love we ask you show the world Christ's new commandment
and accompany Negro students to enroll for Alabama University.
This may seem foolish gesture, but the foolish confound the wise.

Dorothy Day, Editor, *Catholic Worker*

TO JUDITH GREGORY
Judith Gregory, a graduate of Radcliffe College, joined the Catholic
Worker in New York for a couple of years before leaving to pursue gradu-
ate studies in political science. Dorothy greatly admired her intellect and
her literary gifts.

JUNE 19, 1963

Sorry you are having all that expense. I'm sure however that it
will pass. It has always seemed to me we are bound to have an ebb
and flow in our lives, like the tides. In the *Imitation*, which I love and
which has always helped me in times of stress, it says somewhere
that God's grace comes and goes, with no fault of ours, and when
we do not have it, we wait patiently and it returns. I do think manual labor of one kind or another is of help and when I get in states
which last, I get to house cleaning, and there is always plenty of
that around the CW and farm, and that is some relief.

But I have had plenty of times when my mind is so dull and
listless and I can't read or think. Don't think I am advising or
anything—we none of us know each other, nor our own selves
either too well, and must just find our way.

Bob [Steed] comes down occasionally to the beach, and to the apartment at Kenmare [St.]. We have one flat on the top floor for Tom Cornell, Arthur Lacey, and visitors, at present three. All behave, no drugs, drink, or women. I am getting a reputation for being a Puritan. *Liberation* is coming out with an issue on Sex, and I am invited to write an article on the subject. To contribute some ancient wisdom I suppose. But I shall try.

My book *Loaves and Fishes*, much deleted, chapters removed here and there, so I do not know whether it is coherent, will be out with some gorgeous pictures, at the end of September. I am not at all satisfied, but they are. At least, in a way, a most unsatisfactory way to me, it brings the CW up to date.

TO TAMAR

SATURDAY JULY 13, 1963

Here is $50 I got for a short article. I was going to use it for the dentist but I can do that later. Had a tooth pulled last week. No sale has gone thru yet on the farm—such delays, and we are so broke. But clutches will not wait. Do get it done right away. I called Forster [in the hospital] and he says yesterday he had a really good day. He begged me to come up today since I have not been there for a week. So I'll get going soon. *The Sign* is publishing a chapter from my book next month on the farm. Not very good. More editing. I am going to print my next book myself with no chapters cut out. All of *On Pilgrimage* sold and so will this new one. *Loaves and Fishes* has some good pictures however in it.

Della from Dobbs Ferry is writing frantically for me to come call, so I may spend the day there tomorrow, tho we have so many visitors on Sundays. I get to feeling torn in so many directions sometimes. You alone do not make demands on me but welcome me when I come and do not reproach me. You do not know how grateful I am for that. You are a real comfort to me always. I guess all working mothers are like this, pulled apart, and this CW is a night and day proposition. I love the work of course or I could not keep it up and I do love to write, and know that what I write comes from the widest and deepest experience.

TO CHARLES BUTTERWORTH

In October Dorothy traveled with Eileen Egan to England to speak at Spode House, a Dominican retreat house.

OCT 15, 1963

SOUTHAMPTON. RMS QUEEN ELIZABETH

It was so good to see you at the pier last Wednesday. In the flurry of leave-taking I do not remember if I did or did not kiss you goodbye. Consider yourself kissed. I don't know why an ocean voyage is so different. I have come and gone on 3 mos. trips to the West Coast, and never had such a send-off—but I guess it is the size of the ship and the magnitude of oceans which make for such farewells.

There is another payment on the farm due November first and I wish you would postpone it until I get back so we could bank it now, separately for a down payment or even ask them to hold it until we have a place. I am praying and hoping you will have a place for me to look at on my return. It is a good time to look at places—one sees all their defects in the winter. Let nothing stand in the way of making some trips. If the car breaks down, go by train and have the real estate man drive you around.

TO JIM DOUGLASS

Jim Douglass, a lay Catholic theologian, wrote articles for the Catholic Worker *on the theology of peace in the nuclear age. At this time he was living with his family in Rome while pursuing studies. He would stay on and serve as part of a small band of pacifists who tried to lobby the Council Fathers at Vatican II to take a stand on nuclear war.*

FEAST OF ST. ANDREW, [NOVEMBER 30] 1963

[Regarding] your article. I have spent twenty-four hours in thanking God for you, Jim, and for your mind and spirit and begging him to give you strength to continue your great work. When it comes to your foundation, it probably will have to be on the personal level, as it is with most of us, and know God will open up all the ways to you.

The article, the review and article, is magnificent. I will send bundles of the issue to the places I spoke recently, a group of business men in South Bend, to the student government body, to the liturgical fair at St. Therese's church (there were six hundred there) and buses from Fort Wayne came too, and many priests, to the St. Joseph novitiate, to the minor seminary, and to three high schools. And next month I speak to the Sacred Heart College and to Emmanuel College in Boston, and January to Harvard Univ. where they want me to stay for three days at Winthrop House to discuss with the students, have seminars, and one large meeting.

I would not be capable of this effort if it were not for such an article as yours, for us to study and comment on. *Pacem in Terris, Mater et Magistra* [*encyclicals on peace and social justice by Pope John XXIII*] and then this applied to the issue of Cuba which is still a vital one. With newspapers here clamoring for the downfall of Castro and talk of the Castro terrorists in Venezuela—such violence in the air. I shall pray *to* President Kennedy about this too. Read the article about him, by the way, in the Nov 30 *New Yorker*. It is worth spending money on.

I hope you meet up with John Cogley in Rome. He used to be editor of the *Chicago Catholic Worker* and was for many years head of our house of hospitality there. Then the *Commonweal* and now he will be a year in Rome. He has a big family too, and a terrific worker. I love him dearly though we differ on many things. The Catholic Worker has been a school, all right. Fr. Putz reviewed my book for the *Davenport Messenger* and talked of the self-styled philosophers and theologians around the CW, and I should like to compile a list, just to go on record (a thing I had never done) of priests, order and diocesan, of teachers, of lay theologians, and philosophers, who have been connected with us, if not directly, then by writing for us and giving us conferences. Do you think I ought to do this, or suffer in silence? What is generally said is that "the gold is ejected and the dross remains." We are the offscourings. I might lose grace by submitting to these criticisms, but still for the sake of the work, should I answer? I will count on your advice.

TO BOB STEED

Bob Steed was visiting Ammon Hennacy out West.

THURS. DEC 5, 1963

It is good to get your letters, though not to me but to Norman and Marge. I think you are doing a heroic job, this exile of yours into Siberia. Have you read *House of the Dead*, by Dostoevsky? He said something in that which I never forgot. He said that to the educated sensitive man sufferings were more intense, that a sentence of one year was equivalent to the sentence of ten years. Ammon is so immersed in himself and his mission, his one-man revolutionism, that he can endure anything. I do not mean to criticize him for that. It is admirable. But not the tone of contempt which he takes toward everyone else, including me. No one can possibly reach his standards. It is just not their vocation. So do not let him intimidate you. You are a stalwart soul and I have absolute faith in your bravery and endurance, though I know you are going to die daily through it all.

I enclose this for an outside meal, for a movie or a book. Let me know if there are any books you want that we may have around here. Books are the only things that keep our sense of proportion in times like these. I am glad you are driven to it in the unutterable misery of your surroundings. Has Ammon a radio? Not that anyone would let you put on good music if they broadcast any out there. I remember during the seamen's strike when we spent so much time on Tenth Avenue, if anyone put on anything good, someone would immediately change it to jazz or news. Keep writing and we will keep writing. It does not matter to whom you write, so don't feel called upon to answer this, if it is an agony to write. But just the same, write *us*, on the farm and beach.

TO KEN GAERTNER

Dorothy replied to a young admirer who had sent her a selection of classical music.

[C. 1963]

First let me thank you for your most wonderful gift and that of your friends. It was a wonderful thing for you to think of doing and made me very happy. Music is my greatest recreation, but being in town all week and then so much company on the farm on weekends, I have not a chance to sit down and enjoy them yet, but the time will come. Will you convey my deep gratitude to your friends, and my friends too, I should say. Next time I am in the Detroit area I'll be coming up to give thanks personally.

About *De Colores*,—ah me, I thought it was too good to last. Treasure those back issues because it will never be so good again. Thomas Merton, Fr. Berrigan, etc. You will find it difficult to get such thinking past the censor. What I keep saying is that lay people have the right to and the duty to explore all possible solutions to the terrible problems of our age. Our Holy Father has urged this. If yours had been an independent magazine and not linked up with the cursillo movement, you could have gone ahead. Well, we will see.

Miracle of miracles, our own diocesan paper, *The Catholic News*, long conservative but now with a new editor, defended me last week in a two-column article, saying that Thomas Merton and I had the right way of combating communism, and more in accord with Christian principles, and it was to be doubted whether any other way were open to a Christian. I could scarcely believe my eyes. God is good, raising up defenders. Anyway, God be with you and keep working. I've read the first story, *The Weekend Visit*, and a grim realistic story it is. You will be outdoing the Russians. I'll read the other soon. Right now, very weak with flu.

TO KARL MEYER

12/19/63

I'm so sorry I did not see you a few weeks ago. I was supposed to go from Notre Dame to St. Paul to speak and had a day in Chicago. The very day I arrived the news struck about the killing of Kennedy and I was so sick at heart I cancelled my St. Paul talk and went home Sunday. I was sick with a cold and did not telephone while in Chicago. Your article is beautiful and most needed. We have to run these risks. John Cort also got t.b. and was in hospital a few years after his stay with us. So do take care and don't work too much. Writing or studying.

Much love to you. I have not written since you didn't—and I thought you preferred dealing with the young ones and men rather than this grandmother of the revolution who should be taking a back seat.

Your writing is wonderful. I wish you could take over editing of the CW some day.

Dorothy refers to the purchase of a new farm in Tivoli, a large estate overlooking the Hudson River.

JANUARY 10, 1964

Paper went to press yesterday. Tom Cornell, Monica Ribar, and Marty Corbin officiating. Have not seen it yet but told Tom to send it on to you at once. I liked your letters, your plans, your desires, your vision, your dream, whatever we want to call it.

You will probably think that I have gone haywire and bought a gentleman's estate. It will be a place for retreats, conferences, a house of hospitality on the land, a farming commune and a folk school, etc.

There—there will be work for a lifetime, 25 acres of woods, and fields, right on the Hudson. We will fish for shad in the spring, when they scoop them out with nets. I stopped eating meat in Sept. but still eat fish. We will raise vegetables; keep goats and chickens, and plant trees.

Do pray for us as we do for you.

TO NINA POLCYN

FEBRUARY 9, 1964

What a darling you are. I'm looking forward to a visit with you when I come out to that horribly frightening lecture which I shall prepare carefully and then wander all around the lot as I usually do. But I could never refuse Monsignor Cantwell, that great pioneer. Pray for good weather. Arthritis in the feet makes it hard to get around still, but if I do a little more fasting in Lent, it may be eased. St. Teresa of Avila said her health improved when she inflicted a little more pain on herself in voluntary mortifications. Some encyclopedia just invited me to write a 350-word life of her, for fifty dollars. The money will be welcome, but how horrible to have to keep within 350 words! How can it be done? I'll have to ask her.

TO DIXIE MacMASTER

APRIL 19, 1964

This morning my spiritual reading was a part of "Love and Unity" in *Seeds of the Desert*, "You will be obliged to reject," etc.

You can see how pertinent this is to my situation, in regard to Cuba, Latin America, Spain, etc. where passions are so strong against the Church.

Such terribly difficult assignments. Yet here again, Father Voillaume gives me just the food I need to nourish mind and spirit. I wish you would have someone type this letter out and send it to him, just so I can let him know my deepest gratitude and loyalty to him, most particularly and to the Little Brothers and Sisters everywhere.

Food for our time it certainly is,—the most radical of all action. For me too, it is the continuation of the "retreat" that I talk so much about, applied to all the situations of our lives.

I wanted to write you most especially this morning because you were the one who brought me so close to this movement, and it is to you I owe so much. And I just wanted to let you know that I feel even closer to it all, tho it is not possible for me to be a recognized "Little Sister," or formally a part of it. I feel this was clearly shown me by all the circumstances which you know of. Mlle Poncet's attitude toward our CW activities and ideas, and her visit to Spring Street and her most evident and expressed distaste for what we were doing, which directly led me to leave the secular institute. You remember I told you I had an "insight," a "light" on the problem when I was making a holy week retreat in a Benedictine monastery on the West Coast. The problem of Cuba had not yet entered in.

When I returned I initiated the meetings of the secular fraternity in Brooklyn in the poor parish where René Voillaume stayed. Nothing was official. There was no formal recognition by the dioceses of Brooklyn or New York.

It was at our yearly retreat that the young priests, 3 or 4 of them, expressed themselves so strongly on my visit to Cuba, which I was to visit right after the retreat.

When I returned from Cuba . . . [*illegible*] . . . association with the fraternity, the attempt made was to split us up—a few CW members to go to other groups—to keep us from being so "ingrown."

And finally, none of us felt we were getting the spiritual nourishment at what were becoming social gatherings of people of widely different views as to the spiritual life. There was little of the meat of Fr. Voillaume's conferences or of Brother Charles's universal friendship. And little emphasis on voluntary poverty or self-denial.

Their attitude toward Cuba (they were full of atrocity stories such as Fr. Machos having his tongue "horribly mutilated" so he could not say Mass) and certainly nothing I said or wrote had any effect on them. I would say it was this attitude of theirs that caused me to leave the fraternities.

That does not mean that I would not like to try again to have a small group of CW people meet once a month to read, perhaps, a conference of Fr. Voillaume, and spend an hour together in adoration, to emphasize the "day in the desert," etc. To follow, in fact, Fr. Voillaume's direction thru his books.

As it is, we try to have a monthly day of recollection but do not always have the priest. When we do, we can have a reading—it may be very short, and a "conversation" together. Will you pray for this?

TO KARL MEYER

JULY 3, 1964

It was only because I was so rushed with work that I didn't write when Ed sent the check. And we should have sent it without your asking. Just the same it would be too bad if we couldn't ask each other when we are in need. Sometimes I think the most important message we have is dependence on Divine Providence. After all, keeping going for thirty-two years is no mean record when you consider the expenses of an outfit like ours.

I am thinking of that expense this afternoon because I was faced with the problem of taking out insurance on the three houses here in Tivoli and after talking to an insurance man for an hour I came to the conclusion that we would be violating principles. So once more we are doing something rash and reckless and leaving it up to Divine Providence to take care of us. But if we had a record of all the harm insurance companies have done throughout the country people would understand our attitude to them. I do like cooperative insurance which is a form of mutual aid where you pay just according to the number of fires, or barns struck by lightning just in one district. Some years you pay nothing and other years expenses are divided up among everyone. There was a farmer's insurance of that kind in Easton, Pennsylvania we dealt with. If you have a mortgage on your house you have to have insurance of course to satisfy the person who holds the mortgage so you probably have it so you have to go on paying insurance until you have paid off your house. How much of a mortgage do you still have? I wish you would look into this kind of thing and write about it sometime, this whole business of house insurance or even life insurance.

TO NINA POLCYN

JULY 17, 1964

What gorgeous stationery! I was just harshly judging some of our nuisances, beatniks on the one hand and drunks on the other, when your note came and the quotes from Chesterton on loving, forgiving, faith, and hope, changed my point of view at once. It is a gem. Can you send me some? Or any cards with good quotes on them. You are a darling.

Traveling is a great recreation, and a great enlightener. I do enjoy it so and am glad you get the same kick out of it. What about our date to go by car to the West Coast this winter? Tamar may take a practical nursing course, one of those government rehabilitation programs, and the first four months will be away from home in Brattleboro, Vt., and I must go and stay with the kids. The last eight months she can live at home and work in the local hospital. She can manage then, somehow or other, the darling. She has weathered many storms. I think she will be good at this, just as she is good with children and animals. It is too good a chance to be missed. So from Sept. to January I will be in Perkinsville. God willing. The course is not absolutely sure yet. But her papers are all in and they have sent for her for an interview.

While Tamar enrolled in a four-month course in practical nursing in Brattleboro, Dorothy did move to Perkinsville to look after her grandchildren.

TO HELENE ISWOLSKY

AUGUST 7, 1964

We were all so happy to hear from you and that you will be home late August. Yes, I am going to Tamar's Aug 28. I will be there four months and hope to get some reading and writing done.

While we can work and be active, we just keep going, and look forward later to settling down like Agnes and Peggy* to a quiet life on the Hudson. But we'll keep writing, you and me, and make tea in my samovar every afternoon! Much love always—and give my love to all up there.

---

* Peggy Baird, formerly married to Malcolm Cowley, was one of Dorothy's oldest friends, going back to their arrest together during a women's suffrage protest in 1917. Peggy ultimately retired to the Catholic Worker farm at Tivoli, where she spent her final years.

TO NINA POLCYN

AUG 27, 1964

I told you, didn't I, at least in the paper, that I would be up there four months, aside from the Labor Day weekend. Tamar is so excited and looking forward to school again. She is so good with children and animals and with occupational therapy, she will enjoy it, I am sure, and do wonders.

Do pray for me. I'm not planning anything at all after January. I'm thinking I should stay home for a bit and get acquainted with the CW again. At this age, and with all the younger ones taking over, I am much freer of course, and things are really going well. If one can call it going well when so many of the miseries of the world descend upon one. It is amazing how cheerful a place it is, just the same.

This place, Tivoli, is so incredibly beautiful, you must visit it. And I am in and out so much I have not even unpacked!

TO FRITZ EICHENBERG

PERKINSVILLE, VT. [C. SEPT 1964]

If you've had time to read the paper you will know that I am now at Tamar's since August 30 and will be here until January to baby-sit for her. It does seem so long since we have seen each other and I certainly think of you very often. Last night I was reading the hunting scene in *War and Peace* and of course with your illustrations, which you were so unhappy with, I felt very close to you. I can never tell you how I appreciate your work. In fact I pore over it to the extent that I neglect the text. Every character you draw is unique. Natasha and her family are just as I have always pictured them.

The boys are hunting each day, rabbits, and I thought of

that scene in Tolstoi. Also I am poring over cookbooks trying to figure different ways of cooking them. It hurts me to think of their hunting unless it is because they are going to eat what they kill. The hunting season only opened up day before yesterday and I'm hoping that they soon have their fill of it. It makes me want to become a vegetarian. But the hard-hearted little children pore over the entrails and wonder at the design of them, and make a physiology lesson out of it all—as well as having the outing in the woods and fields. As I said before, if they eat what they kill, it is all right by me, because we certainly consume a lot of food up here, and it is hard to keep up with these appetites. And when a couple of their friends come in!

Eric is 16 and Nickie is 14, and they still so trustfully put up their foreheads for me to make the sign of the cross on them before they go to bed at night and before they go to school in the morning. I urge them, as St. Benedict did, to short and frequent prayers, as they go down the road to the school bus in the morning but the little ones, Katy, Martha and Margaret (Mary is now a teenager) love very specific prayers at night, describing to God our needs and informing him of how good Nickie has been to fetch water from the brook. "Tell Him something about Hilaire," Katy will say, and so we ask protection for Hilaire who is seven, so that he won't chop off a foot with the ax which he insists on using or get shot by a hunter when he is out with the other boys. He is such a good and serious little boy. "I miss my father," he said to me once. David loved the little ones especially. No one knows his address in Washington. One of our friends ran into him, and he told him he was dishwashing and living in a furnished room. The psychiatrist said it was anxiety and fear of responsibility and so on that led to his collapse. We pray for him that he get a job in a bookshop which might be the beginning of his healing. It is horrible for men to have work to do that they loathe.

Do forgive this awful typing. But my hands are rheumatic

and cooking and washing don't help much. My feet too. Otherwise I am enjoying so much this being with the children and seeing how happy Tamar is with her studies and her work.

Do drop me a line when you can. I do miss hearing from you.

TO DIXIE MacMASTER

OCT 23, 1964

My time is full and I am having a very happy time with the children—it is like a vacation. I still get my hour of scripture in the morning and time for bits of reading during the day. Tamar is so happy in her work but she is dreading the bad winter months, getting the 4-year-old to the neighbor who will care for her and herself getting off to the hospital in Springfield 8 miles away by 7, leaving the other six children to get off to school by themselves. Do pray for us. I'm wondering if I should not stay during the winter if not the full year. I took that year off during the war and had thought then I would do the same every 5 years, but never did. Ours is such a 24-hr a day job. Problems still confront me in the mail each day but it is a very quiet life, and things are going so well at Chrystie St. and at Tivoli. What do you think?

This card [pressed flowers] came from a neighbor who runs a little gift and book shop. Like the seaweeds I pressed, it makes one think of the infinite care of God for beauty. I am surrounded by it here and I am so glad they have it at Tivoli. A constant reminder of our Creator.

TO DEANE MARY MOWRER

PERKINSVILLE, OCT 28, 1964

Got your lovely long letter and do appreciate it. No rain yet up here, and for a bit they closed the woods to hunting and it was a welcome interlude for me. I only believe in hunting if it is because of a need for the food. But it is like pulling teeth to get them to clean their catch properly—I have to stand over them. Then it is a lesson in anatomy and everyone is called upon to admire the perfect design of the innards of the rabbit or partridge. The latter is perfect eating of course and there is not so much dispute about cleaning them. The good thing about hunting is that they are out all afternoon until dark, and they get up as soon as it is light to have an hour on the hills, and they do love these explorations into the woods and fields. You can see how they sense the beauty all around them, and it is something that will always stay with them. I must read again the story of the hunt in *War and Peace*.

My time is so completely taken up I am not getting any writing done or reading. I'll try to get an On Pilgrimage off soon for the November issue. I have brief notes in my diary which will help. I do get an hour in, from five-thirty to six-thirty to do a bit of praying, but my prayers wander off in all directions. Still it is a precious time and if I do not get that in, and the rosary late afternoon (since I cannot get to daily Mass) I find myself getting irritable with the children in those awful noisy hours after supper and before bedtime. It will get worse as the night falls earlier. I find myself shouting at them, the bigger ones, but then one has to shout to be heard. When thirteen-, fourteen- and 16-year-olds start roughhousing, woe to the furniture and the little ones who are in their way. Neighbor children sure let off steam here too, and what with Tamar's permissiveness (she loves the ideas of the Summerville school) it is trying for a 67-year-old. The solution is for me to get out and let them rampage, so I take my transistor and hold it to my good ear and read. But still any cry of hurt reaches me, though all the rest can be dimmed.

I believe in freedom too, but I also believe in the common good, and consideration for others. But no use talking that way to kids in this age bracket. Only thing is to have faith, pray, be silent and patient.

The littlest one is a joy always. She helps in the housework, a real busybody, she draws, she looks at pictures in the big Bible, she prays with me as I read my office, she holds her little Mass book. She is always good and happy. When she starts rampaging, when the others get home, I can have some sympathy because she has been so quiet all day.

My four months are moving along smoothly and I can hardly realize that on December 18 Tamar will be finished at Brattleboro. She comes home then for a vacation until Dec. 26 and starts in work then at the hospital here in town, Dec. 26, seven a.m. I will take a quick trip to New York and Tivoli, God willing, and be back for Christmas Day here and to give her the final week. After that I know she can manage. Though she's frightened of the ice and snow, and the car not working. She manages her car but no one else can, not even Eric. It is a mistake for people to live so far out, and away from villages and the Church.

Give my love to all there. Oh, yes, I had a visitor yesterday, an ex-mental patient from Boston who wanted to come to Tivoli to start his work for the mentally ill. I told him to start in Boston, in a tiny place like Rose Hawthorne did with her cancer home. You should get someone to read that book about her.

Dorothy wrote from a Southern trip, which included a visit to Conyers, Georgia, to visit Jack English at the Trappist monastery.

FEB 8, 1965

What a struggle to get a few minutes to write you. I keep going from six to midnight and it is all very interesting, too, so I am not complaining. But I do not advise anyone to go to the Trappists for a rest or retreat or peace and quiet, at least not if they are in the CW movement. Jack English is the kind that talks day and night. And Father Peter and Fr. Abbot and Father Methodius and so on and so on. The weather is beautiful, warm and mild and the birds are beginning to sing.

In North Carolina in the mountains it was zero weather,

just like N.Y. but warming up in the day. Got my On Pilgrimage written Sunday afternoon, since I had to fill out a questionnaire anyway, an interview for Mr. Sherry, the editor of the Atlanta diocesan paper. I thought it might be good to use it as people are always asking our aims and purposes and the specific questions he asked are of interest to all, especially in view of the attacks made on us which I do not believe in answering directly.

I am staying at a hospital here in Gadsden and talking to the Negro school this noon. Last night to all the sisters in town and this morning at eight thirty to the white school, white because of the neighborhood it is in. Integration in the hospital and bus stations and public accommodations to a certain extent. The CORE group here takes 20 copies of the paper and all the colored section know our work and love us. The young man in charge rushed up to me in the colored drug store and kissed me when we met him there. He is from New Orleans.

The war in Vietnam is certainly escalating, and it is a time for much prayer and sacrifice on our part, so do, please Deane, offer up your sufferings in penance for our sins, and I will do the same in my own small hardships. Don't waste your ammunition. Offer even your bitterness of soul. In Isaiah it is "In peace is my bitterness most bitter."

Therese of Lisieux quoted that and said, "Let us suffer if need be in bitterness, just as long as we suffer, and offer it up." Please excuse me for presuming to say such things. But we are fellow workers.

Much love to you and the others of the family there. Love your enemies, do good to them who persecute you, etc. We begin there. Remember, no righteous wrath, but a calm and peaceful heart. I know you will have Marty or Rita [Corbin] read this to you and we can be personal. Hope you get your column done this month. People miss it. I enclose twenty dollars for you to get tapes with.

TO NINA POLCYN

FEB 22, 1965, AUSTIN, TEXAS

Your letter—with what news!—followed me around and here I am so late with my sympathy. What a miserable thing to have happened. Thank God you have "very little discomfort." But believe me, when I broke my arms as a child it was an agony. And to have to hobble around on crutches! Anne Marie Stokes was incapacitated for a year what with her broken bone in her ankle. She did a lot of suffering too. And she was the one who walked on picket lines with us, and for miles along the beach on Staten Island.

Thank you for the check you sent and God bless you. What with this generosity, if God sends back a hundredfold, you are going to be a millionaire before you're through. In graces anyway.

Remember how we planned to drive west this year? And here I am going on without you. You will see by the paper my route. Had a grim time in Mississippi, harrowing. Trying to write a little here in Austin, in a half day of leisure. They sure do not give you much time on one of these speaking jaunts. This is the first time I've been west since four years ago. I am already dying to get back home where I certainly do not work so hard though I'm kept continually busy. But I'll go on, and probably won't strike Chicago until the end of March. I'm very anxious to see our new places in Oakland, and Ammon's place in Salt Lake City. By now you have your copy of his book [*The Book of Ammon*], which I only had time to pick up, but in spite of heresies, and I understand the last chapter is awful, almost a rejection of the church, it is always engrossing. God help him. I cannot help but worry about him too.

I sometimes think he is aiming at an interdict, just so he can think of himself as fighting the great Holy, Catholic, and Apostolic Church. God forgive me for such an accusation, but his pacifism takes the form of aggressiveness for sure.

Trouble is the clergy like to hear him criticize, say the things they would like to say. Then they are not patient enough to instruct.

Tamar is half through her course, has six months to go at the local hospital. She can live at home since all the kids are in school, except Katy who is staying with our cousins, and Tamar misses her terribly.

I had a wonderful time the four months I was there, but Tamar really didn't want me when she was able to be at home. There is no room for two mothers in the kitchen, and so on. And they are crowded in winter in the only heated part of the house. I am going back there in the summer and spend some more months there, God willing.

Internationally things look very bad. We need to pray hard for peace.

TO A MARYKNOLL SISTER

EASTER SUNDAY 1965

Dear Sister,

I can only greet your letter with the greatest sorrow. The older I get the more I feel that faithfulness, perseverance are the greatest virtues—accepting the sense of failure we all must have in our work, in the work of others around us, since Christ was the world's greatest failure and see the marvelous success of the Cross. Dom Hubert von Zeller brings this out so well in his little book, *Approach to Calvary.*

It does seem to me that when one enters religion, it is as though one contracted marriage, and even if one feels as though one had made a terrible mistake, one has to be faithful to it. I have many times advised people to stick it out in religion, until they are thrown out. If God wants you out, from the place you are now, He will see to it that you *are* out. Or transferred, or something or other.

When you say you are going to join us, I can only say that within a very short time after you do that you will be most disillusioned with us (whether we deserve it or not is not the question) and finding another apostolate. You will then wander from one to another. It is the usual pattern, and how little peace there is in this.

I pray for Fr. [Felix] McGowan daily, that he persevere, go where he is sent, accept *the little way,* which we are forced to accept in the long run whether we want to or not, and accept the personal poverty which means the hardest work of all, stripping oneself of all desire for novelty, great works, appearances of poverty, successes, and so on. We are born bourgeois in the U.S., rich in many things, and feel guilty and ashamed and try to escape it. I wrote a book on the Little Flower because it is wonderful to see how she dealt with these things. I am sending you a copy under separate cover.

Please, I beg of you, wait a year before taking such a step as you contemplate, and then make a move only with the consent of your spiritual advisor. This is the advice I gave once, long ago, to a young seminarian in Baltimore [Jim Rogan] and he obeyed. Then at the end of the year he came out, took charge of our little house in Baltimore, was a conscientious objector during the Second World War, got training as a male nurse in the Alexian Brothers hospital in Chicago, after the war, married, had two beautiful children, and this little family were the first lay missionaries to Durban, South Africa, where he nursed in the hospital for Africans and Indians for three years until he was too sick with the hepatitis to continue.

I warn you, you know nothing of our work when you announce that you will join us (after traveling for a time!) and if you do come to stay with us you will find nothing to satisfy you here. If God chooses to take the "offscourings of all," which we are, and give some kind of teaching to the world through us it is not because *we* do anything, or deserve anything. If I, with long experience (I am 67), find the work utterly frustrating and full of most humiliating failures, I do not know how you could stand it. However, if at the end of a year, with the consent of your spiritual director, you still wish to come, we will gladly accept you with great love.

Meanwhile, write and do let me know Fr. McGowan's permanent address. I pray daily he persevere, not only in his radicalism, but in obedience.

With love, in Christ, Dorothy

TO THOMAS MERTON

ST. JOHN [BAPTIST] DAY, JUNE 24, 1965

Yesterday Dr. [Karl] Stern telephoned me from Montreal asking me to ask the Trappists and my friends the cloistered Maryknoll Sisters for prayers for a great trouble he has. We are having a retreat here right now and reading the prison meditations of Fr. [Alfred] Delp [*a Jesuit executed by the Nazis*] with your introduction, and I thought of you right away. The call came right while we were at dinner. So first of all, I am asking you to pray most especially, and begging you to ask the community since there is no time with God and prayer is retroactive accordingly. I am sure that already his weight of sorrow is lifted somewhat, or that he has had an increase of grace to bear it. He is a daily communicant, and a deeply suffering man. I sometimes think that without his writing and his music he would collapse.

I have been intending to write you for some time, just to thank you for your writings. You will never know the people you have reached, the good you have done. You certainly have used the graces and the talents God has given you. I am afraid I lack the discipline to do the work I ought to do, being occupied with many Martha-cares. Right now we are having a retreat for priests, a small affair, ten of them, and Fr. Hugo remains afterward to give a laymen's retreat.

As usual during retreats there are great distractions. One of our family, who had spent a good many years of his life in prison, in Sing Sing and Dannemora, who had broken his parole and was threatened with a life sentence, who had sanctuary with us for the past ten years, died after much suffering with emphysema, if that is how you spell it.

There were the details of grave digging, the pleading with the undertaker for a plain pine box instead of the satin-lined casket. He told us only Jews used them, and Jewish cemeteries always smelled what with the decay coming up through the ground. Perhaps he really believed it, perhaps he was taught this—a sales pitch.

When Peter Maurin was buried in 1949 the undertaker tried to bully us with tales of handles falling off of cheap caskets, and inexperienced pall bearers dropping the coffin and the body being spilled out on the church steps. How horrifying! There should be a committee in each parish to take care of those details of burial so that poor people need not be harassed and exploited at these sorrowful times.

It was such a happy release for our poor man that we could only rejoice at his liberation and I did not at all mind fighting with the undertaker. But the expense anyway! It cost $400 to bury the dead at the very cheapest. And this is what they charge welfare also, to bury the destitute.

On top of our other troubles, two young drug addicts tried to take refuge with us the night before. And refuge for them means a harbor in a libertarian atmosphere, where they will not be interfered with. The peace movement seems to be plagued by such. On the Quebec-Guantanamo march they had to exact a pledge from the marchers not to indulge in drugs, liquor, or extra-marital intercourse. "And what's wrong with that?" six young freedom riders asked me when I expelled from our midst two young people, one an ex-seminarian, who were keeping girls with them in our rooms which they shared with men from the Bowery. I could only explain that people were not sending us money to support them, but to support the destitute. That they should get work, and it was available to them, and support themselves in the way they wished to live. Peter Maurin's philosophy of work, an understanding of it and a living by it, would do a great deal to discipline these young lives.

So you see by this, I am having a hard time right now and I am begging your prayers for me, myself. I am sending you also something I have written about problems in the city. If you know of someone who could help us, do pass it on.

AUGUST 11, 1965

Our Pax weekend was very good, thanks to Jim Douglass. He has been urging me to go to Rome to try to reach the bishops directly and at that very weekend a friend gave me $500 to go. So I beg your prayers. We will be there by the 15th of Sept. Martin Corbin and I cannot thank you enough for the Maximus article ["St. Maximus the Confessor on Nonviolence"] which we will use in the Sept. issue. The Aug. issue was all directed to the bishops of the world.

Jim Douglass is outstanding—a daily communicant, most disciplined, strong and gentle. The best of all the peace group. Jim Forest gets better all the time. Tom Cornell is in deep trouble over a critically ill wife. The Pax group, Eileen Egan and Howard Everngam, grow in numbers among the older, more conservative. All of us count on your prayers and continued work. God bless you always. With love from us all—

TO JACQUES TRAVERS

Jacques Travers, an instructor of French at Brooklyn College, extended Worker-style hospitality from his own apartment in Brooklyn.

AUG 4, 1965

You are not the kind of person who will take advice, evidently, so after repeating what I said before about not leaving the Professor and Ray Leach there in your apartment, I won't venture to advise you again. You said you were not warned that the Professor drank. We never gave him any money for that reason, just paid his room rent and gave him his meals. And as for Ray, the same there. He does not drink, but he *accumulates*. Usually from ash cans. When you come back you are liable to find your apartment stored with papers, books, and boxes of trash of all kinds, usually in cartons, which, if you move out the door, he will move in the window. He is a sweet and good person, but I am afraid he is the kind who is only at home in the slums. We have another like that, and have had others. They get the apartment so filled up, one cannot get in at all. So I warn you. Go to Europe but I do not know what you will find on your return.

TO DELLA [DAY] SPIER

Among all her relatives, Dorothy maintained the closest relationship with her younger sister Della, who lived with her husband Franklin Spier in various towns in the New York area. Since childhood they had especially enjoyed trading notes on their travels and reading, and over the years Della's home was a frequent site of rest and recreation. Unfortunately, very few of Dorothy's letters to Della have survived. In this one, she writes from Rome, where she had traveled to lobby the bishops at the Second Vatican Council to take an active stand on behalf of peace. As part of her efforts there, she planned to join a group of international women in a ten-day fast.

SEPT 18, 1965

I have just finished my first week in Rome and it seems as though I had been here for a year. I have a tiny room, comfortable bed, one flight up in the apartment of a spinster daughter of an attorney, who rents two rooms only and gives no meals so the place is very quiet, except for the courtyard onto which many apartments look out and it sounds like Mott Street. But there are grape vines in the courtyard and birds in cages singing, and the sky is bright above and plenty of light in my room, so I am very comfortable at one dollar a night. Continental breakfast is only coffee and brioche, but I am used to it now. Lunch is never served until one or two and dinner at night at eight thirty. What hours.

This morning, Saturday, there being no council meeting, I am meeting two cardinals, one at ten and the other at one. In both cases the engagements were made by their secretaries so it is no doing of mine. I could happily spend my time sight-seeing and bus-riding and sitting at a corner café and watching the world go by. But one must work, that is, lobby. Discreetly to find out if the reverend feels the same as we do about our hellish weapons. And secondly whether he will get up and speak at the Council, so that when votes are taken, he will have taken his stand.

Strangely enough bishops are also inarticulate about such world issues and feel they do not know enough to speak out. They feel military experts should speak up, and the scientists (but then they have!). The problem is that they accept war as a means of righting wrongs,—most of them living in the Middle Ages still, and the time of chivalry. Of course most of us wish to be defended, naturally speaking. But what an example the Quakers set. Douglas Steere is here from Haverford College and I am certainly going to try to see him. A really great man.

Fortunately I have friends here so my time is well occupied, otherwise I would be homesick indeed, so far away from home. Mail reaches me immediately, care of the Notre Dame Center. I have been getting mail from the office and from Tivoli. I wrote you on the boat so you should have had one letter from me.

SEPTEMBER 28, 1965

How good to get your letters, yes I got one and 2 and the last which was so good and cheering a one. It is certainly better to be so needed, to have every instant taken, so that some reading at night is a luxury and most enjoyable. So much better than always being "on one's own" as I am over here, a solitary in a way, seeing new people, new friends, but who can never take the place of our own "loved ones." That phrase is trite, but true.

In two more days I will leave my little cell of a room to go to a convent near the catacombs of St. Priscilla and join 19 other women (none of whom speak English) and undergo our fast. The demons of war "can only be overthrown by prayer and fasting," the Lord said.

Meanwhile I have had 3 weeks of meeting bishops and their theologian advisors both on the boat or here, to ask of war and peace and to urge ample provision for conscientious objection.

At night I've been reading *The Betrothed* by Manzoni, an old classic but very good indeed. Finished it last night. Jim Douglass, another of our lobbyists, a professor, is reading *Kristin Lavransdatter*. I sleep like a log, get up to *cold* coffee in my room, then Mass across the street—then brioche and black Italian coffee with milk afterward for breakfast. People take a toasted sandwich at 12, lunch at 1:30, a siesta, then work again from 4–8. Everyone dines at 8. What hours! Hard to get used to.

Did I tell you my room was a dollar a night? No baths, no hot water. So I bathe in cold, a washbowl bath, and portable bidet. It is so warm one does not mind the lack of hot water. You can go to the station and have a hot bath and a two-hour nap however. A wonderful service for travelers. My pedicure worked wonders. So well done my sore toe does not hurt at all. Only my bones. But no cramps at night either, which is strange considering the walking. It is really standing which is bad.

What a gossipy letter. Did I tell you I go to press briefings in the morning—12:30. Then lunch, then a panel discussion at three, other meetings at 4:30, etc. Time is filled up so there is little time for sight-seeing really except by bus.

But it is travel itself I enjoy, seeing people. Still, I have no associations with the Italians as I have with the English, what with our love of literature. And language barriers are terrible. What ignoramuses we are, not to study other languages. I'm going to get back to my Spanish!

Do excuse hasty note. Seeing bishops and priests constantly to talk about conscientious objection and war.

Love to you and Franklin—Dorothy

TO DEANE MARY MOWRER

SEPT 29, 1965, ROME

I am glad all at the farm read my letter, because surely I don't have time to do much writing. Every moment of my day from the time I get up is taken and I don't even have time to take a bath, which one has to do at the railroad station. Just washbowl baths in cold water ever since I was here. For the last two days it has poured intermittently and I am glad I have that rain coat which I grabbed from the office door the last minute. Also a plastic kerchief. It is still warm here, but with a little chill in the air which makes my red wool dress comfortable. But not rayon which the rain causes to shrink up to my knees. Wool or cotton for me hereafter.

Today I see Archbishop Hurley, and tomorrow Abbot Butler of Downside Abbey, England. Every day there is a briefing at noon, 12:30 or one, according to how long the Council lasts that day, and a very brilliant summing up by Fr. Heston of Notre Dame, who will be broadcasting for one of the big networks during the Pope's visit. Then lunch with priests and bishops, one or the other until two thirty and then a panel discussion on the latest that has taken place on the floor which sounds much like a CW roundtable discussion, with questions coming from the floor on such issues as to where is Heaven and is there a personal devil, such questions being brought up by skeptical newsmen, because of such allusions in speeches. They miss all the intellectual content sometimes and fasten on something which will make the church look ridiculous. They are going to town now on the new Jesuit Fr. General. His language has given them strong meat for their condemnations.

406 ALL THE WAY TO HEAVEN

Many of these clergy need public relations men as well as better ghostwriters. Yesterday I had lunch with Fr. Putz who told us how various influences here at Rome mislaid every message from the very large commission which studied at Notre Dame the problems of population and family limitation. Not one of their three attempts reached the official commission at Rome, so he gave it out to the press. A missionary Holy Cross Bishop from Africa said he would probably lose his head or some such comment. I am always running into people at whose schools I spoke in the States.

Monday I was invited to an afternoon discussion at a meeting headed by Cardinal Suenens, which is meeting to discuss lay application of the Council work in the world, after the Council is over. That afternoon they were honoring Frank Duff, pious Irishman, truly a noble soul, who started the Legion of Mary and spoke of its growth in China and Africa where, because of its lowliness and lack of influence, it had reached the people and actually inspired them with martyrdom in China. Certainly they were integrating in Africa long before we began to hear about it.

Martin Work of National Council of Catholic Men and also the editor of the *St. Louis Review* got up to talk of more significant work, and their comments not being specific fell rather flat so I was urged to get up. We had all, about fifty of us, introduced ourselves and when I said Catholic Worker the whole place applauded, which was not too gratifying since no one pays much attention to all our work on peace. They were just welcoming a little stimulus.

We were in a great villa looking like something out of Hollywood or La Dolce Vita, overlooking all Rome, on the top of a high hill with a view of the Alban Hills all around, and the place was very crowded. So I told them about my contact with the Legion of Mary in jail with Deane, and how one of the correction officers had started a little group of prostitutes and drug addicts to study the lives of the saints, and this, of course, on her own time. And how that kidnapper and three women charged with murder amongst a group of others, on another occasion, another year, when we were held without bail, gathered around this Italian woman's bed and recited the rosary. It gave me a chance to talk of the dignity of the human person which Schema 13 stresses so much, and also to talk about our witness for peace coming from the level of the market place and the street corner through demonstrations.

Afterward Cardinal Suenens came to me and he thanked me, he speaks English well, and of course many others as well. The direct action, the appeal to their compassion had an immediate response.

When Dorothy returned from Rome she was immediately confronted by a succession of dramatic events reflecting the mounting protest against the Vietnam War. On October 18, Catholic Worker David Miller became the first person arrested for burning his draft card after Congress passed a law making this a specific crime. On November 6, Dorothy and veteran activist A. J. Muste lent their public support to several young men, including former Catholic Worker *editor Tom Cornell, as they burned their draft cards in Union Square. And then on November 9—a terrible day—Roger LaPorte, a young volunteer at the Catholic Worker, sat in front of the United Nations, doused himself with gasoline, and struck a match. "I am a Catholic Worker," he said to hospital workers. "I did this as a religious action. I am anti-war, all wars." He remained alive for thirty-three hours.*

Roger LaPorte's death was a great blow for the CW community, not least for Dorothy, who was widely blamed for encouraging this "suicide." The reaction of Thomas Merton particularly stung. On hearing the news of LaPorte's death he sent a telegram asking to be removed as a sponsor of the Catholic Peace Fellowship. He felt that the peace movement was succumbing to a kind of madness. It appeared to Dorothy that he too was blaming her for this desperate act—something she never forgot. Even many years later the memory remained a source of anguish.

TO THOMAS MERTON

NOVEMBER 15, 1965

Excuse me for writing your name wrong on the envelope ["Father Thomas Merton"]. We are so full of distractions these days. I am sitting by the hospital bed of our oldest resident, Agnes, widow of a coal barge captain, who herself lived in barges for thirty years. She has been with us for 15. I look upon her with admiration and wonder and hope I have the sweetness and patience at the close of my life.

About your telegram—we are so glad you know about our tragedy, being assured you are praying for us.

I am certainly behind the boys who burned their draft cards—Tom Cornell has been with us for years, and David Miller and Jim Wilson all summer and working all day, every day, with the poor. As for poor Roger [LaPorte], he was only living with us a few days, while he searched for another apartment. He had worked for Columbia two years and was going to school. When I came back from Rome, I met him for the first time. Since he only came in occasionally to serve tables or to attend our Friday night meetings, I had never actually exchanged a word with him. But he seemed to me older and more mature than his twenty-two years. The pictures in the press were high school ones.

If anyone had ever dreamed he contemplated such an action, he would have been watched day and night by the other young ones such as Jim Wilson, David Miller, Kathy, Nicole and the others. They are all in their early 20s and very much "in love" with each other and with life. None of us can understand what happened.

I am only hoping that your reaction, as evidenced by your telegram, that is, holding us responsible, is not general, but I am afraid it may be. We have already received two bomb threats and I myself have been threatened at a public meeting at N.Y. Univ.

Of course, as members of one Body we are all responsible for each other.

The November issue of the CW will have short comments by other members of our group. Do you receive the paper regularly? Did you receive the July-Aug. issue directed to the bishops of the world, with articles by Jim Douglass and others?

In view of the terrible things that are happening—the accidental bombing of friendly villagers, the spraying with napalm of our own troops yesterday, there is bound to be increased protest.

I am glad that there are so many now. The Catholic Worker has borne the burden for 33 years—protesting wars, Chinese-Japanese, Ethiopian, Spanish, World War II, Korean, Algerian, and now this.

My nephew, David, (my only sister's son) is reading *Seven Storey Mountain* now. He and his wife are agnostic (she would say atheist) and she refuses to read it. Or rather, in her fear of what the book may do to him, she calls it a bore! They have a three-year-old who has no legs and only one arm and he suffers terribly. One other child is ill. They are caring for my daughter's youngest who is 5, the same age as their oldest. Will you please pray for him? I think he is close to the Church. We all love you dearly and please keep praying for us.

Merton subsequently apologized for the desperate tone of his telegram ("a rather ill-considered and immediate reaction to the sad news of Roger LaPorte") and expressed his confidence in Dorothy. In her reply she refers to Father Daniel Berrigan, a Jesuit priest and poet, who was emerging at this point as a prophetic voice for peace within the Catholic Church. His superiors had specifically charged him to maintain silence on the subject of Roger LaPorte's death. When he seemed to defy this order by sharing reflections at a memorial service, his superiors ordered him to leave the country for an indefinite assignment in Latin America. Dorothy thought this term of "exile" might do him some good.

DECEMBER 2, 1965

I hasten to write to thank you from my heart for your most reassuring letter and to tell you that I agree with it in many ways. I am in agreement with the draft card burners because they are young men liable to the draft. You are a contemplative priest and your vocation is another one. Our faith does not count for much if we did not believe that your vocation to bring the suffering world and the individual in it before the Lord in prayer was infinitely more important than anything else. We have always talked about the primacy of the spiritual and during the Second World War, I took a year off in order to spend my time in prayer and study in an old convent down on Long Island. It was on that occasion that Cardinal McIntyre, who was then Bishop, called me into the chancery office, asked me where I would be during the coming year, and told me that they would hold me responsible for the work then as well as any other time. This I took as a mandate to continue—a very indirect one.

When I saw Father [Daniel] Berrigan a week before the draft card burning, I advised him not to come to these meetings where there was about to be violence of one kind or another, pointed out to him that the lay person had a distinct vocation to work in the Temporal Order, and I was glad to see that he did not come. I think all of his writing and his speaking have done a wonderful amount of good and even now, his silence will cry out in what people consider his exile in South America. However, my feeling is that he is in some ways young and inexperienced—and that being sent off on such a tour is to his advantage.

I base my judgment on two things. One is that some of my friends said that in answering objectors in Detroit, he became pretty sarcastic. Perhaps it was his first experience with the man of the streets—the kind of people who read the *Daily News*. So many priests are used to a collegiate atmosphere and never come up close to the kind of people who come in our bread lines. These are the masses we will have to reach if we are trying to change men's attitudes. This is the distinctive thing about the Catholic Worker—that in all our houses the majority are these men the world calls derelicts and who really are men who have done much of the hard work of the country. We are not just talking to each other, as so many in the pacifist movement do.

And my second judgment was that he was too excited, in his actions—emotional, overwrought. Perhaps I am wrong, but such transfers will deepen his experience and knowledge. I will not protest it, though the others disagree with me.

I just received your book today and thank you from my heart for it. God has given you a great grace to keep writing as you do—an inspiration to us all.

I count on your prayers. Remember the girl I told you of who said: "Thank God for Thomas Merton"? She was going bad, men and marijuana, and these last two years she is fine—has a good husband, a child and has retreated to the countryside. I am sure you are holding us up in your fruitful solitude. God bless you.

Love from us all. In Christ, Dorothy

TO FRITZ EICHENBERG

Her beloved friend Fritz Eichenberg was going through a painful divorce. Dorothy wrote to offer her support.

DEC 13, 1965

I hasten to write before you leave for Mexico. It is a good step you are taking, I am sure. Tamar had to go thru the legal business of separation. Such suffering as you have gone thru. . . . I should say nothing, perhaps, but I feel the need to say that I feel very strongly you are doing the right thing. The Eastern religions (India's) talk of 3 periods in a man's life—and you have finished your middle period very clearly and your third period should be seeking God and, thru one's work, a giving to one's brothers in general as a true way to find Him.

Again, love, Dorothy

TO KARL MEYER

JAN 13, 1966

Since your telephone call last week, I have had an invitation to speak in Georgetown, in Washington, at the Department of Health, Education and Welfare of the Public Health Service. Can you not make your meeting for another date? I will not fly, so to come in the middle of the conference would be no good. Who else are you having on the platform beside Ammon? He spends so much time attacking me for what he calls my sexual repressions and sense of obedience, etc. that I do not particularly like to be on the same program with him. He is better alone, being himself, our highest example of a sense of personal responsibility and the importance of the individual and what he can do. He is the most self-disciplined person who ever worked with us, and we owe him much.

TO DIXIE MacMASTER

FEB 1, 1966

I keep putting off writing till I can write a "real" letter. "The best is the enemy of the good," the old saying goes. I should keep up if only with cards.

You know of course how grateful I am to you for sending me Fr. Voillaume's letters. They are a great source of comfort to me. We have, or rather, I myself have been getting so many attacks lately. I feel quite buffeted, rather stunned and uncertain sometimes, as to whether I should not retire into silence.

I'm reading *Pope John* by Balducci—a wonderful essay on death to begin it. And the spiritual journals were so good. They made me happy to read them.

I do pray things are working out for you—your brothers-in-law, your mother, etc. Let us drop cards to each other, when things have been too overwhelming for letters. Roger [La-Porte's] death, Jean Walsh's leaving us after 5 years with us, Peter Lumsden's leaving the farm—these things have meant much heartache. But our dear Father knows what is good for us all—draws great good out of it all. And what marvelous spiritual direction is available to us now, at all times.

TO ALICE AND JOE ZARELLA

Dorothy enjoyed hearing from old friends like Alice and Joe Zarella, who met and married at the Catholic Worker in the 1930s—one of the first Catholic Worker marriages.

FEBRUARY 3, 1966

If you could see the volume of mail always you would forgive me. I do thank you with all my heart for your remembrances—Joe's gift, also the Guadalupe Virgin, my favorite. You are always filled with loving kindness. God bless you.

I'm sick in bed with cold and arthritis at the moment and my hair is falling out by handfuls. Just getting older, I guess. My other "faculties" seem unimpaired—that of enjoyment for instance. Just read *With God in Russia* by Fr. [Walter] Ciszek [*the story of an American Jesuit's 22 years as a prisoner in the Soviet gulag*]. A marvelous book. Makes you feel like a luxurious pipsqueak! What a man! What a priest! People give us credit for so much and we do so little. It is the idea or the ideal they esteem. We fail miserably.

The belaboring I have recently received in the press is usually for the wrong things, but as my mother used to say, "You never get a lick amiss."

TO MSGR. STEPHEN J. KELLEHER, *Archdiocese of New York*

Monsignor Kelleher wrote Dorothy on behalf of a committee correlating suggestions from the U.S. bishops for revision of the Code of Canon

Law. From Dorothy he requested "a memorandum" of her own views on the subject.

APRIL 5, 1966

I was deeply moved by your letter of March 30, thinking of it as another indication of Cardinal Newman's influence now both as felt in the work of the Second Vatican Council and in the present work to bring the Bishops and the people closer together.

Pope John said in his journal that secularism and nationalism are two great evils of the day and Peter Maurin defined secularism for us as a separation of the spiritual and material. Since you are indeed consulting the laity, as Cardinal Newman suggested, and as St. Benedict advocated in his rule (calling upon the Abbot to consult the youngest and least of the order), I must admit frankly that I know nothing of canon law so as to be able to think specifically in terms of reorientation of the law.

Peter Maurin used to speak much of the Prophets of Israel and the Fathers of the Church and their teaching, and in view of the great renewal of Biblical studies and the writings available for study clubs in the field of Scripture, it certainly seems to me that canon law should be considered in light of Scripture, in the light of the new dispensation of love, rather than law. This should surely apply in the field of education, parochial and secular, seminaries as well as in colleges, since priests and religious come from the laity.

I know of great advances in these fields as well as great abuses. In the realm of marriage, the status of women, church and state, war and peace—it seems to me the laity have much to say. It is wonderful that Committees are going to be set up where the laity too can hear and be heard and can participate in the study of these problems. Probably most of all in the problems of poverty, the Catholic Worker has had most to say and is least understood. This problem is more fundamental than the problem of war.

Let me conclude by saying that I became a Catholic forty

years ago because I longed for a "rule of life and instruction" and that I take most seriously the duty of obedience in spite of my acts of *civil* disobedience. Pope John's motto was Obedience and Peace, and it is in this spirit that I answer this letter.

TO THE PRESIDENT OF SAINT JOHN'S UNIVERSITY
Collegeville, Minnesota

With the passage of years, Dorothy came to be offered many honorary degrees from Catholic colleges and universities. "If you live long enough," she observed, "you come to be regarded as a venerable survivor." She made a practice of declining such honors, partly on the basis of her respect for "holy wisdom," but secondly, as a protest against the entanglement of Catholic universities with the defense industry and military training.

APRIL 5, 1966

Dear Father Colman [Barry],

This is a terribly difficult letter for me to write, especially since I am answering it late. I have been in misery as to how to express what I feel, since I am refusing the great honor you have offered me. Let me say, first of all, that I love Saint John's and have loved the Benedictines ever since the days of Fr. Virgil Michel who was so great a friend of Peter Maurin. From the beginning of the Catholic Worker I have always been made welcome there. I am myself an oblate of Saint Benedict of Saint Procopius Abbey and many of our former Catholic Workers are oblates. This letter would be too long to tell all we have learned from Saint Benedict.

But I cannot accept the honorary degree you so generously offer. I have had to refuse two other honorary degrees from two other Catholic colleges (Jesuit and Christian Brothers) offered informally by telephone so that neither they nor I would be embarrassed.

I am sure you understand, dear Father Colman, especially right now in view of our country's involvement in Vietnam, our opposition to ROTC, and our own involvement in civil disobedience, draft refusal (not draft dodging), etc. Since this trip takes me to the University of Minnesota Newman Club for their meetings April 13th to 16th I would be most happy if you would write me there. Otherwise I would feel not at ease in visiting Saint John's as I usually do when my work takes me nearby.

Please understand and forgive my late reply, which was not my fault since I only just received the letter last week.

Gratefully yours, in Christ, Dorothy Day

TO DIXIE MacMASTER

JULY 1, 1966

I'm afraid you will just have to think of me as having gone into a tunnel or off on the desert where there are no mail deliveries. Anyway, the work gets so piled up I just go dumbly on, one letter at a time, one visitor. We are swamped with young people, the Bowery, students, teachers, etc. etc.

I was on a trip recently, to Minnesota and St. Louis, Chicago, Detroit, Cleveland, and Pittsburgh—all very wearing but enlightening too. I had the great joy of seeing Little Brother Roger and Little Bother John, in Detroit, and it did me much good to see their equanimity, the peace they maintain, because I have troubles, what with the two CW groups in Detroit, the young and the old, with the young going in for the new morality and the new theology—the young contracting alliances not only out of the church but out of the law also and the old and the poor generally disregarded by the young ones, who feel they have to take over the world which *we* made such a mess of. However, the work goes on, and in one way or another all are seeking God.

We had our retreat last week, five days, which Fr. Hugo

generously flew in from Pittsburgh to give us. My sadness during the retreat was the fact that only 14 came of the fifty people at the farm, and of these 14, most were in opposition, wanting to argue points on the last day, so that Fr. thought he had been quite a failure. However, it was the usual, "In the Cross is joy of spirit," and I shall try harder next year to have a better kept silence, and a more publicized retreat, for those who are hungry for the spiritual meat of the Gospel. It may be the Gentiles will come, while the Jews, our own, will stay aloof.

Deane Mowrer especially attacked it, even attacked Fr. Hugo. We can only say "abandonment to divine providence." As I type I am in the city, sitting by a window on Kenmare Street with traffic jams and trucks and cars laden with holiday luggage going by. Roads will be jammed and I am staying in town a few days more before going back up to the farm.

I am reading *The Problem of Pain*, by C.S. Lewis. Do you read him? He is one of the best theologians of our day, Fr. Hugo says. Much, much love. Please do write if only a card. I do not deserve more, but I am just not well organized, perhaps am entering into my dotage, as they say—68 in November. But even if it's just a card, I will be answering. In His love, Dorothy

SEPT 9, 1966

What a joy that last letter was. About the saints and the Angels—about the *invisible* world. I've always felt so happy we have guardian angels and pray to them in a group. Angels of God, our guardians dear.

Here is my news. My oldest grandchild Becky, 21, is getting married Oct 1 at St. Mary's, Springfield, Vt. And I will go up to help Sept 27.

Now Tamar has only 6 at home! Thank God she has her work—she is very happy with it. I beg your prayers for Mary, 15, the oldest girl at home, who is sweet and good but thinks only of boys. She spent 3 weeks with us at Tivoli, but I could not get close to her. Very silent—if it were not that she were good in school and at games, I'd think she were just in a state of euphoria. How little we can know each other and how wide the gulf between youth and age.

How desperate we'd feel sometimes without the consolations of prayer.

We are buying a home and I am hoping being under one roof will bring us closer together and will concentrate more on the poor and less on students who tend to take advantage of our hospitality in summer.

The summer has been a very busy one at Tivoli—but we do need a priest to stay with us. Our local pastor says Mass only 2 or three times a week, and often does not show up at the Masses listed in the bulletin. There may be a chance to have a priest with many difficulties [Jack English], who is leaving the Trappists. I am inviting him but he is also invited to go to the Bahamas to work with the Benedictines. May God's will be done.

We have with us a laicized priest and a nun—I often think— are there any problems in this world we do not have a sample of in our midst?

Love in Jesus Caritas, Dorothy

SUNDAY NOV 20, 1966

How inexcusable of me not to have telephoned you before I left, especially since I had expected to drop in again Monday morning before I left. But my toothache increased little by little and I did not get done all I had intended or promised. Please forgive me. It was so wonderful to see you again and talk to you, and always there is much more to say.

Do pray for these grandchildren of mine. The one great sadness of my life has always been that none of my own dear family has become a Catholic and now there is the added tragedy of Tamar and David, and the 5 oldest not getting to the sacraments, the 2 youngest, 6 and 8, quite indifferent, as yet, and only little

Martha and Maggie faithful. When Tamar ceased getting to Mass, after her separation, the others of course felt themselves relieved of the obligation.

John Cogley too says he can no more talk to his children about religion than he can about sex.

I am terribly afraid of intruding on people's personal inner lives. But when I write personally about myself and my own religious feelings, it is because my heart yearns toward others, that they may know the happiness I do.

Well, my great comfort is—God loves them more than I do, and God, our Father, wills that all men be saved, and when I pray Thy will be done, I'm praying for their salvation. Deane and I offer each bead of the rosary for someone.

TO EMILY COLEMAN

DEC 3, 1966

Jack English left the Trappists and is with the Benedictines in the Bahamas, wildly happy because he has, together with some other priests, a solid black parish, poorer than any southern parish. Jack is drinking again, has been for a few years. Trappists are trying to be his disciplinarian. But men go there to be held in line, their only safeguard. Oh dear. Jack came up here—said Mass, half lit, and John McKeon went to Communion and so did some others who had not been for years—none of them of course bothering about confession! The younger ones say they "are rebuilding the church in the shell of the old." Oh dear. I am just an old conservative.

Older I get the less I understand people. Did I tell you Tamar and the children no longer get to Mass? Adolescents—all of them. Do pray. I love them so.

TO FRITZ EICHENBERG

DEC 29, 1966

I write from Tivoli where I am spending the week with Tamar and her nine, tho now it is ten with a new son-in-law, and several neighbor children too. What a crowd—what noise. We fall into bed at night exhausted. I am answering Christmas mail to the tune of rock n roll—very incoherently.

God bless your generosity. And how happy I am to see the steel workers appreciating your work—not the first union to use your cuts, and many of them without permission, and others, individuals, even profiting by them, selling them as Christmas cards—it makes me angry sometimes, for you. I mean, to be exploited. And yet I know our paper is not copyrighted and in a way we should be happy that the work is so appreciated. I find my articles reproduced in textbooks too, no permission asked, no compensation. But I am glad to have it so. It means we are truly dependent on God's Providence and each other's generosity. You can never know how I appreciate yours.

TO FATHER LEO NEUDECKER

Father Neudecker, a priest from Minnesota, was a long-time friend of Dorothy. She joined him on a pilgrimage to Mexico in 1958. He later invited her to visit his mission work in Guatemala—a trip several times postponed and in the end never undertaken. It was a time of great ferment for the Catholic Church in Latin America as priests and religious, inspired by the teachings of Vatican II, applied the Gospel to the conditions of social injustice and "institutionalized violence." Dorothy supported these efforts. She was disturbed, however, by reports of clergy and missionaries who were lending their support to armed revolution.

JAN 7, 1967

I'm anxious to visit Guatemala and see the work you have started there. It makes me sick to see priests go all romantic over revolution. Fr. B. gives rousing talks in support of armed revolt in Latin America; knows nothing of Gandhian nonviolence; wants to follow the tradition of priests leading armies in South America.

Every revolution has just led to another revolt down thru the centuries. People are losing sight of the primacy of the spiritual. Excuse this blast.

Love and gratitude to you for all you are doing, so quietly—with so little fanfare.

TO A SUPPORTER

JANUARY 17, 1967

You must excuse me for bothering you again, about the letter which I so unwittingly destroyed but I am sure you must understand my anxiety as to its contents, especially since I found another letter from you in the files in which you say you sent the enclosure, a generous check "for people in need," and ask us to "please spend it purely for the relief of the poor and destitute." Since the check you sent at Christmas was so very large, almost two thousand dollars, I feel it very necessary to tell you a little bit in detail about our activities. I am sending you also two clippings. In addition to the care of the men on the breadlines, there are about eighty which call themselves part of the family and who either live with us in little apartments (five for men) or who have a meager pension of say forty a month which enables them to pay their own rent, and they take their meals with us. This takes place in the main house, on Chrystie Street, the business offices of the work, the meeting place, the dining room and kitchen.

By business office I mean the files, addressograph, stencils and all necessary for the mailing out of about eighty thousand papers, the rest being sold on the streets. This mailing list is rather like a poor congregation who put their pennies in the plate on Sunday and do not worry too much about funds to support the "plant" of church, rectory, convent and school, etc. It will always keep going they feel. Also ours is an unpopular message, of voluntary poverty, disassociation from the finance capitalist system, from war, and an emphasis on personal responsibility and the "little way," of prayer and penance and alms-giving, in the spiritual order, and credit unions and cooperatives in the material order. People have come to accept state aid and wonder why we bother ourselves at all, when the State can do it all so much more efficiently. Our books show we take in about $80,000 a year and from this money we support the main house, ten apartments, and the dozen or so workers and students, three of whom are married and have little apartments of their own.

You will note that the clipping about a new women's shelter is supposed to cost $700,000 and will accommodate 50. Since we are paying in all over a thousand dollars a month in rents, we felt we owed it to our contributors to try to buy an old house and remodel it for our work. This we have done, buying a place for $35,000 with ten thousand down, two mortgages to pay off over ten years. The greatest obstacle is remodeling the house to comply with the building and fire laws and this will take another $25,000. To raise this we are mortgaging our farm here at Tivoli (there is no mortgage on it now). Since we are living in cold apartments which have to be heated by gas, in what they call railroad apartments, with one room running after another and no privacy; toilets in a cold hall with the water freezing up in the winter and of course the trial of vermin; and the men who have a hard time taking care of themselves two blocks away in five apartments, we think we are making good plans for the work. We have one of our own group who has gone into real estate in order to learn how to start some cooperative apartments for poor families in Harlem, a lawyer, a contractor,—all graduates you might say of the Catholic Worker who are trying to make long range plans for those poor who can help themselves, once given a start. Part of the farm is going to be used as an extension of this project.

There may be much space given to the young men fighting the draft and the war, and space to the intellectual discussions which stimulate us to action, but it is this work for the poor which is basic and which takes most of our time. We are trying to attack poverty on every level, poverty, the cause of wars as the Pope has said. So voluntary poverty and the works of mercy are basic. These are what take up most of our time, living in most close intimate contact with the destitute.

I try to do some writing and *House of Hospitality, On Pilgrimage, The Long Loneliness,* and *Loaves and Fishes,* deal with these problems of poverty, much of it written to ease an aching heart and a discouraged mind. And a most effective way of working things out for oneself, as well as trying to make others understand. I do hope you will excuse this long letter. I have put your money in escrow for the house. Shelter is the most difficult and important problem. But I do want to know whether you sent this money for us or for some other purpose. I remember once one of our readers sent us two thousand dollars to purchase CARE packages for the poor overseas which we were happy to do.

And I should also say that I have always considered writing as a way to earn a living which each of us is bound to do as far as he is able before depending on others, even though we may act as stewards for others, and the servants of all (and get entirely too much credit for a work for which we have a vocation). Right now I am trying to write a pamphlet or booklet on the works of mercy for John Todd, pay for which will give us enough money to pay the rent on a few of the apartments for one month. Writers are notoriously underpaid. I earned more working my way through a year of college at 20 cents an hour for housework, plus four hours work a day for board and room.

TO THOMAS MERTON

JANUARY 29, 1967

Do please forgive my long silence. I don't remember if I ever thanked you for your wonderful article on Camus ["Albert Camus and the Church"] which has had wide repercussions, teachers writing for a score or so copies for their classes and many individual responses. We get so overcome with visits that we are all overworked and the mail piles up, as you well know. When I thought of it, I thought you would probably rather not hear from one extra person. I am at present enjoying your *Conjectures of a Guilty Bystander*. We all feel that way. I am enclosing the last issue of the CW in which I had to write about Cardinal Spellman, not only to cry out in grief, but also to point the fact that we are all guilty.* We can never do enough praying, fasting, penance and I'm glad and happy as usual that Lent is beginning, and I can start anew and try harder. A rather childish feeling, because I know how comfort seeking I am. Our life is incomparably rich in many ways, in our reading, in our liturgy. I even feel guilty about that, feeling that I am spiritually self-indulgent. However there are deserts too to cross. But women always have the good remedy of housework, meals, people to take care of and that pulls us through.

This is a babbling letter. Please excuse it. It is just to thank you from my heart and to beg you to send us any material you have which we always welcome with great joy.

---

* In an article in the January 1967 issue of the *CW*, "In Peace Is My Bitterness Most Bitter," Dorothy shared reflections inspired by Cardinal Spellman's call for victory in Vietnam. "Words are as strong and powerful as bombs, as napalm," she wrote. "How much the government counts on those words, pays for those words to exalt our own way of life, to build up fear of the enemy." She pointed out the common guilt we all share, the rich of the world, in the suffering of the poor. And she concluded with Jesus' new commandment, "to love others *as I have loved you*." It is a hard saying, "'a harsh and dreadful thing' to ask of us . . . but it is the only answer."

TO EMILY COLEMAN

FEB 19, 1967

I am sitting in Agnes' downstairs room which is big and pleasant and next to the bathroom, and she is snoring away in the midst of a catnap from which she awakens now and again with groans. She has cancer of the throat, and is slowly fading away, suffering great discomfort, and yet welcoming visitors and insisting on talking in a voice very hard to understand. We are taking turns to be with her, and I sleep here nights. Hence my silence. I owe you a letter and you graciously wrote just the same. I so enjoy hearing from you. I'm glad you got the articles from *Ave Maria*. They were hard to write. The new morality means free love and trial marriage, etc. No confession, just go to the Sacrament anyway. It all breaks my heart.

Jack English left his monastery, was accepted by a Benedictine bishop in the Bahamas, a very good man but is behaving badly down there, and I am afraid he will end up again with us. I pray our chancery office will give him faculties if he does arrive. There are all kinds of priests wandering around loose and offering "underground" Masses, they call them. Fr. Jack said Mass here in transit and was drunk when he offered the Holy Sacrament. A good altar boy helped him along. John McKeon and others received Communion from him (not having been to confession).

Now John is living with a former Maryknoll sister—an anarchist marriage, they call it. God knows how long it will last. I had to ask them to leave the farm. They were causing open scandal. Life gets harder and harder. The birth pains of a new order, and hard to live thru.

Yes, I remember you and yours, and you remember us. All we can do is *love* and pray for them all. And accept our miseries as penance. Agnes said "Come visit us, we love you." We do.

TO CAROLINE GORDON

The novelist Caroline Gordon was an old friend. In the 1920s, with her former husband, Allen Tate (whom she divorced in 1959), Gordon had been part of the New York literary set in which Dorothy traveled. They had fallen out of touch after Dorothy's conversion, but the friendship resumed many years later after Gordon's own conversion to Catholicism.

2/24/67

Did you ever get thanked? God has to make up for our deficiencies. Christmas time is so hectic and so much sickness around some mail gets neglected. Jack English calls up every now and then from the Bahamas—feels the Bishop there will not put up with him very long.

Seems to me when a man goes to a monastery for discipline he should get it. Permissive abbots! Giving up their freedom is the reason men go there. Their most precious possession. Anyway. Fr. Charles will probably end up at Tivoli. He came on his way to the Bahamas (circuitous route) and was in bad shape. Do pray for him. Tom Sullivan, Marge Hughes, various others tried to hold him in check but he was irrepressible. I groan when I look ahead. Well, we will get what we deserve, what God sends us. Community is sure penance. We have 5 hermits now. Expect to find me immured in a cabin on the hillside one of these days.

Do write. Hope you are still in Florida basking in sun. Sand and fragrance of citrus blossoms. Foretaste of heaven.

TO JIM FOREST

Jim Forest joined the Catholic Worker community in 1961 after his conversion to Catholicism and his subsequent discharge from the Navy as a conscientious objector. Dorothy had quickly recognized his literary talents and put him briefly in charge of editing the paper. He left the Worker in 1962, following a disagreement with Dorothy: she wanted him to travel to Tennessee to write about a civil rights project while he felt obliged to take part in an act of civil disobedience in New York protesting nuclear weapons. Their relationship recovered later in the year, by which time Jim was married and working for Catholic Relief Services. In 1964, Jim and Tom Cornell founded the Catholic Peace Fellowship under the auspices of the Fellowship of Reconciliation. When he divorced his first wife and planned to remarry, at the time without an annulment, Dorothy felt his actions were incompatible with his role as a secretary of the Catholic Peace Fellowship.

MARCH 3, 1967

As you can well understand, it is hard to write this. But I have been thinking about this for weeks and wondering what to do. And also what to say to you. In the chapel the other day I was so preoccupied with the problem that I made a few notes as to what to say and here they are.

First, when God asks great things of us, great sacrifices, He intends to do great things with us; though they will seem small, they will be most important. Who knows the power of the Spirit? God's grace is more powerful than all the nuclear weapons that could possibly be accumulated.

Second, when we are asked to show our love for God, our desire for Him, when He asks us as Jesus asked Peter, "Lovest thou me?" we have to give proof of it. "Lovest thou me more than these, more than any human companionship, more than any human love?" It is not filth and ugliness, drugs and drink and perversion He is asking us to prefer Him to. He is asking us to prefer Him to all beauty and loveliness. To all other love. He is giving us a chance to prove our faith, our hope, our charity. It is as hard and painful as Abraham's ordeal, when he thought he was asked to perform a human sacrifice and immolate his son.

The third thing I kept thinking of was how great an organization is the Fellowship of Reconciliation. My association began with it away back when Nevin Sayre had just come back from Nicaragua where he traveled about the mountains on muleback trying to locate Sandino and effect a reconciliation between him and the U.S. Marines. A piece of madness which compelled my astounded admiration. It was Dostoevskyian, Idiot-like. And A.J. Muste's journey to Saigon and Hanoi are in the tradition. He did not mind being a fool for Christ. I can see him sitting between Judith Beck and that other young beauty in front of the Atomic Energy Commission.

These are upright men, these men associated with the FOR. They have done great things, have initiated great deeds, and you dishonor them by setting yourself to be something which you are not, which you have rejected, a Catholic, Catholicism. What's more you certainly dishonor the Church in their eyes, and vindicate in them the anti-Catholicism which I have always sensed there.

To them our priest seems casuistic and it is because of people like you that this is so. To them it must seem that laymen are so weak and despised (so little is expected of them by their spiritual directors, their priests) that no heroic action, no self-renunciation is expected of them. It must seem to them that our celibate priests, who have accepted this martyrdom of celibacy, concede sex to the layman as a necessary evil, a concession to their poor weak human nature. It must seem to the Protestant that sex itself is dishonored, regarded as a physical necessity like food. Marriage is dishonored as a concession to the animal in man, if this picture of Catholicism is presented to our non-Catholic brother. "Oh yes, he can sin, go to confession Saturday night and continue to go to the sacraments," meanwhile hoping he can continue as he is, have his cake and eat it too. Of course, I know too that among you young people confession seems to have been thrown out as a useless sacrament, and I have seen young people going to Communion with the permission of the "underground" priests while they continue their living together, not bothering about marriage either in courts or in church.

To me sex is important, not just a plaything, a pleasure. By our sexuality we are co-creators in a most real sense. Here we are as pacifists seemingly on the side of life, and so many in the peace movement denying life.

Your letters emphasized all the good the CPF is doing, but I assure you that all that means nothing. The dishonesty, the deceit involved negates the good. One might almost say the blasphemy, having married in the Church knowing that it was not going to work out and pledging, vowing yourselves to life together, in sickness and health until death. If you gave all you had to the poor and delivered your body to be burned, it is all nothing but sounding brass and a tinkling cymbal, if you have not charity, the love of God which you have turned from to have the love of women.

Of course it is a beautiful relationship, Linda is a lovely, deeply serious intelligent companion, a once-in-a-lifetime relationship. Don't think I do not feel for you, and know the agony you are going through.

I feel so deeply about this that I am afraid that I must ask you to take my name from your stationery as one of the sponsors. I hate saying this, but I do not think that while you are the head of the CPF it can be considered a *Catholic* Peace Fellowship, if you continue your relationship. I think the manly thing to do would be to resign, if you cannot give up Linda. I would understand that. You could even go on working for the FOR, *provided you did not work as a Catholic;* or in the peace movement in general, from the standpoint of human reason, in the natural order, rather than from one who was a follower of the supernatural teachings of the Church.

You are certainly going through the sorrowful mysteries. But if you don't go through them to the glorious, you will be a hollow man, and considered an opportunist and a fraud. I am putting it as strong as I am able, and hate doing it, but to me the Faith is the strongest thing in my life and I can never be grateful enough for the joy I have had for the gift of Faith, my Catholicism.

With love to you, and to Linda, and begging you to forgive me for the pain I may have caused you.

Dorothy

In the end, Jim remained secretary of the Catholic Peace Fellowship and Dorothy, on the advice of Thomas Merton, decided to remain a member of its advisory board.

TO DELLA SPIER

MARCH 11, 1967

I am reading right now, for an hour in the evening, Johnson's life of Dickens with an analysis of his works, and it is most interesting. I have two Baedekers, one of London and the other of England, and they are full of maps and I love to travel around and follow him in his books. There is a chance of my going over to England again this Oct. for a November 12th meeting of the Peace groups of England, together with Eileen Egan, a Welsh woman, who I went with last time, a very good traveling companion, except that she sleeps until noon each day. Dorothy Weston used to do that. And Marty Corbin does now. But I find it most irritating. They are all ready to keep going at ten at night, when I am ready for bed. The day has only begun. But in a way it is a good sharing of the work, since there are those who are only free at night, and all the meetings too. I like to get to meetings, but then I must have a nap in the afternoon, which they naturally do not take.

Love to both of you always. Dorothy

TO EMILY COLEMAN

TUES IN HOLY WEEK, 1967

I have thought of you so often but could not get down to letters. I am sleeping in the room with Agnes and she is now waking up every hour on the hour all night and insisting on getting out to the toilet by herself, so my sleep is precarious and there is not another soul, at the present, to spell me. So I must be on duty and I thought of the years you took care of your father and were not free. And all the other women I know who are tied to old parents and have no freedom. Women are saved by childbearing, Peter used to say, and also by all these ties of family. How good that is. We are saved in spite of ourselves. I have always found that consoling. We lose our hearing, teeth, eyesight, and so our senses are mortified if we do not do it ourselves. It is a real meditation on death. Was it you who sent me the review, a sympathetic one, of Maritain's last book? The young around here are so intolerant. They are always looking for something new, like the Athenians, and Leslie Dewart's book, *The Future of Belief*, is now the latest craze.

What can I send you? Have you my *Loaves and Fishes*, Therese? There is nothing else I have. I am working on a Works of Mercy pamphlet and a book on the Retreat for Harper. But I get most discouraged and feel how presumptuous I am to try to write about these things. I am dull as ditchwater right now, so pray for me. Dull, but content. The Spring is long delayed. Icy cold here. Agnes suffers,—what long, slow dying. She can scarcely speak or swallow. "My purgatory," she says.

Happy Holy Season and much much love.

TO FRANK DONOVAN

Frank Donovan, an employee of the United Parcel Service, first came to Dorothy's attention through his generous contributions to the Catholic Worker. Gradually he began volunteering on weekends and in his spare time, until he finally took early retirement and devoted himself entirely to the Worker. Eventually he assumed the responsibilities of general business manager. But he offered particularly dedicated service to Dorothy herself—so much so that she later called him the "son of her old age." In this letter she refers to a large anti-war demonstration in Central Park.

APRIL 25, 1967

I was there! The CW crowd was scattered with the religious and pacifist groups. We had CW people from Chicago, Milwaukee,

St. Louis, Cleveland, Phila., etc. We should have identified ourselves with large buttons but so many call themselves Catholic Workers who really ought not to, who are full of class war, and plain frivolous that I guess we just don't want to give people the chance to identify us as someone with a "draft Cardinal Spellman" button, etc. I hate contempt and ridicule, when we should love *all* men, enemies outside and in—love our own selves even, with all our failings, because God loves us. I did not really march. I went to the Sheep Meadow—met many friends, had chance to talk to visiting groups—then walked to 57th and got 5th Ave. bus to 47th St. Walked to Holy Family Church and the steps were like a reviewing stand.

It was an inspiring day.

I do thank you for your constant help. God bless you always.

TO JUDITH GREGORY

APRIL 1967

How I envy you! You should visit Delano, and find out what's happening under Cesar Chavez. I met all those Franciscans— they sing a beautiful Mass with guitars. Wish you had gone.

If you go along the coast you'll have great beauty but in the valleys there will be the great farms and orchards. Wish you would look into that aspect—as you travel—migrant labor housing, children, work, water problem—just a hitchhiker's account. *Do write.* Once when I was visiting the gov camps years ago—there are none now—I was driving, and picked up an Okie who said, "Nothing I like better than to be out in a big field chopping cotton." I'll never forget it. The love of earth and sky and sea. Reminded me of Tolstoi's haying scene in *Anna Karenina*. Except his was solitary labor. He was trying to earn enough to send for his wife and children. Read *In Dubious Battle* by Steinbeck. I read it the day my father died, to distract my mind, and never forgot it.

Agnes Sidney is dying and I sleep in her room with her and catnap between her wakings which mean bouts of pain and pills. I don't know how long it will last. Nothing like contemplating the fact of death night and day. Reading St. Paul is a great joy. That little psalm book is a gem, and a small Testament to match brings me great happiness. Read I Corinthians Chap 15, beginning v. 35. A most amazing and glorious promise. Agnes and I are most companionable. Peggy keeps her in wine—a 3 oz. drink at noon and before bed. She has cancer and can take only liquids. She reminisces and smiles and every night tosses holy water around her. She received Communion all Holy Week and is anything but fearful. Such calm acceptance. Very beautiful and happy.

I signed a contract with Harpers to have my book "All is Grace" done by Nov 8, but feel too stupid to write in the midst of the furor going around in theological circles.

Do keep writing and I am now a collector of postals—pictures of work of all kinds especially—mines, orchards, cotton fields, etc.

Oh what fun! I wish I were younger or had the strength in the legs of Aunt Betsy Trotwood (*David Copperfield*) and I'd go walking too.

My love always. Don't forget the picture postals.

JUNE 15, 1967

I have to speak at Mike Gold Memorial meeting Friday night and I dread it.* Town Hall and a stage full of sponsors. I am being exploited politically of course and will probably be shot for it one day, but I feel there are few ways when we can make contact and find concordance and in the presence of death is one of them—Mike's death.

Much love to you always, Dorothy

---

* Mike Gold, the author of *Jews Without Money,* was a leading figure in the Communist Party and editor of *The Daily Worker.* He was one of Dorothy's oldest friends.

TO CHARLES BUTTERWORTH

AUG 31, 1967

I will be 70 in November, and I feel like a grandmother wanting to get things settled for the children before going on to the next world. To finish the book, "All is Grace," and get ourselves moved and started off again on the more disciplined life of a House of Hospitality, instead of all these apartments—these are my immediate aims. It has been a particularly bad summer with so many young people using the place as a "pad" who do not even know the CW, but are just referred to us as though we were diggers or hippies.

Good news for me. Marguerite Harris is paying my way to and from and my expenses there, to Rome to attend the World Lay Congress, October 11-18. I sail on the Rafaelo on Sept. 30. Eileen Egan is trying to get me accredited as an expert, but I want to go just as a journalist and pilgrim. There are thirty Americans representing accredited Catholic organizations such as National Council of Catholic Men and Women, etc. and are accredited by their bishops.

TO THOMAS MERTON

SEPTEMBER 13, 1967

Please excuse me for my delay in answering your most welcome letter. I read the article you sent on Auschwitz ["Auschwitz: A Family Camp"], and it is an overwhelming account. I told Marty Corbin November would be the best month when we are thinking of the dead and meditating on the four last things. The most awful part of it is how the Germans so soon forget and we so soon forget.

I have had the wonderful good fortune to be going to the Lay Congress and I am sailing on the 30th of September. A dear friend who says she owes her conversion to the Catholic Worker is paying my fare both ways and my upkeep in Rome.

Jack English was visiting us here for three days. He was fine while he was here but New York is not good for him. I understand that he is now back in the Bahamas but I have a strong feeling that he will be our chaplain here eventually and we will be happy indeed to have him. You probably know his weakness and one of the best things I can say for Cardinal Spellman is that he has never hesitated to give faculties in this diocese to priests who are in difficulties. Whereas the Philadelphia Archdiocese, back in the days when we had a farm near Easton, Pennsylvania, informed us that his Eminence was not at all pleased that we had some of these difficult situations with us. Do please pray for Jack.

And there is another situation I am begging your prayers for and I ask the prayers of the community also. A young girl named Barbara, a widow with a child, is in a truly crucial situation. She is living with the husband of a family Jim McMurry brought up here last summer, a man who went berserk up here, smashing furniture, threatening people, etc. She rashly took him in along with a few others we were not able to handle. Now the others have left, she has thrown away her plans for college, and we hear he has a "sixty dollar a day habit." She seems to be in a state of delayed shock and the future can only be grim for her unless a miracle intervenes.

God bless you always. With love and gratitude.

Merton wrote, "It is a joy to send things to the CW, precisely because it is a simple, humble, honest paper that goes its own way and cares nothing for anybody's establishment."

SEPTEMBER 28, 1967

I enjoyed your letter very much. The thing I love about the Little Brothers of Jesus is, they really know how to do nothing. They go settle themselves and there's an aura of peace and joy, not to speak of manual labor and prayer, that surrounds them. I visited them in Detroit and between the conflict of a new house which didn't last too long, made up pretty much of a dissipated young crowd and the older CW group who have kept two houses going for the last twenty years, there was quite a struggle going on and Brother Roger in a beautiful state of detachment brought peace to both sides and certainly to me too. What a tremendous amount can be accomplished by just doing nothing. I am sure you know what I mean. Certainly working a full day in a factory and coming home and spending an hour on your knees when you could be falling over with fatigue of both mind and body is not doing anything.*

TO DELLA SPIER

NOV 1. 1967, LONDON

Here I am in bed, right around the corner from the British Museum, innumerable bookshops, Kegan Paul publishers, tea rooms, etc. Arrived from Rome at 2:30 p.m., a 2½ hour trip by plane which would have taken 24 hours by train, and not a thru train at that.

I love my traveling companion Eileen [Egan] and it was her courage in dashing off to Trieste and to Israel on her job (Catholic Relief Services) that gave me courage to take the step to fly. But she likes to sleep until 9:30—or 10:30, and when you are sharing a small room (the cheapest) it is most difficult. So I have to silently sneak out, as I did this morning, at seven and here I am down in the basement dining room (they serve only breakfasts) and in peace and quiet, read or write. A young cleaning girl (in a micro skirt) and bare legs, is cleaning upstairs in the

---

* Thomas Merton would die suddenly on December 10, 1968 while attending a conference on monasticism in Bangkok. In an obituary in the December issue of the paper, Dorothy, who had frequently prayed for Merton's perseverance in his vocation, would quote from his many letters to calm speculation that he had been planning to leave his monastery.

sitting room and television room and showed me down here. They will not serve breakfast for an hour, she said, but fortunately I had my instant coffee and hot water from the faucet and had my black coffee. This place is spotlessly clean.

The place is so very quiet I'm sure it will be all right for Eileen too, tho she is enamored of the high up room, looking down over the back of the Museum. Trees surround it, like the Metropolitan, and it was good last night to see the grounds, the sidewalks, with their wet fallen leaves. I love the Fall and hate to miss it. And rain and fog do not depress me. I will, however, have to buy a raincoat. Right in front of the Grisham there is a bus stop, and a sign with the numbers of six buses, and I will take them all, in all directions, and see London. And today, I will go to Cook's and see if there are any tours this late in the season to Yorkshire. At least there will be a sightseeing tour of London. I could spend all my time here very happily.

I cannot tell you how happy I feel at having broken that block about flying. It is not more expensive actually, all things considered, so I could not use that as an excuse. It means, I'm afraid, that I'll do more traveling, God willing.

I'm so happy to be here where one understands one's fellows, radio, and television and newspapers are in English and the food is familiar. One gets very weary of Italian food. Can you imagine eating 3 meals a day for a month in a Chinese restaurant?

Anyway, one can get tired of Italy. I can understand the English, Germans, Russians, etc, going there for the sun, as we as a people go to Florida. And I can certainly understand them going to hotels where other English go. But hours of meals, 8–2–8, and the 1–4 siesta when every shop, every institution, every church even is closed and shuttered tight.

So today I go to the British Museum and begin on my [Danilo] Dolci and [Ignazio] Silone interviews. One must write while things are fresh in the mind.

TO DIXIE MacMASTER

DEC 1 1967

I'll be praying for you daily, most especially. One of my favorite prayers is O dear Lord, deliver me from *fear*. We know God's grace is sufficient but our poor flesh recoils from pain. They have such wonderful anesthetics now. One touch of sodium pentothal and you're out, until you are back in your bed, and it is all over. Eliz, a convert, very good, and I are wishing to start a secular fraternity, just as there are contemplatives in many orders. I mean she and an ex-soldier, Ron, and I would like to begin a secular fraternity within the CW to deepen our prayer life and eventually to go live among the migrants in South Jersey, or Long Island, or Delano, Calif. The whole problem of the rural destitute is much on my mind always. They are so much worse off than the city poor who have better health, educational and recreational opportunities. I need one or two more girls to make the venture with Elizabeth.

TO A YOUNG PEACEMAKER

ST. JOHN'S DAY, DEC 27, 1967

Thank you and God bless you all. I'm interested not only in your peace work but also the work for the mentally retarded. Glad you are helping in it. Thomas Merton wrote me today that his friends who went to the Washington Oct 21 day [*march on the Pentagon*] told how newspapers distorted everything. It is a terrible thing to see *hate* on the faces of our brothers. But they are *afraid*. We have to love and pray for them too. "Deliver us from the *fear* of our enemies," not from the enemies because we are all brothers. A gang from our crowd gives all their time to the protests, the resistance, but my arthritis keeps me down. So I stick at letters, writing, and travelling and speaking. But I envy the young ones with the strength to sit out vigiling all night. Thank God the protests are increasing. Please pray for my 20-yr-old grandson [Eric] who is [being inducted into the army] January 2. It is so hard to resist in a small town.

TO EMILY COLEMAN

JAN 7, 1968

I am running around like a chicken with its head off, as my old New England forebears used to say. But like always, farm and city both claim me, and there are speaking engagements and overnight stands, and I went to Tamar for Christmas.

Christmas was lovely for Tamar and me too, but rather sad, what with Eric [Hennessy] being drafted. He left for the induction center Jan 2, and no word since. We do not know where he is so cannot write him. He is so like Forster. I am afraid he will crack under it. Maybe he thinks letters will make him all the more homesick. He is terribly attached to home and Tamar and she to him. My mother was the same about her oldest son.

I have found some book of yours in our library at the farm—cannot remember the name—about a young actress in love with another actor who does not love her. I just looked into it one evening. I will send it on to you when I get back to the farm. Stanley said it was something you had looked for once and valued. Very cold here. Eight below zero in New York but I got an electric blanket for Christmas, and am looking forward to going to bed with it and a good book.

2/2/68

I'm traveling—a 2-weeks stay in Minnesota and stopping by Milwaukee to visit the houses there. I am almost overcome by longing to do nothing until spring—I'd like just to crawl into bed and hibernate. I'm all aches and pains with arthritis. Penance—needed penance. When I arrived home 2 deaths, many illnesses around, heaped up mail. But I've thought of you so often—and that cold room. Do get an electric blanket. . . . I read [Jacques] Maritain's book [*The Peasant of the Garonne*]—yes, it is a cranky book and I did not like it. He is so much alone, and suffering. I'm disappointed in the English? group—Catholic Leftists. There is now a "theology of violence" in the air with missionaries joining guerrilla forces and marrying. They are indeed going to the world! I want to do as you have done—be a hermit in the world—a contemplative in the city. We'll be moving into our new headquarters in the city by spring.

FEB 27, 1968

I start the day writing to you, when I should be getting out a batch of letters. I read that C.S. Lewis was at his desk at eight in the morning and here it is ten. But it is Ash Wednesday, and people came into the apartment to breakfast, oatmeal and coffee and we talking of penance—unless you do penance you shall also perish. And here one of the young couples is getting married in Lent, and there is always dissipation and parties, and beer, and now marijuana around, and some of the young c.o.'s as tho they had done enough by taking their stand, are dissipated too, and it keeps me thinking of Roger LaPorte who immolated himself in front of the U.N. He felt the horror of the time we are living in, just as the saints did, and I am convinced offered himself in sacrifice. We certainly are not doing enough at the CW. Fr. Hugo said, or rather quoted, "He who says he has done enough has already perished." He said St. Augustine is author of that terrifying phrase.

This sounds gloomy, but here I am with ashes on my forehead and feeling joyful that Lent and also spring is beginning. But the forecast is snow and I think of your cold, and penances, and you too have immolated yourself as a hermit, and I love you for it.

Paperwork is piled high, but I have been going to the doctor for high blood pressure and arthritis, and taking pills and vitamins, etc. Now he says I must have all my teeth pulled. They are abscessed and worthless and should be abandoned. But the wedding at which I must be (two of our best workers this past year) means that I should not have it done until March 18, just after the wedding. So I guess I'll go up to the farm before the promised snow begins, and settle down there to work for ten days.

I am a slow starter. I should have told you the news first, that Jack English is with us, with his faculties, and is saying Mass and giving the most beautiful homilies and is stimulus and joy to us all. But before he came up he was on a bender. Also his abbot wrote—they had given him up, he was a cause of grave disturbance in the monastery, and the bishop in the Bahamas where he was for the last year, also Tom [Sullivan], was in despair about it. But right now he is all right. I imagine when he wants to go off he will go to the city. But he insists on wearing his collar and throwing his weight around. Poor Tom, and Natalie, and all his friends who truly love him. So please pray, won't you?

Quoting scripture, as I've been doing, reminds me that there is one book I want—which is very expensive, the English edition of the English Jerusalem Bible, which is big but not so huge as the American one, which is too cumbersome to hold on a lap. If you could find what it costs I would send the money on to you at once. I'd love to have it for Lenten reading, as I must be so much of the time in the city, so you could send it here, marked personal.

How I would love to see what you are writing. Is it in longhand? Do you have it copied? If you do, please have a carbon made for me and I will send it back, and guard it with my life.

I think what we write is important. I think our insights are important and that we must write.

Did I tell you that I have been offered five honorary degrees, the latest Fordham? The others, St. John's, Holy Cross, LaSalle, Boston College. That is three Jesuits, one Benedictine, one Christian Brothers. I have refused them all of course, what with ROTC and their tie up with the State and war.

I am not boasting. It is to emphasize that it is important about writing what we write.

TO DANIEL BERRIGAN

Dorothy felt much affection for the Berrigan brothers—Daniel, a Je-suit, and Philip, a Josephite. Both had taken courageous action in op-position to the Vietnam War. In October 1967 Philip, along with three companions, had destroyed draft files in Baltimore. In 1968, while still awaiting sentencing, he repeated the deed, this time joined by Daniel and seven other Catholics, who poured home-made napalm on draft files in Catonsville, Maryland. Suddenly, the two brothers were the most notorious priests in America.

MAY 31, 1968

I wrote the enclosed letter for your brother Phil at first and then went on to mean it for both of you, though the sentence he is serving is for the first act of sabotage. Neither that act, nor the act which you took part in, in any way injured any individual (those who wished to be drafted can enlist) and I could only think that it was a very strong and imaginative witness against conscription. I am sure that both you and your brother counted the cost. I cannot tell you how close I feel to both of you, though I am not able to get around much these days what with bad ar-thritis in my knees, and very pressing duties at all times in our very large family here at the Catholic Worker. We are so sur-rounded by the sadness and tragedy of life, the destitution of body and soul, the broken minds, the aged, the fatherless chil-dren and those who no longer know what they believe, and there are so few who have the energy to work, that those of us who can, are kept doubly busy. It is hard to write to you both— what to say in the face of these harsh sentences that are being passed out. I am convinced that sooner or later we are all going to end in a concentration camp. You have both been on my mind continually, and in my heart too. If I sound disjointed it is because of fatigue and because I am surrounded by too many interruptions. Be assured of my love. We have never had a chance to talk over some smaller differences which are not important really. When you see Fr. Phil bring my letter to him.

With love in Christ, Dorothy

TO PHILIP BERRIGAN

Phil Berrigan was sentenced to six years for the action of the Baltimore 4.

MAY 31, 1968

We all heard with such a sense of shock about the heavy sentence you received last week. It is hard to write to you when I do not know whether you will receive the letter, and of course knowing that it will be read. I can only say that I will be praying for you daily, as I pray for all prisoners. Fr. [J. Léandre] Plante, a priest from Canada, remarked once that freedom was so precious that an animal will gnaw off its own foot to get free from a trap. I met prisoners at the women's House of Detention who with a two-year sentence would never look out of the window to the Village streets around them. All counted the days. Just today I got a letter from a friend in the Springfield, Missouri prison which tells of the long weekends in prison when there is no work. He was considering the matter of non-cooperation, "thinking of it almost constantly. It is impossible not to think about it. And the others here, in similar positions to mine, worry too. All I can say is that at present I have chosen to do what I have to do to get out. Perhaps not a very admirable decision, but under the circumstances, I personally do not feel able to do anything else."

At this point I began worrying about what he meant—whether he was going to accept army training and going to Vietnam, or what. But he goes on to say, "How this would affect parole I can't say."

So I guess he means just that he would cooperate in the prison and do whatever work is assigned to him. I certainly would do the same. There is work to do in prison, after all. Ammon Hennacy always did the work assigned and I am sure had quite an influence on the other prisoners and even the guards.

I have long been worried about the hostile attitude, the attitude of contempt present in some protestors. Fr. [John] McKenzie's writing on Scripture has affected me profoundly lately. His comments on Jesus' words, "Resist not evil," does not mean of course that one obeys man rather than God. In fact it is so hard to explain what I mean that I am going to write a much longer piece in the CW about it, when I have time to think. *You* have never shown such attitudes of hostility, and I am sure that the present desperate act springs from your keener sense of the horror of our presence in Vietnam and the devastation of that country as a result of our presence.

Is there anything we can send you from the CW in the way of books? I'm hoping that you will be able to do a little writing in jail but I know that the impact of your fellow prisoners will be such that it will be hard to think. I know that you will be receiving mail from your brother in Syracuse and that I can send you messages through him. It is the way we reach our other friends among the prisoners. Yours is most truly a witness, a revolutionary act, or rather a series of revolutionary acts, and I know you have counted the cost. Certainly if a Ho Chi Minh and other revolutionaries can spend much time in prison, you also can endure the coming years. Years! It seems terrible to be saying it. But others feel your strength and do not doubt it. My love to both of you, and I shall be praying for strength and for the peace of Christ, for you both. This letter is for both of you.

TO DIXIE MacMASTER

JULY 3, 1968

I think so often of you and your mother and how completely you must rely on Divine Providence. But God loves us—we can be so confident, so trustful. I say that over and over about my grandchildren—who are going thru, the older ones, such turmoil. He, our Father, loves them more than I could ever do, and will watch over them. I pray for them all daily. What an example of faith the [Robert F.] Kennedy funeral was. What strength it brings. What joy even in the midst of suffering, tragedy.

This is just a note to ask you to remember me as I did you on retreat. I love you, and hold you in my heart.

TO FORSTER BATTERHAM

There was a long gap between Dorothy's previous letter to Forster in 1932 and the resumption of their regular contact, although Tamar had, in the meantime, served as a link between them. A turning point came in 1959 when Dorothy accepted an invitation from Forster to help care for his long-time companion, Nanette, who was dying of cancer in their bungalow on Staten Island. After her death, they again parted ways, but over time the occasions for contact become more regular—visits in the hospital, the exchange of gifts, the occasional letter. In her last years, Forster would call almost every day. According to Tamar, he took pride in Dorothy's accomplishments—keeping a scrapbook with every newspaper clipping about her, and, after her death, attending her funeral and a memorial service at St. Patrick's Cathedral. He also preserved all of Dorothy's letters, which he eventually passed on to Tamar.

JULY 19, 1968

We have had such a busy summer that I am way behind in my correspondence as well as in everything else. Usually I try to keep track of Tina, and Dickie Maruchess at Rockland, and John and Tessa, and Della and Franklin, but we have started a day-care center up here for the migrant children and have hordes of visitors besides. And in town we are moving into our new house, and the last moving should be done by August first. We bought a place on East First Street, right off Second Avenue, and the repairs alone cost $40,000 so I have been writing, speaking, and scrounging around for money to keep going. Five of our young editors are in jail now, in four of the Federal prisons, and I suppose more will go too. The protest is still growing. Our friend Fr. Phil Berrigan and other priests have been doing a good anti-war job too, and Fr. Phil is in for six years and God knows how much more he will get for burning the records.

Tamar is here with me for the summer with Mary 17, Maggie 14, Martha 13, Hilaire 10, and Katy 8 years respectively, the five youngest, and all beautiful children. She has the same propensity I have of hospitality and she brought two others with her from neighbors both with family trouble. Eric, 19, is in the army at Fort Benning. Becky is married and living in New Hampshire and they both work—two years married and no children yet. Susie has contracted a free alliance with a young Brazilian she met in Montreal. She graduated from nursing school in Montreal and so can work anywhere and they have been in Sudbury and she nursed while he worked in the mines. She is working in a children's camp now for the summer so that is pleasanter than a hospital. Nickie is going to get married soon. His girl, a neighbor is already pregnant, so I, (and you) will be great grandparents.

That is really why I felt I had to sit down and write you. It is a thrilling experience—this about to become a great grandparent. Tamar is taking the summer off—she has worked very hard and certainly needs more of a rest than she is getting . . . Just now a fearful storm has started and she had left the children swimming at a little lake at Elizaville and has had to go after them. I'm only hoping no blown-down trees have blocked the road and I'm as bad as Victor Maruchess about the lightening, so I worry about the children. But Tamar seems to be up to handling any crisis. Thank God we are getting the rain we so badly need. She has one of those old Corvairs that that fellow got into so much trouble about and was so persecuted by the auto corporations. Supposedly a dangerous car. All cars are dangerous though.

Storm over—still just as hot. Tamar cannot sleep and feels nervous and depressed. She is sick of her work—it is nerve-racking and very heavy. Mostly very old people filling up the hospitals, people, families, trying to get rid of them, she says. It makes her very cynical about human nature. She'd like work in a greenhouse or a pet shop—she is crazy about fish and has a wonderful large fish bowl—all kinds of fish. I told her I was writing you and she says—"Ask him if he has any books about fish!" I do hope you are well—and cheerful. When I get back in the city again I'll telephone and perhaps reach you. Perhaps you are with one of your sisters.

Tamar sends love. Me too, Dorothy

TO DELLA SPIER

AUG 26, 1968

So glad to get your letter which was forwarded to me by Stanley [Vishnewski] at the farm. You knew of course that I was going to have to go to Washington for that Liturgy and Revolution conference and just before leaving I got a long distance call from my friend Marge Baroni here in Natchez that I must come down. We were able to make stops at Conyers, Georgia, where the Trappist monastery is where Fr. Jack English was stationed for eight years, and at Fort Benning where Eric was. They were both on a direct route. He has finished his course and is graduated as a ranger and after a few weeks in the swamps of Florida and then in the mountains of Georgia, he will have his final leave of one month and be shipped to Malaysia. He evidently can stand the heat.

I have been asked to do a book for Macmillan (my friend Betty Bartelme is religious editor there) and so I must get rid of my obligation to Harpers by sending them a collection of essays, reprints of articles from various magazines which I have written over the years, with an opening article "All is Grace" summing up the things I was trying to write in a book and in which I was thoroughly bogged down. If they do not take it there is no time lost as Marge Hughes typed all the mss. for me and it is all but ready to go. Then I will start on the Macmillan book which will be a travelogue through Catholic America. That is, I will tell what tremendous changes in the church are going on—the breaking up of monasteries and seminaries, the influx into secular life of the clergy and nuns, the work of the priest in the field of racial and social justice. I am starting here in Mississippi since this is the most backward part of the U.S., the most benighted, and I have all these friends here.

Much love to you and Franklin. We must look up Malaysia.

TO KARL MEYER

OCT 22, 1968

Please write. Only a few weeks ago I saw your communication in *WIN* [magazine of the War Resisters League] and gave it to Marty [Corbin] to use, to reprint in the CW. About taxes. The only word I have had from you is that which I received from Mike [Cullen] when he paid a flying visit to New York. God is trying you certainly, but He has you in His hands and knowing all the things that have happened to Catholic Worker families—all the martyrdoms suffered—I cannot but feel that He has given you the grace to take whatever comes, whatever has happened. Mike was obscure. But I take it you and Jean are living elsewhere now and perhaps you will do more writing. There might be too much activism, you know. God may take it in hand one way or another. He does push us around. Those in prison are immobilized and under an obedience of a kind even if it is slavery. But suffering certainly is the surest following of Christ. The old should learn more silence, but I cannot help but remember always all the tragedies in the families of the CW. I wrote an article once for the CW, "What did they expect, Suffering or Utopia?" in one of my sermonizing moods. But we walk alone in such things, and little can be said.

I used to think, "Thank God for Karl,—perhaps he will some day come on to New York and help edit the paper." Now I'm thinking perhaps there may be another mid-west paper, or a Chicago paper. Do write more. And please write to us. We think of you often.

TO MIKE AND NETTIE CULLEN

Mike and Nettie Cullen were founders of the Casa Maria Catholic Worker house in Milwaukee. In September 1968 Mike joined the Milwaukee 14, a group that included Jim Forest and others close to the CW, in destroying draft files with homemade napalm.

OCT 22, 1968

Dr. [William] Miller from Marquette was here last week and he is much concerned about support for Nettie and the children. I cannot worry about that when I have had so many years of experience, of how God takes care of those who trust Him. He is unfailing and will send us what we need, and of course she has her family behind her. Sometimes we are driven by circumstances to do what God wants rather than what we want and afterwards know that it is all to the good.

You are almost as bad as we are about not writing. So I know you understand our silence does not mean we are not thinking of you. We have two brand new babies here, one born at the place, the other is the Corbins'. Are you afflicted by strange mad people who come and stay and want to take over the place, claiming they are led by the Spirit? That happens to us periodically and aside from calling in the police to evict them, it is all but impossible to convince them that it is not their vocation to take over. This couple is one example. It has happened before, under the same circumstances. The girl is about to have a baby and one must care for her. She is a lovable little creature of 20,

Jewish and gentle. He is 45 or more, and is like a wandering player, ex-Shakespearian actor. Then there is an eighty-year-old woman recovering from a cancer operation. Life is precious and she enjoys every minute of it.

Today the sun shines. I was reading St. Teresa of Avila, her Foundations, to refresh my soul, and she said, in effect, all may not be capable of mediation, or contemplation, or visions or ecstasies, but "all are fit to love." What a beautiful thought to begin the day and how it makes you start loving all over again, even all the unwanted and fantastic and disagreeable ones! Disagreeable people are those who *disagree* with us.

Much love to all of you. If you can send a postal once in a while, I'd love it. And you.

TO GORDON ZAHN

Gordon Zahn, a sociologist and activist, devoted his life to the cause of peace. A conscientious objector during World War II, he later wrote influential books about the role of Catholics under Nazi Germany, including the first biography of Franz Jagerstatter, an Austrian layman, who was executed for refusing to serve in Hitler's army. Zahn was one of the most articulate and effective figures in the Catholic peace movement during the Vietnam era. Yet he had misgivings about the draft board actions in Catonsville and Milwaukee. For him the question was whether this was "effective as a symbolic communication." As he noted in a letter to Dorothy, "I think it is not. The only people who will be impressed are those who are already in their corner, so to speak. Others . . . are more likely to be 'turned off' than won over." He also worried about the effect of siphoning off the best leadership of the movement into prison. "I think the price is way beyond the gains accomplished."

At the same time, he confided his own personal crisis of faith in light of "the awful failure of the official church leadership." He found himself wondering "if this failure may not be evidence that the formal structure of the Church is really a block to the fulfillment of the Christian vocation."

OCTOBER 29, 1968

First—will you review Jim Douglass' book [*The Nonviolent Cross*] for us?

Now I will get on with my apologies for delaying these 29 days in answering you. You can be sure I've done plenty of praying for you.

I too was not invited to join in any of the burnings and they knew I had misgivings too. But that did not mean that I was against *them* doing as they did. Once the act was done, we must all stand by and defend them, and point to the possible good (and pray for it) their acts may do. The shock value of the act, the waking up of the bishops to the knowledge and admission of how far they are entangled in the State and in the economy. And those who did these acts of sabotage were also perhaps doing penance for their own inadequate lives, their self-indulgence in comfort, drink, and so on. They have expressed to the world their willingness to embrace, and joyfully, the hard life of jail—and most of them do not know how hard it is. You certainly fling yourself on God's mercy there. That first time I was in jail in Washington in 1917 I wept for a week in a punishment cell. I related so completely with the life of the others. The first time we defied the Civil Defense law there were about ten women and girls, and thereafter only 2 others besides Deane Mowrer and me. You cannot go to jail as a gesture. It is a real suffering. Up here in Rochester McVey said to me, "You changed your mind about the Catonsville 9, now. You were against them before." So I seem to be inconsistent.

Didn't you find the response of youth inspiring in Baltimore? I do have faith that God will raise up other leaders in the peace movement, who will feel diffident and unprepared but who will study and learn, and spread the word. We see them at the CW. Just out of college and this is true all over the country.

Far more serious is your own personal crisis, and you can be sure there was not a day I did not pray about it. Words are so inadequate. As a convert, I never expected much of the bishops.

In all history popes and bishops and father abbots seem to have been blind and power loving and greedy. I never expected leadership from them. It is the saints that keep appearing all thru history who keep things going. What I do expect is the bread of life and down thru the ages there is that continuity. Living where we do there certainly is no intellectual acceptance of the Church, only blind faith. I mean among the poor.

The gospel is hard. Loving your enemies, and the worst are of our own household, is hard. Please, Gordon, struggle on, resist this temptation. Be faithful. You don't know how we depend on you, nor how much your leadership means to us. By now maybe this trial has passed.

Meanwhile be sure of my love and prayer.

Dorothy

TO FATHER LEO NEUDECKER

NOV 23, 1968

Fr. Casey was here (New Ulm) and advised me to accept your most generous invitation [to Guatemala] even though I didn't feel up to it now. But of course it appeals to me mightily. Usually someone offering to pay my fare is what starts me out on a trip. And Eileen [Egan] is a marvelous traveling companion. But it is hard for her to get away too. I am fascinated by all the approaches to work in Latin America. I'd love to be with you and learn about what you've been doing and what your friends have been doing. We've gotten acquainted with a young Capuchin from Honduras who is working all alone up in the mountains on just such self projects as yours. What a contrast to the Melvilles.* It breaks my heart to see this adolescent romantic infatuation with violence. I

---

* Tom and Marjorie Melville, formerly a Maryknoll priest and Maryknoll sister, were expelled from Guatemala in 1967 because of their contact with guerrillas. Leaving their religious communities, they married in 1968 and both took part in the Catonsville 9 action.

met an Irishman in the bus station in Montreal who was working in Brazil, on brief leave, who had the book about Camilo Torres in his pocket with my introduction, a very ineffectual one. He said that all the young priests are talking of Saint Che and Saint Camilo. I too admire them both but cannot help but mourn such wasted material and the terrible lack of teaching of the Gospel in the seminaries. Maybe you do not at all agree and we would argue if I came along. But I think we understand each other.

Another thing. If I went so far, I'd like not to come back by plane but take a bus to California and visit Chavez who has visited us several times in New York. So if you'd take care of my fare there, and my subsistence in Mexico, I'd somehow get up to Calif. and back home. People would pay to get rid of me, send me on my way.

I'd love to come. Please excuse this delay but it is my terrible lethargy, an aftermath of this flu. However I am now inoculated, I hope.

TO KARL MEYER

Karl had written Dorothy of his decision to move out of the Catholic Worker house in Chicago.

DEC 21, 1968

I wanted to write you both and wish you a happy Christmas but my heart aches about the whole situation too. No, I do *not* think it is a good thing for women to put their feet down. I am no feminist. I believe men have the vision and women must follow it. Without Peter, I would never have done a thing. I tried to do what he wanted and his example and guidance gave me the courage. I do know a home with *both* mother and *father* is most necessary so God will surely see that "all things work out for good for those who love Him." Ammon loves that quotation. Marriage is an enormous risk when one is engaged in a revolution. I only hope you do not make Jean suffer for the sacrifice you have made. It would not be good for the love you share. Be cheerful—rejoice—and I beg you, *write*. We have too few writers on the CW. Please write a monthly column or 2 or 3 for us. On whatever you are thinking, reading or observing. Be our Midwest editor—Ammon's last column was a rehash—all about diet—and Mary left it out.

TO FORSTER BATTERHAM

DEC 28, 1968, PERKINSVILLE, VT.

Here we are snowed in, 15 below now, and a promise of snow and sleet tomorrow. And I am due in the city Monday! I came up last week between snow squalls—driving in my 1958 VW which has 150,000 miles on it. They do wear forever, and cost so little in gas. The whole family were here. . . . Eric will be shipped, or rather flown over to Vietnam and Malaysia in mid-January. He arrived last Friday and is out with his friends every night of his leave. But just the same this is a better Christmas than last when he was waiting induction Jan. 2. Strangely enough he has enjoyed his training, after he got thru basic. It was all survival training in the mountains of north Georgia, in the swamps of north Florida and paratroop training. He loved the South and he loved the rigors of life in the wilds. They walked 26 miles a day and starved in the swamps and mountains. He ate rattlesnake meat and one fellow ate a lizard. They didn't give them time to fish or hunt. They were allowed one ration a day.

Loving the outdoors and mountains as you do you will understand how he enjoyed this part of the training. They're not Green Berets, but they are in some special service and those that complete the course are staff sergeants and their companions are both Navy Seals and West Point men. Why is it that, when forced, men are capable of so much, and do so little when no compulsion is put upon them. Tolstoi said men are naturally lazy. I know I enjoy being up here away from all the work I ought to be doing in the way of correspondence and writing. We've been sewing, knitting. Reading, watching the astronauts on television, on which we get poor reception what with the mountains. Tamar has tropical fish, 3 tanks, a wild squirrel, a mouse, 2 canaries, 3 dogs and about 8 cats (only 2 in the house). This is an old 14-room house, and was full of rats when they moved in, but none now. There are all kinds of plants in every room it seems—Xmas cactus, all the begonias, African violets. I've started a cactus garden at my room in Tivoli and have a terrarium of mosses too. One can neglect them all so they don't suffer from my absence, and travel.

It's bitter cold so now to bed. There's an oil furnace here which heats downstairs—but many drafts. Much love to you from us all. Your gift to Tamar helped a lot and she'll get around to writing you soon.

Dorothy

TO FATHER LEO NEUDECKER

FEB 3, 1969

I'm glad the trip [to Guatemala] is put off but I do look forward to a future one, in the late fall or whenever you say. I want to write about the "little" unglamorous way of hard work, that the missionaries and local priests are putting in—the *nonviolent* way, the slow martyrdoms, and the need for U.S. parishes sponsoring mission parishes. But I don't know about Miguel Hidalgo. Was he one of the violent ones, leading a revolution which led only to more revolutions?

I prefer the saints who are out of fashion now. So perhaps you won't want me along. But tell me about St. Miguel Hidalgo. When you have time. When you get back from your quick trip.

Love and gratitude, Dorothy

TO KARL MEYER

Karl had published an article in the CW about the need for sanctuaries for the homeless.

FEB 7, 1969

You emphasized the idea of large-scale shelter (like that at Graymoor in Garrison NY and the Municipal Lodging House.) To make it human, young men would have to share with the others, or take turns sharing the hospitality of the shelter. Maybe for months at a time, draft themselves to do this, like the Little Sisters of Jesus in Belgium and in Sao Paulo, Brazil, going to jail to be with the others for six months at a time.

During the Depression, which you do not remember, the city did just the things you proposed, turning piers down over the East River into day shelters or places with many little shops where unemployed tailors and shoemakers could repair clothes and shoes, where there was a reading room, game room, etc. And then the huge dormitories on the piers, with double-decker beds, all run by holy mother the city, and run very well. No churches opened their doors, their auditoriums, or turned their lower churches into shelters, that I ever heard of.

None that I know of now. Fr. Dempsey in St. Louis ran a shelter for many years, and it is still running as far as I know. Our own municipal lodging house has become much more human of late. Do you remember Gorki's stories, *The Lower Depths,* and *Creatures Who Once Were Men*? They remind me of our lodging house and how it was for a long time so that men were afraid to go there, and were in danger of being robbed and beaten. But now St. Vincent's Hospital cooperates with a project there and has supplied doctors and psychiatrists and the lodging house has given over a floor to take care of alcoholics. They are given a three-day treatment "to dry them out" and certainly to build them up and supply the vitamins and nourishment they need and three or five days complete bed rest does much. Camp La

Guardia, not too far upstate, is another project of the city which is always spoken of by the men who have been there as first rate and many have stayed in the country for long periods.

The shelters you proposed, yes, in time of transition, in time of crisis. But hasn't the Church as well as the State always done a great deal of this in the past? I remember reading of St. Ephraim, how he came out of his monastery in the desert to feed the hungry during a famine. Also that the monks raised enough wheat on the irrigated land to feed the hungry. And there was not enough poor to feast on their abundance. This beautiful tale continues.

Since the growth of the modern state, the welfare state which numbers and cares for men from womb to tomb, the Church has done less, and has been paid by the State for what she has done.

But, and I cannot stress this enough—we must never forget our objective and that is "to build that kind of society where it is easier for people to be good." This is what Peter Maurin taught us. To follow the gospel teaching of the works of mercy. If your brother is hungry, feed him, shelter him. How can you show your love for God except by love for your brother? He who does not love his brother whom he has seen, how can he love God whom he hasn't seen?

This is a beginning. We are also trying to make that kind of society where such wholesale practice of the works of mercy are not needed.

We want a society where men will have work as well as bread, where they can choose their vocations, and where every child will have a chance to develop their talents and capacities. In Cuba, I saw billboards, "Children are born to be happy."

We have to work on many fronts in our attempts to build here and now a decentralized society in which men will have a voice. There is much preparation necessary in the field of education, unionism, and in the cooperative field. We must keep in mind that we are active pacifists-anarchists. Or peacemaker personalists. Or libertarian pluralists, decentralists,—whatever you want to call it. It certainly needs to be presented in many lights, this teaching of revolution, nonviolent change where we begin now within the shell of the old, to rebuild society.

Students need to read and study much to follow their calling in this great revolution. They need to study the works of Gandhi . . . They need to study Martin Luther King's writings. They need to keep in touch with the work of organizing in the union field, and among agricultural workers most especially and to study farming communes as they are developing in Russia, China, Cuba, and even here in the United States where the hippies have started farms, unfortunately with little theory of revolution. Peter Maurin used to quote Lenin as saying, "There can be no revolution without a theory of revolution." We need to make more of a heaven here, and have a long range view of a new social order wherein justice dwelleth, which is neither capitalist nor communist nor totalitarian in any way. How to accomplish it by nonviolence and not by warfare?

It is good to read the life of Ho Chi Minh or Che Guevara and be warmed and inspired by their fierce dedication to the common good. But how much we need to study, how much we must learn to endure. What dedication and self-sacrifice is needed.

TO DONALD POWELL

FEB 22, 1969

Your dear gift came just after I had an argument the night before with Deane and when I announced your gift she was so happy she forgot the argument! Everyone gets cabin fever at this time in Tivoli—tho we have a most spacious cabin to live in, warm too!

Tamar and her 5 youngest 8-17 were visiting us. Two of the girls and Nick are married and Eric is a Ranger in Vietnam, a staff sergeant. She and I are sick over it.

Have you read Berdyaev's Dostoevsky chapter on human freedom and evil? Explains a lot for me. One cannot do evil that good may come of it. But we are all involved in evil—all are guilty.

Don't think I'm gloomy. All day I've been listening to the Wagner cycle which began at 9:30 a.m. and just ended at 11:30 p.m. I'm surfeited with Wagner and feel thoroughly rested, having been so far removed from reality all day.

It makes me happy to have a friend like you, who writes me once a year and sends me presents, tho I've been a Carrie Nation these many years and cannot take his suggestion as to how to spend his gift. Having given up cigarettes and meat, the former in 1941, and the latter over the Vietnam war, I went for a good shrimp chop suey dinner with my assistant Pat Rusk and bought her and me a book.

Have you read Martin Buber's *Paths in Utopia*? It's in paperback.

Love and gratitude, Dorothy

TO DELLA SPIER

MAY 11, 1969, ST. CLOUD, MINN.

It is early morning—no one up yet and I'll seize the time to send a note. No time in St. Paul to write. Here I meet with 3 Catholic Worker families all of whom have boys of draft age so much worried about the war. Hippies here as all over. Actually some get exempt because of extreme long hair! They do not get c.o. status but "unfit for army." They are marrying young—17 and 18, and taking to the woods up by the Canadian border and building houses for themselves—becoming pioneers again. It's as tho they were determined to live—to get out of the war atmosphere they have lived in all their lives—a new generation entirely. Even tho WWI broke out in 1914, we were far removed, and had a quiet childhood behind us.

My plans are very uncertain. I want to go on west and visit

2 Hutterite communities and the Indians in Washington who are fighting for their fishing rights. But the Milwaukee 14 are going to trial Monday and I know 4 of them well and they want me to go to the trial. But you can imagine I get sick of war—writing about it—and want to write about communities, etc. So I'm not sure yet. By flying one can skip a lot of the fatigues of travel, but lose a sense of leisurely travel.

Don't be irritated with me. I know how little leisure you have. How nursing when you are not well yourself is a desperately hard existence. I just want to chat a little with you on paper, when I can. I will keep in touch. So expect cards from here and there. If you write your letters will be forwarded.

Much love to you and Franklin,

Dorothy

TO DIXIE MacMASTER

JUNE 19, 1969

I have just had all my teeth out and my gums ache indeed. Tuesday I went into the chair and it felt like they were tearing down a stone wall. But they were gone, eight of them, and the doctor and dentist said they had to come out. So now to wait for the healing and the plates to be made, or rather an entire new set. I feel naked to the world. My mother used to say you make your own mouth, though God makes the rest of your face. Meaning, the expression, I suppose. And my face is grim, down at the mouth, mean looking and narrow lipped and I shudder to see myself. What vanity we have! But I can talk reasonably clearly so continue to see the household here (there are ten volunteers) and the house is full.

Across the street we have two Little Brothers of the Gospel living in a fourth floor apartment with a tiny chapel, the house an enormous old tenement with Puerto Ricans. A neighboring Italian says they risk their lives. Not true. How afraid people are of each other! These brothers are a blessing. Two postulants are with them. Some of us go over for Mass once a week. They are Italian, not French, one an artist and the other working as a messenger to get money to pay the rent. The latter speaks English. Another member of the Fraternity, Victor Avila, has prayer meetings in his house, or apartment, once a week to which some go. Catholic Pentecostal. We also have a Franciscan seminarian with us who is manly and devout, a dependable sort. We are blessed this year.

Dixie, darling, you say not a word about yourself and your condition. I pray for you, and you do me good just to think of you, a tower of strength! How strange it is. We must be ready for anything. But how I wish you could be with us, with a companion to care for you. We have so few who are without serious troubles of mind and body,—no one we can depend on right now. Do write and let me know how you are, what your plans are.

The short breviary is a treasure always, and I get my reading in in the morning. Much love to you always. Do write soon.

SEPT 7, 1969

I was so overcome by human miseries when your letter came that I misread it and did not see that you would be gone before my letter to Montreal could reach you. My human misery was because of Tamar, who is in such a state that she condones everything and the summer was a hell with all the teenagers staying up until two or three and keeping others awake, and any attempt to curb this was greeted with such hostility on the part of the rebellious middle age group, Rita [Corbin] and Tamar, who believe in permissiveness, that disorder prevailed. The few that worked used our place as a play place and treated the others to movies and all were sleeping together, and when this was protested, one was called evil-minded and making judgments. Amorality prevailed. On one occasion marijuana was brought in, and LSD, and only fear of a police raid cut that out. If I tell people to go others let them come back.

So I have decided to sell this place [Tivoli] and try to find something smaller where we will return to our work for the poor. The PAX conference was wonderful and prayerful and serious, but they were all older people, disciplined in their professions of teaching and law and so on, and in their thirties and forties.

My having to be in N.Y. so much, with dentist appointments did not help matters much and Deane kept insisting everything was my fault for not being here. When I tried to straighten things out, Tamar said I was another Deane who did not understand youth. All her hidden resentments of me and my life seemed to come out strong, probably because she was troubled too. My own disorderly life was cited to me by young and old alike, individually of course when I tried to talk to them. You can imagine what a failure I've been feeling.

I have not spoken of all of this except in confession and I am telling you to let you know I am in dire need of prayers and the light to know what to do. Meanwhile school has started again and some order will be restored here and at Tamar's in Vt.

I do need your prayers. That is why I am pouring all this out to you. This last week I have had strep throat so feel worse about everything of course. But better now.

TO WILLIAM MILLER

NOV 17, 1969

How are things going with you? We have been extra busy and I've been having a fruitful time traveling. My visits to Chicago and Milwaukee and my visit to the archives were most pleasant. Right now I have another box ready to go. Did you get all the others I sent on to Marquette? Do you still want me to send stuff on to you first? I could use my judgment and send only those things which would be most useful. Let me know. I'd like to get my room and office cleared out for the New Year. Also, at 72, who knows what will happen next.

Stanley has collected everything he can lay his hands on pertaining to me, my life, comments on my work, favorable and unfavorable, dissent, conservative currents, etc. which he says he will sell. I do not like especially his writing articles about me like the one in the *Catholic World,* which I have never yet seen. He does not show them to me, and if he undertakes to write a biography of me, God knows what it will be like, since I know there are very many points of disagreement. He is a most fearful soul about the future of the work. Deane's tape library comes on apace, and I think will be very valuable as a record. Everyone who knew Peter or the beginnings of the work, she gets to make a tape and you must get up again to see us all, and to listen to them. Or she could send them.

Eric is coming out of the army December 20. His friends in Vt. are out or coming out, and one released for some months has reenlisted. That is what war does for some of them. They find they like the life. God help us! Eric writes that he and his friends will treat Vermont to a New Year's that they will not forget. These things are a great worry to Tamar and me. You can imagine. Sometimes it looks as though I have the world today, youth today, in microcosm in my own family.

NOV 22, 1969

I would love to come down to visit with you and to talk over the things you speak of in your letter. And to bring some of the personal stuff with me.

As for my biography, I'd be glad to have you do it, if you promise to take ten years at it. Knopf has asked several people to do it, including John Cogley, and I forget the other. Anyway, I refused. But I am at home with you. We are both converts. Someone will do it, so I will rather it be you. You have the understanding. *The Village Voice* had an interview last week. *Look* is going to have a story later in the spring. A photographer [Bob Fitch] has been following me around for them. We all like him. He has been doing pictures of the Cesar Chavez pilgrimage around the country.

TO DIXIE MacMASTER

DEC 5, 1969

I have been so much on the go so I am late in answering your letter. I had been worrying about you and it was with great joy that I heard from you. How I wish I could talk to tell you more about my sad summer—I know you would be a comforter. It is my granddaughter, Mary, 18, that caused me such grief, and of course Tamar too who seemed to turn against me, accused me of making cruel judgments against young people, even saying a number of times that the old seemed to hate the young. I have not seen her and the children since August but we do keep in touch of course, by phone and letter. Another thing that has happened is that three of the most wounded young people have taken refuge with her, and she enjoys having them—there are only 4 at home—and feeling needed, and part of the CW, as if her home were a sort of annex to the CW, to Tivoli.

She is right in many ways, such as not judging. But it is a grief to me that none of them are practicing their faith. Eric is due home from Vietnam the end of this month and I know she worries, as I do, as to what the war has done to him. And Sue is in Brazil with her husband and baby, and does not write, and the political situation down there is ominous. Some of the Grail women, Brazilians, have been imprisoned for several months at a time and have been tortured, because radical students took refuge with them on one occasion. We are so much in the midst of the violence of the world, here in N.Y.

This week I have had speaking engagements at Regina Laudis and at Maryknoll, to the nuns in both cases. The breath of the spirit is everywhere! There is a great deepening of prayer life, thank God, and one can feel it. We ourselves, a few of us, in addition to vespers each night and a few chapters of the Jerusalem Bible, are having a Pentecostal prayer meeting on Tuesday nights when we continue after Vespers with an hour or two of silent prayer and some quiet prayer, directly to our Father, and asking the Holy Spirit to guide us, asking also for the baptism of the Holy Spirit. "Through Thee may we the Father know, through Thee the eternal Son." There is a growing movement of Catholic Pentecostals, there are 40,000 of them, it is estimated, in the U.S. and all with a deepening devotion to the Church and her sacraments, and a great growing in Faith. I'll send you a book on the subject if you wish, but I do not want to burden you with more reading. So I am enclosing a clipping to begin with. Let me know if I should send the book.

I myself have only gone to five other Pentecostal meetings, and am most impressed. They have them at Fordham, as well as small meetings in the home, like our Tuesday night prayer meeting. At first I was very self-conscious about praying in this way, I have such a love of the liturgy. But I have gotten over that, and they bring me much peace and quiet, even healing.

PART VI

All Is Grace

1970–1980

As she entered the last decade of her life, Dorothy remained vitally active and engaged in the mission of the Catholic Worker. Her travels expanded to include Russia, India, and Tanzania. She was arrested for the final time while picketing with striking farmworkers in California; a famous photograph by Bob Fitch shows her with a look of utter tranquillity seated between two armed and imposing officers. She showed equal tranquillity in staring down the Internal Revenue Service when confronted with the charge (correct) that she had failed to pay federal income taxes. In her last years she undertook a major new project, opening up a second house of hospitality in New York City to provide shelter for homeless women. It was there, in Maryhouse, that she finally retired and spent her final years.

And yet for all these activities, her energy was clearly declining. Heart failure finally stilled her restless travels. Increasingly she was confined to the city, and then to Maryhouse, and finally to her room on the second floor where she enjoyed a view of the activities on Third Street and the sunlight on the tenement rooftops.

It was a time for letting go, for turning over the reins to the "young people" who continued to be drawn to her cause. After the frantic activism of the 1960s, she welcomed the signs of spiritual renewal and the growing interest in such themes as decentralization, ecology, and the "small is beautiful" philosophy popularized by E. F. Schumacher. All these were extensions of the constructive program advanced by Peter Maurin—not simply protesting, but announcing and "building a new world in the shell of the old."

With age came increasing signs of recognition. Honorary degrees were offered (and declined); Notre Dame conferred on her its distinguished "Laetare Award"; a publisher reissued paperbacks of her books; she was invited to speak at the Eucharistic Congress in Philadelphia in 1976; Pope Paul VI sent her personal greetings on her 80th birthday.

Such attention meant little to her. "Fools' names like fools' faces, always seen in public places," she quoted her mother. Far more important was the fact that young people continued to take up the cause of peace, carrying on the works of mercy, and finding their way to the faith that had sustained and guided her. And what, she was asked, would happen to the Catholic Worker after she died? "It doesn't matter," she answered. "If it is God's will, it will continue. If not, it will fail."

She had time to consider her personal failings—particularly her tendency to anger and judgment—and she reached out to old friends to make amends. Rather than the leader of a movement, she felt more like the mother of a large family, whose joys, sorrows, and anguish were her own. She suffered over the struggles of her grandchildren and other young people, remembering the floundering of her own youth.

Though she noted with sorrow the ongoing troubles in the world—poverty, violence, the ongoing threat of nuclear war—she trusted in God's Providence. She felt no fear.

She continued to take delight in small things: fresh bread; letters from friends and family; the Saturday afternoon opera on the radio; the beauty of picture postcards.

As she liked to quote St. Catherine of Siena: "All the way to Heaven is Heaven, because He said, 'I am the Way.'"

TO MIKE CULLEN

Dorothy had initially expressed her support for the draft board raids conducted by the Baltimore 4 and the Catonsville 9. She admired the courage of these bold activists and their willingness to endure prison for the cause of peace. But when the office of the War Resisters League was vandalized (presumably by government agents) she began to have second thoughts about the destruction of property. These second thoughts were too late for Mike Cullen, who was already in prison for his part in the Milwaukee 14 action.

[C. FEB 1970]

Today Tom Cornell is on his way to Washington to be with the DC 9 at their trial. They too have asked me to send a message. If I tried to write, it would be at such length they would not read it. Besides, as you know, I disagree with these actions. I understood the grief, the horror, which caused their planning and execution. But I do not think them right. In this I stand with the War Resisters and Peacemakers in the long-enduring, patient suffering struggle to change the hearts and minds of men so they will refuse to fight. They work in the philosophical-anarchist tradition. "Wars will cease when men refuse to fight."

Going after the top brass, the machinery of war, is working from the top-down, instead of from the bottom up. It is sabotage. It is using force to get the attention of government, industry. But if they will not hear the screams of children burned by napalm, do you think they will hear the breaking up of files and office furniture?

"The wrath of man does not work the righteousness of God." "Anger, hatred, violence" were termed the unholy trinity by the Fathers of the Church.

True, Christ scourged the money changers out of the Temple

but He also said to all of us, "He who is without sin, let him cast the first stone."

The noblest aspect of these acts is not the rebuking the sinner but the willingness to go to prison, to give up one's dearest possession, "Freedom."

It is almost an axiom in the radical movement that the words of men in prison cry out more loud and clear than those of men enjoying that most precious possession, freedom. The exercise of one's free will to choose one's steps, one's occupation, associates, surroundings, not to speak of studies, recreation, etc. etc.

A Father [James] Groppi, in his years of protests against the imprisonment of the poor in their destitution, against the limitation of their choices in every way by their poverty, has given up his freedom too.

I wrote the life of St. Therese because she exemplified the "little way." We know how powerless we are, all of us, against the power of wealth and government and industry and science. The powers of this world are overwhelming. Yet it is hoping against hope and believing, in spite of "unbelief," crying by prayer and by sacrifice, daily, small, constant sacrificing of one's own comfort and cravings—these are the things that count.

And old as I am, I see how little I have done, how little I have accomplished along these lines.

When I went to jail in the fifties for civil disobedience—and a few of us were arrested each year for six years—I felt glad as I entered my cell that now at last I could be really poor for a time, for a day, a week, or a month, that for no matter how small a time, I was at last sharing a little the misery of the poor. In a way it was true. I was stripped, prodded and searched for drugs, pushed from here to there, interminably, caged half the 24 hours like a wild beast—yes, I had just enough of it to teach me to suffer more keenly for the rest of my life over the plight of the prisoner. And not only the *grown* prisoners but the little children, in their detention homes, "youth houses," or whatever the city and state call them. And what of the refugee? The "displaced," the "relocated"?

Being in prison was dramatically to be "poor," but I soon reached out for the luxuries of something to read, the letters sent in to me, the something to eat. Yes, as soon as I was permitted to go to the commissary I got me a jar of instant coffee and so could indulge myself early mornings before the cells were unlocked, with the luxury of hot water from the tap (think of it, an open toilet in the cell, and tiny washbowl).

How can I condemn the expensive drinks of the activists in the peace movement when I myself hang on to my comfort, my own addiction—"judge not."

I am convinced that prayer and austerity, prayer and self-sacrifice, prayer and fasting, prayer, vigils, and prayer and marches, are the indispensable means . . . And love.

All these means are useless unless animated by love.

"Love your enemies." That is the hardest saying of all.

Please, Father in Heaven who made me, take away my heart of stone and give me a heart of flesh to love my enemy.

It is a terrible thought—"we love God as much as the one we love the least."*

TO DIXIE MacMASTER

APRIL 21, 1970

I keep waiting till I feel better to write you. What the doctor called my breathlessness and fatigue was "heart failure"—and he forbade me going to Guatemala as I had been invited—too high up—and told me to take it easier. Fr. [Pie] Regamey says haste is a form of violence so I have indeed slowed down. I've found myself rushing on the typewriter to make a deadline, to get an article finished to be on time somewhere. Everyone tries to do too

---

* Dorothy attributed this line to Father John Hugo. She repeated it often.

much—usually of what he wants to do, not the daily grind, and feels frustrated. The daily chores of cooking, dishwashing, cleaning, taking care of two incontinent people takes up so much time and is never done. The three young mothers, or rather four, have to give all their time to feeding and care of children—so folks quarrel about the lack of justice, etc., etc.

This letter has been interrupted twice. It may be very disjointed. And now, sitting before my window at Tivoli, I see more visitors arriving. They are "movement visitors," so predictable. Far more difficult are two young people who came a few days apart and went away together with new signs on their suitcases, "just married," to enable them to hitchhike.

A teacher visiting us from a private school told us 2 15-year-olds announced themselves to be "man and wife," saying they no longer believed in marriage! What a time we are living in! And the abortion laws!

The only thing is to keep plugging along at the works of mercy and all that teaching implies and "to be what you want the other fellow to be," as Peter Maurin used to say.

TO FRANK DONOVAN

JUNE 4, 1970

I was so overwhelmed when I opened your envelope that I tried to call you at home but you were not yet in and now I'll wait till tomorrow, but write you a note too. With what you give us you could buy a car, a boat, or take a trip around the world, or take the summer off and loaf on the beach and read, and here you are stripping yourself of all self indulgence and leading a life of hard work and then more hard work. The only way I can show my love and gratitude is by trying harder to get that book out. I'll try to match your diligence, taking into consideration of course your youth and energy, and recognizing my own limitations.

I just looked up that word diligence and a diligent person is the opposite of a dilettante. One who is diligent perseveres and is selective (has chosen). Diligence means to "esteem highly to select." (*Webster's New Dictionary.*) And I feel you have chosen our work at the Catholic Worker, "esteeming it highly," and it makes me very happy. Please excuse these wandering thoughts but the word diligent started me off. It's not a word I have ever used. Anyway. If you have chosen us to be your adopted family, don't ever give us up. Who knows, you may be called to other work, other cities, but you will always belong to the Catholic Worker family.

Love and gratitude. Dorothy

TO DIXIE MacMASTER

JUNE 7, 1970

I've been thinking of you a lot and wondering how you are. Hope your silence does not mean you are ill. Myself, I have been having trouble with my heart, water on the lungs, and have to take digitalis and some kind of pill to eliminate water, which also drains me of potassium, which meant I felt terribly low until the doctor said to drink two glasses of fruit juice daily. So I am careful to do it and am better, but still am pretty breathless and must walk slowly and take the two or three flights of stairs, which I must navigate three or four times a day, slowly. The more people there are, the more work there is to do, but they are a very good bunch of young people who are coming in from the schools to stay a few months during the summer. And some very good young women. So I must be with them, and get acquainted.

Our street and neighborhood is becoming more of a community, mostly Puerto Rican, and a wonderful consciousness among the young that they must try to "make a new world where it is easier for people to be good," as Peter Maurin used to say.

We have daily Mass of course and Vespers each night, and one does get a sense of searching amongst the young, and a desire to grow in prayer. That Pentecostal movement is growing among college students. You read in the *CW* perhaps about the Ann Arbor meeting I attended. I spoke at a Day of Renewal last month and the meeting of two or three hundred young families for singing and praying together, with a picnic supper, and scripture reading—it was a most restful and lovely day I've had for a long time. These take place monthly. I would attend regularly if I were in one place. The hymns especially, in both words and music, are haunting and remain with you a week after. There is enough repetition to make you remember them.

There is a deep piety here, and an emphasis on the place the Holy Spirit plays in our lives. True prayer of praise and thanksgiving. I of course am a little fearful when I see too much anxiety to have manifestations of healing and prophecy, speaking in tongues. Smaller meetings I have given up, though that emphasis, "where two or three are gathered together" is good. The trouble is around here it turns into a discussion club, not a good meeting of prayer, as it has been at the farm. There we say Compline first, then read Scripture, then spend the rest of the hour in silent prayer. It is very good. They gave it up down here and have only Vespers.

But everywhere I go I find people are leading more prayerful lives because of this Pentecostal movement, and in *America,* the Jesuit magazine, the editors say that there is hope for the Church in Latin America because of it.

Much much love, and do forgive my remissness in writing. I do hope you have at least been getting the paper. Drop me even a postal [postcard], just so I hear from you.

TO A CARMELITE NUN

JUNE 9, 1970

It made me very happy to hear from two or three of you and to know that you are praying for us. And I do want to ask you to pray especially for two priests, Fr. Charles [Jack English] and

Fr. Cajetan, who both of them are drinking priests and are in a retreat house for priests a good part of the time. Every now and then they are sent out to a parish and find themselves surrounded by priests who are able to take it; but the example is bad, and neither of them after some years seems to be getting any better. At that, however, they are in a way in a better state than a lot of the priests who are so filled with doubts and who are letting go of a great many of the most beautiful teachings of the Church. These two are very good solid priests. It certainly is a mystery how the Lord leaves you in your weakness so often. I do feel that in a way they are victim souls who are bearing the humiliation and the suffering for a great many others who get away with it, if you know what I mean. I know that both suffer deeply; so I do beg you all to pray for them.

I am just answering a letter from a young priest, twenty-nine years old, young enough, he says, to learn and grow, asking for guidance and counsel, who is in prison out in California for protesting the war. He has been suspended by his bishop under Canon 2367 whatever that may be; and he has give up institutional religion. So I will write to him and scold him.

TO DEANE MARY MOWRER

At this writing Dorothy was on the tail end of a worldwide tour with Eileen Egan that took her from Australia to India, Tanzania, Rome, and finally England. Deane was writing a monthly column from the farm at Tivoli.

SEPTEMBER 22, 1970

Just arrived in London last night and your splendid article in Sept CW was there to greet me. Thank God for news from home. Your article was beautiful—I can hear those chickens! Also, a first-rate report on PAX [*the Catholic peace organization*], and the ecology meeting, and prep for Third Sunday and the writing was so clear, so satisfying to mind and heart. . . . My silence was due to being caught in a flood in Calcutta, down with dysentery in New Delhi and Bombay, but Africa was splendid and now I am better again. I am to speak at War Resisters International Thurs and BBC next Tues and Pax meeting Sunday. Then we will be starting home. Whether by ship or plane, who knows. Everyone is terrified of hijacking. A real war scare. How good it will be to be home. Hope you are having daily Mass. We are resting today after our journeys.

TO A YOUNG WOMAN *regarding marriage troubles*

JANUARY 27, 1971

I hasten to answer your letter to say that in a situation somewhat like yours Fr. Damasus at Elmira (the Benedictine Monastery) was a great help. There was a case of an old friend of ours, a printer, whose first wife was in a mental hospital and who married out of the Church. Fr. Damasus was his advisor later, and he told Tom, who was by that time the father of 3 or 4 children, that the situation was such that he had to go on with the marriage and that the thing was to see that the children were getting a religious education and going to the sacraments, and that he also should do as much as possible in the way of getting to Mass and the sacraments; that undoubtedly the grace necessary is there. It has been a good marriage and by now they have 10 children. My daughter is godmother to 2 of them, and I think Fr. Damasus was a good guide in this situation because he did what was possible.

A long time ago there was an article called "Unwilling Celibates" (*Blackfriars*, in England) and they talked of those who, because of desertion of one party or the other, had to live celibate lives. This was Dominican advice, not Benedictine, and they talked even of going to the sacraments . . . as often as possible.

I don't exactly know what they meant "confession and the sacraments," but it was an article that was so good that the *Catholic Digest* printed it and the Bishops got so upset they ordered it recalled. Certainly, in your case, with such a happy relationship and your children, we have to accept a good deal of the uncertainties and frustrations.

From your letter I take it that you are worried about the marriage question and validation. I don't know exactly what you mean, but certainly, legally, the marriage ceremony, even a religious ceremony, without the legal requirements of our society (that is, a certificate of health and the license) might not be considered legal and might involve the legitimacy of the children in case of inheritance.

My child is a child of common-law marriage, since my anarchist husband did not believe in either a marriage before a priest or a justice of the peace, neither a civil nor a religious ceremony. It was a mutual consent. Since there are no papers written out, or formal witnesses to the mutual consent, it would not be considered legal. But a child can be legitimized by the father going and filing a paper acknowledging his parenthood. I know that this is the case with my daughter, and I know that some of the girls who had babies at the Catholic Worker farm saw to it that the men responsible acknowledged their fatherhood. I know too little about it to say more than this. Actually, I don't know right now of any priest there to whom you could go. However, here in New York, Fr. Alfred Martin (of St. Francis of Assisi Monastery) is highly thought of in his work in personal and marriage counseling. You might wish to write to him.

I was very happy to hear from you and can only say, as a much older woman, let not your heart be troubled, but keep on praying.

TO FRANK DONOVAN

2/25/71

As soon as you are able to get to the phone, do call me, though I know that you will only say you are feeling much better and getting along well. You never complain about anything, in fact your behavior in general is so perfect I wonder at you and feel shamed at all my own failings, complaints, dilatoriness, lack of attention to others, etc., etc. I have just finished telling Joan that we must observe holy silence for the rest of the afternoon so that I can get some work done. Sometimes she seems a compulsive talker and never stops coming to the door to say something completely unnecessary and I lose patience when I am trying to get some work done. Somehow people think that if you have a book in front of you, or are writing, you are not working, and they can keep up a conversation. I am using you for my wailing wall for the moment. Actually, I am just gossiping to give you news and the atmosphere of the place at the moment, here where you call it your other home.

Fr. Damasus Winzen said one time that the kind of love and concern and compassion we should have for each other is that exemplified in the Old Testament story in the account of either Elisha or Elias, who, when called on to restore the widow's son to life, went and placed his own body on the child's body, his eyes on his eyes and his mouth on his mouth, and so restored him to life. But it certainly indicates how close we must be to each other! And here we are all running away from each other for privacy. I am guilty of it all, closing my door and seeking privacy as I do!

I was going to see you this afternoon and company came in and kept me busy until three so hearing that Harry went up, I shall go to church and pray for you. As a matter of fact, you are so much on my mind that I dreamed of you the other night and cannot remember what I dreamed. But I do worry about you and pray daily you will recover completely, and have the good sense to take a rest at home or with your family. We love you dearly, Frank, and you have worked yourself to the bone literally. You cannot afford to lose weight. You are thin enough.

TO TAMAR

FEB 27, 1971

Here it is, your birthday again, this Sunday, and I cannot get up to see you yet. Tho the weather here is sunny and no snow on the ground, I'm afraid March will be full of blizzards! I guess it will be April before I get up there. Forster called the other night and seemed so pleased at hearing from you. He actually boasted, "We've done pretty well, haven't we," meaning all the grandchildren and great-grandchildren! Anyway his health seems good and he suggests when his sister Rose comes back from her travels—she must be 85—we must have lunch together. I wish he'd send you a nice birthday present! As for me I'm only sending a pittance, as the saying is, but will send more later. No word from Susie [Hennessy] yet. She's coming east later in the spring. Your house will be bulging! When I visited the Spencers and saw and heard some of their troubles, I felt how minor your troubles are. You are blessed with wonderful children—and I can't tell you how happy it makes me to see how you and they are appreciated by the young gang at Tivoli. You have a house of hospitality in the realest sense. We are really all of us foundering towards a better life, a better social order—a real accomplishment in this day and age.

    Much, much love—Granny

TO NINA POLCYN

MARCH 16, 1971

Here I am laid up again—cold, flu, virus, pleurisy, leaky valve, breathlessness, pain in my right side (liver? lung?). It surely looks as tho all indications are I'm staying home—here at Tivoli, to conserve my strength or rebuild it after my last year's travels. After all, born in 1897, I've seen a lot of this world, and I'm not much longer in it. That is, unless I take pains to conserve my energy, sit in the sun, walk a little instead of being *propelled* everywhere. I would like to have ten more years to write, to live the life of a hermit, here in community. So, much as I love Russia, I'll use maps, and guidebooks, and literature to do my traveling, I'm afraid. Why don't you take one of your nephews and nieces—what a break it would be for them. Do go—you are so much younger than I that it will be only joy and recreation. But now, for some time, I've been at a low ebb.

I'm sorry to be a gloom. But I'm really ill. A "comeback" takes a long time.

Much, much love—

Dorothy

TO THE PRESIDENT OF CATHOLIC UNIVERSITY

APRIL 12, 1971

Dear Dr. Walton,

Please forgive the delay in answering your very beautiful letter of March 18, but traveling, not to speak of the difficulty of answering you as I must, meant delays.

It hurts me to say it to you, with the feeling I have for all things Catholic, and especially for the Shrine where I prayed in 1932, on the Feast of the Immaculate Conception, for guidance. (The answer God sent meant the beginning of the Catholic Worker movement). It is with all humility that I must refuse your generous offer of an honorary degree.

The Catholic Worker stands in a particular way for the poor and the lowly, for people who need some other kind of schooling than that afforded by universities and colleges of our industrial capitalist system. I have had to refuse seven other colleges and universities for the reason that they had ROTC and are one way or another closely allied to federal government. In many cases they receive research grants, many of which have to do with war and defense. We very definitely are working for the new man and the new way so often spoken of in the Gospel and Book of Acts, and we would like to see the kind of an educational system envisioned by a Julius Nyerere, Catholic president of Tanzania. We talk of these things when invited to speak at colleges around the country and try to stimulate the young to study ways by which they can change the social and educational system nonviolently, rebuilding society within the shell of the old, as Peter Maurin, our teacher and founder always insisted.

Please do not misjudge me, or consider this effrontery on my part. I have a deep conviction that we must stay as close to the poor, as close to the bottom as we can, to walk the little way, as St. Therese has it. I have never publicized these refusals of mine, and I am afraid I have given offense to some of the schools, but not St. John's, Collegeville; Fordham, New York; and Bard College, from all of whom I have had understanding replies, among others.

Will you please convey my deep appreciation to the Academic Senate and the Board of Trustees for the honor they wished to confer on me? God bless them for their kindness. We beg their prayers.

TO WILLIAM MILLER

[UNDATED 1971]

Happy Easter! Finally I am coming to life again, recovering from my cold. But I lost 25 lbs this winter, had colds, fever, pleurisy, and had a hard time keeping going. Excuse me if I sounded cranky about too much emphasis on me—not enough on Peter [Maurin]. But I know you understand.

I'm so glad you've almost finished the book [*A Harsh and Dreadful Love*]. You must be weary of the job and wonder why you ever undertook it. I'll be glad to read it and so will Marty [Corbin]. Stanley [Vishnewski] is coming to the city for a month to visit his sister, but he will be prompt when your book comes—to read it. But he absolutely refuses to send his archives to you—only Marquette. He is sending books in which CW is mentioned, articles, etc., etc. He won't even let me see them. He has a great collection on me, praise and blame. As a Lithuanian he has always been anti-Communist. Anti a good deal that we stand for. Yet always a devoted fellow-worker.

TO FRS. DANIEL AND PHILIP BERRIGAN

The Berrigan brothers were in prison for their role in the Catonsville 9 destruction of draft files. It is notable that Dorothy did not write them here in her capacity as a long-time champion of peace, but as the mother of a large family, troubling over the breakdown of morality, the ensuing unhappiness, and the need for greater self-discipline.

MAY 14, 1971

FEASTS OF PACHOMIUS, CARTHAGE AND MARY MAZZARELLO

Dear Fathers Dan & Phil,

Please excuse me if in writing a letter of gratitude I also write a long letter. You as I do must get too many long letters.

Every morning I take my Penguin *Dictionary of the Saints* which Donald Attwater, an old friend, collected, and I turn to the saints of the day to find some encouragement and inspiration,—some instruction to keep me going.

Today, May 14, the patrons range from St. Pachomius to St. Mary Mazzarello, companion of St. John Bosco. There were 2 others listed, a Basque priest and St. Carthage of Kerry, Ireland, and founder of monasteries (mention is made of the jealousy of monasteries having adjacent lands!) All this reading from a "dictionary" took only half an hour but started a train of thought, about us, and today. Pachomius started as a hermit and ended by founding the first communities, two of them for women. Turning to my larger Butler's *Lives* [*of the Saints*], I found he was drafted, age 20, when he was a student of "Egyptian sciences" by the Romans, and when the Nile boat with its recruits arrived at Thebes, he met for the first time some of the many Christians there who made it their business to help all those in distress. The Christians made so great an impression on him that when his service was over he returned to Thebes, became a Christian, and went to the desert to learn to pray without ceasing (the psalms and the Our Father) and manual labor for his own subsistence and to help the poor.

There was all kind of misbehavior among the hundreds of monks who gathered around him,—luxury, self-indulgence, frivolity (a former actor and buffoon), etc, etc.,—it seems many came to escape conscription and wars and the disorders and dangers of that day. These tales should not give me comfort but they do, in my frequent discouragement and sadness at seeing the drunkenness, noise, and disorder of our houses, and the laxity of our houses of hospitality on the land, and how few the true communities.

Another saint of the day, Mary Mazzarello, a penitent, and so well used to hard labor, was a companion of St. John Bosco, who started trade schools for the young, tailoring, shoemaking, and other trades, and Mary started similar work for girls. John Bosco and Mary were peasants and had been brought up with habits of work and piety.

And what have we done? Nothing, except that we have endured, we continue hoping against hope. The children in our neighborhood in the city torment the men on the "lines"—run over the roofs, down fires escapes, thru the house, "ripping off" in several senses of the slang phrase. Drunkenness and drugs around adults means windows broken and repaired, trees planted and uprooted, pandemonium, and a vision of hell. I read Chekhov's "Ward No. 6" and can call our houses on many occasions Ward No. 7.

On the farm we have parents afflicted with drink, or fatherless children, and mothers unable to cope and abandoning the children to the care of the community. The adults take refuge in building hermitages for themselves and planting individual gardens. Individualism, not personalism, is the order of the day. And the hunger for love leads to couplings and scandal. 14-year-olds begin to look upon sex as an amusement, and when one looks for direction or solace the only comment I got from one of the priests with us was "Sex has its comic aspects."

Sometimes I think sentimentality and romanticism are the besetting sins of the day, both of the pious and the impious, the self-indulgent and the austere.

And yet—and yet—there are so many strong and amazingly good and hard-working young people continually coming to the Catholic Worker, both at the farm and the city. And when I look at the vices of some, I can say their virtues outweigh their vices, and my own sloth and self-indulgence should provide my mind and heart with occupation, rather than mourning over the failures of the CW in general or over individual cases of adultery and fornication (what harsh words!).

However, I have seen such disastrous consequences, over my long lifetime, such despair, resulting in suicide, such human misery that I cannot help but deplore the breakdown of sexual morality. After all it involves *life* itself. We are aghast at the continuing and spreading warfare in the world—the waste of human life, and at home too with abortion used to save the resulting consequences of our acts from suffering, from the cross we impose upon them.

The educated Blacks have called our national policy genocide, and perhaps their attitude is the correct one. What a way to deal with poverty and "over-population." It is "over-consumption" by the so-called Christian world which is the problem. We are all guilty.

My only solution for myself is more self-discipline, more manual labor, more silence, prayer, and of course with all that, even the constant new beginnings mean more joy. Joy (as distinguished from happiness). Even tho we must begin again and again and again. Discouragement is a failure in *cour-*

age, and Ammon Hennacy used to extol courage as the greatest need.

So this private letter is a morning meditation. I could not possibly print it—it would discourage others around the CW who could rightly accuse me of lack of charity, of hope, even of faith in them all.

Scripture gives the best direction (no matter how exciting, inspiring, and instructing the lives of the saints). "Rejoice, again I say rejoice. Judge not! I do not even judge myself," as St. Paul said. Forgive 70 x 7 my own failures too.

So I beg your prayers for me and my family, natural and supernatural. For two, especially, of my grandchildren who are in the utmost misery over the consequences of their "love" affairs. "What did you do at our age, Granny?" one of them said to me, not in malice but in despair.

I love this large family of mine, here and in Vermont, and certainly tales of woe are poured out to me daily, and love brings suffering indeed.

Please forgive me for sharing my suffering with you. Praying for you daily as we have at Vespers these last years, you are bone of our bone and flesh of our flesh. As you are to many.

TO NINA POLCYN

Dorothy was alarmed to hear that Karl Meyer, just sentenced for tax resistance, had "lost his faith."

MAY 21, 1971

Bad news from Karl [Meyer]. His letter was not forwarded to me so I did not go by way of Chicago to get home. So missed the trial [for tax resistance] which was Monday, the day after our boat ride. He got 2 years and $2,000 fine. The saddest thing is he has given up, has lost his faith, not only in the church but in Christianity.

All I can do is pray. I would feel it is my fault, my failure, if that were not vanity. I'll remember him dearly, in prayer, at Mass. He is one of the best.

TO KARL MEYER

MAY 28, 1971

God bless you always and give you strength to continue. This card has St. Therese's message—the Little Way. Your reputation and influence are great, an example of integrity and hard work—to us all. Your letter caused me grief but I know all works out for good eventually. Wish I could get out to see you but am in bed at the moment. Plain fatigue. We remember you daily at Vespers in town and Compline here at the farm. Of course you are always part of the CW family. We're proud to have you and love you. We all must grow in courage and love, Dorothy

TO DONALD POWELL

JUNE 22 [1971?]

A succession of troubles around the farm has certainly fouled up my correspondence and I cannot remember whether I thanked you for your generous remembrance of me. Anyway, my memory is slipping for sure—I notice it every day. Yesterday a succession of visitors kept me doing nothing all day but sitting out in the sun up here at Tivoli, just visiting. Really beautiful weather, and I don't get up here very often. Nor to Tamar's. But I cannot really say that. I do get up there about three times a year, and enjoy them all very much, though there is plenty to worry about there too what with unemployment for the three oldest right now.

Did I tell you I have four great-grandchildren all told? Another worry, unless I put my mind to remember my own youth and my present faith. I do indeed believe in guardian angels.

And saying the Little Office. Only the Blessed Mother can take care of all the women I have in my prayers. My own darling granddaughters, and the kind of women, old alcoholics who come in the CW from the Bowery. There are a couple of young ones too who are in a terrible state—young, pretty as can be, but on their way to destruction with drugs and drink. And in the midst of all this, even here at the farm, families with young children who literally have nowhere else to go.

Do remember us in your prayers, even if you only say "God help them." He certainly keeps us going so we have living space, sufficient but most monotonous diet. But such decent poverty keeps everyone tilling the soil up here, and now in the summer we live on vegetables and rice, creamed cod, and baked beans. We did fatten one pig, and ought to fatten a few calves for food, as Tamar is doing, but you have to hire a butcher to slaughter them. "If you eat 'em, don't name 'em," the saying is, and we all love animals.

TO DIXIE MacMASTER

Thanks to a gift from a wealthy benefactor, Dorothy was planning a trip to Russia. Her traveling partner would be her old friend Nina Polcyn.

JULY 10, 1971

Next Thursday I set off for Russia! So I must get off a few lines to you before I go. Nina Polcyn, who runs St. Benet's Bookshop in Chicago, is going with me, but otherwise it is a peace tour on a chartered plane, with a theological professor from Yale leading it. They gave me a travel fellowship—that is how I get to go, and Nina is paying her way. We may be the only Catholics in it. I won't know till we all—fifty or so—meet at the airport next Thursday evening. Nina and I are going to get there early to visit the church at the airport and make "an hour."

Dutton the publisher wants a book about the tour and I

may do a pilgrimage one, especially if they lure me with an advance. For a long time I have had a dream about getting a little place, in a village in Nova Scotia, or Cape Breton, to be used as a retreat house or house of prayer. Maybe just rent it for a time, to see. I must be on the sea. Some friends of ours have moved up to a little place called Meat Cove, Cape Breton. I would like to drive up with my granddaughter Sue and her little girl, two years old, this September, to see them, and that means I will see you soon. I pray and trust God will make it possible.

Certainly we are fruitful in suffering. People come to us with the most terrible problems and take refuge with us and the burden is hard to bear. But we are blessed at having this last year a priest with us who understands the Cross and preaches beautiful homilies, and works hard and is otherwise very silent, so we are blessed in that way. I do long to see you for a good long visit.

I do not have your letter by me to answer your questions, if any. I'll look again for the correspondence we talked about. I would like to get your feelings about it. The new morality, even the new theology! Sometimes one does not know what to make of it. I still read the *Imitation* regularly, and am glad Pope John set the example. Also Fr. Voillaume's communications. The Little Brothers are near us, on Fourth Street.

Could you get me some automobile maps of Nova Scotia and Cape Breton? Also any real estate news you might glean from priests? I would like to rent a place for six months at least and finish writing my retreat book there. It should have heat and water.

Much love in Jesus Caritas, Dorothy

TO DELLA SPIER

WARSAW, JULY 19, 1971

Here I sit in a Warsaw hotel lobby after an hour and a half visit with the prime minister where we were all served black coffee in little blue and gold cups (and cookies) around two long tables (there were 50 of us) while Jerome Davis handed him a list of 5 questions which he answered at length. We had spent the morning with a peace group. I had dodged evening meetings, etc., and slipped out of other sessions with our group to explore and so today I was good and did my duty. We had a grand tour yesterday going to Chopin's chateau and an open air piano concert in the park around the house, a visit to a state farm, and an evening at the opera, all about Seneca and Nero and Poppea, composed by Monteverdi in the 17th century. Maybe you heard it in Riga.

On the way we stopped at Amsterdam—a beautiful city—at Brussels, which seems very poor in comparison, in East Berlin, very poor—and we've had three full days in Warsaw—a beautiful city. Benches, parks, flowers everywhere—not much traffic—much rebuilding still. The country is much poorer—little farm houses, narrow roads.

Tonight we will be sleeping in Leningrad.

TO FRANK DONOVAN

HOTEL RUSSIYA [MOSCOW], SUNDAY 1971

All my resolutions to write to everyone are broken. It's one of these planned trips with every moment taken, and the most insane schedule of plane rides. Up and down continually in crowded plane, as plain and unluxurious as our Trailways buses. We are indeed seeing the world. One Monday in Moscow and we will be on our way to Sofia, Bulgaria, and then the Black Sea for a few days, etc.

Today was lovely. Mass at the American Embassy. Only one Roman Mass in the city. Fine young priest. Then brunch at the Canadian Embassy's secretary's house. Then a museum to see some of the most famous ikons, etc., etc. Every museum is full of people, but no music, no concerts. I've walked my legs off and rested all evening, while poor Nina had to spend it in a seminar. In no time at all I'll be home and at my typewriter, disentangling my copious notes.

I miss the home folks very much.

Take care of yourself, Frank—do not get too tired. Just "be" there. See visitors, don't keep working. People need to be talked to and listened to. Much love to you—pray for me.

TO DELLA SPIER

HOTEL BALKAN [SOFIA, BULGARIA], JULY 31, 1971

A wonderful tour of Communist countries but it does make you love your own more. This is a happy country—so far. Moscow is frowning—here all smiles. But Mike says this is more Communist than the Communists. "The daughter outdoes the mother," he said. Climate marvelous—wonderful fruit—music and dancing—tourism is big business. But I remember Dracula lived in these mountains! We drove all thru them, dark and terrifying—wild drivers. I did much praying. But everyone—seasoned tourists—admits this is a terrifically tiring trip. Planes are smaller, more cramped, crowded. Little food—biscuit and coffee—rough runways—noisy planes—hot, etc. Buses in U.S. are more comfortable. But much beauty—nice people. Bus loading now.

Love, love, love, Dorothy

TO KARL MEYER

AUG 13, 1971

A fine friend I am not to have written before. But life in summer is so hectic with everyone in the world traveling and wanting to take in the CW, along with the United Nations and Lincoln Center and Radio City, that we go crazy around here. No time for mail. And then I became a traveler myself and accepted a travel

Fellowship from Jerome Davis and some Quakers who run peace seminars to Eastern Europe and spent the last three weeks on a mad whirl which I would never do again. A tour is a taste, however, of the four countries we visited. I saved the postals to send when I got home, because postage was so exorbitant and the mails so uncertain. I am sending on a few. Churches are show places and ikons are valuable museum pieces and the color is beautiful in them.

Jim Douglass wrote me recently accusing me of suppressing part of your letter which we printed in the last or next to the last issue [June 1971] of the CW. I take it to mean the part when you tell me you no longer felt yourself a Catholic. I felt that I did not want to bring so personal a problem to our readers. You must know the deep unhappiness I felt and do feel. I have felt so many periods of dryness and heaviness and confusion myself, but also felt that I could only keep saying, "Lord, I believe, help thou my unbelief." And to try to keep my own deep sadness and discouragement from others. I think there are many periods of dryness, of searching and waiting for light in our lives. There is such a thing as deep spiritual fatigue, as well as physical. One can only "wait—and do nothing," as the psychiatrist in Eliot's *Cocktail Party* said.

Maybe you'd rather I did not write about these things in my correspondence to you. What I feel about the institutional church for instance. For me it is the place in the slum, in our neighborhood, where it is possible to be alone, to be silent, to wait on the Lord. The sacraments mean much to me. The daily bread we ask for is there. To sit in the presence of the Sun of Justice is healing, though I have to force myself to remain in fatigue and fullness and misery often. But the healing is there too. No matter how corrupt the Church may become, it carries within it the seeds of its own regeneration. To read the lives of the saints has always helped me. We've had corrupt popes and bishops, down through the ages, but a St. Francis, a St. Benedict, a St. Vincent de Paul, a Charles de Foucauld will keep on reminding me of the primacy of the spiritual. Peter Maurin used to tell us to study history through the lives of the saints.

But I don't want to bore you with what may seem meaningless to you at this time. It has been so hard to write too. You have stood for so much in my life, your emphasis on personal responsibility, your courage, your very aloneness. To me you have been someone with absolute honesty and integrity and this sudden blocking out of one aspect of your life comes to me as a shock. I won't write anymore. It has taken me all morning to write this. Please don't take me off your mailing list and I'll try to do better.

Love to you and Jean and the children, Dorothy Day

Writing to Dorothy from jail, Karl Meyer noted: "I have no inclination toward a public repudiation of Catholicism. . . . If I say to you honestly, in the presence of Jesus and of all the saints, that I do not now believe in the preeminence of Jesus and of Christian doctrine over all others, I do not believe that this honest statement constitutes a break with Jesus or his disciples or you, because there remains that intimate communion of all of us who have earnestly sought truth and worked for universal brotherhood. . . . Though we are talking only of a gentle drawing apart of ideas within an intimate communion of values and purposes, perhaps I can understand some of the deep sadness you feel in watching the gradual dissolution of the goodly company of those who sat at the Roundtable of Peter Maurin, the steady attrition of us who might carry on his message in all of its wholeness and purity. . . ."

TO CHUCK SMITH

Chuck Smith opened a Catholic Worker farm in West Virginia and started a journal, The Mountain Worker. *Dorothy took heart from these ventures, which seemed to reflect the enduring relevance of Peter Maurin's message.*

SEPT 3, 1971

I have not written because of much turmoil at the farm. One can endure the problem of drink and keep hanging on to John, Mike, Alice, etc. to keep them from dying on a barroom floor. But even so it is hard to see them getting worse. We have no real leadership at the farm. If you have any suggestions, any advice to offer, it would help. Do you think we should sell out, get a small farm, near yours for instance? Are you in danger of being held in prison for refusal to be inducted? If you were not there, it would not help us much to try to be near you.

It would take the next year to liquidate and start over, keeping with us the helpless and most needy. Many of the younger ones should be on their own or working actively. We must do something. The corruption of children, or allowing it, is a serious sin.

You see I am in quite an uncertainty as to what to do. I feel that all the young men here are here as in a school and are not seriously considering CW as a way of life. Very good, but not wanting responsibility on the land. They are thrilled by the city, getting out a paper, running a house, but not really inclined to the land.

Do pray over this and make suggestions. God will show the way, the Spirit will lead us. But we need to counsel one another. It is late and I've been writing letters for hours.

TO WILLIAM MILLER

SEPT 22, 1971

Latest developments on the CW front: every so often the federal income tax people are on our heels. I referred them to our lawyer, John Coster, and the zealous agent spent 4 hrs. with him one day and 2 another. They class us as a political group, not a charitable one, which is paying us a great compliment—we are indeed trying to do more fundamental things for justice and peace than feed a soup line, run houses of hospitality. It all goes together, as Eric Gill wrote.

Dr. Miller offered Dorothy the loan of a car—a marvelous luxury. "It relaxes me to drive," she noted.

OCT 5, 1971

Today I got the plates, so now I can settle down and feel guilty at my luxury. But it does not go very deep. Now that my legs give way on occasion under me, and my heart is tired and I pant at too much walking (and I did love walking!) it makes me happy indeed to be able to go out, jump in the car, and go to the laundromat, insurance man, real estate office, post office, etc., etc., and just take a rural ride with Stanley or a small pilgrimage with Deane.

All is suddenly going peacefully here, and I know there is plenty of good work going on here—the old, the mental, the crippled, the men off the road—last week a dozen blacks from Florida kicked off a large farm without their pay (they got it finally after going to Albany—the employer was notorious), etc., etc.

It is the young ones, their new morality, their religious justification of it, their conviction that we will just have to accept it (another affair is budding before our eyes) that makes one feel that these surroundings are not right for us now. Or not right for them. Life on the land should have its discipline, its hard work, so that people sleep instead of staying up making music all night. Poor Deane. She comes from a farm and knows how people have to work.

I worry about the car. Are you sure you are not depriving the young ones of your family? It is such a tremendous help to me. Do you know that when I go from here to Tamar, I've had to take 4 buses—Red Hook to Hudson, Hudson to Albany, Albany to Rutland, and Rutland to Springfield where Tamar meets me.

It relaxes me to drive.

Love and gratitude, Dorothy

TO FRITZ EICHENBERG

OCT 5, 1971

I'm weary so I'll be all but illegible. I do miss seeing you, and think of you so often. I got your last note of Aug 5 when I got back from Russia, together with a suitcase of mail held for me, some of which I am still answering. Do you get deluged in this way? So many lonely people, and we speak to their condition, and I know how people look for mail, so I try to answer all of it. And so neglect my friends. But I know you are as busy as I am.

Are you in N.Y. as before at the Graphic Arts? Can't we meet? You must talk to me about Simplicius Simplicissimus [*a book Eichenberg was illustrating*] and I will talk to you about Alexander Solzhenitsyn and his novels. We both have our personal tragedies—our children's unhappinesses—but we have our work, a God-given work, a vocation which brings happiness, contentment, also. There are always two sides to the coin, joy and sadness. "In peace is my bitterness most bitter," is the old translation of a biblical text. I can understand it. But the Peace and Joy are there just the same. God can bring good out of evil. Ammon used to quote "All things work for good to those who love God."

TO DEANE MARY MOWRER

SAN FRANCISCO, NOV 16, 1971

The time is flying and I am flying around too. I feel well and am learning a lot. I cannot tell you how busy I've been. I had one meeting at Santa Clara and Joan Baez showed up, or rather came early to meet me, stayed for the meeting and sang afterwards to the delight of the audience, made up of all ages. She came also to the Cathedral here in San Francisco yesterday afternoon (Sunday) with her mother, and it was a packed house there too, as in Santa Clara, even though no one knew she was coming either time. She is beautiful and very sweet and evidently loves the CW, which should make us all happy. She wants to come to visit the farm some time.

Now tomorrow I go to Sacramento, and then down the state to Cesar [Chavez's] new place, La Paz [*headquarters of the United Farmworkers Union*], which is an educational center with a dozen families living around it. Fred Ross is going to come to help organize the educational program. We had a good talk yesterday. He feels Cesar has a great vision and is truly a great leader. I told him about Julius Nyerere and he is going to study him. His people call Julius Nyerere *Malimu*, or teacher. Ross asked after the Brazilian [Paulo] Freire and his writings on education [*Pedagogy of the Oppressed*]. He is very hard reading, for me.

I always think of Peter Maurin's statement that there can be no revolution without a theory of revolution. And Fr. Tompkins always said that study groups, indoctrination, clarification of thought, came first. Then the credit union to provide the money for starting projects too, besides giving aid to the membership.

As I learn more about these organizing and educational ideas, I'll write again. I know you feel as I do about the land, the family, and communitarianism, and we both suffer over the difficulties and conflicts. Cesar has what could be called a small community of families living in trailers right now at La Paz, which I go to in a few days.

Here I am the guest of Ephrata House which is a center for the deaf and those who communicate by sign language and lip movements. I spoke here yesterday morning at Mass, and my little ten-minute talk was translated into beautiful sign language, which is like a dance of the hands if it is done slowly and lovingly. There are three Sisters living here in a little community, and there is a cursillo center next door with chapel and dormitory and dining room. The young priest, Father Cane, is wonderful. (What extravagant language I use. I am afraid I am guilty of enthusiasm, in Fr. Knox's sense.*) Anyway, I've been very happy this last week in this little community and most comfortable. Mass every afternoon, and I have time for my Scripture reading in the morning, a good hour of it.

I am trying to keep my diary, my notes, in the morning, when I am fresh and then perhaps I can read over what I have written. If I write at night I can't read my own handwriting.

Much love, Deane, and I do hope your weather there is good and sunny and brisk.

TO FRANK DONOVAN

LOS ANGELES, NOV 18, 1971

Had a bunch of meetings in San Francisco and Joan Baez sang at two of them. A thrill. Glad to be here in Los Angeles with friends. Now resting a few days before going to the Ammon Hennacy [CW] House. Everyone says they are all very young there and I'm afraid they regard me as an old traditionalist. I've never had a word from [Dan] Delaney except a mimeographed newsletter. He is a priest, married to a nun, you know, and I think they are both very young, too, so he may be afraid of me. How awful! I rather dread meeting them all. I see Chavez next week, then San Diego. Then Mississippi and then home!

SAT. DEC 4, 1971

You cannot imagine how hard it is to live at the Ammon Hennacy House here. No prayer, no Mass-going, not even on Sundays—a terrible bitterness on the part of Dan Delaney against Cardinal McIntyre and the "institutional" Church. Just six people in the house, and not a practicing Catholic among them.

---

* Fr. Ronald Knox, an English Catholic writer and biblical translator, was the author of *Enthusiasm*.

However Cesar Chavez makes up for it all. I spent 5 days at La Paz, a great deal of it with him. He is truly devout. He fasts and prays and gets to Mass and Communion, not daily but certainly weekly, and as often besides as he can. He fasts, no meat, fish, cheese or eggs. Bread and vegetables only. He lives like a desert father. He says "work like this means sacrifice." "To be a man is to suffer."

Did I tell you I had three days in San Diego and Tijuana? The terrible contrasts, destitution and luxury.

TO KARL MEYER

JAN 21, 1972

I'm sitting in my room at Tivoli watching a grey dawn lighten the hills across the river, reading my prayers and thinking of you as I have so often this last year. It is 1 Peter, chapter 1 which engrosses me, about belief in Jesus—in the power of His holy Name. And my own joy and gratitude to Him, and the whole problem of faith, which is so precious it must be tried as tho by fire. I pray daily for my grandchildren, for my children, that God will draw them to Himself, thru Jesus, as He has promised. And you know I pray for you.

You have been especially on my mind because of a call from a Mr. Spiegel and his arrangement of a meeting in Chicago where he wants me to speak. He is a high pressure salesman alright but I said I would only speak if you asked me. So I grabbed the only paper I can find at this early hour to write and ask your advice, your desires along these lines. And would what I have to say prove acceptable at all? Trusting as I do in Jesus (and I am not what they call a Jesus "freak") and His words in the Sermon on the Mount, I have lost faith in "resistance" and believe in voluntary poverty, as you do, as a solution to tax problems, and in accepting authority in taking alternate service even tho protesting the draft.

There is such suffering in the world, in prisons, mental hospitals, youth detention homes that I can only think such work is blessed. To serve the poor because Jesus Christ demands it in Matthew 25 (not because the State does). In fact it is the only way to get into these places (youth prisoners), and to be meek and humble of heart means loving the officials of the state, respecting all men, and taking this opportunity to serve the poor.

It is only faith in Jesus and His words that makes me speak as a Christian anarchist. When I explain this Christian anarchism, many accept it but prefer the word "personalist."

Please excuse this scrawl. Drop me a line if you can. I would love to speak if you want me too. I can only believe "an injury to one is an injury to all," the slogan of the IWW, in the sense that we are all one in Christ Jesus, members of one another. So I sign,

With love in Christ, Dorothy

TO MARY HENNESSY [*one of Dorothy's granddaughters*]

JAN 29, 1972

Things have been not too good at Tivoli. We are looking for another farm, out of Dutchess County, either north of Albany (and so nearer Tamar) or west of it on the other side of the [Hudson] River. We are really decentralizing. Especially since we are having trouble with the Internal Revenue Services about tax exemption and have been sent a bill for $300,000 for back taxes and penalties. They are trying to suppress the peace movement or make it ineffective. Of course we are guilty of not filing returns, etc. But we have our case and our defense mapped out and it will come to court sooner or later.

We have two good lawyers and there will be delays I am sure. At any rate we must think in terms of cutting down expenses and will get a farm which will be cheaper to keep up— one building and a barn, outhouses perhaps, even oil lamps, who knows? Anyway, subsistence place. Everyone will have to work more but we will be together, those who are really in the work. We are taking it all very quietly and will go ahead and survive, I know. God has watched over us and provided for us all this time, so I am not worrying. What He wants will happen. It will all be for the best. As Ammon used to quote so much, "All things work together for good for those who love God."*

I must tell you how happy it made me to have you three girls with me at Mass on Christmas morning. My greatest joy would be to see all of you practicing the faith. You have to practice it to make it grow, and what a strength and joy it gives, to young and old, in good times and bad times.

Much love, your foolish old grandmother, Dorothy

TO A YOUNG COUPLE

A young ultra-orthodox Catholic couple from Saskatchewan visited the New York Catholic Worker communities and afterward wrote Dorothy a series of long accusatory letters expressing their disapproval of conditions they had encountered. A typical passage from one 12-page letter included these observations: "In the Catholic Worker you permit a situation where it is very hard to be a true Catholic. You let in illegitimate priests and let them run rampage over the faith of the people there. . . . At the CW it is hard for a person to keep his Catholic faith intact without compromise, when you yourself pretend to preach anarchy and call it the teachings of Christ. . . . You teach the abolition of authority and its imposition in whatever form, thereby denying that Christ could institute a Church to transmit in an authoritative way the message of salvation. By this you are undermining the plan of Christ and his Church and leading others to do it."

---

* In the end, the IRS agreed to drop its claim against the CW. According to Dorothy, the government lawyer "shared with us the conviction that we would continue to express ourselves and try to live the Catholic Worker positions as best we could, no matter what steps were taken against us by the government."

FEBRUARY 1972

Your letter telling of the cold and how you are surviving is certainly fascinating, but there are so many questions unanswered. How far are you from a church? A Catholic church. Can you get to the Sacraments? How do you get to church, are there any neighbors to pick you up or do you have a dog sled or what? You have not been to Mass since Christmas? But even the desert fathers got to Mass once a week. You certainly seem to be doing without the Church, just as we, practicing the works of mercy, try to do without the State. I do think you have missed the point completely of what we are trying to say in our articles and in our lives.

You must remember that the Church has not withdrawn from us our privilege of having the Blessed Sacrament with us at Tivoli. Our local bishop has visited us twice. Dear Fr. Cain has helped us many a time, coming to say Mass when there was no other priest and visiting our sick and burying our dead. Count the number of the works of mercy there. The number of sick taken care of—heart, brain tumor, old age, epilepsy, mental illness. Of course there is sin everywhere. Where sin abounds, there does grace abound. We have that assurance, also, of being forgiven seventy times seven. We also have Christ's words in Scripture, Judge not.

Are you truly reading and meditating on Scripture? Do you think we are not mindful of the desperate situation there? What we are working toward is a complete decentralization. We are selling the place [Tivoli]—it is in the hands of real estate people now, and the Corbin family will get a start in a place by themselves, as families surely should be; there will be a house of hospitality for the old ones, perhaps in Staten Island, so we can be nearer; and there will be a farm, primitive, perhaps even with outhouses and no electricity, a place where some of the young ones can work with Marge [Hughes] and Fr. Andy, without the help from the CW, no check, after the initial purchase.

Please take care of your own anarchistic souls, and pray for us with loving kindness, and quit writing those long and difficult to read letters, for one whose eyes are growing dimmer and who is seriously overworked trying to answer mail and take care of the truly immense work here in New York. I go to the farm when I can and remember St. John of the Cross, "Where there is no love, put love, and you will find love." Also "Why see the mote in your brother's eye and do not see the beam in your own?" And meditate on the story of the publican and the Pharisee. If it makes you happier, call us personalists, or decentralists. "The less you have of Caesar the less you will have to render Caesar."

May we call you both cop-outs from both Church and State in your flight to the wilderness? But why call names. We'll play Mary's cassette or tape and thank her for it and not wonder why she has the means of making one or whether it is in the spirit of St. Francis. We are only too happy to have it.

Anyway, let us cease this unfruitful correspondence and subside into holy silence for Lent. Until you stop your arrogant presumption of being guide and preceptor I will just return your letters unopened as I have no time nor inclination for controversy.

Meanwhile, love to you both.

TO WILLIAM MILLER

TIVOLI, APRIL 15, 1972

Dear Dr. Miller,

Or rather Dear Bill

I'm tired, the place is crowded, the weather is grey and cold and I've just answered, tho briefly, a batch of mail. But I do love it up here—it is beautiful and I sit by the window and breathe fresh air. Also I can read and read. My room is very quiet too.

Bill, I do not want you, or anyone, to write my biography. So please respect my wishes in this, now and after my death. Not that I think of it as imminent. Aside from a tired heart I'm in good shape. Give my love to your wife and family. It was touching to hear of your old relative's death. And her kissing the hands of those who helped her. Drop me a line when you can.

TO FATHER LEO NEUDECKER

MAY FIRST, 1972

I'll be 75 Nov 8 this year and a paperback company [Curtis] is publishing *The Long Loneliness, Loaves and Fishes*, and *On Pilgrimage*, 1960s. A nice present.

Tonight we have Mass here in the house in the dining room after supper. All of the young people and neighbors, black, white, and Puerto Rican. (A simple Mass, not one of these folk Masses which I don't much care for.) I'm afraid I'm pretty much a traditionalist. We say the rosary (and Compline) on the farm, and down here Vespers. All the young here now get to daily Communion at the 5:30 p.m. Mass, or 8:15 a.m. Do remember us in your prayers. I've been canceling and turning down speaking engagements—time for quiet. Plenty to do right here at home. I'm so glad you get in some traveling. I still would like to make a pilgrimage, but no more speaking trips. For a year anyway.

My last trip, every meeting was packed—standing room only. Bad for my pride, to see how the CW appeals to people.

I still hope to get to the Holy Land.

TO FATHER STANLEY MURPHY

JUNE 5, 1972

Your letter and most generous gift (May 17) finally caught up with me and this is a rather late "thank you." I've been having trouble with a "tired" heart—too much traveling and speaking, so I had to cancel all my engagements which began piling up again. But I had to go to Notre Dame of course [to receive the Laetare Award], and to be there at a commencement was a great privilege.

As for politics, both McGovern and Humphrey have shocked me by their statements about Israel and their pledges to go to their aid, even with nuclear weapons. This was last night on television! I'm an anarchist and decentralist so have never voted.

TO FATHER LEO NEUDECKER

AUGUST 2, ST. EUSEBIUS

Eusebius fought the Arians and was exiled and mistreated and went on hunger strike in protest! according to Donald Attwater in the Penguin *Dictionary of Saints*. Lots of Arians today. Karl Meyer says he is so overwhelmed by Christ's humanity he cannot see (believe) the divinity. Please pray for him. And I have grandchildren going in for yoga! Life gets harder.

You were a dear to send me that present. I do have an account at the Red Hook bank up by the farm and suffer from guilt feelings. Some royalties go in that for my daughter who is poorer than any of us here with her 9 children and 5 grandchildren. Always troubles, sicknesses, etc. But it is a close family. No father there for 12 years.

Yes, I do thank you. I love St. Teresa saying she was so thankful a person she could be bought with a sardine.

I do agree with you in all you are doing. Work is even more necessary than bread. The waste and squalor in the slums is appalling. Government checks but no places to live—exorbitant rent, no work, means more drinking. But the dear Lord pushed us into this work and we are like an extension of a mental hospital. Do pray for us all.

Don't get tired of our pacifism, our seemingly futile work. I love to think of our pilgrimage to Mexico.

TO WILLIAM MILLER

SEPT 26, 1972

I hate to bother you with inquiries but how come Liveright is doing the book [*A Harsh and Dreadful Love*]? And have you seen the scurrilous ms. of John Stanley together with Isadore Fazio which the former claims has been accepted by Liveright too? Meanwhile the *Publisher's Weekly* carried a full-page ad of Curtis about my 3 paperbacks coming out in Nov. (*The Long Loneliness, Loaves and Fishes,* and *On Pilgrimage,* the 60s). On the next page a short ad of your book which was advertised as "A Harsh and Dreadful Thing—Dorothy Day and the Catholic Worker Movement." I am so tired of that quotation being used and ascribed to me rather than to Dostoevsky, as the Paulists also used it in advertising *Meditations.*

I rather think I'll go into hiding in November. Meanwhile I think of you often with deep gratitude as I use your car going back and forth to my sister (only an hour away) or with Stanley to a rummage sale where he is always finding treasures of old books like *Co-op* by Upton Sinclair, which I have long wanted.

Tho I dread the publication of your book (because of title) I will certainly read it. I have a block about reading manuscripts. Actually I have 3 on hand now which dear friends have sent me to read and still another which I enjoy—Helene Iswolsky's memoirs, which she gives me chapter by chapter.

Please do write me. I miss your friendship.

TO DELLA SPIER

TIVOLI, SUNDAY, OCT 15, 1972

Here I am stuck in my room once more for a few days—not answering the phone even, and with a new sneezy cold and runny nose. When one gets run down, it is hard getting up again. But

I'm getting the best of care. Since I'm going to be here all winter, God willing, I've moved to a front room where there are 5 windows—three in front and one facing east, one west. The three face south and the sun pours in. Very cheerful.

Going down to the city for 4 days meant coming back a nervous wreck—on verge of tears all the time just from weakness. I've gotten to this state only twice before (after flu usually) so I know it means only rest. Marge [Hughes] brings my meals to me—I wonder at her strength and endurance. The work would fold up (at least here) without her.

But I'm sleeping and reading, writing a few letters and refusing to see people. They come up anyway. And then I have to make an appearance just to stop rumors I'm on my last legs. Seventy-five seems a terrific age.

Enough now, I'll keep dropping you lines. Cheaper than telephone and I'm not going downstairs.

TO WILLIAM MILLER

OCTOBER 28, 1972

Thank you for your good letter, and I was happy that you are happy—now that your work is finished.

I'm sorry I hurt you by saying I did not want you or anyone to write my biography. Knopf some years ago wanted John Cogley to write it but I refused (John said he knew I would). So your *title* bothered me somewhat. Just as the Paulist Press blurb did. If people are going to quote Dostoevsky's Fr. Zossima— "Love in practice is a harsh and dreadful thing compared to love in dreams"—why do they attribute it to me? It is not honest. I told the editors of the Paulist Press. They may change it on the next edition of *Meditations*.

And now to see James Finn announced by [John] Deedy in the *Commonweal* as writing my *biography* and the history of the CW movement!! I knew he was writing about the *CW ideas and movement* and I'm only too glad to have brainy men write about them. Those ideas, which Peter Maurin emphasized as Gandhi did, of such utter simplicity, need to be written about more and more.

I may travel but not to speak anywhere. Speaking brings in money—not writing, as you well know. But I will have to have increased faith and trust in God, because literally I am worn out. I'm visiting Tamar now, a good relaxed atmosphere, and a happy one, though they live in utter confusion. Most of the week I've been lying in bed reading.

Dr. Robert Coles also has a book coming out about us [*A Spectacle Unto the World*]! with illustrations by Jon Ericson. All this and my 75th birthday, is like a 9-days wonder, a tempest in a teapot.

But I do know, of course, that *we are on the right track* and that we will miraculously survive. One cannot suppress an idea, no matter who gets elected.

I've been reading Lanza del Vasto's marvelous book *The New Pilgrimage*, printed in 1956 and which certainly needs re-printing. It makes us feel we have only begun, but most truly begun, what with the rejection by our young of the present social order. Their beginnings at practicing survival. There are aspects of a "new barbarism," as I think you and I were saying once, but spending the last 23 months on the farm I'm learning a lot. I'll write, I hope, this year, fruitfully. And read, and rest. And not answer mail except to special friends.

And above all study the Sermon on the Mount, the New Testament. And I want to take to heart "Judge not." And the Lord's Prayer, "Forgive us, as we forgive others."

TO DONALD POWELL

DEC 26, 1972

I don't have 6 secretaries. None at all. We're a bunch of rugged individualists around here. No personalists, no communitarians.

Mostly isolationists, ten shacks, three houses on our 86 acres—each one playing hermit or Thoreau, or the Idiot, etc. etc. What's Peter doing up there, not taking better care of us? Yes, we women do survive, out of plain stubbornness and deviousness too, making successes out of most evident failures. Plenty of flop-houses, houses of hospitality, but no farming communes, no clarification of thought.

During these bombing days [*the massive "Christmas bomb-ing" campaign over North Vietnam*] I console myself or rather try to strengthen my weak knees by reading *500 Days* (Salisbury) and *1914* (Solzhenitsyn) and realizing we never will have peace on earth but that we will survive and keep happily proclaim-ing the good news that men (and women) have tremendous capacities for spiritual growth. That little prayer of Ivan Deni-zovich on the Baptist, that strange joy lights up the world for me.

I am in love with such men. Did you read the *Cancer Ward*, *The First Circle*?

These times worse than the Thirties. Why don't you visit us at Tivoli?

TO WILLIAM MILLER

DEC 28, 1972
The book is beautiful, jacket, printing, type, and pictures—also index. When I get it out of Stanley's hands, I'm browsing in it as I lie in bed. He is taking care of it so it doesn't disappear out of our hands!

Considering my captiousness (is that the word?) you have been an angel in putting up with my lack of cooperation. But I know you understand. Our paperwork, Stanley's and mine, is enormous.

Liveright is an old and honorable name so I'm glad it's com-ing out with its imprint. When I get my strength back (and I feel it coming) Stanley and I may go south showing slides on the way. But it won't be till May, I know.

TO DIXIE MacMASTER

For the first time in months I went to NY last week to "attend" two Masses—one Fr. Dan Berrigan's for Peace, at United Nations church (Holy Family) which was packed, and the other at the Paulists. Both had urged me to be present. At the second they wanted me to give the homily! I refused of course. And I'll go to no more of such Masses when the laymen make up the Mass, except the consecration, and you can't even hear these long, composed prayers. The Mass, as generally accepted now, has been hard for me to get accustomed to, shortened as it is, accompanied as it is by guitars, and feeble music. But times past have been hard times too, and the Church survives it all, thank God. Enough complaining.

TO A YOUNG WOMAN IN DISTRESS
After spending the morning in a "good talk" with a young woman at the farm (as she noted in her diary), Dorothy "wrote her a long letter about suicide and abortion, prayer, salvation." This letter is notable for the references to her own abortion and two suicide attempts—events from her youth, long before her conversion, which she seldom, if ever, mentioned in writing or conversation. Despite her criticism of the climate of moral laxity, Dorothy (remembering her own troubled past) felt enormous compassion for the sufferings of the young.

TUESDAY FEB 6, 1973
Dearest Cathie—

Please forgive me for presuming to write you so personally—to intrude on you and your suffering, as I am doing, but I felt I had to—because I have gone thru so much the same suffering as you in the confusion of my youth and my search for love. I cannot help but feel deeply for you and for your mother, your family, because now I go through these sufferings over my grandchildren—one or another of them. In a way, to use old-fashioned language, I feel you are victim souls, bearing some of the agony the world is in, Vietnam, the Third World, "the misery of the needy and the groaning of the poor." But just the same it is a very real agony of our own, wanting human love, fulfillment, and one so easily sees all the imperfections of this love we seek, the inability of others ever to satisfy this need of ours, the constant failure of those nearest and dearest to understand, to respond.

But God has been so good to me, again and again, to make one know that when I cry out, even so feebly as calling, "God help me," He answers. "What have I on earth but Thee? What do I desire in Heaven beside thee? Hope thou in God," the Psalm goes on. "Hoping against hope," it says some place in Scripture. And "In peace is my bitterness most bitter"—such mysterious words—and yet it is hope, fragile hope,—and a ray of peace, even if faint.

I'm praying very hard for you this morning, because I myself have been through much of what you have been through. Twice I tried to take my own life, and the dear Lord pulled me thru that darkness—I was rescued from that darkness. My sickness was physical too, since I had had an abortion with bad after-effects, and in a way my sickness of mind was a penance I had to endure.

But God has been so good to me—I have known such joy in nature, and work—in writing, as you must get in your painting—in fulfilling myself, using my God-given love of beauty and desire to express myself. He has given me, over and over again, such joy and strength as He will surely give to you if you ask Him. "Taste and see that the Lord is sweet."

Again, I beg you to excuse me for seeming to intrude on you in this way. I know that just praying for you would have been enough. But we are human and must have human contact if only thru pen and paper. I love you, because you remind me of my own youth, and of my one child and my grandchildren. I will keep on praying for your healing, writing your name down in my little book of prayers which I have by my bedside at home.

May love grow in your heart, and help you to express this love in joy and peace.

TO WILLIAM MILLER

FRIDAY FEB 16, 1973

Here I am lying in bed writing letters and someone brought me the *Commonweal,* which made me very happy. A good review of your book and a very humorous tone throughout, which does not bother me in John Cort, since I know him so well! But it does point very well why you and I had a tension between us. Mainly because of the title—focusing on me. What I wanted was emphasis on *Peter,* and the influence he has had—on many great men, not just on me. John Cogley and John Cort always told funny stories about Peter, which really downgraded him, who was in truth a great *teacher.*

But the NY *Times,* and this *Commonweal* article—I'm sure many more reviews which Liveright will send you—are doing justice to your hard, hard work and atoning for my lack of sympathy. I'm happy for you—and beg your forgiveness.

APRIL 21, 1973

CHRIST IS RISEN

Thank God my strength is coming back little by little. The reviewers were puzzling but since you used my name in the title, it gave the reviewers the excuse to ignore what they did not understand. When the review in the *Nation* mentioned that you had dispelled the romantic image of me as a radical (in their sense) I really began to want to read the book! I'm looking forward to it, but my nose is kept to the grindstone around here of mail, and seeing visitors, etc. Publicity has increased our work but not our income. But we get what we need.

MAY 12, 1973 11 P.M.

I don't know what you mean about people at the CW wanting to stone you or why you talk of "slipping in and out." It is *me* they want to stone for getting all the attention. You never spent any real time around the CW—the complaint is you never hung around and got acquainted, and it is a valid criticism, I think, that you put too much emphasis on me and disregard all the wonderful and exciting young people all over the country who *do the work* while I go around and make speeches.

I saw that expressed in one review. Perhaps you are too shy, too reserved, find it hard to mix with such a diverse crowd which changes all the time, and the young people are shy too, especially of people who want to write about them.

I am deathly sick of all the interviewings and publicity I got around my 75th birthday, and exhausted from all the visitors, telephone calls, and requests for talks, etc. I have turned down at least 14 honorary degrees, but accepted some awards because they meant something to me, like the [Eugene] Debs one, for instance. I am truly in a state of exhaustion right now.

Anyway . . . Your letter hurt me—telling me *not* to read your book. That suggestion that the CW as a whole do not like it. Those who have time to read (how little time most of the young have—and how they seem to long to get away from books) *do like it.*

But please forget us as people to be written about for a while and do come see us, just to visit and take Peter's stuff back to examine at your leisure.

Love (and sympathy), Dorothy

P.S. Please be cheered and forgive my grumpiness. I am now feeling much better.

I have 2 texts to guide me in my attitude to the aberrations of the young around me. "Judge not" and "Forgive seventy times seven."

Here in N.Y. they *all*, 16 or so, get to daily Mass and Communion and Vespers every evening. We never had a better crowd these last 2 years. The farm still has its problems. "The Sexual Revolution." Three or four situations among the very young. But they must learn the hard way.

TO DELLA SPIER

JUNE 17, 1973

Last night I read *A Once and Future King* by [T. H.] White in paperback. The best book I've read for a long long time. It is the story of the youth of King Arthur. *The Crystal Cave* by Mary Stewart, which I found so fascinating, is about the youth of Merlin. In the White book Merlin is an old man, a tutor to Arthur. Both books have the charm of the *Idylls of the King*. It is all history of the time of the Saxons and Britains. The incredible age of England and Wales compared to our America. Do read both—they are paperbacks. They take me so out of my troubles and physical miseries, aches and pains. They take me back to the joys of youth—those afternoons in Lincoln Park when I felt Scott's *Lady of the Lake* came to life in that beautiful park. Remember?

TO SUPPORTERS OF THE CATHOLIC WORKER
Dorothy writes to John and Margaret MaGee, formerly of the Boston CW, about plans to purchase a new house on Third St.—Maryhouse—as a shelter for homeless women.

JULY 3, 1973

I'm sorry indeed for the long silence, except the brief note to Margaret. Now I am recovered, but it is hard to write what with the influx of visitors, especially priests and brothers as well as people passing through to and from vacations. And the work increases—with the people, men, women, and children around us in this Bowery area. The hardest thing to face are the old women, with all their earthly belongings in shopping bags and sacks who sit around our place until eleven when we close and then go out to live in empty buildings or doorways. The one shelter run by the city for women holds 45 only. St. Zita's and Joan of Arc residence are not taking our kind of destitute, deranged, and otherwise damaged females. So they hang around us.

Now we have suddenly come upon a place on Third Street—a music school settlement house is up for sale, and it has many small practice rooms which would be ideal for the homeless women who are so suspicious of each other—always accusing each other of stealing, etc. Each one tries to help us in her own way—cleaning, washing, sewing, etc.—but all are hoarders, collectors, from our clothes room, or even from wire trash baskets along the street corners. It is these habits of clinging to household goods and material goods which make them hard to deal with. So the Salvation Army at present has three good shelters for men but none for women.

The price of the building on Third Street is $150,000—an immense sum, but Ruth Collins says it is a bargain. There is a sprinkler system and sturdy fire escapes there, but additional baths and fire-retarded halls would be necessary. I wish you could see the place.

We have never had a better group of volunteers—all of them daily communicants at Nativity Church around the corner and present too at Vespers and Scripture reading every evening. Always the dear Lord sends up the help we need—young people just out of college, accepting our place as a school, one might say, and going from us into the professions, but learning definitely what they want to do in life.

TO THE BISHOPS OF CALIFORNIA

While picketing in California on behalf of the United Farm Workers, Dorothy was arrested along with several hundred protestors. She and the women were held for ten days in a prison camp, where she drafted this epistle to the bishops of California. (It is not clear that it was ever sent.)

AUGUST 7, 1973

From a prison in Caruthers, Fresno County, California—called an Industrial Farm: A letter to the California bishops, and I trust you will not think this letter an affront. Call it brain damage from bumping my head every time I sit up in this lower berth of one of 24 double-decker beds where I lie, resting, looking out on green fields, trees, vast fields in this magnificent valley. There are 99 women in two barracks, 30 of them Sisters. In the corridor of this low elongated cage in which we are imprisoned there are two other barracks for the strikers.

A group of Mexican women, most of them young mothers, are playing jacks, as I write. The Sisters from various religious orders around the country are fasting. Their 8th day now, and they rest only in the afternoon. They go to the kitchen and dining hall barracks, and take their places while the rest of us eat—3 times a day. It doesn't bother the Sisters at all. They are upheld by the prayers of all of us and their Sisters of their various orders.

This place is a farm for rehabilitation—a place for men—and they teach them to use farm machinery, and courses are given by local colleges in the winter months. Most of the prisoners are young and Mexican, Filipino, and Arab. Here in our women's barracks I've never been with a more beautiful crowd of women and girls. Warm and loving, pure and clean of life and speech. They are women of great dignity and recognize in the struggle of the United Farm Workers against agribusiness the importance of La Causa.

As news comes of more Teamster contracts signed they

realize the long fight there is ahead. They may seem to be losing or to have lost, but the strike goes on against growers, corporation farms, child labor, poisonous insecticides. We will be calling on all our readers for support—money, the boycott, the picketing—the giving of time, study and money to this important movement which strikes at a basic evil in our American Way of Life, the love of money. You cannot serve God and mammon. Many translators use the word money. "Sell what you have and give to the poor. Sow sparingly and you will reap sparingly."

We all see what is happening in our "American way of life," corrupting politics, presidents, lawyers, labor union officials—the Church itself. We must admit it. The Church began to stumble and falter right after Jesus said "Upon this rock I will build my church" and he chose Peter—who wanted to start building right after the Transfiguration, who denied Him 3 times, tried to keep Him from laying down His life, who was called by Christ "Satan" (the adversary). James and John (one can call them Bishops) wanted to sit in high places. They made their mother ask it for them. (She shared in this ambition.) Even after He died, rose again, and they walked and ate with Him, they said, "Are you going to start the kingdom now?" The Holy Spirit had to renew them before they glimpsed the road ahead. (Excuse me for reminding you of what you already know.)

Joan Baez came and sang to us this morning, a Guatemalan reporter and photographer visited, and we talked of nonviolence and Cesar Chavez and the farm workers' struggles.

We agreed that this nonviolent struggle is a great and mighty movement and could not in the long run lose. As for violence on the growers' side, I saw men sitting in the vineyards with rifles the other day. Each day on the picket lines we were faced by rows of police with long clubs and guns in their holsters, and a new kind of handcuff I never saw before made of plastic. Some of the strikers said they saw cans of mace, a horrible weapon to use against the weaponless. I saw three carloads of men in plain clothes, whether police or men (I hate to call anyone a goon) hired by the growers or Teamsters union—all carrying long sticks with the end sharpened to a spearhead. Bob Fitch, West Coast photographer, got a picture of a hand-cuffed Mexican worker on his knees, hands behind his back and a policeman standing poised to beat him. "We are here to keep the peace," the police told me. "We are here to protect you." But when I asked the police to disarm these men armed with sticks and clubs they did not answer. They did not move. They "protected" them, they protected the growers, not the people, the farm workers.

This morning here in a grassy yard the bishops of El Paso offered the Mass and several hundred received communion. But where are the other bishops of California? We want their pastoral visits. Visiting the prisoner is a corporal work of mercy commanded by Jesus in Matthew 25 as of vital importance. "Inasmuch as you did not visit the prisoners, you did not visit me." Surely the farm workers—Filipino, Mexican, Arab, Chinese, and so on (all men are brothers) are "the least of these, His brethren." He who was consorting with publicans and sinners. How hard it is to separate the sheep and the goats. All men are members or potential members of the Mystical Body of Christ, St. Augustine wrote.

But the bishops will lose the support of the growers, it is said. How wonderful it would be for you to embrace holy poverty by having wealth taken from you! It is hard to know how to go about divesting oneself when there are a dozen consultors, priests and laymen, in a diocese who might not agree to selling your superfluous holdings and giving to the poor. The Quaker method of waiting to reach a unanimous agreement is intolerably slow. You certainly would quicken the process of acquiring voluntary poverty by visiting the striker or nonstriker prisoner and taking the consequences.

The papal states were taken over by the people in Italy and the papacy has grown in stature since. It is true Pope Paul's words at the UN have not been heeded, "War no more!" But we have had great popes, and great and inspiring encyclicals from them. . . .

Rejoice, rejoice when Sunday collections are falling off and bequests stop coming in. "Your Father knoweth you have need of these things"—vocations and food, clothing and shelter, schools, clinics, shelters. Saints will rise up to take care of these things.

Parish schools are closing, novitiates are closing. Huge buildings stand empty up and down the Hudson River Valley, unused, untaxed, making the burden for the poor heavier. I suppose the condition is the same everywhere, here too in California.

Cesar Chavez has an income so low it is untaxable. There are the Forty Acres owned by the union with hospital, clinic, hiring hall, cooperative gas station, and the strikers use their community hall for a strike kitchen. . . . How many families of farm workers during this long struggle could be set up this way on Church property. Such a change will be wrought not with violent revolution as in Mexico, Russia, China, France, etc. etc.

Forgive me for being presumptuous but Christ's words are so clear—"Sell what you have and give to the poor." "Your Father knows you have need of these things." "If you sow sparingly you will reap sparingly." The trouble is—after every revolution the Church starts getting her own back again.

This has been a strange jail experience. . . . My only complaint [has been] the complete lack of privacy—fifty women in one long room, and 5 toilets, ranged along the wash room. Very inhibiting. But I am forgetting I am writing to bishops—about most serious affairs. They are our dear fathers who in turn ordain other fathers who provide us with the Sacraments—the water of salvation, the "knowledge of salvation through forgiveness of our sins"—the bread of life, and shall we not thru them as thru Him, receive all good things?

I'm most serious about this letter and these suggestions. I see empty convents, institutions, academies, novitiates, and Jesus said "Sell what you have and give alms." "Feed the hungry, house the homeless, visit the sick and the prisoner."

You will reap a hundredfold.

TO THE EDITORS OF *COMMONWEAL*

Dorothy enjoyed a long relationship with Commonweal, *the independent lay Catholic journal, to which she made her first contribution in 1929. To mark her 75th birthday in 1972, the editors asked Dorothy for an article of reminiscence and recollection. She replied with this letter, which was published in the August 20, 1973, issue.*

Dear Friends,

I hope you do not mind my responding to your letter for a short "reminiscence" by writing you a rather disjointed letter. I am inspired today by a great sense of happiness and gratitude to God and to *Commonweal* too and a desire to share it. I wonder how many people realize the loneliness of the convert. I don't know whether I conveyed that in my book, *The Long Loneliness*. I wrote in my book about giving up a lover. But it meant also giving up a whole society of friends and fellow workers. It was such a betrayal of them, they thought. One who had yearned to walk in the footsteps of a Mother Jones and an Emma Goldman seemingly had turned her back on the entire radical movement and sought shelter in that great, corrupt Holy Roman Catholic Church, right hand of the Oppressor, the State, rich and heartless, a traitor to her beginnings, her Founder, etc.

Anatole France introduced me to the Desert Fathers in his book *Thais*, and even in that satire the beauty of the saints shone through. George Eliot introduced me to the mystics. Her Maggie Tulliver read the *Imitation*, so I read it too, regardless of the fact that George Eliot rejected formal religion. Did you know that Tolstoy has Pierre read the *Imitation* after his duel with his wife's lover? That Gandhi and Vinoba Bhave have read the

Imitation? And Pope John? It still nourishes me. I'm tired of hearing eminent theologians disparagingly quote that line, "I never go out into the company of men without coming back less a man." But how much idle talk in all our lives, dishonesty, equivocation, and so forth sullying each precious day! I go down on my knees each night and say, "Dear Father, Jesus told us you were Our Father, repair these slips, mistakes, even sins I have committed with my tongue during this day—the discouraging word, the biting criticism, etc." Even this article.

Of course "my bitterness was most bitter" over and over again, not at Holy Mother the Church but at the human element in it. But thank God, there were always the Saints. . . .

God forgive us the sins of our youth! But as Zachariah sang out, "We have knowledge of salvation through *forgiveness of our sins.*" I don't think anyone recognizes the comfort of this text better than I do. I have not yet been attracted by the present tendency to bring everything out into the light of day by public and published confessions. Were we not taught by Holy Mother Church to respect the modesty of the confessional? Or is that a silly expression? But oh the joy of knowing that you can always go there and be forgiven seventy times seven times. (Even though you wonder, in your distrust of yourself, whether you *really* mean or have the strength to "amend your life.") I hope your readers can read between the lines from the above and recognize what my positions on birth control and abortion are. . . .

Thank God we have a Pope Paul who upholds *respect for life,* an ideal so lofty, so high, so important even when it seems he has the whole Catholic world against him. Peter Maurin always held before our eyes a vision of the new man, the new social order as being possible, by God's grace, here and now, and he so fully lived the life of voluntary poverty and manual labor and he spent so much time in silence, and an hour a day in church, besides daily Mass and Communion (while he was in the city), that all who knew him revered and loved him as the leader and inspirer of the Catholic Worker movement. . . . Peter was delighted when people praised him and even seemed to boast of the college presidents who listened to him. He thought prestige helped the work. "We need to build up the prestige of these young men," he said to me and he himself did it to such an extent that many a time he was foolhardy in his trust and estimate of others.

I must illustrate my own explanation of why I have accepted the awards that have been accorded to me in the past few years, by a little story. This is called "reminiscing" and serves to remind people that I am *very, very old*, as one of my grandchildren said to me once. She said it as she handed me a crude drawing of a ten-tiered, high-riser birthday cake, "because you are *very, very old*," she had printed underneath, and have nine grandchildren to eat that cake, she neglected to add.

The story is this. A girl called Katey Smith way back in '34 was sent us by St. Vincent's Hospital; she had been operated on for tumor of the brain. (She recovered.) She loved to join in all our activities and accompanied us on a picketing expedition one day on 34th Street in front of the Mexican Consulate because renewed persecution of the Church had broken out. A passerby asked her what the picket line was about and she answered, "None of your damn business."

I would feel like Katey Smith if I refused some of the honors offered me, honors which call attention to and pay tribute to Peter Maurin's idea. I have refused honorary degrees because of my respect for Holy Wisdom, just as much as for my abhorrence of our military-industrial-agricultural-educational-complex-conglomerate. I compromised when I accepted the Laetare medal from Notre Dame this year. Fr. Hesburgh threatened to come to First Street and present it there if I did not come to the Midwest. At the Notre Dame graduation and conferral of degrees, a dozen or so honorary ones, I could be lost in the crowd, I thought, so I accepted. . . .

I write this from my place of semi-retirement at Tivoli, New York. The spirit of youth today rejects our old names, *Maryfarm* and *St. Joseph's House*, but still keeps the name "Catholic Worker

Farm." It is not the kind of farming commune or agronomic university Peter Maurin envisaged, but we can boast that whereas the average age of most "communes" in the U.S. today . . . is nine months . . . our own commune has lasted thirty-eight years. . . . Fidelity, constancy, are beautiful words, but we must confess there is much plain stubbornness and very real poverty, even destitution, which holds us together too.

Thank you for your patience. If you don't want this letter-article, send it back and I will use or expand on it for my next "On Pilgrimage." . . .

Love and gratitude to all of you always.

TO SIDNEY CALLAHAN

Sidney Callahan, a professor of psychology at Mercy College, in Dobbs Ferry, New York, was emerging as a prominent lay Catholic voice on issues of the family and the role of women in the Church. Despite Dorothy's own record of transcending traditional female roles and stereotypes, she found it hard to relate to the emerging feminist movement.

SEPT 17, 1973

Can't find any stationery. I'm not home yet, that is in N.Y. house of hospitality, which I consider home and where they considerately acknowledge mail when I am away.

About "softening up" on honors—I got the notice of the Laetare medal [*from Notre Dame*] before I was given a chance to refuse. Besides—having a house and a farm and a group there over the years made it easier not to make a fuss.

But I do draw the line at honorary degrees! I've been offered 16 to date, and my reasons for not accepting them are twofold, and only one, I'm sure applies to your college. That is, I am not a scholar but a journalist, and have too great a respect for learning, for the hard labor put in by the young in obtaining degrees, to accept them gracefully. Also, the second reason is all colleges are so tied up with the government and funding.

[Robert] Hutchins said they were the heart of the industrial-military conglomerate and so on.

So do excuse me.

A compromise—I'll come speak some time about my recent adventures in jail in California, about the grape strike—about the use of spiritual weapons, etc. etc. It would be a rambling discourse.

I've been traveling since July 30 and feel fine. Recovered from the London flu, which laid me low last winter. I'll keep up the semi-retired fiction to cut out most of my *speaking* and continue to enjoy traveling.

Could you come to N.Y. some time and speak to us on Women's Lib? I feel badly at seeing formerly happy women friends, bitter and angry at all they have suddenly discovered they have suffered. And they get angry at me for not being angry.

After all, even dear Orwell considered some things as *sin* and wrote that we should make a note of it and do penance by going out and planting a tree! Isn't anger a sin?

That was a nice peaceable meeting we had at Tivoli—you and Rosemary Haughton and all of us admiring women. You both stand out in our minds as valiant women. It's just too much, Marge Hughes said afterwards, that you should be beautiful besides.

Love and gratitude (for the help too) that you should have thought of me for that honor.

TO DANIEL BERRIGAN

OCT 25, 1973

What a crowded life we all lead. It was good for all of us to hear from you. We're all in it together and feel close. A good feeling.

Life is so crowded, 4 old women in the next room begin knocking on my door at 5:30 a.m.—all a bit mad. I have to visit the hospital daily, my dear daughter's father [Forster] has had 6 operations while I was in Calif. and is feeling low. Two years older than I. He likes to see me hobble in and out—with a cane. I'm so happy he hangs on to me. Only when he's sick. Usually over the years Mother's Day or Xmas. Family is family no matter how extended. I'll keep your mother in my prayers. I have a list and read it over daily, when I awake and pray (comfortably) in bed. Give her my love and you write and tell her to remember me too.

Put on plenty of warm underwear while picketing! We need you. We love you.

TO FRITZ EICHENBERG

CHRISTMAS, 1973

I must tell you that our Friday meetings are constantly interrupted now by John Stanley and Isadore Fazio who both come to sing a hymn of hate against me and picket and hand out leaflets.* There is such madness going around. I guess we all have to share in the suffering. We've known both for years and love them, so it all hurts. But my mother used to say, "One never gets a lick amiss," meaning, in case you do not understand old New England ideas, that if the blow seems undeserved, there is some other sin which deserves it.

TO CESAR CHAVEZ

Cesar Chavez was the founder and leader of the United Farm Workers Union. Dorothy had supported his cause from the beginning and she regarded him—a dedicated Catholic, an exponent of nonviolence, a champion of the poor—with unlimited admiration and affection.

---

* John Stanley, a former Trappist who gravitated to the CW, had at first venerated Dorothy. Eventually, after becoming disillusioned, he used to picket the Worker and hand out leaflets denouncing her hypocrisy.

MONDAY JAN 21, 1974

It is 4:30 a.m. and I could not sleep any longer for some reason or other, probably because mail to answer is piled up and I have another piece of writing to do, writing an introduction to a little pamphlet, *The Practice of the Presence of God*, by Brother Lawrence back in the 17th century.

But when I started to say my morning prayers—the Creed, the Our Father, and Hail Mary,—I began thinking of you and thought I should write you. Especially not to be discouraged. I feel so sure of your mission that God is with you and is using you and that before the world you are an example of nonviolent action, that at this moment when all seems to be lost (no contracts, the Teamsters victorious—the largest union in the world, a disgrace to the labor movement), you and your people are bringing to others courage to persevere when all seems hopeless. I was reading the 63rd Psalm this morning and it was like a promise. I am really writing to ask you two things—to pray for the Indians who are going to be tried for the Wounded Knee takeover, who are remnant of a conquered people, and who are also our people. They are a constant reminder to us of our sins. You are a link between them and us, part Indian and part white, so you represent us both. And you mean much to the Latin American world.

The other things I would ask you to do is to go to Medellin [Colombia], the conference being held there at the end of February, a small conference of the nonviolent people. It would not take you more than a week I should think, and I could raise the fare to and fro. Dom Helder Camara, I understand, will be there, and Hildegard Goss-Mayr, a woman of great faith in "the little way," and Gordon Zahn, our friend too.

I do firmly believe that in the midst of the violence and threats of our time, this little band of people represent a great truth, which Gandhi brought before the world so unforgettably.

Leave your own immense problems of the Farm Workers Union in the hands of our Lord who loves them far more than you can, and make this pilgrimage of faith, of solidarity with the poor, the destitute of Latin America. You are part of them. They are your people too.

This letter has taken me an hour to write, lying in bed and thinking of you and what you represent and reading again the Magnificat in the first chapter of Luke and the Canticle of Zechariah, and about how God exalts the humble—the poor of the world.

So rejoice that you have such powerful adversaries and go join that small band at Medellin for a few days. God bless you always.

Love and Peace, Dorothy

TO CATHERINE MORRIS

Dorothy had met Catherine Morris, a Holy Child Sister, during her visit to the Ammon Hennacy House of Hospitality in Los Angeles. Here she responds to news that Sister Catherine planned to leave her order to marry Jeff Dietrich, another long-term member of the L.A. CW community. While Dorothy often expressed concern about priests and religious who abandoned their religious vows, in this case she welcomed the union with genuine warmth.

FEB 2, 1974

I am happy indeed for you and Jeff and the Ammon Hennacy house and kitchen, etc. Only today your letter arrived—it had gone to England, Dublin, and only back in the mail at First Street today! I opened it on the Staten Island ferry on my way down with another woman to our beach house to see about freezing pipes. No telephone near—no change—I was tempted to telephone you, I felt so upset at the long delay. You must have wondered at my silence, my seeming indifference, or even suspected me of disapproval of your vital news. So I'll get this in the mail tomorrow and hope it reaches you and does not go wandering as yours to me.

I hope "the criticism which is resulting" is only from the Order, not the house. Our place has been greatly enriched by newly married couples. With children it is different. We have families at the farm. I don't think a house of hospitality is a place to raise kids. My Tamar always lived on the farm.

I'm still traveling and speaking. Last week, 4 days in New England—colleges, Paulists, Trappists. Great response. The Trappists want to get rid of their stocks and bonds but find we are not tax exempt! One can only perform works of mercy with permission of government. We embarrass government greatly.

So we will always have trouble and poverty too! Yet we are being given money for a new house just the same. This work has its exciting moments. Hope you and Jeff give your life to it.

Love to both of you, Dorothy

TO JIM FOREST

Since leaving the Catholic Worker Jim Forest had dedicated himself to the cause of peace—as a founder of the Catholic Peace Fellowship, as a member of the Milwaukee 14, and at the time of this letter as editor of Fellowship *magazine. He had never ceased to feel connected to the CW, and, with Tom Cornell, he had edited* A Penny a Copy: Readings from the Catholic Worker. *Seven years had passed since Dorothy's critical letter to him of March 3, 1967. Now, at the beginning of Holy Week, she evidently felt the time had come to make amends.*

DETROIT, PALM SUNDAY, 7 APRIL 1974
I'm visiting the Detroit CW. Only stationery I can find is this! Lou Murphy is in Henry Ford Hospital with t.b. and I flew out to see him. Tomorrow to Avon, Ohio to see Bill Gauchat, dying of cancer! Home Wednesday.

But I did want to get this letter off to you before Easter to apologize for my critical attitudes and to promise to amend my life!! or attempt to by "mortifying my critical faculties." I don't remember ever hearing you criticize people. Every time I look at *Penny a Copy* I'm grateful to you for working with Tom on it.

So I send you my love this Easter time, and God bless you and yours.

In Christ, Love, Dorothy

TO LOUIS SHEAFFER

Louis Sheaffer was the author of a Pulitzer Prize–winning biography of Eugene O'Neill. Dorothy was among those interviewed for the book.

APRIL 10, 1974

Your book on Gene is the best which ever will be written! I'm engrossed in it. I saw "Moon for the Misbegotten" and "Iceman" both this year. Read the first—reminded me of Chekhov. He, Gene, undoubtedly was a genius as playwright. His last days were tragic. I pray for him often. "May he rest in peace," as Catholics always say. But he'd never be in peace if he could not write and produce plays. So better say "May he be with God." God is truth, Love, wisdom, etc. and somewhere in the Old Testament is the saying "Wisdom is the most active of all active things." Or something like that.

That finale to the "Moon" was the Pietà. Showed his craving for confession and absolution. "We are all sinners—anyone who says he isn't is a liar," St. James wrote in the New Testament. A fact of life. The whole theater seemed to participate—they wept. They also shouted with joy at such theater, such acting! Your book brings me that enthusiasm, hence this letter on recycled paper. Someone ripped off my 1st Vol of yours when Peggy Baird died at our farm. Like ghouls people divide or grab the possessions of the departed. Where can I get a copy? Maybe you can lend me one. I'll keep it under lock and key. Someday I'll write an account of my nights walking the waterfronts with him.

Love and gratitude, Dorothy Day

TO DIXIE MacMASTER

JUNE 7, 1974

One cannot write too much about the new house [Maryhouse], or the details. Conditions are getting so violent in the streets— three of our old women murdered recently. We had been alluding to their plight and a Trappist abbot told me to go find a bigger house for them and he would pay for it. So we are getting an old music settlement with many little private practice rooms and we paid cash—$100,000 for it. But the city has its regulations—more baths, steel, self-closing doors ($350 each) etc., so it will be in the Fall before we're in. We'll have to keep two houses which will be a great expense—but Divine Providence!

Our 85-acre farm, all under cultivation, and practically the "powerhouse" of the county to which the highway police mercifully bring old men in off the road, and other problems, is in danger. The county wants to take over all the old mansions and land around them and make parks and historic sites of them. So we may be moved out yet.

Somehow we manage and find young people recovering from breakdowns and old people dying peacefully with the last rites and loving family around them.

More and more young volunteers are coming as to a school, and then go back to train as doctors and nurses and lawyers and teachers—all this does my heart good. Regular Mass, daily in city and 3 times a week in country, and Vespers and Scripture reading each night.

We have a little house of prayer—really a shack, down on Staten Island, not far from our old place and I am here alone this week, reading Scripture and praying but not being able to get to Mass because the church is 2 miles away and my car broke down. But I begin to feel rested and am looking forward to seeing the abbot (I had never met him) at Piffard N.Y. next week. It is near Buffalo and I have an engagement there, a Franciscan convent.

One of the reasons I have taken these talks is this—the Church has overbuilt and convents are half empty. In Denver last year I came across one Franciscan convent in the center of the city which had given over its entire ground floor to a house of hospitality. Many nuns have left because pastors have built $100,000 places for 8 or 10 nuns, with Sisters with private baths! Many Sisters then go to the other extreme, give up their teaching, become social workers—forget the primacy of the spiritual and embrace voluntary poverty as if that were everything. But it is a scandal—more and more slum clearance and nothing built up in its place for the very low income people. More and more terribly luxurious banks, insurance companies, office buildings— but people sleeping in doorways. I've never in my long life on the East Side—I lived here when I was 18 or 19—remember it so bad. Rents are enormously high for the same old rat-traps. Rents up to $100 or $125 a month for what used to be $18.

TO WILLIAM MILLER

AUG 29, 1974

Here I have been staying at Tivoli for some weeks, surrounded by boxes and boxes of my diaries, notebooks, and engagement books, and am so strongly tempted to throw them in an incinerator that it is hard to resist. What vanity is in us all. They are all so personal, so illegible, so repetitious that I truly do not see how any researcher can get anything of any value out of them. Surely my books are enough—and they too will do a bit of good and then be forgotten.

And yet, and yet! Every time there is a death around here at Tivoli, like Peggy [Baird's], or Emily [Coleman's], everything they possess suddenly disappears. People descend on a room like ghouls to take lamps, blankets, etc., etc., not to speak of books. It is strange and rather terrifying to think of one's death in this context. I will be 77 in Nov. and I am writing you seriously about this. If you want my papers do drive up sometime and take them away.

P.S. I sound rather somber, but I was assured by a heart specialist I would have to rest—too many speaking engagements in the spring, so I cancelled them all. I'm getting much enjoyment out of reading and *not* seeing many visitors. The city where I spent most of the last year or so between trips was too hard—noise, violence, etc. and here it is so quiet, so beautiful.

TO JAMES DOUGLASS

Dorothy had revered Jim Douglass, the lay theologian and activist, as "the best of all the peace group" when she worked with him on the peace lobby at Vatican II. But, as in similar cases, she had pulled back upon news of his divorce and remarriage outside the Church. In light of her recent conciliatory letter to Jim Forest, Douglass evidently hoped her attitude had softened enough to accept one of his articles for the paper.

SEPT 23, 1974

I don't know why I never sent a letter to you when I wrote to Jim Forest, but I've been exhausted, mail is too much for me, times are certainly worse. Nationally and locally, etc. Anyway, I stopped fretting about my venial sins which accumulate with age and feebleness—and neglected the letter to you. I do repent of being judgmental as Jim F. called it, but I cannot condone the irregularity of the lives of our young people and I suffer with the sufferings of the children especially, deprived of father or mother. I've sinned enough to know that most miserable suffering follows for the innocent as well as the guilty.

I'm sorry we cannot use your article. I say *we*, especially thinking of its great length. How could you possibly think we could in our small 8-page paper, use it? My letter to Jim F. probably was not very clear. I did not write about his marriage as I am not writing about yours. I write to say I was sorry I was so judgmental. Personally I have warm feelings of friendship for both of you, talented, adventurous young people (and not so "young" any more) and my very affection makes me suffer that you have lost faith in the Church and its leaders. I really can't consider either of you "Catholic." You see I'm really "rigid," my old Communist, radical background.

Love, nevertheless, Dorothy

TO JEFF DIETRICH, *Los Angeles Catholic Worker*

NOV 11, 1974

I cannot tell you how grieved I was, how shocked to hear the tragic news about Jim's loss of an eye.* What a horrible thing to have happened. I would have written before but I've been sick—some kind of nervous exhaustion which makes me weak and shaking and full of tears. A sudden feebleness, an inability to cope. I did write you a terse note—a line—urged on by Pat about the house. A meaningless gesture, but trying to let you know I was keeping both of you in mind. My further advice is to wait and do nothing about it until the Lord pushes you, one way or another. My sister and I saw "The Cocktail Party" years ago by T.S. Eliot, and in it the psychiatrist advises, "Wait and do nothing," which we take to mean, "Go on doing what you are doing"—and God knows I will keep you closer in my prayers to make up for my not answering you, or trying to comfort you in your misery.

Tell me more about Jim. Is he still with you? Shall I send him a tape recording this Christmas to make up for not being

* A deranged guest at Ammon Hennacy House had attacked one of the volunteers.

able to read easily? Having a totally blind person with us like Deane Mowrer who was blinded late in life (55 or so) makes me more conscious of the tragedy.

Tell your dear wife [Catherine Morris] to write me. We are just sending out our Fall Appeal and maybe will be able to help you more later.

Please pray for me that I recover from this state of feebleness. It should not be this bad at 77 years of age! I'm afraid I aspire to the vigor of Mother Jones. God bless you all there. Oh yes, I meant to ask you—do you have Friday night meetings? Ours are most stimulating and bring in more people to help.

Love and Peace to all of you, especially Jim, Dorothy Day

TO DOROTHY GAUCHAT

NOVEMBER 15, 1974

I have to answer your letter immediately, because certainly you have the hardest kind of suffering and you are paying with blood, sweat and tears for the success you've had, which is just as important in keeping your work going as all the money that has come in to support it. You and Bill and Collette are really paying for the happiness and joy you've brought all these little children. What different crosses we all have. I have just come back from visiting Tamar and have been sitting and weeping this morning because not one of the nine children is practicing the faith and Tamar only speaks of the Church with bitterness, which is certainly like a knife wound in my heart. You should know that I look upon you with envy for such a wonderful group of children and I know that your patience in the past has been an example to me. Your endurance and your suffering in the past over Bill has made me realize that prayers are really answered. I ask you to pray for Tamar especially, because I am sure she left the Church because she could not keep her marriage vows "until death do us part." She just couldn't take it any more and yet blames herself, I am sure, because she couldn't take it any-more.

Give my love to Eric, and David and all of the rest of them, and my special love to Collette, who is another little victim soul. I have been feeling very low physically, all my own fault, after traveling too much and doing too much speaking in the spring and early summer.

TO JOHN EUDES BAMBERGER

John Eudes Bamberger, a psychiatrist and Trappist monk, was abbot of the Abbey of the Genesee in Piffard, New York. The abbey's generous contribution made it possible for Dorothy to purchase Maryhouse, a shelter for homeless women at 55 E. Third St. Dorothy wrote to apprise the abbot on progress toward the opening of the house.

JAN 23, 1975, FEAST OF ST. RAYMOND

Both Ruth [Collins] and I agree you are the kindest of men and we are immensely grateful to you. I am writing in the early morning and I do not want to take up too much of your time by overmuch letter writing.

"The law's delays." But our dear Lord is always with us and there must be some meaning for all this frustration, these impossible demands made on us, always city and state increasing their objections, as to size of rooms, furnishings—everything to be complied with before permit is given. Now another state board, this time of social agencies.

It is *they* who are protecting the poor from well-meaning religious fanatics who would endanger their lives by fire hazards, health hazards, etc. etc.

We are certainly forced into great overcrowding at St. Joseph's House. Even the basement (which has a good toilet and washroom) is occupied at night by 5 "shopping bag women." "Ladies," the social workers call them. I prefer the name "women." Jesus used it too!

Fortunately our guests, who always become permanent, do not mind the crowding as long as they are sheltered and warm. They even sleep in the hall or mailing room, lying on the floor, daytime or nighttime, they do not care. (Social workers say these particular types refuse to go to the one municipal lodging house which holds 45, I think, because their bags and layers of clothing are taken from them and they have to undergo humiliating physical examinations. As a doctor you may be shocked at this, but there is one large public bath on Allen Street where anyone can go, these women included, and under all these layers of rags they are reasonably clean. Also they do not mind (nor do we) using our baths and toilets in each of our 5 floors counting basement. Only occasionally we have found vermin on ourselves which is small penance for the comfort we well know how to make for ourselves.

A holy old Dr. Koiransky, a Russian exile, said to me once it was a miracle we all did not come down with t.b. But he added that soap and water are the best disinfectant. He visited us often, years ago, and knew well how we had to wash the soup bowls every morning after each serving on the "line," perhaps several hundred men mornings, and a hundred of us in the evening. The young people all take their turns cooking too. We get much fruit and vegetables free at the big N.Y. market—stuff which might not keep over weekend. Often Friday nights we have a big fruit salad. People bring us much food, too. It is really shelter which is the great problem.

We cannot write too openly in the CW about Maryhouse, but actually six or eight students from St. Benedict's and St. John's at Collegeville have stayed over the holidays. We have to have 2 men there as night watchmen. We have a night watchman at St. Joseph's too. We are managing, "As deceivers, yet true," as St. Paul wrote. We will be getting into the new house by little and by little. I suggested we move our offices and mailing room over right now and work there so releasing our 2nd floor for women. Those who work with us, Anne, Jane, Terry, and some of the men, have apartments of their own down the street and take in families, runaways, emergencies, and to help them get more permanent care from the City or State. These are compromises we have to make.

Actually all these troubles will work out to our good, to our increased dependence on God, in practicing the little way. We are always being forced back to "the little way." Every home with a Christ room, giving away one's cloak and coat, sharing one's meal. God will not permit us to get too big. He wants us small. My great comfort and joy is that what we do wrong He will correct, as we go along. As in life our senses are "mortified" by increasing age, so also our work.

So I will rejoice that He hath care of us, and all our business. He loves these destitute women more than we do and will temper the wind to the shorn lamb. I am talking to myself in this writing. Patience, patience. It comforts me that the word means suffering. "We are accounted worthy to suffer." So I'll rejoice that you are our friend and helper—that we have your prayers. You see how effective they are. I am truly comforted, writing all this, telling myself too, these things.

I send my grateful love to you and your large family. Looking forward to visiting you in the spring.

TO PAT AND KATHLEEN JORDAN

The Jordans had met and married while living at the New York Catholic Worker, where Pat had also served as editor of the paper. After leaving New York they spent time at Dorothy Gauchat's house in Avon, Ohio, and then at the San Francisco CW community. Later they would return to New York and settle in a cottage on Staten Island next door to Dorothy's island retreat.

ST. SCHOLASTICA, FEB 10, 1975

A bright sunny day at the beach house, St. Teresa's. No wind but a still cold. Such quiet. It is early morning and I am having my hour of psalms and scripture in general. A fountain of refreshment. Ruth Collins to whom I gave a Short Breviary years ago says she now could not do without it. (She pronounces Lauds "Louds," the way I too was taught in public school Latin.) She just says Lauds before beginning her busy day. I'm sticking to *Prayer of Christians*, which is rather cumbersome to carry about. But traveling, I find just a paperback Psalm book and the Gospel of St. John the best "library" to have with me.

I was thinking as I read this morning that after the hard labor you have held up under these last 5 or 6 years, you must both be feeling let down. Especially not knowing what is ahead of you. Just traveling is good—you made a wise choice to get those 60-day tickets. Over the years I found those bus trips not just hardships—they were certainly that during WWII days— but times in the desert, alone on my way, tired from speaking, incapable of anything but still resting in the hands of the Lord— being renewed, in a way. Rest your eyes from reading too— look off into distances and wait for the Lord.

You see I am very much with you. We all love you so much! Miss you so much, but feel you are with us just the same. Such friendships the Lord has sent us in this life. God is good. We can't thank Him enough. Thank you, thank you, Lord, for everything but friendships especially. We are not alone.

I'm writing steadily—an article on the 30s compared to the 70s depression. My last column was pedestrian compared to the other wonderful articles in the paper!! Congratulations, Pat. I'm a terribly slow reader so St. Thomas More was snatched from me before fairly begun. Can't read too much while writing. The article mentioned above is requested by *Newsday* in L.I. Then on with my childhood chapter in my real autobiography.* Even so,

---

* Dorothy entertained the notion of writing a "real autobiography," as opposed to the "story of her conversion" recounted in *The Long Loneliness*. At the same time she wanted to write a book called "All Is Grace," that would tell the story of the CW retreats and the holy priests who had played a role in her life. Neither book ever took shape.

it won't be all—I believe in some reticence for my own sake as well as that of my family and others. A great problem. What do you think?

Much love in Christ. Wait on the Lord, Dorothy

TO KARL MEYER

[FEBRUARY?] 1975

It made me very happy to hear your voice this morning.

Physical weakness, nervous exhaustion, has forced me into taking a quiet time on the beach—you know how I love being near the bay. It is a joy to see the sunrise and the gulls and terns and grebes, to hear the waves. I'm busy with correspondence and trying to write "All is Grace," which has been long in the planning—a mish-mash—story of my childhood, a chapter on the priests I have known—reflections on the changes in the Church, the Pentecostals, the social worker emphasis, etc. etc. Reflections, obituaries, etc. And about death too—in 2 Timothy 1:10 it reads, "Christ Jesus has robbed death of its powers; he brings us light thru the Gospel." Reassuring myself and others too, if this notebook is published.

So many women are writing notebooks—Doris Lessing, Anais Nin—have you read them? I cannot—there is such an absence of the sense of the supernatural.

I'm bold to write you a handwritten note, which doubtless will reveal to you my spiritual and physical states! The *Wall St. Journal* had a front-page column on many businessmen who have applications for employment processed by a firm of handwriting experts.

However I trust in your love and friendship to be tolerant and understanding.

Did you know I now have 11 great-grandchildren, the last three born this winter—all boys? I see little of my dear Tamar, and the nine grandchildren. I feel venerable in the face of all this youth in Vermont and West Virginia. Thank God they are all on the land. Enough. I have piles of mail I should be doing and my 2 or 3 pages daily of "Reflections."

TO BECKY HENNESSY, *Dorothy's oldest grandchild*

APRIL 16, 1975

Just came across St. Justin in an old missal—April 14th. All the old books are obsolete now—they've tossed out half the saints as fairy tales, but we all love fairy tales just the same.

I should put all you families on the mailing list so you can read the columns and get the news.

Will you send me a list? Are Mary, Sue, Maggie, Jo Ann, women lib people and by their own names? I'm always puzzled. Tamar was always Tamar Batterham in school and now too in Forster's will. He calls me up regularly once a week to find out how you all are! Quite proud of *his*! numerous progeny!

I do love you all so much, "you and yours," I always say in my prayers—and *name* you. I treasure the folder of John's [*Becky's husband's*] drawings and have one of his cards,—a branch in one of my prayer books. So I do keep each card and everyone in mind. John does such beautiful work. I hope he keeps it up.

Much love to all of you, Granny

TO JOHN EUDES BAMBERGER

SPRING 1975

Last week I had to go in to an eye doctor. Looking out on the bay I was seeing double, one ship on top of another. While I was in town I stayed at Maryhouse together with five other women. Did I mention that we were taking in all who come to our doors all winter (not those referred to us by agencies), the street women, old and fearful? Two young men going to college help at

St. Joseph's house in their spare time, sleep on the top floor. There are none except five windows being broken. It was wonderful to be at the house the four nights and get a feel of the place. I have been in fear and trembling many a time, you may be sure, at the largeness of this undertaking, especially when I talk so much of the Little Way.

Did I tell you that there are forty or more little houses of hospitality around the country now? But this is in a way the heart of the work, the synthesis of what Peter Maurin used to call "Cult, Culture, and Cultivation." Religion is the basis of everything in our lives, all beauty and joy, music, art, study, sculpture, stained glass, even the gargoyles on the Cathedrals teaching us the joy men expressed in their work, the work of their hands.

At St. Joseph's we have a Mass every Monday night and people feel so at home at the CW that more and more are coming in, and the deep reverence and quiet are most impressive, and this from the most troublesome of the street people, men and women. At our Friday night meetings we have had sisters and priests, Sister Caridad of the Philippines, Fr. Janda, S.J. about the Sioux Indians, Father [Henri] Nouwen on hospitality, and many laymen too. We try to make the place beautiful, not like an institution, and people feel free there, part of a family, helping fold papers, put stickers on, mail out the 85,000 copies of the paper sent out nine times a year. (And they like to see their names mentioned, as part of the work.)

We cannot mention it in the paper but we have had as many as four disturbed or drunken women sleeping in our basement, on benches drawn together so they will be wide enough. They do not hesitate to come in and stretch out on three chairs for a daytime catnap. Many of them are like wild things who will answer no questions and if you try to probe or talk to them even, they will flee to their streets or empty buildings or cellars or wherever it is they take shelter.

Sometimes the place is orderly and quiet and one sees nothing out of the way. Sometimes it seems to me like a school, or a Quaker work camp where young people pay to come to work and learn about conditions. But it is a school in its way, and Sisters spend vacations with us and college students and graduates, staying until they have made up their minds exactly what they want to do with their lives. Pat Jordan was such and what a loss, that after five years he has gone back to California, he and his wife. We miss them sorely. They literally washed the feet of others, old people, crippled people, etc. Kathleen finished her nurse's training course while she was with us.

 With love and gratitude, Dorothy

TO WILLIAM MILLER

TIVOLI, JUNE 20, 1975

Here I am at the Peacemakers meeting—we are 100 or more, including a gang of little kids. Very sultry, and people have poison ivy and lice, bird lice and human, one or two cases, and I have mites. Did you ever hear of them? They end in scabies, always associated with dirty people! I scrub daily—fortunately I'm next to the bath, but itch nevertheless. Penance I do not do. I have it inflicted on me! The dear Lord knows what I need—penance for my lack of charity.

 When this peacemaking group are gone, I'll call the family here at Tivoli together and discuss the practically of a sale, and decentralizing, getting back to the "little way." "Small is beautiful."

 Which reminds me—we did not talk of Peter Maurin and Ralph Borsodi, with whom he spent much time. He was all for the ideas of [E.F.] Schumacher, Bob Swann, Borsodi, etc., which I did not understand, nor take to at the time. The land, decentralization, intermediate technology, the money problem, all these ideas occupied Peter. I'm afraid I was a disappointment to him. There was much I left out. Money, interest, etc. Bob Swann talked at our Friday night meeting last week. Very good. On Land Trusts.

P.S. Next day. Two "lights" came to me as I did my spiritual reading this morning. One—why not *lend* me your car? Two: I must make a will to leave all my papers and notebooks to you. I've seen too many of my fellow workers die in the CW movement, i.e. Peggy [Baird], for instance, and their books and papers scattered. (I feel well so do not think I'm morbid.)

How you can bear to mess about with so much paper, I don't know. You tell me to save stuff, so I do, but it means my desk is a mess, my room is a mess. Evidently I am not a "detached" person. Too much self-esteem. Why do I consider my ruminations, the "lights" that come to me, important? To justify myself, I'd say it is part of poverty. I'm like the poor who surround themselves with clutter. I'm like the "shopping bag ladies" who accumulate more and more! Oh dear, please excuse me, for thus excusing myself, an untidy, disorganized person.

TO EUNICE SHRIVER

Eunice Shriver, sister of President John F. Kennedy and the wife of Sargent Shriver, was a friend to Dorothy and a supporter of the Catholic Worker. As founder of the Special Olympics, she achieved international recognition for her work on behalf of the mentally handicapped.

SUNDAY JULY 6, 1975

Thank you for your letter, and for your offer of an air conditioner. But really I do not need it. I'd rather have open windows, with variations in climate—I love all the changes in weather and the moods it puts one in.

I meant to write you before to ask if you read the two two-page accounts of the one-tenement project in Harlem which a few of us have been working on for some years. They are badly in need of a grant and surely this is a family project. My heart goes out to slum families. Our work in the Bowery area is surely the "folly of the Cross," seemingly, but the Lord seems to want it.

Right now I am staying at the Tivoli farm, New York, and did not answer your letter because I left it in New York and did not have your address. We have just had a conference of young people—almost 100 of them, and our usual population of about sixty people, including a number of mothers for thirty children, a score of old men "off the road" whom highway police bring in to us, and college students. There is a good staff and 12 acres of garden, half-a-dozen goats and a cow. We are right on the Hudson River in an old mansion and two other buildings. I am getting plenty of fresh air.

I meant to write you before to thank you for your hospitality and to tell you how much I enjoyed being with the children that night. What with my own daughter, nine grandchildren, and eleven great-grandchildren I am very much a family person, so I felt at home as your guest.

Belatedly I am sending a set of my paperbacks, marking the package "personal, please forward," so you will eventually get them.

I can write about religion, converts are deeply grateful, but it is hard to talk about. Scripture, the *Imitation of Christ,* and the *Confessions* of St. Augustine are my regular reading. They pull me out of the doldrums.

I have often said "Lord I believe, help my unbelief." Or "In peace is my bitterness most bitter." But faith is always there in spite of dry or bitter days. My mother used to say, "Work is the only thing that helps."

With love, faithfully yours in Christ,
Dorothy Day

TO KARL STERN

Karl Stern, a psychiatrist from Montreal, was a long-time friend of Dorothy and a regular visitor at Tivoli. He was the author of Pillar of Fire, *the story of his conversion from Judaism to Catholicism.*

JULY 6, 1975

This little Sunday morning note is to beg you to suffer in patience my inability to visit, or to get a review finished in time for the mid-summer *CW*, except for mentioning it in my column. I am truly *powerless* to get it reviewed in the *Times* or *NY Review of Books*. We can only trust to prayer. These I am sure are answered. God hears us and sends us what we need. Do trust in Him.

I read the *Imitation of Christ* every morning, a chapter, then the Psalms—often a great cry of woe. I love C.S. Lewis' *Reflections on the Psalms*. You should try to get it. It will nourish your soul.

Tivoli is teeming. So many suffering people—if it were not for the chapel I would be overwhelmed by it. We have no priests with us—"Least said, soonest mended,"—a good old saying. But we have the Blessed Sacrament. We go to Confession and Mass to the Village church, St. Sylvia's.

Excuse this scrawl, and pray for me too.

Love, Dorothy

TO FATHER FRANCIS BUTLER

Executive Director, National Conference of Catholic Bishops
Committee for the Bicentennial

Dorothy responded to an invitation from the U.S. bishops to attend a meeting in anticipation of the nation's bicentennial. The requested topic: "The Role of Christians in Laboring for the Poor." (Although in this letter she appears to decline the invitation, she did end up attending the meeting in Newark, New Jersey.)

SEPTEMBER 2, 1975

Please forgive the informality of this note, but I am in bed with a cold and arthritis, and there being no secretaries around the Catholic Worker, I must answer as I can.

First, let me thank you for asking me to speak or "testify"

or make suggestions at one of the Bishops' hearings that are being held. I am greatly honored and would dearly like to be there and greet again my dear friends Cardinals McIntyre and Manning, as well as others whom I feel I know by reputation and concern with the workers, and with voluntary poverty.

I have had to give up these speaking engagements which take their toll and leave it to the younger members of the Catholic Worker community who are as able as I am to respond to the problems and questions of the day.

P.S. In answer to your own understanding postscript, I'd like to add this: One of our young intellectual friends went to interview Lewis Mumford, a truly great man, and asked him what message would he give the American people during the Bicentennial. He answered one word: "Repent." How can anyone add to that?

TO TAMAR

SEPTEMBER 3, 1975

I'm writing rather than telephoning because Frank Donovan says we are very low in funds—he was paying every bill as it came up for Maryhouse and I have to write the Appeal to mail out Oct first before I come up. I'm dying to see all of you, all the babies. What a family! Even Forster is proud of it and when I am in the city calls up weekly to ask how you all are.

I've cancelled the 3 speaking engagements I had for October because I just felt too weak in the head as well as the body and even my voice was failing me.

The work going on here now is very good. Marvelous garden—we planted more than we can use or can. Better have only root crops, cabbage, onions, potatoes, squash, etc. What can be saved without expense of canning.

Natural gas is going up, as is oil in price, and of course we burn too much electricity. Times now are far worse than in the Thirties, the "Great Depression." Gloomy outlook but the "land movement" is surely flourishing. People look to you and Chuck Smith as models of survival.

Our casino is full of men off the road, young and old, out of jails and mental hospitals. One young girl, Dolores, is going to have a baby and there are other "disturbed young ones" coming out of it and working with us.

Not sure yet when I can get up. But will keep in touch.

It is quiet and beautiful here now, and to be a hermit as well as a member of a community is wonderful. It is not good for man to be alone. I am glad you have your family around you. Never a dull or idle moment! Always some misery but much joy too.

Love always, Granny

TO SISTER PETER CLAVER

Sister Peter Claver, a member of the Missionary Servants of the Most Blessed Trinity, was one of Dorothy's oldest friends. According to an oft-told story, it was Sister who contributed the first dollar when Dorothy was raising money to launch The Catholic Worker.

SEPT 8, 1975

Today is a feast of the Blessed Mother and tomorrow your feast day and I will read the life of St. Peter Claver in my Thurston-Attwater *Lives of the Saints* and think most especially of you.

So long since we have seen each other. My life has become one of physical weakness (heart failure, the doctor says, but that is not so ominous as it sounds). Also much continued hard work—here at Tivoli all summer, and much mail and writing to do, and visitors daily, and my great suffering—to live in the midst of 70 people of whom only a scant half dozen get to Mass at the parish and our own Vespers and Compline daily. And yet when we have a visiting priest, all go.

In N.Y. the group of 8-12 young people are daily communicants (Nativity around the corner, Jesuits, and 3 Masses daily) and at 7 each night recite Vespers together with the daily reading from Scripture. Our readers increase, 90,000 papers go out. Appeals get answered and we have bought and reconditioned another house of hospitality, Maryhouse.

Here at the farm we have had two priests who have now departed. (Least said, soonest mended, my dear mother used to say.) They were loved by the young people, much hard labor was accomplished, but there has been a great falling away of devotions of any kind—including daily Mass. When we do have a priest for Sundays they all go, and receive too. Catholic and non-Catholic! Children (unprepared) and adults (unshriven). I'm considered an ancient, an old fogey, and the more praise given me by the press—by those who do not know me—the more the young edge away from me.

In other words, I can be happy over that jewel of faithfulness in the slum, St. Joseph's house, but sad indeed at the spiritual misery of Tivoli, which is set in the most beautiful surroundings.

So I really should stay here and suffer. We do have a gem of a chapel and permission for the Blessed Sacrament. What an immense consolation. And also I have to learn daily, over and over, not to judge. But how not to? And yet it is far better now than when the two priests were here.

None of my grandchildren practice their faith—only one married in the Church. Yet some great-grandchildren are baptized at once, at birth—I do not like to check up on the others.

So you see I am not giving you any presents, but prayers of gratitude for your friendship and begging your prayers now.

To add another grotesque and horrible misery descended on me—two of the most brilliant women associated with our movement have come to me to proclaim themselves lesbians.

Scripture—St. Paul's writings—no attention is paid to that. It is all "women's lib." And I am just not "with it" any more and you can imagine the kind of desolation I feel.

At the same time, I'm getting much consolation from Pope John's *Journals* and his letters to his family.

"To know how to suffer! This is the great art of living. . . . This is the art of becoming holy without much cost." !!!

Much, much love to you, dearest Sister. I've not been doing any traveling except short visits to my sister nearby and daughter in Vermont.

Again love, in Christ, Dorothy

TO WILLIAM MILLER

Dorothy went back and forth on the question of cooperating with Dr. Miller and his plans to write her biography.

OCT 8, 1975 TIVOLI

I wish you would wait till I'm dead before digging up many aspects of my life I am ashamed of. I cannot bear to read about myself *in any guise*—that is why I have not read *A Harsh and Dreadful Love.*

After all, I am 78 next month, and not active like Mother Jones, so cannot expect to live much longer. Dwight Macdonald asked me once why I had not written of that early marriage—I said I did not write about what I was ashamed of. The confessional dealt with that.

I have always said *"The Long Loneliness* is *not* an *autobiography."*

Please respect my privacy—what I have left of it. Sometimes I wish I had never started this archive business. I feel at times as tho I were being skinned alive, flayed. I suppose I deserve it.

Excuse my petulance. It's the cold in the head.

Love, Dorothy

OCT 20, 1975

About my marriage—I'll tell you more about it some time. It lasted less than a year. I married a man on the rebound, after an unhappy love affair. He took me to Europe and when we got back I left him. I felt I had used him and was ashamed. I never pretended *The Long Loneliness* was an autobiography. That was a publisher's term.*

I enjoyed your long letter. I'm happy at your being near the archives too, and teaching there [at Marquette University]. If you go there, I will surely visit there.

Love to all of you, Dorothy

TO NINA POLCYN [MOORE]

DEC 8, 1975

[FEAST OF THE IMMACULATE CONCEPTION]

An upsurge of strength has meant my accepting speaking engagements—the charismatics in Atlantic City (wonderful experience!)—a talk to the Eastern Bishops!!!—a visit to Alderson Federal Prison for women in W. Va. with Sister Margaret Ellen Traxler and a group of Sisters and two women lawyers. Sister Traxler is head, I guess, of a Coalition of Catholic, Protestant and Jewish women. I think they are trying to get me on their side (women priests, etc.). But I'm just an old conservative.

It is raining and snowing out. Today is our anniversary. In 1932 I prayed at the Washington Shrine to the Blessed Mother to open up a way to work for the revolution!! When I got back to N.Y. Peter Maurin was waiting for me.

I must telephone my sister-in-law Tessa to thank her for her Spanish hospitality. My 100% American brother would have dismissed him [Peter] as an undesirable former associate radical looking for a handout!! But God bless John and Tessa, too. They made him most welcome after I got back.

---

* Dorothy's brief marriage in 1920 to Berkeley Tobey, founder of the Literary Guild of New York, remains a mysterious episode in her life. This terse summary is as much as she ever wrote about the subject.

Tonight we have Mass here at St. Joseph's house. Celebration. My love to you and yours.

TO FRANK DONOVAN

NEW YEAR'S EVE, 1975

A letter from Arthur E.P. Wall (his check enclosed) says he is sending me a *personal present* of the *American Catholic Who's Who*. Do put it in my room. My memory is so poor and my spelling of people's names so incorrect (insulting, such inaccuracies!) that I'd like to see it, or at least have it available. Some books have to be locked up to keep people from stealing. I get tired of offering my cloak too after my coat has been taken. But Fr. Hugo says, or quotes, "He who says he has done enough has already perished!!!" What a man! Will I ever reform? My New Year's resolution—stop complaining!

It is good to be recovering from unutterable fatigue—sitting for 8 and 10 hours straight by Helene [Iswolsky's] bedside. And then the funeral in the midst of snow and sleet! Peggy [Scherer] saw to everything, opening the grave, from the Tivoli end. She is invaluable. I'm glad she'll take a month in the city, to know all aspects of the work. I love her. She has all the virtues I lack—silence, self-discipline, perseverance, etc. to an nth degree.

I must be more like you and not worry about money. I am an extravagant and self-indulgent person in my own ways and you are the most kind and indulgent—to others—and hard-on-yourself man. God bless you always. I do love you and am most grateful to you. This is a Christmas and New Year's letter and my New Year's resolution is to speak less, do more, judge not, pray without ceasing, grow in love, etc. etc.

"It is never too late to turn a new leaf." With this original remark I'll close.

Pass on my love and greetings to all, Dorothy

P.S. When you do not call I think some disaster has happened and you do not want to worry me with it. But I'm sure it is too much of an extravagance to call up here, so don't worry. I know how busy you all are.

TO WILLIAM MILLER

JAN 26, 1976

Did I understand you, did I read your letter aright? Is Marquette really getting *Rockefeller* grants to collect our archives? It cannot be true. Certainly it would mean that from now on, no more materials will be sent. I will also repudiate as historians [*sic*] since from now on we will put the archives in other hands, in some way to save them. Stanley has been taking care of boxes and boxes of them from the first days, even to every leaflet we distributed on the streets of New York, and he feels as I do. I am writing also to Marquette. I am really shocked. You know we refused Ford money.*

I've been ill and only half read my mail. Cannot keep up with it. So I missed your Jan 9 letter telling me this news. Also, I certainly do not want to be interviewed, interrogated about parts of my own story I have left out. Why I have not awakened to the fact that you are doing *my* biography, not Peter's as I asked you, I do not know. Not even the CW story!

I do not mind sending boxes of letters (I never write carbons) and even pages and pages of my own notebooks, but I did not send them *to be published*. They are notes for a continued autobiography which I will do myself. I remember asking you to send me the carbons of the notebooks you had your daughter type before you sent them, the diaries, to Marquette. But you never did.

---

* In 1956 Milton Mayer of *The Progressive* magazine suggested that the Ford Foundation would be happy to extend a grant to the CW. Dorothy declined, citing her commitment to personal responsibility.

However, I won't be bothered with this much longer. Born in '97, I'll be eighty very soon.

Surely you do not forget the Ludlow Colorado massacre, and the recent Attica tragedy. The Rockefeller name continues to be disgraced. We cannot be associated with it.*

TO DIXIE MacMASTER

FEB 5, 1976

How wonderful to have a letter from you with its picture of you and the news of Mother Teresa which is always so inspiring. The two pictures of her relaxed and smiling face, her vigor and joy is so impressive—I love her dearly and regard the time I spent in Calcutta with her as one of the peak experiences of my life, to use a phrase of the pagan [Abraham] Maslow, a professor at Harvard, whom I met several times. And to have that lovely, happy picture of *you*! How grateful I am to you for this rich feast which I had with my breakfast. When I read her schedule, I feel myself to be a pipsqueak, as Ammon used to call us shirkers.

You do get the paper don't you with its news of what is happening? I always feel that my "On Pilgrimage" should be a letter to all our friends. On the other side of this sheet you will see how I spent my Christmas, neither at St. Joseph's House nor Maryhouse, nor Tivoli, nor my sister's, nor my daughter's. I am always so torn between all my loves. It is a simplified, prayerful time for me, a holy time, a happy time.

Also a very mixed up time, what with a great feeling of weakness and a diminishing strength. I am using an electric typewriter and must go slow and try not to make so many mistakes. Also spaced so I can get more on a page to keep the letter from

---

* As Dorothy noted in her diary, "Prof. Miller wrote terse letter . . . pledging himself not to use any Rockefeller funds for archives or his work."

being too heavy. Mail rates have gone up so that we are acknowledging answers to appeals with a card such as the enclosed and pay nine cents instead of thirteen. Our readers love the prayers. We try to answer every note we receive, every dollar that comes in, and people are grateful. I understand from other groups that they never thank their contributors. A tremendous number of appeals go out, my sister's mail box is always full of them, she says, and she tries to discriminate but often sends a little to each one.

I do thank you for the help you sent. I hope you reap a hundredfold in all blessings. Your happy face in that picture, and the two lovely ones of Mother Teresa in the bulletin, also radiate joy. "The joy of the Lord is your strength," writes St. Paul. I am busy with writing, with answering mail and with visitors, and often envy the young their strength as I see them doing heavy housework around here. But I am deeply thankful that we have such helpers. And especially dedicated ones who intend to make the CW their lifework.

Next November I will start my 80th year! Doesn't it seem extraordinary how time flies? I still must take speaking engagements, when I am able, just from pure gratitude for all the help we have been given all over the country in starting this new house. You cannot conceive of the obstacles placed in the way by the state, fire departments, building departments and health departments. In the face of the homelessness around us and people we know living in buildings which have been abandoned, without heat, light, or water (they come for meals to us) we are forbidden to have more than just so many guests, and we had to make changes which cost $125,000 and more before we could move in!

At least we have a certificate of occupancy. We have joyful young volunteers, two or three of them Sisters who are glad to be able to work so closely with the poor. Little by little rooms are prepared and furnished, some only with bed and a chair, but we are warm and sheltered. We are thirty in the house now and there will be room for thirty more. We may get permission to have the Blessed Sacrament with us. But the Church is around the corner and we say Vespers each night.

Will you pray for Tamar and her brood, most of whom are not practicing their faith! Distance from the Church and a sense of distance from the parishioners and a feeling that they are regarded as crackpots in their rejection of "bourgeois values" and living (in a way) in squalor with their spinning and weaving and a house full of looms and handicrafts and even the baby chicks and the goats brought in the kitchen for warmth as they are newborn. But I see signs of their coming back, in their reading of spiritual books and praying and meditating daily as many of the young do.

Also pray for Forster, Tamar's father, who has had one cancer operation after another and gone through a long agony. He always calls me for visits when he goes to the hospital and for a while there I had to visit both him and Helene [Iswolsky] when they were both in intensive care. But he hangs on to life. He is 80. His grandchildren write him, though they have never met him.

Tamar is as taciturn as he, but she always asks for him, as he does for her. In becoming a Catholic I deprived him of a child whom he loved the first two years of her life and he felt her loss keenly. The children (his progeny, he calls them) now number nine grandchildren and eleven great-grandchildren. It rather amuses him, since he always thought the world was overpopulated and with its terrible problem of world hunger. But he asks after them all when we visit and he clings to me, and I tell him I pray for him. So you do too, and I know he will turn to God at the end. Prayers *are* answered.

Much love always, Dorothy

TO BILL OLEKSAK

Bill Oleksak was a friend of many years. He occasionally treated Dorothy and other Catholic Workers to plays or evenings at the opera.

*Dorothy writes here of her recent attraction to the Catholic charis-
matic movement.*

MAY 13, 1976

Did you hear the "Flying Dutchman" the other night? At my
age it is far more comfortable to sit at home and both watch
and hear the opera than it is to go to Lincoln Center. But I
was certainly happy to go together with you; otherwise I
could never have seen the new opera house these times in the
past.

Let me say again how I enjoy the postals you send me, and
that I have a very good collection of them in different parts of
the world, reproductions of paintings, men and women at work
(especially manual labor), and after I have enjoyed them for a
few years, I do some of my correspondence on them so that others can enjoy them too. That's why I like to have blank cards.
It's a great savings of money, on postage.

Much love and gratitude, Dorothy

P.S. Knowing your very reserved disposition, I hesitate to make
this recommendation, but feel I must do it, and that is, that if
you ever get a chance to go to a Pentecostal (Charismatic) prayer
meeting, go. I have been to not more than 4 actual Pentecostal
meetings, but felt that there was really prayer, thanksgiving,
praise, and a sense of joy there. You will just be part of a congregation; you don't have to become involved, except inwardly.
You certainly don't have to speak with tongues, which I think
makes some people feel frightened. The Pope has rejoiced in it
and so has Cardinal Suenens, and I want to share my own joy
with you. So do a little asking of priests and Sisters in whatever
town you happen to be in your travels. And also pray to God that
you find one.

TO THE PRESIDENT OF SANTA CLARA UNIVERSITY

MAY 17, 1976

Dear Father Terry:

I wish colleges would stop offering me honorary degrees which I must in conscience refuse, but wish to refuse with all respect and gratitude. Whoever is responsible for making such an offer to me certainly knows nothing of the philosophy of the Catholic Worker movement, nor of its aims, which are not only to treat all creatures as members of a family, but to so change society that we will be building that kind of society "where it is easier to be good," to use the simple words of our founder, Peter Maurin, a French peasant.

The very offer of an honorary degree means that in a way I have failed to convey—to popularize—Peter Maurin's teaching. He liked slogans. He was an advocate of the "personalist and communitarian revolution," which stemmed from the teaching of such men as Emmanuel Mounier in Paris, Nikolai Berdyaev, a Russian exile, and Charles Péguy in Paris. Small beginnings of this revolution were made in Paris, in the Thirties, through a monthly review, *Esprit*. Peter brought it to America and we learn thru a recent issue of *The Nation* (March 6) that an American priest has been assassinated, others put into prison and exiled, preaching a nonviolent "revolution" in Honduras. (What they were advocating was redistributing land to the peasants, cooperatives, and credit unions, and of course education to achieve these aims nonviolently.) "Unless the grain of wheat falls into the ground and dies, it remains alone. If it dies it bears much fruit." This is one of the promises of Christ. So ideas spread.

The slogans of this revolution used to be "War is the health of the State" and "Property is Theft," which will be recognized as the words of philosophical anarchists such as Kropotkin and Proudhon, not Communists, not Socialists. I am coming to the conclusion that "personalist" is a better word than "anarchist," now that the influence of the word "nonviolent" is beginning to be understood. When Kropotkin and Proudhon and Ferrer were alive, the intellectual context of "anarchist" was understood.

We must keep in mind those slogans, however, recognizing what the United States stands for in the world today.

We must also resist "funding" by our government as well as honors from colleges, many of which are so "funded" in one way or another, for R.O.T.C. and research (often, if not always, military).

To conclude, love of country is not synonymous with love of governments. We wish to be able to grow in that love as we did on learning that the Alexian Brothers turned over their unused property in Wisconsin to the Indians who claimed it as their own in all justice.

When colleges and universities, sectarian and non-sectarian, begin to preach voluntary poverty and restitution, plus the new economics of E. F. Schumacher, the non-Keynesian English economist, and of Robert Swann, the American activist war resister, real beginnings will be made toward a realistic peace, towards building "a society where it is easier to be good."

Sincerely, Dorothy Day

TO HER PUBLISHER

Dorothy wrote to the publisher of Curtis Books, which had recently reissued three of her books in a mass market paperback format and had plans—never fulfilled—to publish her columns from the 1930s, 40s, and 50s. She felt her columns from the thirties did not adequately represent her activities during those historic years.

JULY 28, 1976

I am rather concerned about my own "On Pilgrimage." When I was ruining my eyesight reading through the early On Pilgrimages which were then called Day by Day I became very troubled at the idea of their *representing* the Thirties. I had personally covered a good deal of the organizing in the Thirties, meeting Harry Bridges and John Brophy, attending the first CIO convention in Atlantic City, for instance. We fed the East Coast striking seamen while they were organizing the union headed by Joe Curran, who's as bad as the longshoreman's boss; ran into a lot of trouble with the Church every time there was a strike, such as the National Biscuit Co. strike, the Singer Sewing Machine strike. I wrote articles and editorials on the Spanish Civil War, a war which cut down our circulation by half. I was in Chicago just before the Memorial Day massacre of the steelworkers after I had gone to the priests in South Chicago urging them to be on the side of the workers and visit their union hall; we were practically endangering our lives covering anti-Semitism in Brooklyn.

And then I see your preparation to bring out the Thirties columns so filled with sweet nothings about my little daughter and Freddie Rubino that I protested to Betty. Betty's reply was that you had ordered her only to paste up articles *signed* by me. And I do hope that some change has been made in the set-up of The Thirties. The very contrast between our idyllic lives around the Catholic Worker headquarters and the turmoil the world was in at the time was brought out very clearly in the paper. I am sure that my personal articles in the column were an appeal to the people to take a more human view of what was happening and to come out of their apathy and their prejudice and their indifference. I've called you several times but I have not been able to reach you, probably on weekends when I had more leisure, probably a foolish time to try to get you, or Betty either. I am hoping you have not already gone to press but if you have I certainly would like to be able to write an introduction to the book bringing out some of these ideas.

TO JOHN PAPWORTH

John Papworth, an Anglican priest, was an economic advisor to President Kenneth Kaunda in Zambia. Dorothy was delighted to receive his

*book about alternative economics, in which she found concordances
with the philosophy of Peter Maurin.*

AUGUST 12, 1976

I cannot tell you how happy your letter made me and I woke up
this morning with a sense of joy and a feeling that I must write
to you at once. The Holy Spirit is certainly moving in the world.
Peter Maurin, the founder of our work, used to talk constantly of
the "primacy of the spirit," and every day saw him going to a
noonday Mass and spending an hour in adoration in the church
which certainly gave him the energy to continue late in the
night his contacts with people and conversations with them. He
brought to us Emmanuel Mounier and his emphasis on the life
of the spirit. They called it the Personalist and Communitarian
revolution, and recently in Honduras, according to the *Nation*, a
liberal magazine, young priests have been exiled from the country or imprisoned and, in one case, assassinated for preaching
the Personalist revolution. Recently, at the 41st World Eucharistic Congress, I met Dom Helder Camara, who embraced me
with such warmth as you only find in the Renewal movement
which is so strong in Latin American and South America.

Perhaps you can write to us about it and tell us what is happening in Africa. I am going to make copies of your letter and
send them to friends who are more immersed in the communitarian aspects, or the social aspects, than in the life in the spirit.

Meanwhile, I send my love and do beg that you will drop
me a line personally if you have time. Since your letter is not a
personal one, I feel at liberty to reprint it in the *Catholic Worker*.

TO FATHER PAUL LACHANCE

*Fr. Lachance, a Franciscan, lived in a community of "worker priests"
in Chicago, but often visited the Catholic Worker. Peggy Scherer and
Chuck Matthei, whom Dorothy mentions, came to the Worker by way
of Peacemakers, a pacifist movement dedicated to nonviolent direct*

action against war. Peggy stayed on at Tivoli and later became man-aging editor of the paper. Chuck was more of a "one man revolution," as Ammon Hennacy would have put it. Though he never called him-self a Christian, it was Dorothy's conviction that he lived more faith-fully by the Sermon on the Mount than anyone else she knew.

AUGUST 12, 1976

I woke up this morning with a feeling that I ought to write to you to beg your prayers for Chuck Matthei. Ever since Peggy Scherer's return to the Church, and I am sure he must feel this too, I've felt how good it would be if this very ardent and very intelligent worker for social justice would have the joy that we have in the sacraments. Probably I shouldn't say return to the faith because I don't know if he ever was a Catholic—but then I felt the same way about Peggy—I thought she was a Protestant in her Christian ded-ication to peace and was amazed when her stepmother told me that she had returned to the faith since your visit.

I would love to see you again to tell you of my own joy in the Renewal which I can see taking place all over the world and to my great joy is emphasizing the needs of the poor and afflicted. I recently had a letter from Zambia from John Papworth, the former editor of *Resurgence*, which we consider a companion paper to ours in England. He and [E. F.] Schumacher, the econo-mist who wrote *Small is Beautiful*, are to my mind very impor-tant to the whole movement, especially when I hear of the developments in Augusta, Georgia and Houston, Texas, where people in the Renewal are literally selling what they have and building up communities where they can share with the poor.

When I look at Peggy and Chuck in their youth and energy, I feel that we must pray for them to have the strength to work for peace and justice which can only come with a strong life in the spirit.

P.S. I just learned that Chuck is descended from a long line of Orthodox Rabbis!

TO TAMAR

AUGUST 19, 1976

Here I am in Pittsburgh again making one of Fr. Hugo's famous retreats, a time of silence in a beautiful convent in a suburb—like Oakmont was. Good meals, beautiful weather and complete silence. We are on top of a hill, looking over valleys to houses on the top of other hills. Everything green—surrounded by orchards and pine trees—only the hum of the city far away. Only 8 of us, each with a private room.

After having to speak at the Eucharistic Congress in Philadelphia to 8,000 women, the silence and rest are wonderful.* This weekend I'll go over to Dorothy Gauchat—not too far away. Cecilia Hugo will drive me. It will be good for her to see the work there with all the little brain-damaged and crippled kids. When they are 8 years old they are supposed to give them up to the state to end up in big institutions. But Dorothy has extended the work to another house nearby, a little farm and a big house, and they can stay there as adults even and have gardens and crafts, etc. Two of our NY staff, Kathleen and Pat [Jordan], are living there now and will take care of that end of the work.

Our summer at the farm, what with Peggy in charge—she is 25, a former Peacemaker who came back to the Church—is all going smoothly now. Joan Welch helps me with letters and taking dictation.

TO VIRGINIA GARDNER

Virginia Gardner helped arrange for Dorothy's trip to Russia. She often sent Dorothy books by Chekhov and other Russian authors.

---

* On August 6, Dorothy spoke at the Eucharistic Congress in Philadelphia on the topic "Women and the Eucharist." She used the occasion to link the Sacrament with the cause of peace, noting the anniversary, on that date, of the dropping of the atomic bomb on Hiroshima.

[C. SEPTEMBER 1976]

How good you are to think of me. Thank you! And here I burden you with another request. I want to read Marx. I visited his grave in London and the British Museum where he wrote, and yet never read *anything* he wrote. My sister-in-law [Lily Burke] who worked at the Marxist library tried some years ago—should have asked her then. My ignorance is colossal. I'm having a good rest here at Tivoli but will come down when the equinoctial storms come.

Sitting out in the sun now reading *China Shakes the World* by Jack Belden—a good travel book. Much love to you. You'll have to come to dinner in my suite at Maryhouse on 3rd St. when I come to N.Y.

TO FORSTER BATTERHAM

MONDAY SEPT 14, 1976

What with a heart attack—a coronary, the doctor said—I've been ten days in bed. Have to stay in bed another week. Then to the hospital for a cardiogram (?). We have a doctor friend in Kinderhook, N.Y. where Della lived, and his wife is the librarian there so I've known them a long time. Thank goodness he did not put me in the hospital intensive care. He believes in home care, thank goodness.

The best part of my illness was being able to skip a gathering here at the farm of all the East Coast Catholic Worker houses. There were 60 people besides our own staff of 40 or so, and much talk. Weekends are crowded, but days quiet, so these last sunny days I have sat out in the sun and watched the river and shipping, large and small, going by. Today, Monday, it was beautiful and I am feeling better after all the sleeping I've done. Thank the Lord for radio. I have a good one and get good symphonies thru Albany Medical College Station. Tamar drove down or rather was driven down with Nicky and one of his friends Sunday afternoon and was on time for the baptism of your latest great-grandchild—Charlotte Rose. We run to girls you notice. In case you forget—your grandchildren are Becky, Susie, Eric, Nickie, Mary, Maggie, Martha, Hilaire, and Katy. 9.

And great-grandchildren: Lara and Justin,—Tanya, Kachina, and Charlotte Rose, Shawn Patrick, Sheila, Joshua, Jude, and another due this month—Forest—Oak—thirteen *great*-grandchildren in all. All these are your progeny! None live in the city, all raise their food, and hunt and fish. A good life. They enjoy it.

Much love to you and Pat. Dorothy

TO MARGE HUGHES

Marge Hughes first came to the Worker in 1939. She served as Dorothy's secretary and raised her family on a succession of CW farms—Easton, Pennsylvania, Newburgh, Staten Island, Tivoli.

OCT 5, 1976

St. Bruno says nature—the beauty of nature, is very healing. I believe it. (But I wish we were down on the S.I. beach. What a wonderful winter that was!)

When I sat out yesterday I saw a flock of wild geese (and what a noise!). That was the second following the river route south. It is very still today, no shipping, no trains, since I came out. Dead calm water, mountains clearly distinct. I love to look off into distances—the bay, the prairie, etc.

After supper, 7 p.m.

Notice the raindrops! [*water stains on paper*]

Had to go in and the house was colder than outside.

Outside again at noon, eating lunch.

Deane and I are sitting out in the absolute calm and silence of a fall day. Not a breath of wind but a little damp chill coming up from the river. An old electric blanket, now dry, clean from three downpours, is on my knees. It is like being on a ship.

I told the real estate people we were not going to sell, much to Peggy [Scherer's] amazement. I must say she has perfect control and never gets upset at me and my proneness to make arbitrary decisions. I have great confidence in her and Bob Ellsberg [managing editor of the CW]; she is 25, he 20!!

Enuf! We all enjoyed your letters but all say—you must visit us this winter. Write soon.

Love from us to *you* most especially too. Dorothy

TO NINA POLCYN [MOORE]

FEB 4, 1977

Cleaning my desk 2 letters from you a year old. One letter was about Risa—a lovely name. Here another woman (she is just past college) and I are reading Chaim Potok's books. *The Chosen, The Promise.* Because of her interest this young woman volunteer in the house is studying Hebrew (she is a good Catholic). The Potok books are about the Hasidim, whom I had encountered through Martin Buber's books. We really are closer, Jews and Catholics, than Catholics and Protestants, I think.

You had sent me last year, and so many times since, help for our work and also fare to visit you, which I certainly plan to do if I survive this winter. I have always loved travel, and nothing would give me greater joy right now than to go by bus, swinging across country, to visit you, but I must wait for milder weather. Right now I'm in a feeble state. Too conscious of my 79 years! But Mother Jones, the great labor organizer, tramped the country from Colorado to West Virginia at a great age! It is truly awful to feel debilitated. When we went to Russia together I felt the same age as you. We had such a holiday—never laughed so much. A joyous memory.

Pray for us all, and for me that I get my strength back and can renew myself, come spring, in a little travel again.

TO MARGE HUGHES

MARCH 30, 1977

I've been thinking of you so often and wishing you would be able to get up to see us some time. It would be a treat for us all. But especially I wish you would come for next winter. Try to plan on that. Things have gone pretty smoothly all this last winter until a recent terrible storm when two tall pines fell over our telephone wires and power lines (and this just recently) and the house froze up and I got chilled to the bone and just took off for New York, much to the shock of everyone here who thinks I ought always to be around like "mother." It was good to get down to the beach again where Kathleen and Pat [Jordan] and their two-year-old (and she is expecting) have that little pink bungalow across the road. I had a few delightful days, though it was cold, and the toilet was stopped up, which inhibits me greatly. Oh, for the good old outhouse! That plumbing is my only beef against the beach. Pat and Kathleen have inside plumbing, but I don't like to go into other folk's house for that. For dinner, yes.

Joan is doing a lot of difficult letters for me, such as refusing honorary degrees and speaking engagements. I really do want to feel retired. Mail will keep me busy always. Stanley [Vishnewski] is raring to go to Minnesota again and gets very angry at me for being away. Peggy Scherer wants to go to Mexico and stays in N.Y. for the time being to study Spanish.

Do write a May Day issue article for us, which will commemorate Peter. People grow in love for him.

Do you want a book on Simone Weil? Or did I send it? Love, Dorothy

TO DEANE MARY MOWRER

MAY 15, 1977

I am writing now early in the morning after reading my psalms, while I still feel the strength God has given me thru good sleep. I cannot tell you the state of nervous exhaustion I've been thru. It's been like a constant trembling of my nerves, a need for solitude and no responsibility. With everyone else taking responsibility, and having taken it for so long, bearing so much, I feel like an utter failure—wrung dry.

But I am beginning to recover from the miserable state of depression, this sense of a nervous breakdown has put me in. Meanwhile I pray, listen to the radio, and thank God that great [anti-nuclear power] demonstration at Seabrook is over. It got great coverage over radio and press.

I'm praying I'll be able to be at the Memorial Day conference but am not sure. I have still a great weakness, tho the nervous depression is leaving me. I could not even telephone, nor have I tried to.

TO SISTER PETER CLAVER

7/28/77

So good to hear from you and I do thank you for the *Ordo*. Remember how Jesus said, "It is written, it is written, it is written," when he was tempted? I suddenly realized He read the Scriptures— O.T., and Psalms also. True God and True Man! Sorry to miss our retreats but I am "poorly" as the saying is. Travel and the excitement of retreats is too much. I am on the beach, very beautiful here.

TO DELLA SPIER

SEPTEMBER 1977

It is getting on September and the Fall days are still muggy and the humidity is 100%. It seems it has been this way for weeks. Grey days, hard to work in. The summer has been bright and cheerful, much company, much work, but the melancholy days are here.

The September issue of the paper has just arrived from the printer and by the time our readers get it, it will be late in October. People enjoy the mechanical work of mailing out the paper, sitting around tables, folding them and stacking them and another group putting stickers on them. There is no speed-up around the CW and people enjoy stopping to talk and get a cup of tea, and perhaps a piece of sweet bun which our baker sometimes brings in to us together with the enormous amount of day-old bread we put out each day before the soup line.

Now that we have the women's house on Third Street, Maryhouse, with its cheerful red brick and white picket fence (iron of course) there are twice as many to feed, more than that since in Maryhouse we have families sometimes.

Thank God for the cheerful little children playing around the dining room every night after the leisurely meal. A great deal of the cooking is done at St. Joseph's house on First Street and then the big pots are put in a high baby carriage and wheeled over to us—our share, that is. Sometimes we are given coffee cake, or pastry from some bakery, sometimes the Holy Name mission sends us the leftover from the banquets which have been given to them. We eat well usually. Though sometimes there is too much seasoning in the soup.

Having been away, living on the beach a good part of the summer, my room needs cleaning up—which means removing books which have accumulated on my shelves, and sending them down to the library on the floor below. It gets so I do not worry about people walking off with books, though I do miss my *Master of Hestviken*, Sigrid Undset's masterpiece.

Sigrid Undset visited us at Mott Street during the Second World War. She had been lecturing on one of my books when the Germans invaded Norway and escaped by the skin of her teeth, through Finland and Russia and Siberia, thence to America. Perhaps she took the same route Peter Kropotkin did when he walked out of the Siberian prison camp. It was good to be rereading these books this summer in the same atmosphere as the first time I read them.

Do write and let me know what you are reading now. I know you were reading all of Smollett, but I have never been able to get into his work. I had started *The Warden* but did not finish it.

I worry about not hearing from you, so do please write. I know I have been remiss, but I have had a period of melancholy too. Declining years, I guess. Eighty my next birthday. Do let us keep in closer touch. I do miss you. The bell will be ringing soon for 5:40 Mass and after that dinner, and after that Vespers, and bed with a good book, as we used to say.

TO DOROTHY GAUCHAT

OCT 5, 1977

Your beautiful butterfly [*a stained glass piece from Ade Bethune's studio*], symbol of the Resurrection, hangs in my window at Third St. and I do thank you for it. Please pray for me—I am going thru a period of depression and weakness and feel utterly useless! I know you have had such periods too and have come thru them valiantly. So when I am "down" and look at your gift I'll remember and feel cheered. "All things are passing," including these moods. Right now I am trying to write a story, reminiscence, and am wishing Mary Lathrop would come in so I could dictate it to her. But I'll struggle with it today (for the next issue). Frank [Donovan], our business manager and editor, who is the most dedicated and generous person in the world, is on jury duty this week and I miss him. He types my handwritten articles often. Bless him. Pray for us.

TO NINA POLCYN [MOORE]

2/1/78

Tamar is spending some weeks with me and doing a lot of knitting for her *grand*children, who are beauties. Her father, Forster, calls me almost every day and Stanley makes my illness an excuse to abandon the rural life for a time and be a gallant amongst all the young lady volunteers around here. . . . He and Tamar go for walks, exploring bookshops, and bring me back presents. This week it is a wonderful book on China.

We have Mass twice weekly here at the house. The Little Brothers of Chas. de Foucauld are around the corner . . . and come and inspire us.

TO THE SEATTLE CATHOLIC WORKER
In response to a request from a new CW community to name their house "Dorothy Day House":

JANUARY 17, 1979

Please, no. "Fools' names like fools' faces always appear in public places!" My mother taught me this! Call it Peter Maurin house.
    D.D.

TO NINA POLCYN [MOORE]

3/21/1979

Here is our Polish pope [John Paul II], our dear sweet Christ on Earth, as St. Catherine of Siena called him.

Much love to you. Do write. I'm living a life of leisure, plenty of volunteers, young men and women for both houses, in city and country. Sometimes I feel like a relic. Treasured and pampered and spoiled "rotten," as my mother used to say. I wish you could see the luxury in which I live—large room and private bath, so much space it becomes a dumping ground. Where is my voluntary poverty? Two 5-shelve book cases crammed with books, good and bad.

Everyone is always giving me things of beauty so I sometimes think that in addition to running a library I am in a museum.

After my morning Psalms and sticky oatmeal breakfast I am looking at an Australian illustrated calendar and remembering my trip to Australia years ago. Rome, England, Australia, Africa—surely I've seen the beauty of the world! God has been good to me! How wonderful it is to travel.

I have a shoebox full of picture postal cards and Mary Durnin, formerly of Milwaukee, has become a world traveler—at least, England and Europe—and sends notes and cards regularly. She makes her home in London. Wonder what became of her large family of children—are they all married and settled? She had a tragic marriage. She sent me pictures of Rome and the new Pope—he is blessing the world. So good he got to Mexico, and blessed Castro as he flew over Cuba.

4/17/79

Easter greetings! We had wonderful Holy Days around here, fastings, vigils, services packed in both houses. St. Joseph's on First St. and Maryhouse here on Third. All mail is at a local station, collected in the morning by Frank, or "dear soul" Arthur J. Lacey, whose "vacation" is always spent at a Trappist monastery. He prefers that at Conyers, Georgia, where Jack English finished his days. We have always been so close to the Trappists, north, south, and Midwest, and they were "activists" where we were concerned. They have kept us going with their prayers and as far as Gethsemani and Piffard, N.Y., were concerned, with financial help. Also cheeses! Frank makes me a toasted cheese sandwich every day! I am pampered. "Joyous I lay waste the day!"

Right now I listen to the Masterwork hour on radio. At night television! And what reverential programs during the Holy Season! Thinking of you, I envisioned you serving the shut-ins and prayed you would not be overtaken by a Minn. blizzard and be buried alive. Terrible thought.

Stanley [Vishnewski] is a great help around here, taking the disconsolate out to feast, and cheering people up. He was responsible for getting my *Therese* reprinted by that small press in Illinois [Templegate]. He spent the Holy Days at Maryknoll.*

Did I tell you I hear from the Zarrellas in Tell City, Ind.? And a fellow called Seaman (in Montana) sent a half dozen old pictures of when we were at Easton! And oh! How young and fair I was then! Vanity, vanity! I am a generation ahead of all you young ones!

Someone at the door! Signing off!

Love to you and yours!

Dorothy

MAY DAY 1979

Remember Julian of Norwich, "All will be well, all manner of things will be well!" I'm a feeble creature these days. Too much celebration here at the house. I know how you feel about neutron bombs, etc.—after Harrisburg [nuclear power plant accident in Pennsylvania]. I sit glued to television on such occasions, and pray. I am cleaning my desk and answering an April 19 letter from you postmarked "St. Cloud" Mn. I have written "check" on it to remember to thank you. If I have forgotten in the past it is because Frank Donovan who works harder than anyone else around here "oversees" me as I open my mail in the a.m. and grabs the "loot" to keep me from going out and living "riotously"! How wonderful

---

* Stanley Vishnewski, the longest-serving member of the Catholic Worker, died on November 14, 1979.

our trip to Russia was! And Warsaw! The day the Pope was elected I wanted to call you and congratulate you. I remember what a big and handsome father you had.

Our House is packed and I enjoy going down to dinner at night and getting acquainted with all the women. What a variety.

Is this a dream or did I get a card from you marked Vienna?

Little by little I am cleaning out my bookshelves. But most important is mail. Such good letters. Yesterday, one from Canon Drinkwater in England. What a privileged life I've had, to meet so many great people!

As for you! How many things to remember—Charles St., the Bremen and its swastika! And our wonderful trip to Russia.

Time of change around here. We are selling Tivoli for a good price and buying a smaller farm at Warwick, N.Y., nearer to the city H of H and cheap bus fare.

I'm staying right here for the time being. Maybe the beach later.

Much love. I'll be praying for you and yours.

Dorothy

2/21/80

Someone gave me these beautiful postals so I hope you don't mind my writing to you this way. The paper (CW) is going to press today and the house is very quiet. Got mail this morning from my sister in Vancouver who suffers so from arthritis that she has to dictate to her daughter. She has much pain.* Thank God I am spared that. It's general weakness, loss of memory too. Living in a house of hospitality is no joke. "Never a dull moment," as the saying is. Some kind of fire started in the room above me and our automatic sprinkler system went on and I got deluged. My room a mess—the drying ceiling flaking off all over the room and paint and calcimine dropping down on desk and

---

* Della died in April 1980. As Dorothy noted in her diary, she was "a most dear sister."

bed, etc. Never a dull moment. We have a wonderful staff. Wish you could see this place—an old music school house.

We have Friday night meetings—a Dominican priest living with us, Mass 3 times a week in our auditorium where there are mattresses piled up in back and often several old "shopping bag women" pull out their pallets, as it were, and sleep thru the Mass. First St. is "St. Joseph's"—3rd St. (us) is "Maryhouse."

Some of the men sleep over here in basement rooms, a priest included.

I'll never forget our trip to Russia and of course Poland. What good lives you and I have both had!

Whenever I get mopey I remember that phrase (Ruskin's?), "Duty of Delight."

Much, much love,

Dorothy

Dorothy Day died in her room at Maryhouse on November 29, 1980, at the age of 83.

INDEX

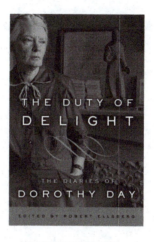